CARBON PROVINCE, HYDRO PROVINCE

The Challenge of Canadian Energy and Climate Federalism

Why has Canada been unable to achieve any of its climate-change targets? Part of the reason is that emissions in two provinces, Alberta and Saskatchewan – already about half the Canadian total when taken together – have been steadily increasing as a result of expanding oil and gas production. Declining emissions in other provinces, such as Ontario, Quebec, Nova Scotia, and New Brunswick, have been cancelled out by those western increases. The ultimate explanation for Canadian failure lies in the differing energy interests of the western and eastern provinces, overlaid on the confederation fault-line of western alienation. Climate, energy, and national unity form a toxic mix.

How can Ottawa possibly get all the provinces moving in the same direction of decreasing emissions? To answer this question, Douglas Macdonald explores the five attempts to date to put in place coordinated national policy in the fields of energy and climate change – from Pierre Trudeau's ill-fated National Energy Program to Justin Trudeau's bitterly contested Pan-Canadian program – analysing and comparing them for the first time. Important new insights emerge from this analysis which, in turn, provide the basis for a new approach. *Carbon Province, Hydro Province* is a major contribution to the vital question of how our federal and provincial governments can effectively work together and thereby for the first time achieve a Canadian climate-change target.

DOUGLAS MACDONALD is Senior Lecturer Emeritus at the School of the Environment at the University of Toronto.

Douglas
Macdonald

**CARBON
PROVINCE**

GREENHOUSE GAS EMISSIONS
1990–2017

Alberta 58% increase
Saskatchewan 77% increase

**HYDRO
PROVINCE**

GREENHOUSE GAS EMISSIONS
1990–2017

Ontario 12% decrease
Quebec 9% decrease

The Challenge of Canadian Energy
and Climate Federalism

UNIVERSITY OF TORONTO PRESS
Toronto Buffalo London

University of Toronto Press
Toronto Buffalo London
utorontopress.com

ISBN 978-1-4875-0721-3 (cloth)   ISBN 978-1-4875-3580-3 (EPUB)
ISBN 978-1-4875-2490-6 (paper)   ISBN 978-1-4875-3579-7 (PDF)

Library and Archives Canada Cataloguing in Publication

Title: Carbon province, hydro province: The challenge of Canadian energy
    and climate federalism / Douglas Macdonald.
Names: Macdonald, Douglas, 1947– author.
Description: Includes bibliographical references and index.
Identifiers: Canadiana (print) 20190231548 | Canadiana (ebook)
    20190231556 | ISBN 9781487507213 (cloth) | ISBN 9781487524906
    (paper) | ISBN 9781487535803 (EPUB) | ISBN 9781487535797 (PDF)
Subjects: LCSH: Energy policy – Canada. | LCSH: Climatic changes – Government
    policy – Canada. | LCSH: Greenhouse gas mitigation – Government
    policy – Canada. | LCSH: Federal government – Canada. | LCSH: Energy
    industries – Environmental aspects – Canada.
Classification: LCC HD9502.C32 M33 2020 | DDC 333.790971–dc23

This book has been published with the help of a grant from the Federation for the
Humanities and Social Sciences, through the Awards to Scholarly Publications
Program, using funds provided by the Social Sciences and Humanities Research
Council of Canada.

University of Toronto Press acknowledges the financial assistance to its publishing
program of the Canada Council for the Arts and the Ontario Arts Council, an agency
of the Government of Ontario.

Canada Council   Conseil des Arts
for the Arts   du Canada

ONTARIO ARTS COUNCIL
CONSEIL DES ARTS DE L'ONTARIO
an Ontario government agency
un organisme du gouvernement de l'Ontario

Funded by the   Financé par le
Government   gouvernement
of Canada   du Canada

Canadä

*This book is dedicated to my fellow Canadians,
in the hope that their future efforts to reduce this country's
greenhouse gas emissions do more to unite than to divide.*

Contents

Tables

Acknowledgments

I first would like to express my gratitude for the financial support provided by the Social Sciences and Humanities Research Council, which has made this work possible, both in terms of past research on Canadian climate-change policy and financial support for this publication. I would also like to thank the University of Toronto School of the Environment – faculty, staff, graduate and undergraduate students – for providing a continually supportive context in which to both teach and research Canadian climate policy. I am also very grateful for the care given me during the writing of this book by Dr Nadine Bukmuz and the doctors, nurses, and support staff of the Princess Margaret and Toronto General hospitals.

Many people helped bring this work into existence. In particular, I wish to thank my researcher during the past decade, Asya Bidordinova, for her cheerful willingness to take on any task, quickly followed by useful results, even while she herself was engaged in a variety of scholarly activities. I am also indebted to the other colleagues who worked with Asya and me on the 2013 SSHRC-funded study *Allocating Canadian greenhouse gas emission reductions amongst sources and provinces: Learning from the European Union, Australia and Germany*. They are: David Gordon, Anders Hayden, Kristine Kern, Jochen Monstadt, Alexey Pristupa, and Stefan Scheiner. I am grateful for volunteer research help subsequently provided by three of my students: Benjamin Donato-Woodger, Stefan Hostetter, and Cynthia Whaley.

Many years ago, at a 2008 authors' meeting for *Canadian Environmental Policy and Politics*, arranged by editors Debora VanNijnatten and Robert Boardman, I presented my still barely formed thinking that one factor holding back Canadian progress on the issue was the way in which emission reduction imposes different costs on different actors. James Meadowcroft suggested I look at the European Union burden-sharing agreement. I did, which led to the 2013 study referred to above and then to this book. Thank you, James, for that and for collaboration (with Glen Toner) on other Canadian climate studies from which I learned a lot. In that vein, I also wish to thank Debora VanNijnatten and Mark Winfield, with whom I have co-authored a number of Canadian climate studies. Working with both has extended my thinking.

An early draft of this work was reviewed by three friends to whom I am indebted: Peter Farncombe, Grace Patterson, and Bob Tyler. Two anonymous reviewers provided insightful and positive suggestions for improvements. One, in a kindly but forceful way, insisted I extricate myself from the quicksand represented by an initial muddled presentation of theory and method. As I attempted to do that, David Houle helped me think through the manner of comparing the cases. The other anonymous reviewer pointed out something directly relevant to the current Canadian impasse. That is the basic continuity in the challenge transportation infrastructure has always posed for Alberta's efforts to market its resources; wheat in the early years of the twentieth century, when the focus was on freight rates, and oil in the early years of this century, when the focus is on pipelines.

I am also grateful for the support and assistance provided by Daniel Quinlan, my editor at the University of Toronto Press. His positive attitude and continual faith in the value of the work helped me through the rough spots. I would also like to thank Christine Robertson and all the others at the University of Toronto Press who helped bring this book into being.

My final acknowledgment of personal help and assistance is by far the most important. The love of my life, my wife, Lorraine Wai Chun Cheng, has always given me unfailing love and support, helping me in more ways than I could possibly list here. She made this book possible.

Abbreviations

AMG	Analysis and Modelling Group
BAU	business as usual
CAA	Clean Air Act
CAPP	Canadian Association of Petroleum Producers
CCME	Canadian Council of Ministers of the Environment
CEM	Council of Energy Ministers (prior to change of name in 2008)
CEPA	Canadian Environmental Protection Act
CES	Canadian Energy Strategy
CoP	Conference of Parties
EABSWG	Emissions Allocation and Burden Sharing Working Group
EMMC	Energy and Mines Ministers' Conference (previously CEM)
ENGO	Environmental Non-governmental Organization
EPIC	Energy Policy Institute of Canada
EU	European Union
FMM	First Ministers' Meeting
GHG	greenhouse gas(es)
HFCs	hydrofluorocarbons
IGR	intergovernmental relations
JMM	Joint Meeting of Ministers
LNG	liquified natural gas
Mt	megatonne (1 megatonne = one million tonnes)
NAICC	National Air Issues Coordinating Committee
NAISC	National Air Issues Steering Committee
NAPCC	National Action Program on Climate Change
NCCP	National Climate Change Process
NEB	National Energy Board (name changed in 2019 to Canadian Energy Regulator)
NEP	National Energy Program
NRCan	Natural Resources Canada

NRTEE	National Round Table on the Environment and the Economy
OECD	Organization for Economic Co-operation and Development
OPEC	Organization of the Petroleum Exporting Countries
PCF	Pan-Canadian Framework (on Clean Growth and Climate Change)
PMO	Prime Minister's Office
UNEP	United Nations Environmental Programme
UNFCCC	United Nations Framework Convention on Climate Change
VCR	Voluntary Challenge and Registry

A Parable of West and East

Your carbon province … walks with a cowboy swagger …

White Stetson … pancake breakfasts …

Fistful of Yankee greenbacks …

Got rich selling oil to the neighbours …

Throws money to brother and sister provinces …

That was fine until people started talking about something called … "climate change."

Your hydro province … walks stiff … nose in the air …

Lives in the east … well, central Canada …

Freeze in the dark …

Ottawa lives in the east …

Why should I sell your wheat?

Hydro provinces got rich by manufacturing … and an Ottawa tariff … cost the west dear …

Not blessed by God with oil and gas to sell …

Sell hydro? *Bien sûr!*

Act on climate change? Help the east, hurt the west …

Heard that song before …

Centre … Hinterland …

The carbon and hydro provinces live with their brother and sister provinces and three territorial cousins in a ramshackle old house, built more than 150 years ago. Way up on one of the upper floors lives a parent who goes by the name Ottawa.

When the house was first built, the idea was that Ottawa would be the big boss. Funny thing, though: somehow over the years it just didn't work out that way. One of the provinces kept saying it was going to run away. To keep it home, Ottawa would give it more freedom: but then, of course, all the other provinces wanted the same thing.

Nowadays, Ottawa really can't tell a province to do anything. Friendly persuasion, small bribes and maybe, sometimes (not very often) the threat (which nobody really believes) of taking a province out to the woodhouse for a thrashing (cutting back on allowance) is about all that Ottawa can do.

Ottawa tries, but it just can't get everybody in the house working together. Cleaning the windows or washing the floors? They'll clean the windows in *their* room: but clean the *common* windows in the living room? Good luck.

This old house is a leaky old house: breezes and drafts everywhere, needs a huge amount of energy to keep it hot in the winter and cool in the summer.

Now that everybody is talking about climate change, the neighbours sometimes say the people living in that old house are part of the problem, not the solution.

Makes everybody in that old house feel real bad.

They tell each other: "We gotta do something." But what? What we need is … We need a plan!

But how can they plan *anything* together?

The provinces will never let Ottawa plan for everyone. And Ottawa? Ottawa doesn't really want to do that. That would make too many people mad at … guess who?

Sometimes the provinces meet up in one of the musty old rooms of the house, without Ottawa. There, all by themselves, they try to plan. But that never works either: carbon and hydro provinces can never agree.

Sometimes provinces do things by themselves. One put a tax on carbon. One of the carbon provinces surprised everybody by *also* (for a while) putting a tax on carbon. Another carbon province swears it'll *never* put a price on carbon. A hydro province says: "That's it; done our share; not doin' much more." Provinces working alone doesn't solve the problem.

Then other times, Ottawa says to the provinces: "Look, we can all work together and figure this out." So Ottawa and the provinces (or most of them) come up with a plan … or, at least, a goal.

Then they all start bragging to the neighbours about their shiny new plan. But you know what?

So full of themselves, never get around to actually doing what has to be done to reach the goal.

So everybody who lives in that big old draughty house …

The carbon and the hydro provinces, the other provinces and territories, and fussy old Ottawa up on the top floor … they all keep on talking about the problem …

They all keep on making a lot of promises to themselves and their neighbours that this time …

Really … believe us … this time … for sure … gonna fix this thing.

But somehow … you know what?

Yes, perhaps you do.

CARBON PROVINCE, HYDRO PROVINCE

The Challenge of Canadian Energy and Climate Federalism

1 Introduction

Since 1990, fussy old "Ottawa" – also known as the Government of Canada – has established a sorry record of setting targets for reduction of total Canadian greenhouse gas (GHG) emissions without having first ensured that between it and the provinces the policies and programs needed to achieve that target are in place. As a result, we have failed to achieve our first three targets. The first was the goal announced by Prime Minister Brian Mulroney in 1990 of stabilizing emissions at that year's level by the year 2000. The second was the international commitment Prime Minister Chrétien's government gave at the 1997 Kyoto summit to reduce Canadian emissions to 6 per cent below 1990 levels by 2012. In 2010, the Stephen Harper government, cynically, since it never intended to act on the climate issue, set a third national target (simply copying Obama's US target), of reducing emissions to 17 per cent below 2005 levels by 2020. All three targets have been missed by a wide margin.

Things changed, however, with the election of the Justin Trudeau government in October 2015. The new prime minister radiated positive energy and optimism on the climate change file – there was no doubting that he personally wanted Canada to do better. However, his government completely ignored the 2020 target, even though at the time it was still five years away. Instead, the focus was on reductions to be achieved fifteen years later in 2030, the subject of the December 2015 Paris climate summit. Continuing its hypocrisy, the Harper government had earlier in the year announced a fourth national target – emissions were to be 30 per cent below the 2005 level by 2030. The new Trudeau government initially sent signals it might adopt a more ambitious goal, but then retreated from any such thought. It did, however, launch a new effort to work with the provinces to develop coordinated national policy, something not seen since the Chrétien government's previous federal-provincial effort had collapsed in failure in 2002. In consequence, on 9 December 2016, the prime minister and most of the premiers and territorial leaders, excluding those from Saskatchewan and Manitoba, signed the Pan-Canadian Framework on Clean

Growth and Climate Change, a program of action by both levels of government intended to achieve the Paris 2030 goal.

During the next few years, however, the degree of policy coordination and therefore potential effectiveness of the Pan-Canadian Framework (PCF) program declined significantly, as a number of provinces withdrew. Even at the time of signing, however, despite the breath of fresh air and hope brought to the issue by the new prime minister, the Pan-Canadian Framework was a further continuation of the stale dynamic of an announced target without the necessary accompanying programs. Analysis shows that the PCF cannot by itself, using only the programs set out in that document, achieve the 2030 goal (Environment and Climate Change Canada 2017; Government of Canada 2017; Sawyer and Battelle 2017). The PCF document itself (PCF 2016, 44) says that the target can only be met by putting in place "additional measures." A report published by Environment and Climate Change Canada in 2019 stated that based on actions by governments, business and others up to September, 2018 emissions were projected to be 4 per cent below the 2005 level by 2030 (as stated on the previous page, the target is 30 per cent below); taking into account "additional policies and measures that are under development but have not yet been fully implemented" emissions were projected to be 19 per cent below the 2005 level by 2030 (Environment and Climate Change Canada 2019a, 5). In 2016, once again, a national program had been put in place that was relying on *future* action to accomplish its goal, rather than being based on programs *already in place*.

The four Canadian targets referred to above are shown in table 1. The table shows the goal of stabilizing or reducing emissions so the total will be a specified percentage below a base-year level and shows the year by which that is to be accomplished. The right-hand column shows the "emissions target," which is the planned total of Canadian GHG emissions in the target year. Emissions are stated in megatonnes (Mt); one megatonne is one million tonnes. As can be seen, the emissions targets are not that dissimilar. What is different is the target year. Canada has been trying to achieve roughly the same target since 1990, while continually pushing forward into the future the date for bringing about that reduction in emissions.

In order to advance suggestions for change, this work examines the question of why Canada over a period of something like thirty years has consistently been unable to put in place greenhouse gas emission reduction programs that are sufficient to meet the goals committed to at the international level. Some answers are obvious. This is a large country, with enormous energy needs for transportation and for heating in winter and cooling in summer. Beyond that is the fact that Canada is a fossil fuel energy exporting nation. We produce GHG emissions not only because of the fossil fuel energy we use ourselves but also because of the energy needed to extract and transport coal, oil, and natural gas for sale abroad. Public attitudes do little to push governments towards effective

1 The four Canadian greenhouse gas emission reduction targets

Total Canadian emissions in 2017: 716 Mt

Year announced	Context	Reduction	Emissions target (Mt)
1990	Green Plan	stabilize emissions at 1990 levels by 2000	613
1997	Kyoto summit	reduce emissions to 6% below 1990 levels by 2012	576
2010	Copenhagen summit	reduce emissions to 17% below 2005 levels by 2020	620
2015	Paris summit	reduce emissions to 30% below 2005 levels by 2030	513

Sources: Commissioner of Environment and Sustainable Development (2017); Environment and Climate Change Canada (2019a, 2019c); Government of Canada (1990).

action; only about two out of three Canadians register support for increased government action in opinion polls, and many are dubious about such things as rising electricity prices attributed to greening the electricity supply or the possibility of paying more for gasoline. More significant is organized political action by powerful actors such as the oil and gas industry, the automotive industry, and other industrial sectors whose profitability is linked to fossil fuel consumption, plus insistence by all business leaders that for competitiveness reasons Canadian policy must not get ahead of that put in place in Washington. More recently, Conservative politicians have agreed action is needed, but have devoted most of their energy to railing against one form of such action, a carbon tax.

Clearly another reason is the fact that for nine of those thirty years Canada was governed by a prime minister who, as was often pointed out, had great difficulty enunciating the words "climate change" let alone doing anything more. Finally, we might point to the usual political process of governments promising they will give us the moon and stars tomorrow, while being reluctant to impose attendant costs today.

While these and other explanations for Canada's policy failure to date are important, they do not tell the whole story. For that, we need to pay attention to other more basic, underlying factors that pose major challenges to significantly reducing Canadian emissions. Without understanding those underlying challenges, we are doomed to spend another thirty years on our hamster wheel of futility, making empty promises to the world while all the time running faster and faster to give ourselves and others the appearance of meaningful action. The argument made here for how Canadians can address those challenges and begin to take action that will achieve an international commitment is summarized in the following three sections.

A Coordinated Federal–Provincial Program Is the Only Option

The first part of the argument is that Canada can only meet a target for reduction of total Canadian emissions, as opposed to a given province or city meeting its own target, by coordinated federal-provincial action. We cannot meet a target such as Kyoto or Paris by relying on action by Ottawa alone, using only federal government laws and policies. As discussed in more detail in the section on jurisdiction in chapter 2, in a legal and technical sense, Ottawa by itself could certainly meet any of the targets set to date or a more ambitious one. Taking into account political realities, however, it cannot because the provinces, on a file so important to them, will never accept a situation in which they are not setting their own climate-change policies and action is being taken only by the Government of Canada. Nor can we meet a Canadian target by relying only on provincial policies, with no action by Ottawa. We know that is so because during the Harper regime from 2006 to 2015, when Ottawa did virtually nothing on the file, the provinces *were* acting – but in the absence of federal leadership the sum of those actions was always well below the national target (NRTEE 2012). A coordinated federal-provincial program is the only means of achieving a given target.

Any Such Federal–Provincial Program Faces Three Challenges

The second part of the argument is that any federal-provincial effort faces not only the difficulties of high energy needs, weak public opinion, and other factors outlined above, but in addition three more fundamental challenges. The first is what is termed here the West-East divide, which has a number of facets but at heart stems from the fact that the fossil fuel producing provinces, most notably Alberta and Saskatchewan, have economic interests respecting energy and climate change very different from those without fossil fuel resources, such as Ontario and Quebec. The provincial economies of Alberta and Saskatchewan are heavily dependent upon fossil fuel export and associated emissions have been steadily rising even as they have fallen in other parts of the country. The challenge of getting all parts of the country moving in the same direction of declining emissions is augmented by the deep historic roots of the West-East divide. Conflict between Alberta and Saskatchewan on the one hand and Ottawa and central Canada on the other dates back to the creation of those two provinces in 1905, when they were unjustly denied what all other provinces had when they entered Confederation: ownership of the natural resources located within their borders. The West-East divide respecting energy and climate policy is wide and deep. The fact that it is the latest evolution of one of the major regional fissures threatening national unity makes it almost unbridgeable.

The second challenge is the inescapable fact that the total emission reduction needed to achieve any given target, expressed in megatonnes, must be allocated among both sources of emissions, such as transportation or buildings, and provinces – action on a source such as buildings leads to x Mt reduction, while spending on public transit leads to y Mt reduction; plus, the real rub, British Columbia reduces by z Mt (translated into a per capita figure), while Newfoundland and Labrador only reduces by half that per capita amount. Immediately, the cry is heard ringing from west of the Rocky Mountains: THAT'S NOT FAIR! But we never do hear that cry because British Columbia, not surprisingly, having been privy to those numbers long before the national program is decided on, let alone implemented, moves to kill in the egg the particular policy option that led to that per capita difference (something it has considerable power to do, given the consensual, nonvoting nature of the Canadian intergovernmental process).

A real-life example of this jealousy among provinces was provided on 27 October 2018, by Premier Brian Pallister of Manitoba. Speaking of the Justin Trudeau's government's backstop carbon tax imposed in provinces that do not themselves have an equivalent carbon price, Premier Pallister complained that Trudeau was "allowing … [Newfoundland and Labrador] to have a lower carbon tax than Manitobans are being forced to pay." The premier then made a comparison with another province: "Quebec, which submitted a less stringent plan than ours, is getting a 40 per cent lower carbon tax" (Pallister 2018). Another example of the allocation issue at work was provided at about the same time by a newspaper comment on planning being done by the Ontario government for a new climate change plan. "Ontario is planning to issue one [a climate change plan] this month that will argue the province is already doing its fair share to meet Canada's emission-reduction targets – which, by implication, places more of the burden on Alberta and Saskatchewan to cut emissions" (Clark 2018).

Indeed, the Ontario plan released 29 November 2018, referred to "continuing to do our share" while it announced that the target of a 37 per cent reduction from the 2005 level by 2030, set by the previous Liberal government, had been reduced to a new target of a 30 per cent reduction by 2030 (Ontario 2018, 21). The Ontario plan stated that: "Measured against the same base year as Canada's target under the Paris Agreement (2005), the province's total greenhouse gas emissions have dropped by 22 per cent – even while the rest of Canada saw emissions increase by 3% during that time" (Ontario 2018, 7). The

implicit message was that Ontario already *had* done its share and so was justified in reducing its level of ambition. Federal environment minister Catherine
McKenna responded by also implicitly discussing burden sharing when she
said the other provinces would have to do more because Ontario had reduced
its target. The prime minister made the same point at a First Ministers' Meeting
on 7 December 2018, to the great distress of the Ontario premier. The issue of
allocation of the total reduction among provinces is always lurking just below
the surface.

Even if programs are put in place without any regard to allocation among sectors or provinces, those calculations will be made and the results will become
part of the negotiating dynamic, raising charges by some that the allocation is
unfair. That, in turn, will inevitably exacerbate the regional conflict inherent
in the West-East divide, in particular because per capita reduction costs are
higher in the western, carbon-intensive economies. The European Union has
twice found a way to allocate its total reduction effort among member states,
once in 1997–8 and again in 2008 (Macdonald et al. 2013). A central argument
made in this work is that Canada needs to follow that example and negotiate a
burden-sharing agreement that all see as being fair.

The third challenge is the fact that effective national climate policy cannot be
made by Ottawa or the provinces acting alone, as set out above, but instead must
be generated by that extremely ineffectual governing process, federal-provincial intergovernmental relations (IGR). This poses a major problem, since any
Canadian government can opt out of a federal-provincial process at any time, as
did, effectively, both Alberta and Canada in 2002 as each chose to abandon the
federal-provincial climate-change process and instead take independent action.
In the same way, Saskatchewan, and later Ontario and other provinces, chose
not to participate in the 2016 Pan-Canadian Framework. The fact that all governments have this right to leave a federal-provincial process without penalty
gives each a form of veto power, which moves intergovernmental agreements
in the direction of lowest-common-denominator, ineffective policy solutions.

The problem represented by these three underlying challenges is compounded by the fact that they stem from basic causes, about which we can
do nothing. The starting point is the empirical fact that oil and gas are found
in some parts of the country and not others, giving rise to differing regional
and provincial government motivations. This is connected to a second aspect
of physical reality – climate change is a global issue that can only be solved
by cooperative global action, meaning Canada must adopt just one national
reduction target. If that one target is to actually be met, the total reduction must
then be allocated among those differing regions (something we have avoided to
date by the simple stratagem of missing all targets), which raises the issue that
the carbon regions face much higher per capita reduction costs, and so are most

likely to make the charge that the cost distribution is not fair – which leads us back to the West-East divide. For all the well-known reasons going back to the Plains of Abraham, in 1867 Canada could not come into being as a unitary state. Canada could only be created as a federated state, and the trend since then has been towards extreme decentralization and weakening federal power. However, since the failures of constitutional change represented by Meech Lake and Charlottetown, governments and the Canadian public have no interest at all in further attempts to amend the Canadian constitution. This leaves us with a governing system ill-equipped to address the first two challenges, hinging as they do on regional conflict played out by constitutionally strong, highly motivated provinces, but a system that effectively cannot be changed.

We Cannot Keep On Ignoring It: We Have to Start Talking about the West-East Divide

The third part of the argument is that to date Canadian governments have addressed the challenge of the West-East divide, combined with the inherent need to allocate a given reduction among sources and provinces, by pretending that neither exists. If we don't talk about challenges, maybe they will not appear. However, as shown by the case studies examined below, the West-East divide has *always* appeared, whenever Canadian governments have set out to forge national, federal-provincial energy or climate policy. Strongly motivated fossil fuel producing provinces such as Alberta, whose economic interests are certain to be affected by national energy or climate policies, have always exerted considerable influence on those policies. Governments have only been able to sidestep the West-East divide by putting in place ineffective climate-change policy that does not threaten western energy interests. Instead of ignoring those challenges, we must in future acknowledge them and put them on the table for discussion. However, we must be careful in doing so, since there is a very real danger any such discussion will descend into mutual recrimination and stalemate. What must be put on the table are not the things that divide us but rather the things that can bring us together, in particular the ways in which we can accomplish a fair sharing of the costs and benefits associated with achieving a given climate-change target. In that way, we can open the door to effective national policy that achieves a Canadian international commitment to act on the problem of climate change.

Subject

The subject of this work is national, federal-provincial climate-change policy-making intended to achieve a given Canadian international reduction commitment. (Today the three territories are always included in the process and efforts are made to ensure some participation by Indigenous actors; the term "federal-provincial" is used here and in the following pages as shorthand for policymaking by Ottawa, the provinces and the territories, with an Indigenous role; the term "the provinces" should be read as "provinces and territories.") That subject necessarily includes federal-provincial energy policymaking. The global atmosphere is changing largely due to human use of fossil fuel energy sources. Climate-change policy, therefore, focuses in large part on energy choices, the stuff of energy policy. Nor yet can energy policy now be made without considering its climate-change implications. Finally, ever since about 2010, pipeline siting, something at the heart of energy policy, has become central to climate-change politics. For these reasons, it is virtually impossible to discuss action on the climate-change issue without also considering action taken, or not taken, with respect to energy. Recognizing this, the late Jim Prentice, former minister in the Stephen Harper government and premier of Alberta, who sadly died a premature death in 2016, called for a full integration of Canadian energy, environment and climate change policies (Prentice 2017). Accordingly, in order to fully understand federal-provincial climate change policymaking, this work examines intergovernmental policymaking on both the energy and climate-change files.

In the pages that follow, we will examine all the major instances to date of efforts by Canadian governments to develop coordinated federal and provincial action on energy or climate-change policy. There have been five such federal-provincial processes, as follows: 1) efforts to revise Canadian energy policy following the first world oil price spike in 1973, culminating in the Ottawa-Alberta conflictual negotiations associated with unilateral announcement of the National Energy Program (NEP) by Pierre Trudeau's government in the federal budget of 28 October 1980; 2) the first attempt at developing national climate change policy that was made by the Mulroney and Chrétien governments between 1990 and December 1997; 3) the second attempt, referred to as the National Climate Change Process (NCCP), from early 1998 to late fall 2002, which ended in the collapse of the federal-provincial process; 4) the provinces-only Canadian Energy Strategy (CES), which was first discussed by premiers in 2005 and culminated in release of the CES document in July 2015; and, 5) the Pan-Canadian Framework (PCF) on Clean Growth and Climate Change, the result of a multilateral national process initiated by the Justin Trudeau government shortly after it was elected in October 2015, eventually signed by all provinces and territories except Manitoba and Saskatchewan on 9 December 2016, followed by subsequent withdrawal of a number of provinces. Accordingly, the time period covered here is for the most part 1973 to 16 April 2019, the date on which Jason Kenney was elected premier of Alberta, bringing to five the number of provinces unwilling to themselves implement the carbon pricing measures called for by the Pan-Canadian Framework program. Energy policy development and the evolution of Canadian intergovernmental relations prior to 1973 are briefly reviewed.

Within each case, four subjects are examined. The first three are the challenges set out above and more fully in chapter 4: the West-East divide, the inherent need to allocate a given total emission reduction among sources and provinces, and the weaknesses of the intergovernmental relations system. The fourth subject is the strategy used by the lead government actor (the government that most wants to see coordinated national policy put in place) to induce behaviour change on the part of other governments. In four of the five cases the lead actor was the federal government. In one case, that of the Canadian Energy Strategy, Alberta played the role of lead government actor. Since that case shows a province cannot lead a national policy effort because it has insufficient means available to influence other provinces, the subject of lead government strategy effectively is strategy pursued by the Government of Canada.

As discussed in the methodology section below, the three challenges are examined in order to learn more about their nature, so that they might be more successfully addressed in the future. Strategy of the lead government actor is examined for the same reason – to learn from past success and error to better inform future action by a prime minister and government wishing to lead another national climate-change process.

As necessary, analysis of these five case studies includes relevant aspects of the context within which national energy and climate policy are made. The first of these is US politics and policy in the same fields, not because that country brings pressure to bear to influence Canadian decisions but because the two economies are so integrated that it is impossible for Canadian governments to ignore the implications of their decisions for that trading relationship. The second, given that Canada is a fossil fuel exporting nation, is the nature of world oil and gas markets and prices. The shock of the 1973 OPEC price increases brought the first case study into being, while years later a sufficiently high global price, combined with technological advances and changes to Alberta and federal tax regimes that favoured the industry, made possible exploitation of the oil sands. The third contextual element is the current state of energy technology. Not long ago, coal was the cheapest energy source, which put a barrier in the way of successful climate-change policy. Today, however, costs of generating electricity from solar or wind are competitive or lower than coal, with associated policy implications. At the same time, fracking has given access to new supplies of oil and gas in different parts of the country, with again implications for both policy and its underlying regional dynamic. While fracking in central and eastern Canada was not a factor in any of the five case studies, if it does start to happen in a serious way the basic difference of interest between the oil and gas producing regions and other parts of the country will be altered.

Use of the terms "carbon province" and "hydro province" here is closer to a literary device than a precise categorization of Canadian provinces. That is because some provinces, such as British Columbia, both export fossil fuels and generate hydro-electricity. While it cannot be applied in a precise manner, the term "carbon province" refers primarily to Alberta and Saskatchewan, since they export the largest quantities of oil and natural gas and Alberta is the one province planning to significantly increase its oil exports, by attracting further investment in the oil sands. British Columbia, Newfoundland and Labrador, and Nova Scotia also benefit from fossil fuel resources. The first two, however, also generate hydroelectricity, and so it is difficult to place them squarely in either the carbon or hydro camp. The term "hydro province" refers primarily to the central Canadian provinces of Ontario and Quebec, which have historically benefitted from development of their hydroelectricity resources. Hydro exports play a significant part in the Quebec economic model, much as oil exports do for Alberta. Manitoba also produces hydroelectricity and so is clearly a member of that camp. New Brunswick, Prince Edward Island, Nova Scotia, and the territories are also for convenience placed in the hydro camp, despite the fact they do not all produce significant quantities of hydroelectricity and Nova Scotia does export some offshore natural gas.

By the same token the term "west" is not meant to refer to all of British Columbia, Alberta, Saskatchewan, and Manitoba in every instance. As discussed in chapter 4, the term "western alienation" has the potential to be misleading since the values and identities caught up in that concept vary among the four provinces. The term "west" suffers from the same difficulty. It is used here to refer primarily to the two western provinces that do the most to produce and export fossil fuel energy: Alberta and Saskatchewan. Of those two, the focus is more upon Alberta because that province emits more greenhouse gases, is on track to increase its emissions more than Saskatchewan, and of the two has played a more active role in intergovernmental energy and climate politics. The term "east" can be applied to the six provinces east of Manitoba, but, given their larger economic and political role, refers more often to Ontario and Quebec. Often in western eyes the term also includes Ottawa, beholden as it is to the large number of voters in the two central provinces.

The basic subject examined here is the difference in interest between the carbon and hydro provinces. In terms of energy policy, the interest of the carbon provinces differs from that of others because their fossil fuel production is so important to them, both as contribution to their economies and as a source of government revenues. Plourde gives this data for the fiscal year 2007–8: in Alberta, 28 per cent of government revenues came from petroleum, which also accounted for 15.2 per cent of provincial GDP; in Saskatchewan, 17.5 per cent of revenues came from that source, which provided 8.3 per cent of provincial

GDP; offshore oil production beginning in 1998 brought Newfoundland's GDP close to the Canadian average by 2007–8, while in that fiscal year oil provided 45 per cent of provincial revenue (2012, 97). The historical trend in Alberta has been a decline in the share of provincial revenues coming from fossil fuel resources. Alberta drew 80 per cent of government revenue from oil and gas in 1979, but that figure had declined to 3.3 per cent in 2016 (Hughes 2018). Nevertheless, during the fifty-odd year period examined here, fossil fuel industries have been very important to the carbon provinces. Not surprisingly, they are highly attuned to threats to those industries coming from proposed national energy or climate-change policy.

That provincial interest is reinforced by the political power of the oil and gas industry. Because of their importance to provincial economies and government revenues, firms in those sectors have from the outset held structural power as the basis for their lobbying influence upon provincial policy. Governments in the carbon provinces have always had an automatic interest in furthering the well-being of those firms, long before their premier took a call from the CEO. Although they have engaged in conflict over provincial royalties and sharing of revenues, the industry and governments of Alberta and Saskatchewan have generally been allies as they participated in national energy and climate change policymaking.

In terms of climate-change policy, the interest of the carbon provinces differs from that of others because of the carbon intensity of their economies. Harrison and Bryant point out that "the provinces of Saskatchewan and Alberta have per-capita emissions that would be the highest in the world if they were nation-states" (2016, 504). As discussed below, GHG reduction costs are much higher in carbon-intensive economies than in others. Effective North American climate policy might well expand opportunities for hydro exports, benefitting provinces such as Manitoba and Quebec, but: "Reduction of emissions presents a fundamental threat to the fossil-fuel driven economies of these [Alberta and Saskatchewan] provinces" (Harrison and Bryant 2016, 504).

The other major difference between the carbon and hydro provinces has to do with the historical trajectory of their GHG emissions. Table 2 shows changes in emissions since 1990 for two groups of provinces: those in which emissions have been increasing since that date and those in which emissions have been decreasing. As can be seen, all the provinces with rising emissions other than Manitoba are exporters of oil and natural gas. Harrison (2015) cites extensive academic literature showing that in general, countries and subnational jurisdictions with more carbon-intensive economies tend to adopt less stringent climate policies. While GHG emissions are influenced perhaps as much by changes in the economy as by government policy, the data shown in table 2 indicates that phenomenon at work in Canada.

2 The two tracks of Canadian provincial greenhouse gas emissions

Emissions shown in megatonnes (Mt)			
Jurisdiction	1990 emissions	2017 emissions	change 1990–2017
Canada total	602	716	19% increase
Track One: Emissions Increasing			
Saskatchewan	44	78	77% increase
Alberta	173	273	58% increase
Manitoba	18	22	22% increase
British Columbia	52	62	19% increase
Newfoundland and Labrador	9	11	17% increase
Track Two: Emissions Decreasing			
Nova Scotia	20	16	20% decrease
New Brunswick	16	14	13% decrease
Ontario	180	159	12% decrease
Quebec	86	78	9% decrease
Prince Edward Island	1.9	1.8	5% decrease

Note: Percentages rounded to closest whole number. Calculated using data provided in: Environment and Climate Change Canada (2019b).

Carbon and hydro provinces have very different interests and their emissions are moving in opposite directions. The need to reconcile those differences is the subject matter of this book.

What follows is presentation of the two policy fields of energy and climate change, as they are conceptualized here. "Energy policy" has been defined by Bruce Doern as follows:

> Energy policy as a whole refers to policies aimed at influencing and shaping the supply of energy sources and fuels, the demand for these by various users of energy, and – ever more importantly – the environmental impacts of energy use. Energy policy thus covers sources and fuels such as oil and natural gas, coal, hydroelectricity, nuclear and a host of alternative or complementary sources such as fuel cells, solar energy, wind power, and biomass. (Doern 2005, 4)

What are the primary objectives of governments as they develop energy policy as a whole or policy respecting a particular fuel? Those objectives flow from the basic function of energy in modern society. Until fairly recently, humans had access to only limited amounts of energy, coming from relatively few sources (see Smil [2008] for a review of human use of energy since prehistoric times). Those were primarily energy generated by their own bodies and those of their domesticated animals; wind for transportation by boat and for milling; falling water, also for powering mills; and combustion of fuels such as wood, peat, and coal to provide heat. That all changed when in the eighteenth century the invention of the steam engine meant thermal energy from coal combustion could be translated into other forms of energy used for production in the newly created factory system and for transport of goods, people, and information by rail and ship. This vast increase in the total amounts of energy available made possible by use of fossil fuels, first coal and then later oil and natural gas, was a major factor in the unprecedented expansion of human ability to produce physical goods and the unprecedented economic growth that by the beginning of the nineteenth century had become the hallmark of capitalism. During that century and the one that followed, this increase in the total supply of energy and its application to new technologies, such as the internal combustion engine, were also transforming warfare. This came first in terms of increased mobility of armed forces and their weapons; then, during the First World War, the appearance of industrialized, mechanized warfare that drew upon the full productive capacity of the state; then again by the end of the Second World War with the appearance of a new form of energy, nuclear, initially used as a weapon. At the same time, greater use of energy continued to allow expansion of industrial production. Globalization and the vast expansion of total human material wealth that has occurred since 1945 have only been possible due to ever-increasing supplies of energy. Energy is now of central importance.

This importance is shown by Meadowcroft (2012), who argues that modern democratic governments are engaged in three core areas of activity: 1) ensuring the continued existence of the state by providing military security, which means using coercive force to maintain internal order and repel external attack; 2) facilitating economic growth and ensuring sufficient state revenues; and 3) organizing welfare services. He suggests that providing environmental protection services may now be emerging as a fourth core activity (Meadowcroft 2012). Clearly, energy is central to all four: to the military function and to economic growth, which generates the wealth needed to support both military and welfare activities. Energy also, of course, causes environmental problems. Energy is now vital for the most important functions of the state and, from there, the market and civil society.

Given this importance, a primary objective of energy policy is security of supply. Governments work to ensure that different energy forms are available in sufficient quantities to meet industrial, military, transportation, and heating and cooling needs, among others, either by facilitating private-sector supply or by directly supplying energy themselves. At times, this takes the form of the policy objective of self-sufficiency, ensuring that a country can meet all its energy needs from its own supplies without having to rely upon imported supplies that might be subject to interruption.

A second objective is to see energy supplied at the lowest possible price. Industrial competitiveness concerns and also concern for political waves that might jeopardize re-election, generated by consumer anger over increases in the cost of gasoline or electricity, mean governments dare not be seen as ignoring rising energy and electricity prices. In a country like Canada, however, that relies upon both domestic supplies and imported energy, while at the same time exporting energy, the question of cost is more complicated. As discussed below, industrial sectors buying energy to power their production machinery want low cost, but sectors selling it want high cost.

Since the London smog event of 1952, in which thousands died from breathing air polluted by burning coal, reduction of the environmental and human health impacts of energy use has become another central objective. Smog, acid rain, damage caused by hydroelectric dams, dangers of radioactivity, earthquake activity associated with fracking, water pollution and biodiversity loss caused by conventional and heavy-oil extraction, and, of course, the variety of current and future problems caused by climate change are all issues that must be addressed by energy policy (while at the same time being addressed by various forms of environmental, health, and climate-change policy).

"Electricity policy" is defined here as a subset of energy policy having to do with the use of different energy sources such as natural gas or solar to generate electricity, and also including means of transport; storage options, such as batteries or compressed air under a lake; and degree of efficiency in the use of electricity. When electricity systems were first being established at the end of the nineteenth century, the major policy issue was whether the state itself would supply electricity or whether that would be done by private companies whose prices and profits would be regulated. The major challenge was expansion of the public or private system to include as many users as feasible, expanding electricity from the city to rural areas. After the Second World War, policymakers wrestled with the question of including nuclear energy in the supply mix and shortly after that started to address environmental implications such as acid rain. In the 1990s, various jurisdictions experimented with forms of market liberalization. In the twenty-first century, because of climate change, governments face very different issues associated with electricity. This is the challenge of first phasing out fossil fuels as a means of generating electricity and replacing them with renewable sources, which brings up all the problems of intermittent supply (solar and wind cannot produce electricity on cloudy days without a breeze) and so the need for electricity storage; then, expanding use of this largely fossil fuel–free electricity as much as possible, thereby phasing out other uses of fossil fuels, for instance in motor vehicles or home heating. Electricity policy, which in Canada is the domain of provincial governments, with almost no federal involvement, is now central to climate-change policy. (Federal and provincial jurisdiction respecting both energy and climate-change policy is presented in the following chapter.)

Energy policy is made difficult by three inherent contradictions among its objectives of security of supply, low cost for users and high cost for exporters, and minimization of environmental impacts. These contradictions give rise to equally inherent conflicts among societal actors who place conflicting demands upon governments. The first contradiction is the fact that for an energy-exporting nation, energy works best as a driver of wealth creation when prices are both low and high. The optimal mode is low prices paid by domestic manufacturers and high prices paid by external buyers of energy, but that is difficult to arrange, given the existence of world energy markets and prices. Within Canada, with respect to energy generated and sold domestically, there is an automatic conflict of interest between energy consumers seeking low prices and energy producers seeking high prices. As discussed in chapter 3, until the late 1980s governments in Canada and elsewhere were committed to regulating energy markets, setting prices, and controlling imports and exports, which meant that conflict was automatically politicized. Since then, energy has to some extent been deregulated, particularly in terms of allowing markets to set prices (although less so for electricity), which has reduced, but not eliminated, that political conflict.

The second basic contradiction is between the goal of using energy to drive economic growth and the goal of reducing the environmental impacts of energy use. Setting aside energy producers, the former goal is achieved by means of low-cost energy to contribute to industrial competitiveness in the global marketplace. Broadly put, however, environmental impacts can only be reduced by increasing the price of energy. That can be done directly by pricing, which gives incentive to use energy more efficiently (energy conservation) and, in the specific case of carbon pricing, to switch away from fossil fuels. It can also be done indirectly, by regulatory requirements to change product design, such as catalytic converters on automobiles, or to change energy production processes, such as reduction of methane emissions during oil and gas extraction. This translates into environmental conflict between environmentalists on the one hand and different industrial sectors on the other, both energy industries and those that produce energy-using products such as automobiles or buildings. Citizens, who as energy users buy gasoline for their automobile, pay an electricity bill, and perhaps also pay for heating their home with oil or natural gas, are caught up in that conflict.

Thirdly, the different industrial sectors generating and selling different fuels are all in competition with one another. The nuclear industry would like to see a greater portion of electricity produced from that source, but so too would the natural gas, solar, and wind industries. All such sectors are playing a zero-sum game since at any given time total energy or electricity use is fixed, and increases in the share of one can only be achieved by decreases in the shares of others. Today, now that climate change figures so strongly in energy policy, the basic conflict is between the traditional fossil fuels that became established over a century ago due primarily to market demand and renewable energy sources that have only become established during the past twenty or thirty years because government environmental policy created demand for their products (Lauber 2005; Toke 2011). Originally, when the cost of producing renewable energy was much higher than the cost of fossil fuel energy, that conflict was entirely political. Today, however, as wind and solar electricity generation costs are competitive with coal and natural gas, the conflict plays out also in the market.

Canada, like all other industrialized countries, has seen governments struggle to find a balance among these contradictory energy policy goals, while being influenced by lobbying pressure exerted by relevant actors. Energy policy conflicts have played out in the realm of societal ideas, politics, and markets. However, they have also been expressed as regional conflict, simply because energy supplies in most cases are geographically limited. While sun and wind are found everywhere (although even in those cases there are geographical differences), coal, oil, natural gas, and falling water needed to generate hydroelectricity are found in some places and not others. This means the conflicts outlined above quickly become regional conflicts, which, given Canada's federated structure, equally quickly become conflicts in the realm of federal-provincial intergovernmental relations. Anderson expresses the problem this way:

> Federalism empowers – to a greater or lesser degree – regional governments as well as a national or federal government. Petroleum resources are typically very unevenly distributed among the regions of a federation, so the allocation of powers over the industry and the sharing of revenues can have major consequences for those who live in the rest of the country. (Anderson 2012, 3)

The way in which the internal contradictions and conflicts inherent to energy policy take regional form in Canada is a central theme of this book.

"Climate-change policy" is defined here as actions by governments to both reduce greenhouse gas emissions (mitigation) and to reduce vulnerability (adaptation) to climate change impacts such as severe weather events that lead to flooding, freezing, tornado, drought or, heat wave, plus sea-level rise and northward movement of infectious disease borne by mosquitoes or other vectors. While essential, adaptation policy is not discussed here. Climate change is caused by release to the atmosphere of carbon dioxide, methane, nitrous oxide, and other gases, each with differing abilities to trap heat in the global atmosphere. The most significant greenhouse gas is carbon dioxide released during the burning of the fossil fuels coal, oil, and natural gas. Data for greenhouse gases is usually presented in the form of "carbon dioxide equivalent," which refers to the amount of carbon dioxide that would produce the same contribution to global warming as would the combination of greenhouse gases in question (Government of Canada 2017).

Climate-change mitigation policy seeks to reduce the release of all greenhouse gases and to increase the amount of carbon stored in "sinks" of wood and soil. More specifically, policy works to decrease the use of fossil fuels in two ways. The first is by conserving energy through improved efficiency of use in such things as buildings, vehicles, industrial processes, and appliances. Governments work to achieve that by funding research and technological development; imposing fuel-efficiency standards on such things as motor vehicles, appliances, and buildings; and by funding such things as programs to get older cars off the road and home-energy retrofits. The second main thrust of climate change fossil fuel policy is "fuel switching." This refers to replacing coal, oil, and natural gas with other fuels that do not emit greenhouse gases. For that, policy seeks to "price carbon" – making fossil fuels more expensive than others and so giving an incentive to switch. While considerable controversy surrounds nuclear as an alternative to fossil fuels, increased use of renewable energies such as solar and wind is a central component of climate-change policy (albeit one that is pursued within the ambit of electricity policy). As discussed, a major component of fuel switching is electrification, defined as first ensuring that electricity is generated as much as possible by renewable (or nuclear) fuel sources and then using that electricity to replace fossil fuels as an energy source, such as eliminating gasoline as a fuel for cars and trucks. Electrification is part of the larger subject known as the transition to a lower-carbon economy. That process, which is now underway, requires major social change, not only in replacing the coal, oil, and natural gas infrastructure built over the past hundred years with one dedicated to renewable energy generation, transport, and use, but also wide-sweeping change in laws, markets, and social behaviour. (For a discussion of such energy transformation in the past, see Podobnik 2006.)

Although climate-change policy might be thought of as a subset of environment policy, it differs markedly with respect to both spatial and temporal elements. In terms of the former, many environmental problems, defined in terms of both the source and its impact such as local air pollution caused by a factory, are located within the borders of a given jurisdiction and can be addressed by that government alone, with no need to collaborate with other

governments. That is not the case for climate change, since no causal relationship can be established between a given impact, such as rising sea levels
that increase the damage done by a hurricane storm surge, and the source
of the problem, which in fact is found in millions of sources around the
globe. No government can solve its climate change problem by acting alone.
There is thus an automatic motivation to participate in international regimes
(although motivation differs completely between victims of climate change
such as low-lying island states and fossil fuel exporters such as Saudi Arabia
or Canada). With respect to the second difference, the temporal element is
much more central to climate-change policy than to environmental policy.
Current climate-change impacts, such as coastal flooding due to sea-level rise,
are associated with emissions many years in the past. Emissions today will
generate effects many years in the future. This means those living today are
asked by climate-change policy to pay for actions that will help them less than
they will benefit those living in the future. An issue such as toxic contamina-
tion of drinking water has a close temporal link, since those paying the price
of action today receive the benefit tomorrow. In part because of that, governments began to address toxic chemical pollution not long after Rachel Carson
published in 1962 and again after Love Canal threw the issue of hazardous
waste into high visibility in 1978. Climate change, on the other hand, has seen
a twenty-or-more-year gap between the issue moving onto the policy agenda
and the beginnings of minimally effective government action. Presumably
this delay is in part because the worst effects of climate change still lie in the
future.

Central to Canadian national climate-change policy is the geographic location of the most important sources of greenhouse gases. As can be seen from
table 3, the largest source of emissions is oil and gas production, an activity
located only in the carbon provinces. Other sources such as transportation
and buildings are distributed more evenly in accordance with population distribution, and so do not generate the same regional difference in interest.

Table 4 shows the portion of Canadian total emissions contributed by each
province. As can be seen, just two provinces, Alberta and Ontario, make up
60 per cent of the total. Given that, it is far more important that reductions
be made in those two provinces than in those such as the Atlantic provinces,
where even cutting emissions by a third or a half would do little to help the
country as a whole achieve the national target.

Finally, table 5 shows total Canadian emissions at selected dates since 1990.
The trend shown is consistently upward from 1990 to 2005, followed by a
decrease due to the effects of the 2008 recession and then another upward trend
from 2009 to 2015, followed by a slight decline. Since 1990, economic down-
turn had more effect on emissions than did public policy.

3 Canadian greenhouse gas emissions by sector, 2017

Oil and gas	27%
Transportation	24%
Buildings	12%
Electricity	10%
Heavy industry	10%
Agriculture	10%
Waste and others	6%

Source: Environment and Climate Change Canada (2019b).

4 Provincial shares of Canadian total greenhouse gas emissions, 2017

Canada total: 716 Mt	
Alberta	38%
Ontario	22%
Quebec	11%
Saskatchewan	11%
British Columbia	9%
Manitoba	3%
Nova Scotia	2%
New Brunswick	2%
Newfoundland	2%
Prince Edward Island and three territories	1%

Note: Percentages rounded to closest whole number. Numbers do not add to 100 due to rounding. Calculated using data provided in: Environment and Climate Change Canada (2019b).

5 Total Canadian greenhouse gas emissions since 1990

Year	Total Canadian GHG emissions (Mt)
1990	602
1997	687
2005	730
2009	682
2012	711
2015	722
2017	716

Source: Environment and Climate Change Canada (2019c).

Implications of Integrated Energy and Climate-Change Policy

As noted, in recent years energy and climate-change policy have become increasingly integrated, in that it is no longer possible to implement policy in one field without considering its effects upon the other. This integration has a number of implications for Canadian decision-making in both policy fields. Four in particular are noted here. The first is that energy and electricity policy now have added another objective beyond those discussed above – to reduce fossil fuels in the supply mix, replacing them with other fuels. This exacerbates the competition among industrial sectors supplying different fuels, but perhaps more importantly increases the overall cost of the energy supply, not so much because renewable sources are more expensive than fossil fuels (in recent years they have become competitively priced) but because of the need to fund new energy generation and transport infrastructure. As has been seen in the very vocal opposition to the Site C hydroelectric dam in British Columbia and to wind turbine siting in Ontario, this increased cost is not only monetary but includes as well individual and societal stress.

Secondly, the contradiction in energy policy goals between a low-cost supply of energy and environmental protection has been magnified as carbon pricing has become a primary mechanism of climate policy, a contradiction that will have a greater effect on policy decisions as carbon prices move upward (which they must do, even though other policy measures are also required, if we are to achieve Canadian targets). Previously, the prices of energy supplies and products using energy, such as automobiles, were set by the market and then forced upward slightly by environmental protection measures such as catalytic converters. Now, due to its economic efficiency, carbon pricing in the form tax or cap-and-trade is the preferred instrument for climate-change policy. That preference, however, is bumping up against political opposition to pricing; see Rabe (2018) for an excellent discussion of governments weakening or eliminating established pricing programs. When energy prices are deliberately moved up, the conflict with the economic growth function of energy is played out in demands from trade-exposed industries, such as cement, for exemptions from pricing systems. The contradiction is also displayed as citizens loudly object to paying a higher price for their gasoline.

Thirdly, there is a conflict between the wealth-creation goal of fossil fuel extraction and export and the goal of reducing Canadian GHG emissions. When exported fossil fuels are combusted in another country, the resulting emissions are not assigned to Canada under the rules of the international regime. However, extraction and transport of fossil fuels requires use of considerable quantities of fossil fuel energy in this country, which increases our emissions. British Columbia, shown as having total 2017 emissions of 62 Mt in table 2 above is both a climate change leader in Canada, after bringing in a carbon tax in 2008, and is also actively working to become a major exporter of liquefied natural gas (LNG). Harrison (2015) reports that if those plans came to fruition British Columbia's GHG emissions would double. (In 2018 the British Columbia government introduced a new climate-change plan intended to allow an increase in LNG-related emissions by offsetting decreases elsewhere.) The other carbon provinces are caught up in this basic conflict between a desire to make money by selling fossil fuels to others and a desire to do the right thing by reducing its emissions, as is Canada as a whole.

Finally, another internal contradiction now exists in the policy domain of integrated energy and climate policy – the highly charged issue of pipeline siting. Until recently, regulatory approvals for new oil or gas pipelines were technical issues, securely located within the bosom of energy politics alone and while including opportunities for public comment, attracting little attention from environmentalists or local citizens. As discussed in chapters 3 and 8, after failure of the Obama administration to pass federal climate-change law in the years 2009–10 the American environmental movement shifted its focus to stopping the Keystone XL pipeline. Allied with Nebraska farmers and others worried about spills and other local effects, and with a sympathetic president in the White House, the movement succeeded in delaying regulatory approval until the Trump administration took power in 2017. The political salience of pipelines rose dramatically in Canada as well and Keystone XL, Northern Gateway, Kinder Morgan Trans Mountain expansion and Energy East became fighting words. As discussed in the Pan-Canadian Framework case study, Alberta took the position that it would only participate in the national effort if the federal government approved a new pipeline. Thus integrated energy and climate policy registered another contradiction – in order to lower Canadian GHG emissions by means of the Pan-Canadian program, we need to increase the export capacity of pipelines originating in Alberta, something that will increase emissions within the country associated with the extraction and transport of that province's oil or bitumen.

The argument is made that a pipeline, by itself, does not determine emissions – that policy influencing user demand for fossil fuels is the key factor (Tombe 2016). The argument is also made that if a pipeline is not used to get the oil to users, other means, such as rail transport, will be used instead. It is true that the real solution is policy to reduce demand by efficiency and fuel switching. It is also true that to some extent oil and bitumen can be shipped by rail. However, the actions of the oil industry and the Alberta government, recounted in the CES case study below, show they believe there is a connection between pipeline capacity and emissions. Both argued that lack of additional pipeline capacity was putting an upper limit on oil sands expansion. (This is distinct from their desire for new pipelines to the coasts to allow oil to be shipped to markets that would buy at a higher price than can be obtained in the American market.) Removing that upper limit by construction of a new pipeline would also remove an upper limit on associated GHG emissions, although that is not something they often talk about.

Alberta has imposed a legislated limit, with exceptions, of 100 Mt of GHG emissions per year from the oil sands. However, as judged by its fervent support for the Trans Mountain expansion pipeline, Alberta very much wants to expand oil sands production up to that 100 Mt emission limit. This means there is an inherent contradiction between policy intended to *reduce* emissions, such as the Pan-Canadian Framework, and policy intended to build new pipeline capacity, such as the purchase of the Trans Mountain pipeline by the Trudeau government in 2018, which will facilitate an *increase* in emissions. While the argument is made that pipelines do not increase emissions and that oil can be moved by other means, the two actors most directly involved, the industry and the Alberta government, are not convinced. If they were, they would not have spent so much time and effort pressing for additional pipeline capacity.

The previous pages have presented the importance and major characteristics of energy and electricity policy, including the basic conflict between energy as a source of economic wealth and also of environmental damage; presented climate-change policy and the way in which it is now so closely integrated with energy policy; and, finally, presented the four most important implications of that integration: 1) the drive to switch away from fossil fuels heightens competition among energy sectors; 2) adoption of carbon pricing as a major policy measure heightens the conflict between the goals of low-cost energy to drive economic growth and environmental protection; 3) inherent conflict exists between fossil fuel export sales and emission reduction; and 4) bitterly contested pipeline politics have been added to the already roiling waters of energy and climate politics. Having presented the basic subject matter of energy and climate policy and the way in which, in this country, that subject is strongly fashioned by regional conflict and the workings of federalism, we now move on to the purpose of this inquiry.

Purpose

The primary objective of this work is to provide analysis and recommendations flowing from that analysis in order to help Canadian governments put in place national, coordinated federal-provincial climate-change policy able to achieve a given Canadian emission reduction target. The recommendations provided here could be used to modify the existing Pan-Canadian program or could provide the starting point for a whole new federal-provincial climate-change process. To develop such recommendations, we need understanding of the factors that have to date prevented Canada from reaching its GHG reduction targets. To gain that understanding, analysis is provided of the five federal-provincial efforts to develop national energy or climate policy (recognizing that in four cases both issues were under consideration) that have taken place since 1973.

The five cases are analysed for two different reasons. First, the intent is learn more about the four subjects examined here, the three underlying challenges, and lead government strategy (in particular that of the federal government, which was the lead actor in four of the cases). Since the three challenges will be encountered in any future effort, the more we know about them the better. While Ottawa cannot change the Constitution or the facts of geography, it does have control over the strategy it uses to nudge provinces in the direction of coordinated policy, and so it is imperative we learn from that government's past strategic errors. The role of the four subjects in each case is examined. The findings respecting each subject are then aggregated and discussed in chapter 10.

The second reason for examining the cases is to learn why the national process in question generated the case outcome it did. (The concept of "case outcome," as the term is used here, is discussed on pages 27 and 28.) The outcomes of some cases have been substantial policy coordination. In other cases, we find only minimal coordination; governments work together by participating in a common process that generates an intergovernmental agreement, but do not commit to any significant policy change. Coordination of federal and provincial policies is the goal; we must stop going down the two different policy tracks of increasing and decreasing emissions shown in table 2. Accordingly, in chapter 10 the cases are analysed in order to identify factors that led to greater coordination in some cases than in others in the hopes that lessons learned can be applied in any future national climate-change effort. Suggestions and recommendations for any future national climate policy effort, presented in the final chapter, are developed both by using the findings from the case studies and from an overview of the whole history of Canadian national energy and climate-change policy.

Hopefully this book will be of value to academic understanding of Canadian energy and climate-change federalism, since it fills a gap in that literature by providing for the first time a detailed review of all the federal-provincial efforts to date in the two integrated policy fields. While academic methods are used, an equally important objective is contribution to applied practice. It is hoped that using academic methods to learn from the past will help not only scholars but also both the government officials who get their hands dirty tending to the machinery of energy and climate intergovernmental affairs in this country and also the many non-state policy actors – firms, environmental non-governnmental organizations (ENGOs), First Nations, and others, including individual Canadian citizens – who play different roles as stakeholders and voters contributing to federal-provincial energy and climate policy decisions.

The task facing Canada, given its unique circumstances of geography and constitution, is enormous. To put the matter bluntly, among the many barriers facing national climate policy is the fact that the carbon provinces are being asked to walk away and leave considerable potential wealth buried in the ground. That is a difficult thing to ask of anybody and it must be done carefully and with respect. In addition, it must include an offer to share the cost, material and psychological, of doing so. That bring us to the final purpose of this work – to set forth a coherent argument for future national climate-change policymaking based not only upon lessons from experience to date, but also upon one guiding principle that has informed this project from the outset. Instead of trying to ignore the fact that effective national climate policy, entangled as it is with energy politics, must impose very different costs and benefits upon different parts of the country, we must bring that issue into the light of day and ask ourselves: "How can we make the sharing of the costs and benefits associated with achieving a given Canadian emissions reduction more equitable?"

Methodology

Information presented here was obtained from a number of sources. Those are relevant academic literature; news media reports (newspapers and magazines, including quasi-academic ones such as *Policy Options*); primary documents generated by the actors being studied; and some thirty or more interviews, both confidential and on the record, mostly done in connection with past work on the subject, such as Macdonald et al. (2013).

In general terms, analysis is done using the methods of the qualitative social sciences that seek to explain a dependent variable, in this case almost always decisions made by individual governments or generated by the IGR system, as governments collectively make decisions. An attempt is made to explain those decisions by looking for evidence (information) that allows the analyst to draw conclusions respecting the relative importance of a limited number of variables that help to explain either decision.

The five cases are presented in chronological order. To achieve the case-study analysis objectives set out above, the first task in each is to identify the major policy decisions made during the case process; this includes unilateral decisions (a decision to act made by a government itself, without consultation with other governments, even while it is engaged in the collective decision-making process); bilateral decisions (resulting in agreements between two governments); and multilateral decisions (resulting in agreements made collectively by all or a number of governments). Particular attention is paid to unilateral decisions made by the federal government in its role of lead government actor. As discussed in the next chapter, such unilateral federal action can take either of two forms. In the first, unilateral action might be simply intended to help achieve the national objective – for instance, Ottawa decides by itself it will amend federal standards governing energy efficiency of household appliances, thus complementing and assisting provincial policies. However, unilateral federal action might also be intended to influence provincial behaviour, such as the decision Ottawa made by itself, announced by Prime Minister Justin Trudeau on 3 October 2016, that it would impose a "backstop" carbon price on GHG sources in any province that had not itself already put such a pricing system in place.

This use of threat to influence provincial behaviour is important because, as the case studies make clear, it is a two-edged sword. It can lead to more effective national policy because it influences provincial behaviour in ways that improve policy coordination. Used without finesse, however, as was the case with the Chrétien government, it can also *weaken* the ability of governments to work together; used as a blunt instrument to whack the head of a particular province, as was done by Pierre Elliot Trudeau in 1980, it can damage Confederation for years to come.

Attention is also paid to unilateral action by provincial governments, since that too has implications for the outcome of intergovernmental relations. A province can decide not to participate in a particular federal-provincial process, as did Saskatchewan in 2016 respecting the Pan-Canadian Framework agreement. Provincial governments can also seek to influence the behaviour of other governments by issuing a threat; in their case, it is most usually the threat to opt out of the federal-provincial process unless the collective decision is one it agrees with.

Presentation of each case also includes identification of the "outcome" of the case. For these purposes, the case outcome is defined as the state of national, coordinated policy at the date stated to be the end point of the case. For three of the five cases, the date of the case outcome is said to be the date on which governments signed what seems to be the most important bilateral or multilateral agreement. For the National Climate Change Process 1998–2002, in which no agreement was signed in the fall of 2002, the date of the case outcome is said to be 31 December 2002, by which time the national federal-provincial process had definitely come to an end.

While signing of a formal intergovernmental agreement provides a clear line to mark the end of the case, events after that signing cannot be ignored. For instance, one might argue the first case did not really end until the Mulroney government, after it was elected in 1984, had reversed the major components of Pierre Trudeau's National Energy Policy. Going even further, given the effect the NEP still has upon west-east relations, one might argue that particular case continues to reverberate and so has not yet ended. In the same way, the prospects for the Pan-Canadian framework appeared much brighter on the day it was signed than they did later, once a number or provinces had decided they did not wish to participate after all. For that reason, presentation of the case includes both events up to signing of the PCF agreement on 9 December 2016, and subsequent events up to the Alberta election of April 2019. Thus analysis of the cases focuses upon the policy outcome at the end date, but attempts to also incorporate the implications of subsequent events. The definition of case "outcome" is necessarily elastic.

After presenting the most important policy decisions and outcome of each case, the task is to gain understanding from the case. To do that, each case closes with an analysis section. Discussion in that section is given focus by means of these two research questions: 1) What does the case tell us about the four subjects? and 2) What are the most important factors explaining the case outcome? These two questions are related to the two different objectives of the case study analysis, referred to above – to learn more about the four subjects and to learn something about why energy and climate intergovernmental policy coordination is more possible in some cases than in others. Chapter 10 then uses findings from the five cases in an attempt to provide answers to the two questions. For the first, findings respecting each of the four subjects from the five individual cases are aggregated; there is no comparison of cases. Comparison is used, however, to achieve the second objective. For that, the method is to compare two categories of cases. The first category includes two cases, energy policy from 1973–81 and the PCF, 2015–19, which have achieved a substantial degree of policy coordination (recognizing that PCF coordination fell off sharply in the years after it was signed). The other three cases are in a category of minimal policy coordination. Comparing those two categories allows identification of explanatory factors that help to explain differences in the ability of energy and climate federal-provincial processes to generate coordinated policy.

As previously stated, while it is hoped the data and analysis presented here contribute to academic understanding of Canadian energy and climate federalism, that is not the primary objective. The main goal is to use the examination of experience to date in order to develop practical, politically viable suggestions for how we might do better in future. To do that, the two sets of answers to the two research questions are combined to form one set of "lessons" that can be taken from the five cases.

The final chapter then presents recommendations for future action based upon those lessons from the case studies and more generally from an overview of the evolution of national energy and climate policy since the early 1970s. In what might be seen as a relaxing of the rigour of the method, it must again be admitted that the main recommendation – the "guiding principle" of the need for agreement on equitable cost sharing – was in place, based upon conclusions of previous studies, before the first word was entered on the first blank computer-screen page on the first day of writing this book.

Theoretical Approach

The theoretical approach used here for understanding Canadian intergovernmental relations in the fields of energy and climate change is borrowed from an "interest based" approach to understanding the negotiation of multilateral environmental agreements at the international level. That model rests on the assumption that the interest of a state is the most important factor determining whether it plays a lead, veto, or other role during negotiation of such agreements. Similarly, the model used here assumes that the interests of Canadian governments lead them to play such roles in Canadian energy and climate-change intergovernmental relations. As discussed in the next chapter, while many factors may influence the role played by a Canadian government in energy and climate national processes, the focus is upon three interests: 1) a government's desire to obtain material benefit from fossil fuel energy sales; 2) a government's interest in avoiding climate-change policy that will reduce that benefit; and 3) a government's interest in putting in place effective climate-change policy. It is assumed that latter interest is determined for the most part by ideology of the governing party (a right-wing government is usually less interested in acting on the climate issue than is one on the centre-left).

Accordingly, in examination of the cases of national energy and climate policymaking to date, the focus is upon the relative power of a "lead government" – usually Ottawa – that is working to convince other governments to participate in coordinated national policy, and a "veto government" – which has most often been Alberta, although that province played a lead role in the Canadian Energy Strategy – that is resisting that effort. What follows is discussion of the two variables most central to this model of intergovernmental relations, interest, and power.

The term "interest of a policy actor" is treated here as being synonymous with the objective of the actor. Heclo (1994, 375) provides a definition which includes the concept of objective when he refers to interest as the "self-interested and purposive pursuit of material gain." He suggests that self-interest does more to explain political outcomes than any other single factor but cautions that the variable of interest overlaps with and merges into the other variables of ideas and institutions (actors hold a particular objective or interest in large part due to their ideas, which are in turn influenced by their interests; rules of the game channel behaviour as actors pursue their interests). Exploring those interactions would take us far beyond the theoretical limits of this work, and for that reason discussion here is limited to the different elements contained in the concept of "interest."

First, it is assumed that policy actors have general interests, such as the desire of a government to maintain power by winning the next election and of a firm to maximize return on investment. However, as a government engages in a given intergovernmental policy process it also has a specific policy interest – the policy measure it wants to see governments agree on. As they worked with the provinces to generate the December 2016 Pan-Canadian Framework program, the Trudeau Liberals no doubt were very aware of the implications of their actions for their prospects of re-election in 2019. However, their specific policy interest was in seeing a minimum carbon price in all parts of the country. The analyst must consider both.

It is further assumed, expanding upon Heclo's definition, that policy actors have both material and nonmaterial interests. Schlozman and Tierney (1986, 23–6) refer to "economic and noneconomic interests." A nonmaterial or non-economic interest includes the objective of receiving a psychological benefit, such as esteem in the eyes of others, and also the objective of seeing government act on particular values, such as those related to race, gender, or sexual orientation. Actors often pursue both. Feminists want not only increased esteem in the eyes of men, but also equal pay for work of equal value. The concept of non-material interest is relevant here in terms of the values associated with environmental protection, and also in the form of western alienation, discussed in chapter 4, which leads prairie citizens and their governments to seek recognition from the east, as well as a larger share of the material pie. Non-material interest is also relevant for the case study analysis provided here in terms of ideology of the governing party respecting action on climate change.

Also relevant is the *degree* of interest – how *much* the actor desires a particular policy outcome. Schlozman and Tierney use the term "intensity of interest" and present the concept in this way: "In general, individuals are more likely to be concerned about policies that affect them appreciably than about those whose effects, good or bad, are negligible" (1986, 35). Differing degrees of interest are central to policy issues involving both concentrated costs and diffused benefits (Olson 1965; Wilson 1980). Polluting firms subject to government regulation are highly motivated to influence that policy because they are paying the whole internalized cost, while citizens receiving only a fraction of the total benefit of cleaner air are less motivated, giving a power advantage to the firms. Through all five case studies, the western carbon provinces, receiving a large share of the cost or benefit of energy and climate policy, demonstrated a stronger degree of interest than did other provinces, something which was significant for case outcomes. The degree of interest displayed by Ottawa varies across the cases. More generally, degree of interest is important because it determines the resources the actor is willing to contribute to the political struggle, which in turn is one factor influencing that actor's political power.

It is also assumed that while self-interest produces conflict among policy actors it can also lead to cooperation. Mansbridge (1990) and her co-authors explore the ways in which actors seek to benefit not only themselves, but also the larger society. Beyond altruism, the existence of collective-action problems, in which the actor cannot solve its problem by acting alone, engenders cooperation based purely in self-interest (Hardin 1968). Governments at the international level, facing problems such as climate change or global spread of infectious disease, enter into multilateral agreements perhaps because they are altruistic, but certainly because they recognize that they cannot solve the problem by themselves and so cooperation is the only means available to achieve their own self-interest. It is assumed here that self-interested behaviour and cooperative behaviour are not polar opposites and may often be found together, sitting side by side in the tangled mix of one actor's motivations, due to the existence of collective-action problems and perhaps for other reasons as well, such as a genuine altruism. While recognition of a collective-action problem induces cooperation at the international level, there is little evidence of that in Canadian intergovernmental relations. One of the themes explored in the concluding chapter is how the incentives facing Canadian governments might be changed so that they come to hold an interest in cooperation to achieve a goal they cannot achieve on their own, meeting a given Canadian international climate-change commitment.

The concept of social or political power is a difficult one to use in the social sciences because it has so many different meanings. Clegg and Haugaard describe the problem this way: "What emerges [from a review of the literature] is that 'power' is not a single entity. It represents a cluster of concepts" (2009, 3). In particular, the same term is used to refer to a relationship between actors (power over) and the ability of a system of actors to function and achieve goals (power with). To clarify, the term is used here for the most part in the first sense. While the power of a Canadian intergovernmental system to achieve a given goal is important for the analysis provided here, it is not directly examined. Instead, the focus here is upon the power of individual governments *within* that system to influence actions of other governments. It is assumed that focus is needed because that form of power is one way of achieving policy coordination, which in turn is the source of the power of the system as a whole.

The term power in the first sense (relationship) is defined here as "the ability to achieve self-interest by influencing the behaviour of others." In terms of governments exercising power, we start with the fact that all public policy, to achieve its objective, must bring about a change in the behaviour of relevant actors, be they other governments, firms, or individual citizens. This is because policy is put in place to address a policy problem, which can only be done by changing existing patterns of behaviour. Thus governments as they make and implement policy are continually exercising power by influencing the behaviour of others. As set out in the next chapter, the essence of national, coordinated policy is also behaviour change – governments doing things differently from the way they would if acting alone because they are cooperating with other governments. During that process, they are both on the receiving end of power exerted by other Canadian governments and also seeking to exert power to influence those other governments.

The approach used here to understanding the ways in which actors in a relationship exercise power does not include more sophisticated conceptualizations, such as changing dominant paradigms and therefore the beliefs of actors (Lukes 2005). Instead, the focus is upon the means available in the first instance to an actor wishing to change the behaviour of another. For these purposes, three are considered: persuasion, promise, and threat (Galbraith 1983). If those are the means used by governments to exercise power as they engage in Canadian intergovernmental relations, what are the sources of that power? It is assumed the first is the availability of financial resources, which determines the ability of a government to hire staff, organize expertise and generally to exercise policy capacity. The differing powers of the large and small provinces due to differences in financial resources are discussed below. The second source of power is constitutional jurisdiction (Smiley 1987, 86). A government without jurisdiction cannot act to influence others, which is why Saskatchewan, Ontario, and other provinces hope to convince the courts that Ottawa does not hold jurisdiction to impose a backstop carbon price.

The third source of power is degree of interest, which determines how many resources are committed to the contest and how much pain will be endured in order to vanquish. Fourthly, perceived legitimacy of the actor is seen here as a source of power, flowing from the fact we cede power to those we believe have a right to exercise it, such as a democratically elected government (Beetham 1991). This is directly relevant to Ottawa's constitutional power: what was seen as a legitimate use of federal power in the late-nineteenth century no longer holds today. This source of power is also important here for other reasons. The search for legitimacy by both the oil industry and government of Alberta after environmentalists launched their "dirty oil" campaign in the late 2000s is important for understanding the Canadian Energy Strategy and Pan-Canadian Framework.

It is further assumed that the power of a lead government to influence other governments has two additional sources. The first is skill in engaging in intergovernmental diplomacy, as that government seeks to influence others by persuading them a particular policy change actually is in their best interest, often combined with offering a promise of some benefit in exchange for such behaviour change. Skillful diplomacy enhances the power to influence, while bungling diplomacy diminishes it. The second is a willingness to flex muscle, by either taking or threatening unilateral action in order to influence the behaviour of other governments.

Another factor determining the power of an actor is the extent of countervailing power – how much pushback the actor is encountering. Falkner discusses "countervailing forces" in the form of resistance by states and environmentalists to the wishes of business firms in global environmental politics (2008, 25). The concept of countervailing power resisting either a lead or veto government is presented in the next chapter as key to the approach used here for understanding intergovernmental relations in the fields of energy and climate change.

Finally, the conceptualization of power used here includes the structural power of business that flows from the perceived importance for economic well-being of a given industrial sector or firm (Luger 2000; Macdonald 2007). Governments often do what they think business wants them to do, even if they have received no explicit message to that effect, because they want the firm to open a factory and employ workers in their jurisdiction, thus furthering their chances of re-election. The oil industry, because its investment and operations are so important for the Alberta economy, holds considerable structural power in that jurisdiction but less in Canada as a whole because its operations constitute a smaller portion of total business activity there. The Government of Canada is less dependent upon the industry than is the government of Alberta. For that reason, Alberta policy is at least marginally more attuned to the interests of the oil industry than is federal policy.

Format

The next chapter describes the system of Canadian energy and climate intergovernmental relations and completes the presentation of the theoretical perspective used here to understand the workings of that system. Chapter 3 reviews the evolution of Canadian energy and climate politics since the nineteenth century. The function of the chapter is to orient the reader and to provide context helpful for examination of the five case studies. Chapter 4 then presents in more detail the three underlying challenges which were briefly set out above. Chapters 5 to 9 are devoted to the five case studies. The penultimate chapter provides the analysis of case study data discussed above and draws lessons based on that analysis. The final chapter then provides suggestions for how those lessons can be applied the next time that Canadian governments engage in a national climate-change policy process.

2 Energy and Climate-Change Intergovernmental Relations

In order to set the stage for examination of the five case studies, this chapter sets out the nature of Canadian intergovernmental relations, both in general and more specifically in the two closely connected policy fields of energy and climate change. A brief historical review and discussion of the factors that have led Canadian federalism to take its current extremely decentralized form is followed by presentation of the main IGR mechanisms. The aspects of Canadian intergovernmental relations that make it a weak instrument for generating effective policy are listed. Attention then turns to the central issue of intergovernmental policy coordination: What are the factors that lead Canadian governments to either adjust their policies with the intent of achieving a common goal or to instead take independent action intended to achieve their own goal? The final sections of the chapter discuss intergovernmental energy and climate-change policymaking. Federal and provincial jurisdiction is presented, followed by the factors influencing the prospects for policy coordination in these two specific policy fields and closing with discussion of federal strategy for leading the provinces towards coordinated policy.

Historical Evolution of Canadian Intergovernmental Relations

Since the jurisdiction of each level of government had been specified, those writing the 1867 British North America Act did not see any need to include procedures for governments to work together to develop common policy. Beyond that, it was assumed a high degree of centralization, ensured by such things as Ottawa's power to disallow provincial legislation and to appoint senators and lieutenant governors, would allow the new federal system to function effectively (Simeon 2006, 124). Nevertheless, provincial governments led by Ontario and Quebec came together in 1887 and again in 1902 to discuss their grievances with the sharing of revenues between themselves and Ottawa; the first formal Dominion-Provincial Conference was then convened by Prime

Minister Wilfrid Laurier in 1906 (Papillon and Simeon 2004, 116). With meetings in 1918 and again in 1927, the First Ministers' Conference (now Meeting)
was established in the years following as the central institution of intergovernmental relations (Papillon and Simeon 2004, 117). The need for a government
response to the Depression led to more meetings in the 1930s, as did postwar
reconstruction after 1945. In the period from the 1960s until 1982, first ministers met repeatedly to discuss the constitution, prompted by Quebec demands
for constitutional change, the need to put in place an amending formula, and
Prime Minister Pierre Trudeau's desire for a Charter of Rights and Freedoms.
The 1973 rise in world energy prices meant that during this period first ministers also met to discuss national energy policy.

Beyond these specific issues, the creation of the Canadian welfare state since
the 1950s has required increased coordination between Ottawa and the provinces at all levels, from first ministers, to ministers, to officials. In the postwar
years, just as they did in the other democracies, social welfare, health, and education (areas of provincial jurisdiction) rose to the top of the policy agenda.
Despite a lack of constitutional jurisdiction, the federal government moved into
those policy areas by means of financing shared-cost programs, which automatically require coordination. Similarly, environment became an important
policy area, and since both levels share jurisdiction in that, this again required
coordination. Despite its lack of a constitutional basis, intergovernmental relations during the course of the 20th century became established as an essential
component of Canadian governance.

During the hundred and fifty years of confederation, not only did intergovernmental relations become established as a governing mode, but also under-
went a major evolution. John A. Macdonald's vision of an all-powerful Ottawa
at the head of a highly centralized federal system has been stood on its head.
Starting in the late nineteenth century, provinces such as Ontario and Quebec
developed a manufacturing base and associated government revenues sufficient
to allow the policy capacity needed to challenge Ottawa. During the nineteenth
and early twentieth centuries, decisions of the Judicial Committee of the Privy
Council, which until 1949 functioned as the Canadian high court, tended to
favour the provinces over Ottawa. Smiley gives this summary:

> From the late 1890s onward the Committee embarked on a course of giving
> provincial powers over "property and civil rights" an expansive interpretation
> while narrowly limiting Parliament's general power related to "Peace, Order
> and Good Government" and the enumerated federal power over "trade and
> commerce." (1987, 49)

In 1949, the Supreme Court of Canada replaced the Judicial Committee as the
court having the final say on constitutional issues.

After the Second World War, as noted, the major function of government shifted away from areas in federal jurisdiction, such as defence, and towards social, health, and educational policy, areas of provincial jurisdiction. Quebec's demands for more autonomy led Ottawa to shift jurisdiction down to all provinces. At the same time, social norms respecting the balance of power between Ottawa and the provinces evolved away from top-down authority. It is now difficult for Ottawa use its constitutional powers to disallow (deprive of legal force; effectively cancel) a provincial law or to declare an area of activity to be in federal, and no longer provincial, jurisdiction. Beyond these specific events, the basic nature of the country has always been one of decentralization. From the beginning, Canada has consisted of widely separated, distinct regions with differing economies and cultures, with a gulf dividing the metropolitan centre of Quebec and Ontario from the eastern and western hinterlands. This has been due not only to geography and history, but also in large part due to Macdonald's National Policy and its successors, which have favoured the industrialized centre and disadvantaged the staples-based economies such as fish, wheat, and timber in the peripheries (Stevenson 2012). Thus for a variety of reasons Macdonald's goal of centralization was turned into the current reality of extreme decentralization.

Since the war, intergovernmental relations have gone through successive evolutionary stages in terms of conflictual or cooperative relations. Bakvis and Skogstad (2012a) identify three phases, while recognizing overlap among them. In this view the 1950s and 1960s were an era of "co-operative federalism," marked by federal leadership and generally harmonious relations. This was followed by "competitive federalism" as provinces clashed with Ottawa and one another over high-stakes issues such as the constitution and energy. The era of "collaborative federalism" since the 1990s is one of less conflict and a willingness by Ottawa to see the provinces as something closer to equals than subordinates.

Harrison (2002; 1996b) in the same way sets out different eras of conflict and cooperation in the policy field of environment. In the early 1970s both governments moved into the policy field by passing legislation and establishing environment departments. Cooperation was achieved through bilateral agreements between Ottawa and seven provinces, signed in 1975, and use of an intergovernmental secretariat, the Canadian Council of Resource and Environment Ministers – since 1988 the Canadian Council of Ministers of the Environment (CCME). As the issue declined in popular importance, Ottawa was largely willing to relinquish the field to the provinces. That changed in the late 1980s, however, as popular support for environmental action increased; in response Ottawa began to take a more active role. Ottawa's constitutional jurisdiction respecting toxic pollution was established by court rulings in 1988 and 1997, while another court decision in 1989 required the federal government to give environmental assessment approvals for dam projects in Saskatchewan rather than, as it had hoped to do, leaving that province as the only regulatory authority. All of this led to conflict with provinces. Some measure of harmony was restored, however, by the 1998 Harmonization Accord, an intergovernmental agreement specifying how the federal and provincial governments would coordinate environmental policy in a number of areas.

Similarly, Gattinger (2015) traces the evolution of energy federalism. From confederation until the 1930s Ottawa generally took the lead in establishing policies implemented by federal law related to coal, the main energy source of the time. There was little provincial opposition or insistence that provinces should govern. As in the larger field of intergovernmental relations, up until the mid-1960s cooperation reigned, even as the oil-producing provinces put in place energy regulatory and royalty systems. In the 1970s, however, rising world oil prices provoked intense west-east conflict. Brian Mulroney restored cooperation by moving the federal government completely out of energy policy in the mid-1980s. By the 1990s, however, federal involvement in climate change provoked new energy-related conflict, which has been, aside from the benign neglect of the Harper era, the norm ever since.

Thus we see that while intergovernmental relations was becoming established its form changed fundamentally, from hierarchical control by Ottawa to a system of largely autonomous governments, closer to the international state system than to the more centralized forms of governance found in a federated state such as Germany. We also see that the Canadian system was better able to produce coordinated policy at some times than others. Understanding why we see cooperation at some times and conflict at others is central to the inquiry pursued here.

Mechanisms of Canadian Intergovernmental Relations

Canadian intergovernmental relations are the perhaps inevitable product of the original decision to create Canada as a federated state. Simmons describes federalism in this way:

> In Canada, as in all federations, neither the federal nor provincial governments are subordinate to one another, because this division of policy jurisdiction cannot be changed unilaterally by either of them. In other words, in Canada the two orders of government (federal and provincial) are equal, inasmuch as neither can change the division of powers in the Constitution Act, 1867 without the consent of the other, and in accordance with a specified amending formula. (Simmons 2016, 132)

Bakvis and Skogstad provide the same view when they define federalism as: "shared rule ... and local self-rule ... [in which] neither order of government is subordinate to the other"; a system looking to balance both "unity and diversity" (2012a, 2).

The basic rule of Canadian federalism, summed up by the term "executive federalism," is that it is only governments (the executive, consisting of prime minister or premier and cabinet) that participate in intergovernmental relations. Legislatures and opposition parties play no role, particularly since the results of intergovernmental relations are rarely brought back by governments to their legislatures to be enacted as law. At its most visible, it consists of a meeting of the prime minister and premiers. This was referred to as a First Ministers' Conference until the early 1990s. Since then, in an effort to move on from the high politics of constitutional negotiation and to suggest a less formal approach, the term used has been a First Ministers' Meeting (FMM) (Papillon and Simeon 2004, 114). A First Ministers' Meeting can only be convened by the prime minister, not by the provinces. Ideally, first ministers meet to discuss a given policy problem in order to reach agreement on a shared objective, which will then be accomplished by coordinated action taken by each of those governments. In practice, motives may not be that pure. Rather than including provinces in objective setting, Ottawa may want to convince provinces to accept the objective it has in mind; provincial leaders may be as interested in grandstanding for electoral advantage back home as they are in solving national problems.

The level below the FMM is a periodic meeting of ministers in a given policy area, coordinated by a secretariat such as the Canadian Council of Ministers of the Environment. Prior to finalization of significant decisions in the intergovernmental forum, ministers report back to their government to gain prior assent, just as do diplomats negotiating international agreements. The level below meetings of ministers is meetings of federal and provincial officials. In 1955, a meeting of first ministers established the Continuing Committee on Fiscal and Economic Matters, a body consisting of federal and provincial officials who would meet to discuss issues of the day, after which each official would individually report back to his or her own government (Smiley 1980, 95). During the two national climate-change efforts of the 1990s, which ended in 2002, federal and provincial ministers of environment, functioning through CCME, and ministers of energy, functioning through the then Council of Energy Ministers (CEM – after 2008 the Energy and Mines Ministers' Conference, or EMMC), were supported by an elaborate system of committees staffed by bureaucrats from both levels of government. Individual officials certainly kept their governments informed, but the committees reported as a whole, providing recommendations to meetings of ministers.

Thus the arena of intergovernmental relations can be defined as a decision-making process in which the main mechanisms are either meetings of first ministers or ministers, organized by a secretariat. Each government receives policy analysis and advice from its own officials and on some occasions all governments will receive policy advice from a system of combined officials. The decisions made are then implemented by governments themselves, using their own jurisdictional authority. There is no federal-provincial secretariat, in any policy field, with a mandate and resources to implement IGR decisions.

A Flawed Policymaking Process

Donald Smiley, one of Canada's leading experts on intergovernmental relations, provided this stinging critique in 1979:

> My charges against executive federalism are these:
> First, it contributes to undue secrecy in the conduct of the public's business.
> Second, it contributes to an unduly low level of citizen-participation in public affairs.
> Third, it weakens and dilutes the accountability of governments to their respective legislatures and to the wider public.
> Fourth it frustrates a number of matters of crucial public concern from coming on the public agenda and being dealt with by the public authorities.
> Fifth, it has been a contributing factor to the indiscriminate growth of government activities.
> Sixth, it leads to continuous and often unresolved conflicts among governments, conflicts which serve no purpose broader than the political and bureaucratic interests of those involved in them. (Smiley 1979, 105–6)

These criticisms have as much to do with democratic accountability as with the effectiveness of the policy governments together decide upon. In the same vein, Smith (2004) offers a comprehensive review of the way in which Canadian federalism and intergovernmental relations fail to fully meet democratic standards. The critique offered here has a narrower focus than either of those. Evaluation is provided only in terms of the ability of intergovernmental relations to generate at least some degree of coordination of the policies of participating governments, a first step towards a national program which is sufficiently effective that it can address the relevant problem.

The first problem in achieving coordinated policy, as noted by Smiley, is the fact that the federal and provincial governments meet and deliberate in secret. This locking out of societal actors such as firms and ENGOs means there is not only a lack of accountability and associated legitimacy, but also a lack of formal, public input that can improve the quality of policy decisions. Opposition parties are also excluded, because the results of intergovernmental negotiation, other than related spending measures or laws, are not brought back home by governments and presented to their legislatures. "Intergovernmental accords and agreements are not normally ratified or approved by legislatures" (Simeon and Nugent 2008, 103). As will be seen in the case studies, national energy and climate processes have included multi-stakeholder consultation, but unlike policymaking by governments acting alone, which involves actors such as firms and ENGOs right up to the point when cabinet secrecy takes over, the federal-provincial process may well consult, but it then goes back into its normal mode of closed-door meetings attended only by government officials. This favours industry, which due to its structural economic power has privileged access to government, and can thus pierce the veil of secrecy. Environmentalists and other non-state actors have no such automatic access, although they may, depending upon the ideology of the governing party, have some access.

A much greater problem is the fact that participation is optional – no government is formally required to participate in any given federal-provincial process, although most do, presumably because not to (other than the special case of Quebec under a Parti Québécois government) would appear unseemly in the eyes of that province's electorate. The problem is not so much that governments do not participate, but that while doing so all know that they may leave the federal-provincial process at any time without paying a significant price, either in terms of the reactions of other governments or the provincial or national electorate. By threatening to leave, governments can exercise veto power, bringing decision-making down to lowest-common-denominator results. An example of the latter is the statement by then British Columbia Premier Christy Clark at the 9 December 2016 First Ministers' Meeting on the Pan-Canadian Framework, dramatically made to the news media outside the meeting room just an hour or so before the document was to be finalized, that she was unhappy and thinking of leaving the process. The other governments acquiesced, with the result the text was amended to say that British Columbia, rather than any other government, would decide whether the British Columbia carbon tax would increase after 2020 (something later repudiated by the NDP government that replaced Clark's Liberals in 2017). Premier Clark was thus able to use the opt-out threat to increase the autonomy of her government within the intergovernmental PCF system and to weaken the collective decision. She was able to do that because of her confidence that pulling out would not cost her votes in the next election – quite the reverse, since standing up to Ottawa usually increases the popularity of sitting provincial governments.

Another defect, directly related to the ability of governments to opt out, is the fact that decision-making is always consensual. When Canadian government representatives meet, they discuss and decide, but they never vote. Such consensual decision-making, of course, increases the veto power of each participant, leading to lowest-common-denominator results and thus lessening policy effectiveness. This is similar to the consensual process used by sovereign states to negotiate an international agreement. In both cases, it seems reasonable to assume that the rule of consensus stems from the fact that participating governments are able to withdraw from the process at any time. Since they cannot be bound to accept the result, voting makes no sense. It has also been suggested by one government official working in intergovernmental relations that Canada has no choice but to use consensual decision-making because voting would run the risk of leaving Quebec continually isolated (confidential interview 2010). Given its origins as an international agreement among sovereign states, the European Union originally functioned on a purely consensual basis. That has moved in some areas to qualified majority voting in which member states are bound by the decision, but that decision must be by a specified portion of votes higher than 50 per cent. The system of Canadian intergovernmental relations has not made any such change and the analysis and recommendations presented in the final two chapters rest on the assumption of continued consensual decision-making.

The fourth difficulty with Canadian intergovernmental relations is the fact that the rules governing decision-making are vague and unenforceable, while intergovernmental organizations such as CCME, in terms of both mandate and resources, are weak. The rules cannot bind participating governments, for instance by requiring that they stay at the table and accept whatever decision is generated by consensus, rather than opting out. Organizations such as CCME, which is one of the better funded intergovernmental organizations in Canada, lack staffing and financial capacity, but above all a mandate to provide governments with research, consultation, and development of policy options and to then actively participate in the discussion. Nor are they encouraged or indeed allowed to do so. Canadian governments are very jealous of their autonomy as they participate in intergovernmental negotiations and will not cede power to secretariats (Bolleyer 2009). At the international level, the secretariat United Nations Environmental Programme (UNEP) has played an at least somewhat independent role, working to strengthen multilateral environmental agreements as they are being negotiated (Chasek, Downie, and Brown 2010). Neither the energy and environment secretariats that supported national climate policymaking in the 1990s, or the Council of the Federation that supported development of the Canadian Energy Strategy, have played any such role.

Simmons puts the problem this way: "intergovernmental forums that exist to co-ordinate federal and provincial environmental policies ... are weakly institutionalized or, in other words, largely informal" (2016, 131). Simeon and Nugent (2008) also point to the problem of weak institutions, saying it comes from the fact that the intergovernmental system has no basis in the constitution and intergovernmental bodies, such as CCME, have no foundation in legislation passed by one or more governments. To the extent the rules are weak and informal, they lack the power to influence the behaviour of participating governments. That in turn reduces policy effectiveness. Decisions made by a mob, which lacks any formal decision-making rules, are inherently less effective, defined as capable of achieving rational self-interest, than are decisions made by organizations with powerful rules and clearly defined functions of sub-units, such as the military or business corporation. Bolleyer lists attributes of "strong" institutions (defined as both rules and intergovernmental organizations) such as regularly scheduled meetings, autonomous intergovernmental organizations, clearly specified roles and functions, a formal basis in statute, and intergovernmental agreements that have legal standing and force and that are precise (2009, 25). The Canadian intergovernmental relations system lacks most of those features and for that reason, as Bolleyer (2009) finds in her comparison of Canadian, Swiss, and US intergovernmental relations, is less capable of generating effective policy.

Finally, the formal agreements that set out the decisions made by Canadian governments suffer from a number of weaknesses. The first of these is that the agreements themselves tend to avoid specific statements of obligations and instead describe future actions in vague terms. Presumably this is because of the desire of governments to maintain autonomy, referred to above. Simeon and Nugent say this: "In sum, commitments made by governments to each other are fundamentally ambiguous, which poses a serious problem for policy planning and delivery" (2008, 96). Bakvis, Baier, and Brown give a similar picture:

> Rarely will governments agree on a binding regulatory process. Somewhat more frequently they may commit themselves to joint spending initiatives. Much more commonly, however, after the exchange of information and mutual argument of positions, all that will be released is a general statement of intent, principles or objectives. (2009, 49)

Another factor working to weaken the ability of intergovernmental agreements to influence the behaviour of the governments that sign them is that they are not enforceable. This problem has two aspects. The first is the legal status of such agreements. The courts have ruled that they do not have the status of a law or a contract and hence do not legally bind parties (Simeon and Nugent 2008). The second problem is institutional and political: for most national processes, there is no entity tracking implementation of the agreement and publicly reporting on the results, thus allowing the electorate within a province, or the country as a whole, to apply pressure upon participating governments. Auditor-generals, plus in the environment area the Commissioner of the Environment and Sustainable Development, do not have the power to require policy action, or even to recommend policy. However, by auditing and then reporting their results, they do allow non-state actors to apply pressure to convince governments to improve their implementation of the policies they have put in place. No such mechanism exists, however, for national policy set out in intergovernmental agreements in the fields of environment, energy, or climate change.

These weaknesses of Canadian national policymaking have been summarized by Bolleyer:

> Compared to other federal countries, IGR in Canada remains highly fluid and ad hoc. The process has no constitutional or legislative basis and little backup from bureaucrats. It has no formal decision-rules and no capacity for authoritative decision-making. Most importantly, the scope and the extent of IGR is heavily dependent on whether the first ministers, in particular the prime minister, find it advantageous or not. (Bolleyer 2009, 90)

In summary, when they engage in intergovernmental relations Canadian governments work in secret to produce vaguely worded, lowest-common-denominator agreements that have no legal status and so cannot be enforced, and that lack accountability since limited information is available on the extent to which those agreements are being implemented. It is for these reasons that the defects of Canadian IGR constitute, along with the West-East divide and the inherent need to allocate a given total GHG emission reduction, an underlying barrier to the success of national climate-change policy.

Intergovernmental Policy Coordination

Any group of people working to achieve a common goal must coordinate their activities. In the same way, governments engaged in intergovernmental relations in order to achieve a national goal must coordinate their policies. More specifically in the case of climate change, Canada badly needs improved coordination of government activities to move us beyond the two tracks of increasing emissions in the carbon provinces and decreasing emissions elsewhere. Here we discuss the factors impeding or contributing to intergovernmental policy coordination, while further along in the chapter we apply the general model presented here (set out briefly in chapter 1) to the specific field of integrated energy and climate-change policymaking.

As discussed in the previous section, the original goal of John A. Macdonald that coordination be achieved by means of centralized federal power, using such things as disallowance of provincial legislation, is no longer viable, nor can the Canadian intergovernmental relations process generate coordination by means of majority voting. Making things even more difficult, by and large Canadian governments do not *want* coordination; instead, they want to as much as possible preserve their autonomy even while working with other governments. Bolleyer's findings (2009) make this point clear: her study shows that governments at both levels have a strong interest in policy autonomy, wishing to maintain control over their own decision-making while engaged in intergovernmental relations.

It seems reasonable to think this interest is stronger for the large provinces (British Columbia, Alberta, Ontario, and Quebec) that have more policy capacity and are less dependent upon federal transfers than smaller provinces such as those in the Atlantic region. Bakvis, Baier, and Brown make this observation:

> British Columbia, Alberta, Ontario, and Quebec together account for more than 80 per cent of the national population and more than 85 per cent of the economy ... Not surprisingly, these provinces can devote more resources to the management of intergovernmental relations than their smaller, poorer, counterparts can ... They also tend to be in a better position to say 'no' to the federal government, since they have the resources to provide a cushion. (2009, 51)

Certainly in the area of environmental policy, the large provinces have always actively opposed federal regulation within their borders, concerned about costs that might be imposed upon their industries. Harrison notes that in the 1970s, when both levels of government were establishing their systems for environmental regulation: "the federal government clashed only with the four most populous provinces" (2002, 128). After the federal government passed the Canadian Environmental Protection Act (CEPA) in 1988 and began to take a more vigorous approach to environmental protection: "Provincial opposition was led by Quebec, Ontario, Alberta, and British Columbia, the same four provinces that had opposed the Canada Water Act 20 years earlier" (Harrison 2002, 129).

Both the rules of the game and governments' desire to maintain autonomy stack the deck against intergovernmental policy coordination. Nevertheless, it does exist, as does also intergovernmental conflict and *lack* of coordination. How can we explain either conflict or coordination? Analysts point to a number of factors. Stevenson (2009) suggests conflict may be due to differing economic interests allied with different levels of government, such as western farming interests allied with their provincial governments in competition with central Canadian financial and manufacturing interests allied with Ottawa. Simeon (2006) and Smiley (1987) suggest that the cooperative period of the 1950s and 1960s changed to increased conflict in part due to changes within governments. Increased centralization and creation of new intergovernmental units meant that policy disputes were no longer handled exclusively by front-line officials who were more concerned with the policy issue at hand than with the prestige and status of their government. Once intergovernmental relations were handled less by those officials and more by elected politicians, who wanted to be seen as winning the intergovernmental battle, and officials whose expertise was intergovernmental per se rather than a particular policy field, conflict increased.

(This is the point made by Smiley [1979] quoted above when he referred to the "political and bureaucratic interests" that benefit from intergovernmental conflict.)

Two works of comparative federalism that seek to explain differing levels of coordination found in different federated countries look to the institutional context for explanation. Parker (2015) suggests that the basic structures of the governance system, such as degree of constitutional overlap, degree of centralized power held by the national government, and degree of intrastate federalism, which, as in the case of the German Bundesrat, gives subnational governments a direct voice in national government policymaking, account for the degree of coordination. Some institutional structures (e.g., large overlap, low centralization, and little intrastate decision-making) generate a greater need for coordination than do others. Bolleyer (2009) also looks to institutional factors, suggesting that a greater degree of institutionalization of intergovernmental relations, in terms of such things as fixed meeting dates and agendas and powers of coordinating secretariats, leads to greater coordination. Papillon and Simeon (2004) give a similar view, arguing in favour of greater institutionalization of First Ministers' Meetings, while Simmons (2004) offers evidence questioning that view.

As is the case for many subjects examined by political scientists, there is no one widely accepted theoretical explanation for intergovernmental conflict or cooperation. Parker, whose subject is intergovernmental agreements, which he describes as a "useful means of achieving coordination within federal systems" (2015, 1), says there is "no definitive theoretical treatment of the subject" (2015, 4). Stevenson points out that just as there are competing theoretical explanations for the existence of cooperation and conflict at the international level, in the case of Canadian IGR "it seems that no single explanation will suffice" (2009, 211). The theoretical viewpoint used here, accordingly, is not claimed to be the only one possible. It is simply claimed that it is useful, when applied to the specific IGR policy field of energy and climate change, for understanding the different degrees of policy coordination seen in the five instances to date of federal-provincial policymaking in that integrated field.

The starting point for the approach used here is to place cooperation on a spectrum of all the modes of intergovernmental relations. Bakvis and Skogstad offer five models of the intergovernmental workings of Canadian federalism (2012a, 4–11). The first is "independent governments," in which governments act within the watertight compartment of their own constitutional jurisdiction without regard to what other Canadian governments are doing. Next is "consultation" in which governments exchange information and discuss planned measures with other governments before acting independently. The third model is "coordination," which they define as "going beyond consultation to develop mutually acceptable policies and objectives, which each order of government then applies in its own jurisdiction" (2012, 5–6). The mechanisms used for consultation and coordination are the meetings of first ministers, ministers, officials, and workings of secretariats described above. The fourth model, which appeared in the 1990s, is "collaboration," in which provinces come closer to holding power equal to that of the federal government. In this model, the two levels of government work together to determine "broad national policies" (Bakvis and Skogstad 2012a, quoting Cameron and Simeon 2002, 49); Bakvis and Skogstad point out this can be done by a process involving the federal, provincial, and territorial governments or one which does not include the federal government. As examples of collaboration they refer to three formal agreements: the 1995 Agreement on Internal Trade, the 1998 Canada-Wide Accord on Environmental Harmonization, and the 1999 Social Union Framework Agreement. In each, the provincial and federal governments worked together to determine the national policy objective rather than, as might have happened earlier, that decision being made by Ottawa alone. Finally, Bakvis and Skogstad refer to "joint decision-making," in which governments cannot act alone, but instead must decide collectively "by virtue of either unanimous or supermajority agreement" (2012a, 13). An example is the Canada Pension Plan, which cannot be changed by the federal government without prior agreement of a specified number of provinces.

Gattinger (2015) referring more specifically to "energy federalism" provides this spectrum of types of intergovernmental relations in that policy field: 1) conflict, in which "interests diverge and there is open discord;" 2) independent, in which governments act without considering effects of those actions on other governments; 3) parallelism, in which governments adopt similar policies, but tailor them to local circumstances; 4) coordination, in which governments "maximize compatibility" of policies; and, 5) collaboration/harmonization, in which governments "work together to pursue common objectives."

In both models, we find essentially two things: 1) governments acting independently; and, 2) governments engaging in various forms of cooperation. Bakvis and Skogstad point out that the five models are not mutually exclusive and at times may appear "simultaneously" (2012a, 9). Thus intergovernmental relations involves both actions taken by the federal government and provinces *by themselves* and also *together*. Bakvis, Baier, and Brown describe it this way: governments are "at one and the same time autonomous and interdependent" (2009, 46). Essential for understanding cooperation is the fact that a given government may do both during one intergovernmental process. This is because, in the model of IGR coordination used here, such coordination largely results from the fact that a lead government has taken unilateral action (acted by itself) with the intent of influencing the behaviour of other governments (so that they will act together). In the analysis of the five case studies below, considerable attention is paid to unilateral action taken in the context of coordinated action, particularly such action taken by the Government of Canada. Unilateral action is the opposite of cooperation but is also an essential aspect of cooperation (but, as the cases show, can also *hinder* cooperation).

Bakvis and Skogstad, based on a review of intergovernmental relations in many policy fields, suggest that four factors are most important for determining where a given IGR process falls on the spectrum from independent governments to collaborative action (2012b, 343–5). The first is constitutional jurisdiction. In those few areas in which the constitution clearly assigns jurisdiction to just one level of government, such as local government to provinces, we find the independent governments mode. The second is the history of intergovernmental relations in the policy field, which provides patterns of interaction among governments, conflictual or cooperative, likely to continue. The third is the ideas and interests of governments. The fourth is the international context, which may promote either unilateral action or cooperation.

We return to the third variable, the ideas and interests of governments, when discussing coordination in the energy and climate policy fields, starting on page 55. Here, we examine the essential nature of coordination, in any field of human activity. What does acting together mean? Or, putting the question another way, how is the term "coordination" defined and used here? A dictionary definition of "to coordinate" includes this: "Cause (things or persons) to function together or occupy their proper place as parts of an interrelated whole" (OED 1993, 506). At heart, this definition refers to behaviour change – to function together, parts have to change their behaviour to conform to the behaviour of other parts. In the context of Canadian intergovernmental relations, behaviour change means that a government, because it is acting in concert with other Canadian governments, puts in place policy at least marginally different than it would have had it been acting completely alone.

Bringing about coordinated action is readily achieved within formal organizations because they have both rules and authority. Coordination is achieved in armies or business corporations by hierarchical command, with orders given at the top and behaviour changed accordingly by units and individuals below. Within Canada, one of the most decentralized federations in existence, second only perhaps to Belgium, nothing like that is possible. The federal government cannot order a given province to take a particular policy action; it can induce provincial behaviour change, as discussed below, but cannot order it. Coordination cannot be achieved in Canadian intergovernmental relations by means of top-down command. Nevertheless, Canadian governments do change behaviour to adopt policies aligned with those of other governments as part of a national effort, at least on some occasions, in some policy fields. Beyond the four factors cited by Bakvis and Skogstad and the other explanations referred to above, can coordination be explained by focusing upon the concept of behaviour change?

There are basically two reasons for a Canadian government engaged in inter-governmental relations to change behaviour: 1) changes in government interest (objective) that arise from the basic fact of participating in an intergovernmental process; and, 2) external pressure to change behaviour, coming from non-state actors or other Canadian governments. The first reason exists because external pressure, the most important explanation for behaviour change in formal organizations, does not explain all instances of coordination. We find cooperation and coordination outside formal organizations, in venues in which there is no top-down authority giving commands. Groups of friends are able to agree they will meet at the same restaurant at the same time and change their behaviour accordingly. Sovereign states compromise their sovereignty by agreeing to be bound by rules of multilateral agreements and then change their behaviour, to at least some extent, to comply with those rules. In the one instance of the EU, sovereign states went so far in the direction of coordination as to erect over their heads a new level of government with power to directly order them to change behaviour. Why do these things happen?

The answer was provided in chapter 1, in the discussion of interest as a the-oretical variable, when it was noted that self-interested actors do cooperate, from either altruism or the recognition, when confronted by a collective-action problem, that self-interest can only be achieved through cooperation. Toma-sello and colleagues (2009) report on experiments with humans and other primates, showing that altruism exists at a very early age in members of our species, more than it does in primates to whom we are related. Dinner friends and sovereign states may well be influenced by altruism, but they certainly are also influenced by the knowledge they cannot achieve their self-interest by act-ing alone. Another example of self-interested coordination is given by the indi-vidual members of a symphony orchestra. Each has the option of performing alone, outside the venue of the orchestra, where they would have maximum autonomy and no need to align their playing with that of others. Doing so will produce beautiful solo music. If they wish to create a different kind of beauty, however, such as that represented by Beethoven's sixth symphony, they can only do so by playing as one member of an orchestra. Having made that decision, to achieve self-interest they must coordinate their playing with that of the other orchestra members. Authority and rules certainly exist in the orchestra, which is, after all, a formal organization; the conductor directs and social norms man-date that musicians obey. Surely, however, it is the desire of each musician to create something larger than any of them could create alone, which is the most powerful explanation for coordination in the orchestra. After all, ensembles, jazz bands, and many other groups of musicians manage to achieve coordina-tion without a conductor. One suspects that even while coordination is achieved in formal organizations by top-down pressure, the individuals involved also change their behaviour because they *want* the organization to succeed.

By and large, Canadian provincial governments are self-interested actors, concerned with the well-being of their own province and happy to leave the national interest to the government in Ottawa. They prefer to make solo music, even though nominally a member of the band. Faced with the collective-action problem of the need to win two world wars, however, Canadian provinces responded by ceding jurisdiction without any great objections to Ottawa. "As in 1914, federal powers under the authority of the War Measures Act approached those of a unitary state" (Simeon and Robinson 1990, 104). Whitcomb (2017) discusses the same phenomenon of provincial acquiescence. Faced with a different kind of collective-action problem, the need to put in place welfare state programs that provided roughly the same level of service throughout the country, the provinces allowed Ottawa to spend in their jurisdictional turf and then engaged in extensive cooperation. Is it possible that achieving an international commitment to reduce total GHG emissions could also be fashioned as a collective-action problem, which each province wanted to achieve but knew it could not by acting alone? We return to that question in chapter 11.

As noted, the second factor that can lead to policy coordination is external pressure on governments. Three sources of such pressure seem to be most relevant: 1) from their electorate; 2) from business actors; and, 3) from other governments, particularly a lead government. In terms of the first, once having agreed to participate in an intergovernmental process, governments have a shared interest in at least *appearing* to be working together for the common Canadian good. Their electorate expects it and self-interest makes governments loath to disappoint. Even though opting out is relatively painless, by and large governments choose to continue participating in an IGR process once it is underway.

The effect of this inducement to cooperation is lessened by the fact that governments can get the benefit of giving their electorate the *appearance* they are cooperating, while in fact maintaining full autonomy. To do so, they engage in symbolic policymaking, providing a display of going through the rituals of discussion and intergovernmental negotiation and then at the end of the day signing an agreement that is sufficiently vague and ambiguous that they have committed to nothing. Simmons gives this example: "A skeptic may be inclined to conclude that without identifying who is responsible for what, and without timelines and clearly defined targets, the Canada Forest Accord and National Forest Strategy are effective as public relation tools, but have limited capacity to motivate coalition members to coordinate their efforts, or even modify each government's existing policy trajectory" (2004, 299). The 2015 Canadian Energy Strategy in the same way failed to commit governments to any specific actions. The simple fact of governments reaching agreement is not a sure indicator of behaviour change in terms of new, aligned policies. External pressure from the electorate pushes governments towards cooperation, but governments can evade that pressure.

In terms of non-state actors beyond voters, pressure is most likely to come from industry, simply because it is the most powerful non-state actor. In the first case study, we see that Ottawa and Alberta eventually reached agreement in 1981 because, among other reasons, the oil industry, seeking policy certainty, was pressing them to do so (as were others, including provinces). The 2015 CES came into being in large part because the industry was lobbying for a national energy strategy, believing it would legitimize the business search for deregulation and new pipeline capacity. However, secrecy to some extent insulates Canadian IGR from non-state demands. Even though business has privileged access to communicate with governments, it is not in the room when IGR decisions are made. Perhaps more important, while the oil industry is certainly interested in federal-provincial activity affecting that industry, many IGR agreements, in areas such as social policy or revenue sharing, do not directly touch business interests.

For these reasons, the most significant source of external pressure is that exerted by other Canadian governments. Since the government exerting pressure is seeking to achieve self-interest by influencing the behaviour of other governments it is, in the theoretical perspective employed here, exercising power. As set out in chapter 1, that can be done by means of persuasion, promise, or threat. Although the conceptualizations differ, this is similar to the picture given by Simeon of the "strategies and tactics" used by Canadian governments as they interact in an IGR process (2006, 228). He refers to "partisan discussion," which includes such things as framing of the issue at hand and use of expert data to support an argument, and is essentially the same as the term "persuasion" as the term is used here (2006, 243–7). His second category is "changing reality," which refers to tactics "which actually change the situation which confronts the other actors" (2006, 247). This includes such things as making a new proposal or manipulating the order of discussion on the agenda, and also "the exchange of conditional threats and promises. 'If you do (or don't) do this, then I will ...'" (2006, 251).

Provinces wishing to exert pressure on other governments in an IGR process have two means available: persuasion and threat (promise, in the form of something like a shared-cost program, is not something a province can offer). Persuasion can be done both privately and publicly, with the latter intended to rally support within the other government's electorate. The only threat available is the threat to pull out of the IGR process, thus exerting lowest-common-denominator pressure. As Alberta attempted to do during the CES process, persuasion can be used to bring other governments *up* to a collectively agreed-upon level of policy. Simeon (2006) argues that federal-provincial discussion and persuasion during the Canada Pension Plan negotiations of the 1960s resulted in what all agreed was a superior policy outcome to any of the options considered at the outset. The opt-out threat, on the other hand, can only work to bring policy *down* to a new, less-effective level.

In comparison to the provinces, Ottawa holds much more significant powers to nudge the policy level up or down. In terms of the latter, it can simply refuse to initiate a federal-provincial process, as did the Harper government from 2006 to 2015, thus ensuring that national policy is either not put in place at all or only done so by the provinces acting alone. Like a province, it can persuade, but it can also do something a province cannot do: it can also promise, by offering money in return for behaviour change. Finally, also unlike a province, it can use threat to move policy up towards increased effectiveness. The atomic bomb threat, unlikely to be used today but nevertheless legal, is to indicate that Ottawa might use its constitutional powers of disallowance or declaration. A lower level of threat, although one that still bumps up against social norms respecting use of Ottawa's powers, is the threat to act unilaterally in ways that a province will see as going against its interest. This might include a threat to act alone to introduce a new program that affects a province's citizens or industries, in the design of which the province has no voice. More significant for climate-change policy is the threat of federal regulation within the provincial territory. Discussion returns to this subject in the last section of this chapter.

Energy and Climate-Change Jurisdiction

What follow is a brief presentation of both constitutional authority and practice that decides the powers of the Government of Canada, provinces, and Indigenous peoples to govern and to participate in governing in the areas of energy and climate change.

Energy

Section 92 (13) of the constitution, giving the provinces jurisdiction over "Property and Civil Rights in the Province," is interpreted to provide provincial authority to regulate industries, including energy industries, that are not federally regulated (Webber 2015, 151). The only energy industry regulated by Ottawa is atomic energy. There, Ottawa has sole jurisdictional authority, although it is up to provinces to decide if they will include nuclear in their mix of electricity-generation sources. Perhaps more important for provincial jurisdiction is section 109, which gives to the provinces ownership of natural resources located within their borders. Webber underlines the importance of the fact of ownership.

> In a country as resource-rich as Canada, this control over public lands is one of the principal strengths of the provinces. The administration and sale of mineral

rights, oil and gas concessions, forest resources, hydro-electric power and lands for settlement and industrial development have been a stupendous source of revenue. (Webber 2015, 165)

This fact of provincial ownership of energy resources has two main implications for energy and climate-change policy. First, it explains the differing interests of the carbon and hydro provinces. The former own oil and gas energy resources, while the latter own hydroelectricity resources. Those simple facts underpin the gulf that is making national climate-change policy so difficult. Secondly, as Webber says, the revenues which accompany ownership, and beyond that the energy resource contribution to provincial GDP, are very important to provincial governments. For that reason, energy and climate change are in the realm of high-stakes politics, which makes spanning the gulf that much more difficult.

While the provinces own the energy resources located within their borders, the federal government owns the energy resources located outside provincial territory, in the northern territories and offshore. In those areas, given the fact that to date no Arctic oil or natural gas has yet been extracted and there is a moratorium on Pacific offshore drilling, the most significant energy resource is Atlantic offshore oil and natural gas. As will be seen in the historical overview provided in the next chapter, the question of which level of government would regulate and receive revenues from offshore oil was a source of dispute between Ottawa and the two relevant provinces, Newfoundland and Nova Scotia, until the Mulroney government effectively handed control to the provinces in 1985.

The federal government also holds jurisdictional authority to regulate the movement of energy across provincial borders and in and out of Canada. An anomaly exists, however, in federal use of that authority. Ottawa has always been the government issuing regulatory approvals for interprovincial and international oil and gas pipelines, directly or by means of an arm's length regulatory agency, the National Energy Board (NEB) (in 2019, transformed into the Canadian Energy Regulator by the Justin Trudeau government). On the other hand, Ottawa has chosen not to play that role for electricity lines crossing provincial borders. The NEB Act provided that body with potential authority to regulate interprovincial electricity movement, but the federal government never passed the order-in-council needed to trigger that authority (Blue 2009).

It seems the explanation is provincial resistance to any federal role in electricity. Both before and after the Second World War, successive federal governments expressed an interest in developing a national electricity policy with increased east-west interprovincial transmission, but always met with stiff provincial resistance, particularly from Quebec, for whom its hydroelectricity resource was so important (Froschauer 2000). Nor yet has Ottawa responded to Newfoundland appeals to intervene in its dispute with Quebec over the Churchill Falls contract. That arrangement, finalized in 1969, has given hugely lopsided benefits to Quebec because it allows that province to purchase electricity at

1960s rates from Newfoundland and then sell electricity to New England at a considerable markup. The one thing Ottawa has done is to guarantee New-foundland borrowing for its Muskrat Falls project with Nova Scotia, something that elicited Quebec objections on the ground it had developed its hydroelec-tricity resource with no federal assistance (Macdonald and Lesch 2015). Elec-tricity policy, an essential component of climate-change policy, today is still largely within provincial jurisdiction, even when it is bought and sold among provinces (export and import from the US does require federal approval.) That said, federal officials are working with their provincial counterparts on electric-ity issues as part of the Pan-Canadian Framework program.

The other important aspect of energy jurisdiction is the constitutionally derived power of Indigenous peoples with respect to consultation during the approvals process for a project that may affect their rights. The repatriated con-stitution of 1982 affirmed existing Aboriginal rights, without specifying them. In terms of the right to be consulted and to have views taken into account, that has been done by a number of Supreme Court decisions, starting in 2004. Lambrecht explains the way in which that right is grounded in the constitu-tion: "The Court confirms that the duty to consult and accommodate has a constitutional character grounded in the honour of the Crown and corollary to section 35 of the *Constitution Act, 1982*" (2013, 71). There is now an obligation on the part of governments, given weight by its constitutional basis, to consult in a meaningful way with Indigenous peoples before giving regulatory approval to projects that might affect them. This is an obligation to do more than pro-vide information and listen to views respecting a proposed project, but also to accommodate those views to at least some extent in the design of the project as determined by the regulatory approval. While not giving Indigenous peoples a complete veto, the court decisions have created a right to a voice in decision-making associated with project approval. The courts have quashed prior federal approvals for the Northern Gateway pipeline in June of 2016 and of the Trans Mountain expansion in August 2018 due to failures to adequately consult with Indigenous peoples affected.

Climate Change

In the spring of 2019, the Saskatchewan Court of Appeal ruled that Ottawa's plan to impose a carbon tax in any province that had not itself introduced carbon pricing in the form of either a tax or cap-and-trade system was consti-tutional. That decision is being appealed to the Supreme Court, as will deci-sions in similar cases brought by Ontario and Alberta, which means federal jurisdiction with respect to climate-change policy has not yet been definitely settled by the courts. Law experts, however, are confident that the federal gov-ernment has the constitutional authority to regulate greenhouse gas emissions, since it is a matter of national and international importance (Chalifour 2010). If the Supreme Court ultimately agrees, climate-change policy would be confirmed as an area of shared federal and provincial jurisdiction, similar to the shared authority to regulate toxic substances found in environmental policy (Valiante 2002).

In the areas of both energy and climate change, the federal government holds other constitutional powers. It can "disallow" provincial legislation, essentially cancelling it; Ottawa can also declare a particular undertaking that falls within provincial jurisdiction to be "for the general advantage of Canada" and so transform it into a matter of federal jurisdiction (Webber 2015, 135–6). As discussed, the inclusion of those powers in the 1867 British North America Act reflected the view of the time that Canadian federalism should be organized on the basis of dominance of the provinces by the federal government. Both powers were used extensively in the nineteenth century, but have now fallen into disuse: Ottawa last used them in 1943 and 1961 respectively (Webber 2015, 136). They still exist, however, and are referred to in the energy and climate policy dialogue. In the spring of 2018, before Ottawa decided to buy the pipeline and was still considering all options to overcome the British Columbia government's resistance to the Trans Mountain expansion, commentators suggested use of such constitutional powers (Scotti 2018). Their use today, however, would be seen as an extreme violation of current norms governing federal use of power in its relations with the provinces, and so is most unlikely.

In summary, nuclear and electricity policy fall almost completely within federal and provincial jurisdiction respectively. Since renewable energy is used almost only for electricity generation, it too is effectively provincial (although the federal government has funded research and development for many years). Only fossil fuels are a subject of shared jurisdiction for both energy and climate-change policy and there, with respect to pipeline approvals, jurisdiction is shared three ways, by including Indigenous peoples. This shared jurisdiction, of course, opens the door to intergovernmental conflict. The next section builds upon the discussion above to look at factors that might turn that conflict into cooperation.

Energy and Climate-Change Policy Coordination

The general view of intergovernmental policy coordination given above is that governments are willing to change their behaviour by aligning their policies with those of other governments for two reasons. The first is an interest in cooperation, due to altruism or recognition of a collective-action problem. The second is external pressure coming from others, most notably other governments. The second is far more relevant to Canadian IGR than is the first. This section examines the workings of that external pressure in terms of the interests of Canadian governments specific to the integrated policy field of energy and climate change. That is done, as mentioned in chapter 1, by borrowing from a theoretical approach used in the study of international environmental politics.

Sprinz and Vaahtoranta (1994) offer an "interest based" explanation of international environmental politics, which looks to domestic politics to understand the different positions countries take during negotiations with respect to a given issue, in terms of either favouring or resisting coordinated international action. In the interests of parsimony, their model assumes only two factors are most important for deciding a country's position. The first is the extent to which a country is threatened by the issue at hand. An example is Sweden in the 1960s, which suffered from acid rain pollution coming from Europe and for that reason began to press for international action on the issue. Another example is given by the low-lying island states today, for whom rising sea levels associated with climate change pose an acute threat, leading them also to push for coordinated international action. The second factor in the model offered by Sprinz and Vaahtoranta is the cost a country must bear to act on the issue. An example of a country facing a high cost of action is Saudi Arabia, which sees reduction in fossil fuel use as an economic threat and has historically worked to block progress in the international climate regime. A country suffering from the issue and with a low cost of action will act as a "pusher" advocating for coordinated international action. Conversely, a country with a high cost of action and low vulnerability to the issue will play the role of a "dragger" in opposing such action. In their model, other countries play two intermediary positions.

Chasek, Downie, and Brown use a similar approach to understanding the positions taken by states as they negotiate multilateral environmental agreements. They classify states as playing one of four roles: lead, working to put the new regime in place (comparable to the "pusher"); supporting the lead state; swing, giving support in exchange for some favour; and veto (comparable to the "dragger"), working to block or weaken the lead state effort (2010, 54). Chasek and her co-authors argue that the domestic politics of states determine which role a state will play. While also seeing states playing one of the four same roles envisaged by Sprinz and Vaahtoranta, they suggest that a larger number of domestic political factors will influence the role played by a given state. These include the interests of relative business actors which seek to influence the state position; bureaucratic politics within the state; the influence environmentalists can bring to bear, countering that of business; and ideology of the governing party (Chasek, Downie, and Brown 2010, 55–8).

The implication of the two models is that international cooperation to address an environmental issue, codified by means of an agreement, is unlikely to take place if no country is acting as a lead state, convincing others to participate, or if the lead role is being played by a small, relatively weak state (as in the example of low-lying island states given above). Conversely, the veto role is also key to the ability of states to coordinate their actions. "For a regime to form, [that is, for states to agree on cooperation] veto states must be persuaded to abandon their opposition to a proposed regime or at least to compromise with states supporting it" (Chasek, Downie, and Brown 2010, 49). Veto-state power comes from the fact that if that state does not participate, the agreement will be less effective. In a lowest-common-denominator process, lead and supporting states will agree to demands of the veto state in order to ensure it does not opt out of the process all together.

Modified as necessary, this approach is used as the basis for analysis of the five case studies of Canadian energy and climate intergovernmental processes examined here. The element of cost of action in the two models just discussed can be readily applied to the question of Canadian governments playing a lead, support, swing, or veto role. However, the variable of vulnerability to effects of the issue as a factor determining choice of role does not apply in the Canadian climate-change context.

Some Canadian provinces and territories are more threatened than others by climate change; for instance, the territories exposed to the greater effects of warming in the Canadian north and coastal provinces exposed to the problem of rising sea levels. Since 1990, however, no province or territory has played a lead-actor role because it sees itself as particularly threatened by climate-change impacts. Presumably this is because the climate-change threat has not been seen as sufficiently dire and because they have known that even if they could convince all Canadian governments to act on the issue that national effort, given that Canadian emissions are less than 2 per cent of the global total, would not solve their individual problem. Nor has perception that Canada is threatened by climate change led the federal government to play a lead role in international climate negotiations; usually allied with the US, it has for the most part sought to impede rather than further international progress (the international role played by the Justin Trudeau government is an exception).

While the first of the factors examined by Sprinz and Vaahtoranta is not relevant, their second, the cost of acting on the issue, certainly is. From the outset, we have seen carbon provinces, in particular Alberta and Saskatchewan, who face a high cost of acting on the issue, play a veto role in climate-change intergovernmental relations, just as Saudi Arabia does at the international level. Thus it is assumed that interest in material gain from export of fossil fuels is an important factor determining the positioning of Canadian governments on the lead-support-swing-veto spectrum. As just noted, when that interest is threatened by climate policy (or, in the first case, by Ottawa's desire to keep oil prices below the world level) governments possessing fossil fuel resources are likely to play a veto role. However, that same interest will lead those governments to play a lead role on questions of national policy related to energy export, in particular current debates over pipeline construction. This explains the veto role played by Alberta in the two 1990s climate processes, and also the lead role that province played in the Canadian Energy Strategy.

Two other aspects of fossil fuel export as a factor determining role are relevant. First, it obviously is only a factor for governments that actually possess fossil fuel resources. This means that while it may lead a carbon province to play a lead or veto role, other provinces without fossil fuel resources have no such motivation and are more likely to play support or swing roles. Secondly, the Government of Canada *is* a government possessing fossil fuel resources. Although oil and gas exports are not as important for the economy of Canada as a whole as for the economy of a province such as Alberta, they are important nevertheless. This gives Ottawa an incentive to play a lead role in national policy relevant to fossil fuel exports and either tempers its enthusiasm for effective policy when playing a lead role on national climate-change policy or leads it to pursue both export and emission reduction goals, no matter how contradictory those goals might be.

Beyond material interest in fossil fuel export, the application of the interest-based model used here looks to one other factor as determining the role played by Canadian governments in energy and climate-change intergovernmental relations: interest of the government in putting in place effective climate-change policy, as determined by ideology of the governing party. Generally speaking, right-wing governments have limited interest in doing so. Examples include the Harper government, which did not act on the issue, the Ontario Harris government, which played a behind-the-scenes veto role in the national climate effort of 1998 to 2002, and the Doug Ford Ontario government, which allied itself with Saskatchewan to play a joint veto role in opposition to the Ottawa-led Pan-Canadian program. Conversely, centre-left governments, such as those of Prime Ministers Chrétien, Martin, and Justin Trudeau at the federal level and Kathleen Wynne and Philippe Couillard at the provincial level have worked to put in place climate policy and in some instances to lead intergovernmental climate processes.

Given these and perhaps other factors influencing the choice of role by Canadian governments, the approach used here to understand the degree to which Canadian energy and climate intergovernmental relations produces coordinated action is as follows.

It is assumed that Canadian energy and climate intergovernmental processes are likely to generate coordinated policy:

1) when a lead government does not encounter significant countervailing power from a veto government;
2) when a lead government encounters significant countervailing power but is able to prevail by some combination of skilled use of persuasion and promise and willingness to use unilateral action as a threat to influence

provincial behaviour; all while managing to convince a veto government and other governments not to opt of the process.

It is assumed that energy and climate intergovernmental processes are not likely to generate coordinated policy:

1) when a veto government does not encounter significant countervailing power from a lead government;
2) when a veto government prevails in the contest with a lead government, or, along with a significant number of other governments, opts out of the process.

This model assumes that substantial policy coordination does not require participation of all fourteen Canadian governments, particularly if those opting out have smaller economies and populations. However, it does require participation by a significant number, perhaps at least half or more and, in the case of climate policy, governments representing half or more of total Canadian emissions.

Federal Government Energy and Climate-Change Strategy

The starting point for strategy of any federal government is that government's interest. It is assumed here that the basic interest of any government is to hold on to power by winning reelection. That means governments must give at least the appearance of action on the climate issue. Beyond that, as just discussed, ideology of the party governing in Ottawa influences interest respecting the need for climate action and therefore the role it plays in national climate-change policy. All federal governments, however, whether right-wing or centre-left, share an ideological commitment to capitalism and economic growth and therefore a material interest in fossil fuel energy exports.

As noted in the preceding section, this will influence the way in which a centre-left federal government plays a lead-government role in national climate policy. This was visible but not prominent during the Chrétien years but is unmistakable in the Justin Trudeau government's search for a "balanced" approach that includes both emission reductions, to be achieved through the Pan-Canadian Framework, and emission increases associated with additional pipeline capacity.

Another aspect of the ideological interest of the federal governing party is the fact that Ottawa automatically holds a different view of federalism than does a given province, simply because it is governing the whole country. A province, naturally enough, is focused upon one part of the picture, its own economic interest, but whoever governs in Ottawa must take a larger view (Simeon 2006, 190).

Bakvis, Baier, and Brown discuss the particular interests of provinces and then say: "In the case of the federal government, there is a general sense of the interests of Canada as a whole" (2009, 50). Related to that is the federal concern for national unity. When threatened, survival of the state is the overriding goal of all governments. Particularly since the days of the Quiet Revolution and the razor-thin result of the 1995 Quebec referendum, survival of the Canadian state has been in question. For that reason, the Ottawa interest in national unity has been sharpened. That may help explain willingness to date to settle for ineffectual climate policy and to turn a blind eye to the differing interests and actions of the carbon and hydro provinces. Finally, federal governments hold different ideas respecting the functioning of Canadian federalism. As will be seen, Pierre Trudeau felt the balance of power had swung too far towards the provinces and sought corrective action. Prime Ministers Clark and Mulroney were more willing to accommodate provincial interests, while Prime Minister Harper believed in watertight compartments and disavowed any notion of national intergovernmental programs.

Beyond these material and nonmaterial interests, what other factors guide federal strategy? Here, we start with the fact of shared jurisdiction, which means Ottawa can, if it wishes, act alone to itself reduce some GHG emissions. Accordingly, federal governments planning to lead an attempt to generate coordinated climate-change policy must make two decisions, even if only implicitly: 1) the degree to which they will use their own policy instruments of law, spending, and others to bring about emission reductions – in other words, the portion of the overall reduction effort for which it will take responsibility and the portion to be left to the provinces; and, 2) what means they will use to convince the provinces to put in place policies and programs capable, when combined with federal action, of achieving the overall goal. With respect to the first, the Government of Canada climate plan issued in 2000 stated that federal action would achieve one-third of the necessary reduction (Government of Canada 2000, 2). Federal plans of 2002 and 2005 (Government of Canada 2002b, 2005) and the federal-provincial PCF of 2016 (PCF 2016) do not explicitly state what portion of the total goal will be achieved by Ottawa policies and what by the provinces. However, they do indicate planned actions to be taken by Ottawa alone and, in some cases, resulting reductions. An example is the 2002 federal plan (Government of Canada 2002b), which stated that Ottawa would be responsible for regulating industrial emissions and in doing so it expected to achieve reductions of 65 Mt per year, out of the total target of a 240 Mt reduction. (That was not the total federal contribution; other federal actions were planned to bring about other reductions.)

Ottawa's own climate-change policies are also significant for the second decision referred to above: the means of inducing provincial action. A planned federal unilateral action may be intended to reduce emissions, but also may be intended to function as a threat in order to change provincial behaviour. A federal government has few means available of threatening a province, since it cannot order the province to do anything, and it is difficult to imagine a federal threat such as withholding funding in an unrelated policy area. It can, however, withhold funding in the climate-change policy domain, as has been done with Saskatchewan because it refuses to participate in the Pan-Canadian Framework. The more significant threat, though, is that the federal government will use its own law to directly regulate citizens or firms within the boundaries of a given province unless that provincial government itself takes such action, as we have seen with the federal backstop carbon tax in the PCF. Presumably the provincial government does not want to see that happen because it wishes to be the one deciding how much internalized cost its citizens or firms will be asked to bear. (Although, one could imagine a scenario in which the provincial government is happy to see the federal government take the blame for unpopular action.) Thus the use of federal policy instruments falls into one of two categories. The first is the *actual* use of the instrument to achieve part of the overall reduction. This can be done separately from any negotiations with provinces. The second is the *threatened* use of federal policy instruments, as part of the intergovernmental negotiating process.

Other than threat, the federal government, as noted, has two other means of influencing provincial behaviour – persuasion and promise. Persuasion may well take the form of public appeals to a given province to join the national effort which hopefully will resonate with voters in that province and so bring pressure to bear on its government. Promise most often refers to offers of financial assistance for provinces thinking of coordinating their promises with the national program. The Paul Martin government, for instance, signed bilateral agreements with a number of provinces by which it committed to provide financial assistance for emission reductions in that province. Federal funding assistance is also an inducement to join the Pan-Canadian Framework.

Beyond selecting a combination of threat, promise, and persuasion, the federal government must continually make another strategic decision. Should it negotiate with all or a number of provinces at the same time, or engage in bilateral negotiation with just one (Bakvis, Bauer, and Brown 2009, 51)? Engaging with all increases the number of potential veto points and the complexity of the task. Negotiating with just one is easier and makes provincial alliances less likely to be an obstacle. However, other provinces may object to being excluded (Simeon 2006, 142–3).

A useful summary picture of federal strategy is given by Snoddon and Van-Nijnatten (2016). They argue that when the federal government engages with provinces to achieve coordinated policy it must decide between multilateral and bilateral, and then decide if it will function in one of three modes: 1) imposing action upon provinces, to the extent it is able; 2) setting a goal and encouraging rather than requiring provincial action to achieve it; and, 3) without having first set a goal, bringing provinces together and then acting as one among equals as the goal and plans to achieve it are collectively developed. Drawing on experience to date with coordination of income tax, goods and services tax and harmonized sales tax, and Canada-wide environmental standards, they suggest Ottawa needs to find a balance between inducing provincial behaviour change and leaving room for provincial flexibility.

Their recommendation informs analysis in the concluding chapters below. There it is argued, based upon the case study findings, that Ottawa needs to use at least some of its available power to influence provincial behaviour (Snoddon and VanNijnatten mode 1). However, it must do so with skill, finesse, and above all restraint, not using all available power (a mix of modes 1 and 2). Finally, it must stop setting the GHG reduction target unilaterally, and instead include the provinces in that decision (mode 3). Ottawa should shift towards collaborative policymaking, on the Bakvis and Skogstad spectrum, but should never see itself as merely one among equals. It is the only government with means to influence the behaviour of other governments and thus achieve policy coordination. The basic argument made in the concluding chapter is that in any future national climate-change effort Ottawa must move more towards collaborative federalism than it has to date, treating the provinces as equals in setting the national target while at the same time using skilled diplomacy to persuade them to move in the direction of a more ambitious target. Beyond persuasion, however, Ottawa must take unilateral action to influence provincial behaviour by a combination of promise and threat – an iron fist in a collaborative federalism glove.

3 Historical Overview: Canadian Energy and Climate Politics

This chapter provides an overview of the way in which energy and climate politics and the related policies of individual governments and coordinated federal-provincial efforts have unfolded in this country over the last fifty years or more. Beyond orienting the reader, the chapter is intended to give a sense of the different ways in which the energy and climate issues were viewed at the different time periods when they were addressed by the national policy processes: the oil price shocks of the 1970s, which gave vastly different economic incentives to west and east but raised no environmental concerns; the 1990s, when climate change was starting to become an issue of concern but the science was hotly contested and governments were taking only first tentative policy steps; the 2000s, when expanding oil sands production and pipeline conflicts both fully connected the energy and climate issues and moved that interconnected dynamic to centre stage; and the more recent past, when putting a price on carbon had become accepted wisdom among policy elites but also a source of resentment among many of those asked to pay, stirring all of the west-east passions first roused in the 1970s and becoming a major point of partisan conflict between right-wing and centre-left governments. Since the two periods of the Martin government (2003–5) and Harper government (2006–15) are not covered by the case studies, they are presented in more detail here than are the case-study periods. The chapter follows approximate chronological order, with some movement back and forth across the time period.

Energy Policy, 1867 to 1989

Canadian energy policy is divided in two by the Canada-US Free Trade Agreement, which came into effect 1 January 1989. Prior to that date, the Government of Canada had directly regulated movement and prices of some fuels (not including electricity) and had at times worked to achieve the goal of energy self-sufficiency, reducing reliance upon imported coal and oil. By signing the

Canada-US agreement, however, Ottawa committed to a very different, continentalist, energy path, with prices set by markets and self-sufficiency made impossible by the commitment to never cut off oil and gas exports to the US in order to divert those supplies to Canadian use. This section tells the story of the first half, and a later section in this chapter completes the story.

McDougall (1982) sets out the basic dynamic influencing Canadian energy policy. Since the time of Confederation, the greatest demand for energy has come from the industrial heartland of Quebec and Ontario, but that region, aside from hydroelectricity, has not been blessed with energy resources. Instead, they have been located in the peripheries, with coal mined in Nova Scotia, Alberta, and British Columbia and oil and gas found in the western provinces. This distance between energy users and suppliers has meant that energy transportation costs have always been of vital importance. Alternative energy supplies, closer to the central Canadian buyers and thus with lower transportation costs, have been located in the US, while at the same time American population densities have provided buyers located closer to the Canadian supplies. A desire that energy trade contribute to national unity and pragmatic concerns for security of supply, particularly when strikes in the American mines limited coal imports in the 1920s and the world price rise made oil imports far more expensive in the 1970s, has prompted efforts to ensure east-west movement of fuels. By and large, however, manufacturers' search for the lowest price and energy producers' search for the best markets have meant energy policy has developed along north-south lines. McDougall (1982) paints a convincing picture of the major factors influencing Canadian energy policy: geographic location of resources, the related issue of transport costs, and American policy, which at times restricted export to that country, forcing producers to search out alternative Canadian markets.

In the nineteenth century, Ottawa used tariffs on US imports and transport subsidies to provide the Nova Scotia mines with a market for their coal in eastern Canada; those west of Cornwall bought coal imported from the US (McDougall 1982, 11). By the early years of the twentieth century coal was being mined in British Columbia and Alberta. The regional conflicts endemic to Canadian energy policy surfaced when British Columbia objected to Canadian coal tariffs meant to help the Nova Scotia industry due to fears they would stimulate countervailing US action, limiting the British Columbia market (McDougall 1982, 36). Coal's share of total Canadian energy use (with about half supplied by Canadian sources and the other half by American sources) peaked at 75 per cent in the 1920s, after which it began to decline as users moved to oil and natural gas (McDougall 1982, 36).

Starting in the 1840s, energy in the form of electricity began to be used, first for telegraph and telegram communication and then later in the century for lighting, after invention of the incandescent light bulb, followed by use in urban streetcars. By the early years of the twentieth century electricity had begun to replace coal-fired steam engines for powering industrial machinery. While electricity was originally supplied by the private sector, in 1906 the Ontario government opted for publicly owned generation and transmission through creation of the forerunner of Ontario Hydro (now Ontario Power Generation). Publicly owned utilities were established in Manitoba and Nova Scotia in 1919, New Brunswick in 1920, and Saskatchewan in 1929, while other provinces opted to continue to rely on regulated private suppliers (Negru 1990). While the federal government had regulated interprovincial and international movement of coal since the nineteenth century, it took on no such role once electricity began to cross provincial borders and began to be exported and imported between Canada and the US (although, as noted, federal approval was required for the latter). There has never really been a national electricity policy comparable to the national coal policy referred to above (reserving the eastern market for Canadian suppliers) or to the national oil policies of the twentieth century.

Nuclear power, on the other hand, has always been managed by Ottawa, not the provinces. During the Second World War, the federal government became involved with nuclear power as it worked with the UK and US on development of the atomic bomb and then, after the war, established a crown corporation to provide civilian nuclear power, for electricity generation. Regulation of nuclear safety, as noted, is exclusively within federal jurisdiction, and nuclear is the one energy source that is clearly in the federal domain, presumably because of those origins as a national security issue.

Oil was drilled in Ontario in the 1850s and at Turner Valley, Alberta, in 1914. Most of the oil used in Canada in the early twentieth century, however, was imported (Brownsey 2008). The 1947 Leduc oil strike in Alberta established the modern age of oil production in this country and raised the same question we have seen above with respect to coal: How much of the product would be used domestically and how much exported, and what would Ottawa's role be in determining that ratio? In 1949, the federal government enacted the Pipe Lines Act, giving itself authority to regulate international and interprovincial movement of oil and gas. By the late 1950s, a pipeline system to transport oil and gas within Canada and to US export markets had been established. Highly visible debate in 1956 over the Liberal government's plan for a west to east natural gas pipeline, with federal financial assistance to compensate for failure to select a lower-priced route through American territory, had contributed to that government's defeat the following year. In 1959, the Diefenbaker government established the National Energy Board as an arm's length regulatory agency governing interprovincial and international pipeline construction and oil and gas imports and exports. In 1960 Canada was producing 545,000 barrels of oil a day, 70 per cent from Alberta and 27 per cent from Saskatchewan; natural gas production was located also in Alberta (71 per cent) and Saskatchewan

(7 per cent), with another 17 per cent from British Columbia (Plourde 2012, 90). The oil and gas industry was made up almost exclusively of the large multinational firms such as Shell, Imperial/Exxon, Gulf, and Texaco (Brownsey 2008). Prices were set by the market, and while the NEB regulated international and interprovincial aspects, the producing provinces were the significant regulatory actors, issuing licences for production on crown lands and receiving royalties in return.

In 1961, the Diefenbaker government introduced its National Oil Policy (Doern and Toner 1985). Under that policy, which despite the term "national" was unilateral action by Ottawa and not the result of any formal federal-provincial agreement, Canadian users west of the Ottawa valley would be supplied by western Canadian sources (which were also exporting to the US) while the eastern provinces would rely on imported oil. The impetus for the policy was lobbying by the oil industry operating in western Canada, wanting a guaranteed domestic market to prevent further expansion of imported oil (Brownsey 2008). Just as it had with coal in the nineteenth century, Ottawa was helping an energy industry located in the periphery gain access to the central Canadian market.

The harmonious, non-conflictual nature of Canadian energy politics was then shattered in 1973 with the jump in world oil prices from approximately two to ten dollars a barrel, associated with the OPEC oil embargo. This price increase made the differing interests of the western producing provinces and eastern consuming provinces highly visible – the former, naturally, wanted the Canadian price to increase to the same level, while the latter wanted the opposite. The issue was politically charged because the federal government for the first time assumed the power to set the Canadian price, meaning that whatever it did, one region or another would feel hard done by. The federal and provincial governments throughout the remainder of the 1970s engaged in increasingly bitter conflicts, based in and further widening the West-East divide as they searched for an agreed allocation of the financial benefits associated with oil that had been so dramatically increased by the rise in the world price.

As discussed in the first case study below, Pierre Trudeau's National Energy Program of 1980 relied on unilateral action by Ottawa to ensure that comparable prices were paid for oil throughout the country, to shelter Canadians to some extent from world prices, to reduce the imbalance between Alberta and Ottawa share of oil revenues, and to increase Canadian ownership of the industry. Those goals, of course, were in conflict with those of the western producing provinces. The real problem, however, was the unacceptably draconian method used by Ottawa, which created in the western provinces anger, resentment, and mistrust of the federal government that is still felt today. The program was ended by the Mulroney government after it was elected in September 1984 by means of the Western Accord, signed by Ottawa and British Columbia, Alberta, and Saskatchewan on 27 November 1985. The accord removed a number of federal taxes and ended federal control of the price of oil in Canada (Milne 1986, 107–8). Canadian energy policy was buffeted again by external forces when oil prices fell in the mid-1980s, followed by a complete reorientation as the Mulroney government abandoned price regulation and then locked the country into a continental system by signing the 1989 Canada-US Fair Trade Agreement.

During the time period reviewed here Canadian governments pursued the first two energy policy objectives set out in chapter 1: security of supply and a low price for manufacturing industries, combined with facilitating domestic and export markets for energy industries. Energy was used to further the basic goal of wealth creation and contrary goals of environmental protection and polluter cost internalization, to the extent they were pursued at all for such things as air pollution caused by burning coal, were addressed in what was then seen as the completely distinct policy field of environment. Separate policies were developed for each fuel, and the only overarching energy policy was the implicit goal that all fuels together should contribute to economic growth and job creation. Prior to the 1970s, there was no attempt to develop policy by means of federal-provincial intergovernmental relations. By the time that mechanism was used in 1974, the high world price meant western and eastern interests were so completely at variance that consensual decision-making was impossible. Ottawa then fell back on bilateral negotiation with Alberta and other producing provinces. The intense federal-provincial conflict was only finally resolved by, first, the decline in oil prices, which defused the issue and, secondly, the Mulroney government's reversal of policy and complete capitulation to the interests of the producing provinces. Ironically, it was Prime Minister Mulroney who later rekindled that conflict by putting climate change on the policy agenda, an action seen as a threat to western interests.

National Climate Change Policy in the 1990s

Beyond signing the FTA and re-election of the Mulroney government, 1988 was also the year that the climate change issue appeared in Canadian politics. The Mulroney government was an early leader of action on climate change, hosting the 1988 international conference that put the issue on the policy agenda and speaking strongly at the 1992 Rio Conference in favour of the UN Framework Convention on Climate Change (UNFCCC). As discussed in the second case study below, two years earlier, after little discussion with the provinces, the prime minister had announced that Canada would stabilize its emissions at the 1990 level by the year 2000. Given that provinces hold constitutional jurisdiction as the owners of energy resources, Mulroney's government had no choice but to start to work with them on plans to achieve that goal, with the energy and environment departments in each government being the most heavily involved. After assuming power in 1994, the Liberal government led by Prime Minister Chrétien followed essentially the same path, albeit with a more formalized federal-provincial policy development system. The Canadian Council of Ministers of Environment and the Council of Energy Ministers began to meet jointly on a regular basis to review and make decisions on plans for coordinated policies developed by a system of committees staffed by both federal and provincial officials. The first major outcome of that process was the 1995 National Action Program on Climate Change (NAPCC), of which the major program was a government-industry program titled the Voluntary Challenge and Registry (VCR – ÉcoGESte in Quebec). Firms, hospitals, universities, and others with large annual emissions were invited to develop plans to reduce their emissions and to post their plans on the registry. They could then be held publicly accountable for keeping that commitment. In subsequent years, this use of voluntary action as the main policy instrument was dropped in favour of law-based regulation.

At the third Conference of Parties (CoP) to the UNFCCC, held in Kyoto, Japan, in December 1997, the Chrétien government committed Canada to reducing emissions to a point 6 per cent below 1990 levels by the year 2012, despite the fact it had only a few weeks earlier agreed with the provinces that Canada would commit only to stabilize emissions at 1990 levels by that year. In large part due to provincial resistance to that unilateral action, the Chrétien government then agreed to put in place a revised federal-provincial process, jointly led by Alberta and Ottawa, termed the National Climate Change Process (NCCP). In 2000, that process generated another federal-provincial plan, plus a federal plan for actions it would take itself, beyond its participation in the federal-provincial effort. Having lost faith in the federal-provincial process, Ottawa in the spring of 2002 announced plans to itself directly regulate industrial sources, regardless of what the provinces did. In response, Alberta resigned its position of co-chair of the NCCP, began to develop its own climate change policy intended to reach a far less ambitious goal than the Kyoto target, and prepared for possible legal action to prevent federal regulation within its borders. The provincial and federal environment ministers met for the last time in late October, after which time the federal-provincial process collapsed. Despite objections by all the Canadian provinces, the Chrétien government ratified the Kyoto Protocol in December 2002. Pierre Trudeau had used unilateral action to drive a hard bargain with Alberta; unilateral action taken by Jean Chrétien had the opposite effect, driving Alberta and eventually all of the provinces away from the negotiating table.

The Martin Government

After Jean Chrétien's resignation in December 2003 the Liberal government was led by Paul Martin, who was personally supportive of climate action. The Martin government had inherited the end of the NCCP federal-provincial process and the 21 November 2002 Government of Canada plan for unilateral action on the issue. Although there were no more formal meetings of federal and provincial ministers or officials, the Martin government continued to develop plans for the federal government's own actions on climate change, while signing bilateral agreements for joint action with interested provinces. The main policy instrument to be used was negotiation of covenants with the seven or eight hundred largest industrial sources of emissions, combined with a Canada-wide cap-and-trade system. The ambiguous term "covenant" referred to individual agreements between Ottawa and each firm that were not exactly voluntary, since they were to be negotiated under the implied threat of legally binding regulation. With Natural Resources Canada (NRCan) as the lead department, the federal government began the major task of negotiating those agreements. After the federal election of 28 June 2004, which saw the Martin government reduced to minority status, Stéphane Dion, who came to hold an undoubted and powerful personal commitment to the issue, was appointed environment minister. By 2005, Dion had managed to have Environment Canada replace NRCan as lead department and to change the policy instrument from covenants to legally binding regulatory requirements to reduce emissions (Munroe 2016, 63). In April 2005, the Martin government released its own plan for unilateral federal action, *Project Green: Moving Forward on Climate Change*, and in July 2005 gave formal notice in the *Canada Gazette* of its plan to regulate the large industrial emitters. Before those regulations could be put in place, however, on 28 November 2005, the Martin government was defeated in the House of Commons on a vote of non-confidence.

During the time of the Martin government, while there was no formal multilateral national process, Ottawa did engage with the provinces. Provinces were given opportunities to review and comment on plans for reaching covenant agreements with large sources (Winfield and Macdonald 2008). The federal government also worked to develop bilateral agreements with provinces. For that, it did not wield any sticks, but did offer the carrot of shared-cost funding for emission mitigation projects. The Martin government entered into six such agreements: Nunavut, 31 October 2003; Prince Edward Island, 7 November 2003; Manitoba, 19 March 2004; Newfoundland, 29 April 2004; Ontario, 21 May 2004; and, interestingly enough given that province's refusal to participate in the 2016 Pan-Canadian agreement, Saskatchewan, 24 November 2005 (Winfield and Macdonald 2008). At the time, the NDP, headed by Premier Lorne Calvert, ruled in Saskatchewan. The agreements did not include anything more specific than a mutual commitment to work together in areas such as renewable energy technology development but did provide a basis for subsequent bilateral federal-provincial joint action that might have been forthcoming had the Martin government stayed in power.

The 2003 federal budget included $160 million for federal-provincial project co-funding, a figure increased in the 2005 budget to $250 million (projected to increase in future years to between two and three billion dollars) for a Climate Change Partnerships Fund (Government of Canada 2005). This suggests that had the Martin government stayed in office it would have expanded use of the spending policy instrument, in collaboration with willing provinces. The Martin government's 2005 Project Green plan described the federal-provincial dynamic, anchored by federal funding, in these terms:

> A Partnership among Canada's Governments: Cooperative action is critical to our success in fighting climate change. The Partnership Fund will maximize potential partnerships with provinces and territories. Under the Partnership Fund, governments will identify mutual priorities and share in the undertaking of major investments in technologies and infrastructure development. (Government of Canada 2005, iii)

In an interview, former minister Stéphane Dion stressed the importance of the financial incentive for inducing provinces to cooperate, on a bilateral basis, with the federal government. The approach was to say to a province "show me the tonnes [of emission reductions], I will show you the money" (Dion 2010). All the provinces except Quebec, which rejected joint planning of reduction projects, wanting instead complete Quebec control with federal no-strings funding, were, according to the former minister, happy with that approach (Dion 2010). Of the ways in which a federal government can influence provincial behaviour discussed above – threat, promise, and persuasion – the emphasis during this period was definitely on promise. There is no indication from the public record that its plans to regulate industrial emissions were being used as a means of influencing provincial climate policies. Nor was there any attempt to launch another national, multilateral effort to complement the bilateral strategy the Martin government had been using.

Public Opinion on Climate Change

Although not discussed during the election campaign that began in December 2005, at approximately that time the issue of environment, which had by then become almost synonymous with climate change, started a rapid rise as the unprompted priority issue mentioned in opinion polls. To give one example, McAllister Opinion Research polling data showed these percentages of those surveyed naming "environment" as the answer to the unprompted "Most Important National Problem" question as follows: October 2004, 4 per cent; October 2005, 11 per cent; October 2006, 29 per cent (McAllister, email to Mark Winfield, York University, 2007). This compares with 20 per cent in

1989, at the height of the "second wave" of popular support for action on environment, which had led to such things as the Mulroney government's Green Plan of 1990 (McAllister, email to Mark Winfield, York University, 2007). An example of the visibility given the issue in the news media is the *Globe and Mail* front-page headline of 5 January 2007, proclaiming in large font: "As unseasonable warmth sweeps the country, Stephen Harper adapts to the new climate PM charts a greener course" (*Globe and Mail* 2007). Simpson, Jaccard, and Rivers (2007, 104) note the increased media attention to climate change that coincided with the rise in public interest shown in the polls: "Suddenly, in late 2006, editorial boards, columnists, reporters and editors could not display their interest in the environment fast enough."

This spiking in public concern as measured by pollsters could not survive the 2008 recession. Like the polling results above, Environics found that only 7.2 per cent of unprompted respondents listed environment as the most important issue facing Canadians today in the first quarter of 2006, but that number had increased to 22.1 per cent by the second quarter of 2007 (Environics 2006 and 2007). However, as the economic recession began to take hold in 2008 and 2009, those figures changed dramatically once more. An Environics poll found that in 2009 only 6.1 per cent of those polled believed environment and pollution to be the most important issue facing Canadians today (Environics 2009). Winfield (2012, 206) reports a similar spiking and then falling off during that period.

Nor did that lower level of concern change in subsequent years. An Environics poll in 2015 led to this finding: "Overall, the degree of public concern about climate change has changed relatively little since 2009, and remains well below the level recorded in 2007 when climate change had a much higher profile" (Environics and David Suzuki Foundation 2015, 4). The same Environics 2015 report found that Albertans were marginally less concerned about climate change than other Canadians, but the difference was in no way comparable to differences between Democratic and Republican views in the US (Environics and David Suzuki Foundation 2015).

It seems likely that the 2006–7 upswing in support not only partially explains the Harper government change of policy in 2007 but also increased action by the provinces (both discussed below). We must bear in mind, however, that while public opinion may influence policy at times of high issue salience, as was the case with the Harper government, for the most part it is not the major factor influencing governments. Studies show a correlation between public opinion and policy, but it is by no means clear which way causality is flowing, since often public opinion moves in support of a policy after it was introduced, rather than before (Page 2006). Furthermore, academics studying the subject have found that governments do polling not so much to learn what policies the public wants, but instead to discover how they can best communicate with the public while presenting policies already adopted for different reasons. Herle points to this when he says governments do polling for four reasons: 1) to assess the acceptability or support levels for various policy options; 2) to learn how to best communicate a policy idea; 3) to understand the policy priorities of the population; and, 4) to determine which of their policies to accentuate and which to hide under a bushel (2007, 19). The first and third have to do with policy decisions, while the other two concern communication strategies respecting those decisions. Page gives a similar picture: "interviewees typically indicate that opinion research contributes to communications of policy more than other phases of the policy process" (2006, 78–9). It would be a mistake to think that Canada's inability to keep its international commitments on climate change is due to public opinion alone.

That said, part of the explanation has to be attributed to public opinion. As noted, support for action on the issue had by 2015 not returned to its 2007 level. Polling in 2018 found that only 62 per cent of respondents believed evidence for human-caused climate change is conclusive. The remaining 38 per cent believed evidence for human-caused climate change is either not conclusive or non-existent. Only 60 per cent of those polled wanted government to put more emphasis on reducing emissions. Finally, support for government action varied by region: Atlantic 69 per cent; Quebec 66 per cent; British Columbia 65 per cent; Ontario 57 per cent; Manitoba and Saskatchewan 56 per cent; Alberta 45 per cent (CBC News 2018).

The Harper Government

Climate change policy under the Harper government can usefully be divided into two periods: 2006–8, when federal unilateral action was actively discussed, and the period after the 2008 election of US president Barack Obama, when the Harper government resolutely stuck to its policy of only following the US federal government lead and not taking any independent action on the issue (with one exception, the regulation of coal-fired electricity plants). The 2005 Conservative election platform did not give priority to environmental issues and made it clear that the party considered airborne toxics to be a problem as equally serious as climate change. This low priority was reinforced when the environment portfolio was given to a newly elected MP, Rona Ambrose. This follows a tradition of Canadian governments treating environment as a low-status cabinet post, appointing junior ministers and changing them often as the juniors climb up to more senior positions (Doern and Conway 1994). It was not surprising, then, when the government signalled that unlike its predecessors, it would not even give the public appearance of attempting to achieve the Kyoto 6 per cent reduction goal. Similarly, cancellation of funding for some climate-change programs was in line with the policy direction set out in the party election platform.

While Environment Canada remained the lead department, unlike the Chrétien or Martin governments the climate file was managed directly by the Prime Minister's Office (PMO) (confidential interviews 2007a; see also Simpson, Jaccard, and Rivers 2007). A picture of the prime minister's thinking is given by remarks he made on 10 July 2006, when asked whether his government would work to meet the Kyoto goal:

> I don't believe that's feasible. I think what is feasible is we can make progress, that we can play a role, as Rona Ambrose is, in bringing the international community to a more effective international regime. And, at the same time, we can move forward on some of the issues, the very important issues that Kyoto completely ignores, such as pollution and smog and the various compounds that are involved in that phenomenon, so I can say that we'll have some interesting proposals in the fall, and they will be more comprehensive than anything that was envisioned by Kyoto. (Bonner 2006)

Clearly at this point the prime minister was still committed to the pre-election Conservative thinking on the issue – lack of faith in the Kyoto regime, a belief that toxic air pollution was the real problem, and a commitment to introduce new legislation to address it.

During the summer and early fall the government developed climate and air pollution policy along those lines. Environmentalists were not consulted and in fact were explicitly excluded from the process, but discussions were held with players in the industry (confidential interviews 2007a). Minister Ambrose stated on 9 October 2006: "The oil and gas sector has to be a big part of our plan. We met with them early on and indicated to them that we're moving ahead with legislation and that they will be a big part of it" (Doyle 2006). Rather than stand-alone legislation, the 19 October 2006 Clean Air Act (CAA) was in fact a process of amending the Canadian Environmental Protection Act and other federal legislation (Government of Canada 2006). The CAA addressed both toxic air pollutants from a number of sources and industry GHG emissions. In terms of the latter, the plan was to develop regulatory standards through consultation with industry during the period 2006–8 and to then put in place legally effective standards by the end of 2010 (*Canada Gazette*, 21 October 2006). During the short-term period 2010–15 the plan was to regulate intensity of emissions in such a way as to "yield a better outcome for the Canadian environment than under the plan previously proposed on July 16, 2005" (*Canada Gazette*, 21 October 2006). Other than saying standards would be more rigorous than those in the Martin government 2005 plan, no specific target for industry reductions was set. The overall Canadian GHG emission target was to reduce between 45 and 65 per cent from 2003 levels by 2050 (Government of Canada 2006).

Environmentalists and most other commentators largely ignored the toxins and pollution elements of the CAA and dismissed the climate-change elements as being inadequate. Although the Liberal government climate plans of 2002 and 2005 had also used intensity (ratio of emissions to production) rather than absolute standards without attracting adverse comment, the Conservative intensity standards became a target of criticism. Other critiques included the change in base year from 1990 to 2003, the fact that another four years would be spent consulting and the failure to specify targets for industry reductions. The act was condemned by all three opposition parties in the House of Commons, each promising to vote against it and thereby possibly trigger an election. In response to this pressure, and presumably also the high public support for action on the issue being shown by public opinion polling, on 4 January 2007, the prime minister announced that John Baird would replace Rona Ambrose as environment minister, included environment in the list of government priorities for the coming year, and stated that "We've clearly determined we need to do more on the environment" (Clark and Laghi 2007).

On 26 April 2007, the Conservative government announced its new plan for unilateral action to regulate industrial GHG emissions without provincial involvement. The Turning the Corner plan called for an 18 per cent reduction in the intensity of those emissions, to be achieved by 2010, and then a further 2 per cent reduction each year after that until 2020. The plan was a direct descendant of the regulatory plans that had previously been developed by the Liberals. The 2005 Martin government plan intended to use intensity standards to bring about an absolute reduction in industry emissions of 39 Mt by 2012. The guarantee originally given to industry by the Chrétien government in December 2002 that any costs to comply with climate regulations above $15 per tonne would be paid by the government (discussed in chapter 7, page 169) was maintained in the Martin 2005 plan (Government of Canada 2005). The 2007 Harper government plan was essentially similar to the Martin plan, in that it intended to achieve an absolute reduction of 60 Mt, but from 2006 levels and not until 2020, and also capped industry costs at $15 per tonne by allowing firms to pay that amount for each tonne out of compliance into a special technology development fund (Environment Canada 2007). Like the 2005 plan, it allowed firms to comply by trading or purchasing offsets. Unlike the two previous Liberal plans, however, it was not intended to achieve the Kyoto target. The target date was 2020 rather than 2012, and analysis by the Pembina Institute showed that if the plan was fully implemented Canadian emissions in 2020 would be 2 per cent above the 1990 level, rather than 6 per cent below (2007).

During 2008, the economic recession worsened and public support for government action on climate change lessened. The Harper government was ostensibly implementing the April 2007 Turning the Corner plan, but with few visible signs of activity. That changed in November, when the US elected a president who had run on a platform of climate-change action. The Harper government, perhaps motivated by fear that something like US border adjustment taxes would restrict access for Canadian exports to that country, immediately proposed a Canada-US climate-change treaty, similar to that put in place twenty years earlier for acid rain. President Obama was not interested but the Harper government from that point on took the explicitly stated position that it would only act on climate change to the extent needed to ensure that Canadian federal government climate policy matched that of the US federal government. In January 2010, the Harper government adopted the same goal as the US for action coming out of the 2009 Copenhagen climate summit, a 17 per cent reduction below the 2005 level by 2020. By then it was clear that the Obama administration could not get climate legislation through Congress, which meant policy alignment was a prescription for almost no Canadian federal government action. Turning the Corner was forgotten.

In the 2 May 2011 election, the Harper Conservatives won a majority, meaning the kind of pressures in the House of Commons, supported by public opinion, which in 2006–7 had led the Harper government to change its climate-change policy, were no longer present. The issue could now be safely ignored. The Conservatives did bring in new motor vehicle efficiency standards in 2010, because the US federal government had done so. They subsequently broke with US federal policy when they brought in a regulation under CEPA imposing requirements on coal-fired electricity plants to use clean-coal techniques at some point in the future (estimated to be in the late 2020s) once those plants had reached the end of their useful life. This exception to the rule of only following Washington's lead may have been done at the behest of the electricity industry, seeking regulatory certainty and protection against federal climate regulation before the late 2020s (Macdonald 2011). As discussed in chapter 9, the Justin Trudeau government in 2016 established 2030 as the deadline for this measure, but in the same breath exempted Nova Scotia and Saskatchewan from that deadline.

By this time, oil sands production was in full swing and both the industry and Alberta government were engaged with the need to add to the capacity of pipelines, both those going south to the US and those going to the west coast, from which oil could be transported by ship to Asia. Both had come to endorse the idea that governments could best be convinced to give priority to such new energy infrastructure by placing it within the context of all energy challenges and opportunities in a national, federal-provincial energy strategy. The Harper government initially expressed interest in participation in 2011–12, but then pulled out, leaving the project to the provinces. It did, however, deliver on one part of industry's agenda. In spring 2012, a number of federal environmental laws were amended with the intent of reducing the time required for regulatory approvals of major new projects such as interprovincial pipelines and reducing the scope of the federal Fisheries Act. Through to the end of his time in office, however, Prime Minister Harper stayed true to his vision of Canadian federalism whereby each level of government sticks to its own knitting and neither time nor energy are devoted to collaborative federal-provincial national programs.

Provincial Climate-Change Policies

When provinces first began to develop policies intended to reduce GHG emissions in the late 1980s and early 1990s, they were working within the framework of a national federal-provincial process. As discussed, the Mulroney government had to at least some degree consulted with the provinces before announcing in 1990 the Canadian target of stabilizing emissions at the 1990 level by the end of the century. Federal and provincial energy and environment ministers started to meet to discuss coordinated policies and programs before any individual provinces, by themselves, had started to develop their own climate-change policies. The first to do so was Quebec. On 25 November 1992, the Quebec government adopted an Order in Council supporting the goals of the UNFCCC and adopting stabilization at the 1990 level by 2000 as a provincial objective (Houle 2015, 133). British Columbia adopted the same goal for that province's emissions in a plan put forth in 1995, while Quebec's plan of that same year repeated the stabilization objective it had set forth three years earlier (Houle 2015, 133). In that year, all provinces agreed to participate in the federal-provincial National Action Program on Climate Change. During the next seven years, up to 2002, provinces participated in the federal-provincial program without taking any further action to prepare and publish their own individual climate-change plans.

Accordingly, up to that point all provincial climate policies were aligned with the national effort. The two provincial targets announced prior to 2002 by British Columbia and Quebec were the same as the national stabilization goal. The other provinces had not stated a provincial reduction target, which meant they implicitly subscribed to the national goals of stabilization, and then, after 1997, the Kyoto goal of 6 per cent below the 1990 level (although, as discussed in chapter 7, some Alberta officials saw that as "Ottawa's goal" with the implication it was up to the federal government, not Alberta, to achieve it). That alignment of provincial and national targets changed in 2002, when both Ottawa and Alberta veered away from the national process, the former to develop its own plans for unilateral action to meet the Kyoto goal and the latter also to develop its own plan, but to meet a different goal. The Alberta climate-change plan of 2002 had the objective of reducing the emissions intensity of major sources by 50 per cent below the 1990 level by 2020. This was expected to reduce Alberta emissions by 20 Mt below the "business as usual" (BAU – the level of projected emissions absent any policy action) level by 2010 (Houle 2015, 133). As well as saying that the Kyoto goal did not apply to that province, the plan also differed from the national target in that it did not set an upper limit on Alberta emissions – as long as actions were taken to sufficiently reduce their ratio to production, total emissions could increase without limit. This is very different from the absolute limit on emissions stated by a target of a specified number of megatonnes in a given year, such as the original 1990 stabilization goal, which if achieved would place an upper limit of 613 Mt on total Canadian emissions. Alberta's subsequent plans issued in 2008 and 2015 also differ from all other Canadian government plans in that they do not impose a total limit on emissions (although the 2015 plan does cap oil sands emissions, with some exceptions, at 100 Mt). Table 6 below lists the targets in all provincial plans published between 1992 and 2018.

By 2012, the deadline for meeting the Kyoto goal, the Canadian situation respecting targets was as follows: Canadian emissions were 716 Mt (table 5), substantially above the Kyoto target of 576 Mt; the federal government two years earlier had set a new target of reducing total emissions to be 17 per cent below the 2005 level by 2020; most provinces also had a 2020 goal, which did not correspond to the federal target; and Alberta was still the outlier, the one province which refused to give itself an absolute limit on emissions. While the first provincial plans were aligned with the national goal, ten years later, by 2012, it was clear that provinces were making no attempt to align their targets with Ottawa's 2020 target, or with other provincial targets. The federal and provincial governments were acting unilaterally to set targets, with no attempt at coordination.

Since most provincial plans had been developed from 2007 to 2012, this discrepancy in targets might be explained by the fact that during that time there was no federal-provincial program or, in the case of the Atlantic provinces, because they were setting targets in coordination with US states rather than Ottawa and fellow provinces. That explanation does not hold, however, for the new Quebec target and the two new plans released by British Columbia and Ontario in 2016, during the Pan-Canadian Framework process. As can be seen in table 6, those three provinces did not adopt the national target of 30 per cent below the 2005 level by 2030 – Quebec and Ontario set a different baseline and percentage reduction and British Columbia did not set a 2030 target at all (in 2018, British Columbia adopted new interim targets for 2030 and 2040; the new Ontario government adopted a 2030 target less ambitious than that stated by the previous government in 2016). The fact of differing Quebec, British Columbia, and Ontario targets in itself is not a problem. The basic argument made in this book, set out more fully in chapter 11, is that to be effective a national program should have some rough equality among provinces of per capita reduction cost but not necessarily of megatonne reduction targets. Given

6 Provincial greenhouse gas emission reduction targets, by year announced

1992	Quebec	stabilization goal
1995	Quebec	stabilization goal
	British Columbia	stabilization goal
2002	Alberta	reduce emissions intensity 50% below 1990 level by 2020; 20 Mt below BAU by 2010; no absolute limit on emissions
	Manitoba	Kyoto goal
2006	Quebec	Kyoto goal
2007	British Columbia	33% below 2007 level by 2020; 80% below 2007 level by 2050
	New Brunswick	reduce to 1990 level by 2012; 10% below 1990 by 2020
	Nova Scotia	10% below 1990 level by 2020
	Saskatchewan	stabilize by 2010; 32% below current level (2004) by 2020
	Ontario	6% below 1990 level by 2014; 15% below 1990 level by 2020; 80% below 1990 level by 2015
2008	Alberta	meet 2002 intensity target of 20 Mt below BAU by 2010; stabilize emissions by 2020 at a point 50 Mt below BAU; by 2050 reduce intensity 50% below BAU, which was expected to be a 200 Mt reduction
	Manitoba	6% below 1990 by 2012
	Prince Edward Island	10% below 1990 by 2020
2011	Newfoundland	10% below 1990 by 2020
2012	Quebec	20% below 1990 by 2020
2015	Alberta	objectives such as 100 Mt limit on oil sands emissions and phasing out coal-fired electricity by 2030, but no specific target for total GHG emissions by 2020 or 2030
	Quebec	37.5% below 1990 by 2030
2016	Ontario	15% below 1990 by 2020; 37% below 1990 by 2030; 80% below 1990 by 2050
	British Columbia	80% below 2007 by 2050
	New Brunswick	26% below 2005 by 2020; 46% below 2005 by 2030; 75% below 2005 by 2050
2017	Saskatchewan	plan to regulate industrial sources; no target for provincial emissions
2018	British Columbia	new interim targets adopted: 40% below 2007 by 2030; 60% below 2007 by 2040; 2050 target remains the same
	Ontario	30% below 2005 level by 2030

Sources: Houle (2015); Government of Alberta (2008; 2019); Government of British Columbia (2016; 2018); Government of New Brunswick (2016); Government of Ontario (2007; 2016); Government of Quebec (2015); Government of Saskatchewan (2017); Ontario Ministry of the Environment, Conservation and Parks (2018).

differing provincial per-tonne reduction costs, the overall national target might well be achieved by differing provincial reduction targets. What is surprising, however, about the Quebec 2015 target and the British Columbia and Ontario 2016 plans and targets is that they were released in 2015 and 2016 at all. The new Quebec target was announced on 27 November 2015, by which time it was clear a new government in Ottawa hoped to develop new, coordinated national policy (Quebec, 27 November 2015); the two other governments announced their targets well after that process was fully underway, and yet they still set targets unilaterally.

If Canadian governments truly were engaged in an exercise of developing coordinated national policy, why did those three provinces not wait until that process was completed to finalize and release their own plans? The fact that three provinces could take unilateral action to set their own targets while ostensibly planning their policy in collaboration with other provinces and Ottawa, without a word of public objection from the latter, speaks volumes about the nature of the Pan-Canadian Framework – as described in chapter 9, basically a federal project that asked almost nothing of the big emitters, including British Columbia, Quebec, and Ontario, beyond reaching the federal backstop price of $50 per tonne by 2022. One of the main recommendations made in chapter 11 is that all targets – the international commitment made by Ottawa and individual provincial targets – be set together, by means of collective federal-provincial decision-making, with the prime minister and premiers all assembled in the same room, at the same time.

Beyond the issue of lack of coordination, several other points should be made respecting provincial climate-change policies. The first is to note that Alberta in 2003 was the first Canadian government to enact climate change legislation. As described in chapter 7, that was done not because of a groundswell of popular support for effective action in that province, but instead to provide a bulwark that might stand the province in good stead should it take legal action to try to prevent federal regulation of emissions from Alberta sources. Secondly, there clearly was a spurt of provincial activity starting in 2007. While local circumstances in each province certainly are the major factor explaining provincial plans, it seems likely that the spiking of public opinion in 2006–7, described above, was also a factor. Absent any pressure from Ottawa, provinces that hitherto had not set targets or released any formal plans now proceeded to do so.

The high-water mark of provincial action at that time was the British Columbia carbon tax, introduced in 2008, which was part of a complete reversal of that province's climate-change policy. The Liberal party led by Gordon Campbell had defeated the incumbent NDP government in the election held 16 May 2001, and upon taking office substantially reduced funding available for environmental protection, including climate-change initiatives, cutting the environment department staff by approximately one-third (Bjorn et al. 2002). In February 2002, Premier Campbell was the author of a letter to Prime Minister Chrétien, ostensibly from all provinces but in fact endorsed only by British Columbia, Alberta, and Ontario, which stated that climate policies would have a negative effect on the Canadian economy. Alberta Premier Klein, in a surprise move intended to embarrass the prime minister and generate news media attention, publicly presented the letter to Chrétien at a press conference in Moscow (Bjorn et al. 2002, 61–2; Chrétien 2007, 386–7). In its early years in office, the British Columbia Liberal government was clearly allied with Alberta in opposing effective climate change policy. That position had changed by February 2007, however, when a government Throne Speech announced plans for significant action on climate change, a policy direction that then led to the 2008 carbon tax. Why did Campbell's government reverse policy in this manner? The change is explained in part by changes in public opinion, discussed above, in the British Columbia case spurred by the Mountain Pine Beetle infestation that was causing economic loss to the forest industry. It may also have been seen as a means of stealing votes from the NDP opposition. A major factor, however, was changes in the premier's own thinking, stimulated, he said, by a trip to China in 2006, where he witnessed the effects of air pollution (Harrison 2012).

Premier Campbell's successor, Christy Clark, who took office on 14 March 2011 after winning the Liberal Party leadership following Campbell's resignation, did not share his commitment. Her government embarked on a policy of economic development through liquefied natural gas exports, which, if successful, would have generated emissions far in excess of British Columbia's climate target. In 2016, Premier Clark refused to adopt the advice of an advisory panel that had recommended increasing the province's carbon tax. The mantle of provincial leadership on the issue had by then moved to other provinces. By 2014, Ontario had completed the process of closing its coal-fired electricity plants. While motivated by pressure from doctors and environmentalists to reduce health effects of smog, doing so was the most effective climate-change action taken by any Canadian government to date (Harrison and Bryant 2016). Nova Scotia brought about significant reductions in emissions from its electricity sector by shifting from coal to gas and renewable sources, encouraging increased energy efficiency and due to a decline in demand for electricity caused by closing of two pulp and paper mills. Both Quebec and Ontario, working as part of the California-led Western Climate Initiative, introduced cap-and-trade programs (which Ontario then cancelled in 2018). After the NDP took power in Alberta in 2015 it introduced a carbon tax (cancelled in 2019) and plans to phase out coal-fired electricity generation by 2030, as Ontario had previously done. As discussed in chapter 9, by the time the federal Liberal party took office in October 2015, all provinces had climate programs in place and had moved to use of more effective policy instruments than the voluntary program of 1995.

In summary, three things stand out from this review of provincial climate-change policies since 1990. The first is the lack of coordination in target setting, even while participating in a federal-provincial program intended to coordinate policies. The second is the fact noted in the introductory chapter that unilateral provincial action did not add up to enough to achieve the 2020 target (NRTEE 2012). Harrison and Bryant in a review of provincial policies point to three as being the most successful: the British Columbia carbon tax, Quebec trading program, and Ontario coal phase-out. Nevertheless, they conclude their review with this summary:

> However, for the most part, Canadian provinces' efforts to reduce greenhouse-gas emissions have been piecemeal, symbolic, and largely ineffective. Provincial governments have been unwilling to pursue more aggressive mitigation measures lest they affect the competitiveness of local industry and provoke the ire of voters who resent higher energy prices. (2016, 518)

Thirdly, as noted at the outset, provincial policies have unrolled on two different tracks. By and large, emissions have been increasing in the carbon provinces and decreasing in the hydro provinces.

Energy Policy, 1989 to 2019

Since signing of the Canada-US Free Trade Agreement, followed by the North American Free Trade Agreement (NAFTA) in 1993, Canada has had no national energy policy explicitly stated by any federal government. Ottawa has, however, regardless of party in power consistently worked to implement the implicit energy policy of contributing to Canadian wealth generation by doing everything possible to facilitate export of oil and natural gas – a policy objective clearly shown by the Justin Trudeau government's decision in May 2018 to purchase Kinder Morgan's Trans Mountain pipeline from Alberta to Burnaby, British Columbia, to ensure that a greater quantity of Alberta oil could be exported. This was done notwithstanding the inherent conflict between the goal of maximizing fossil fuel exports and the goal of reducing greenhouse gas emissions. Despite lack of interest from Ottawa, national energy policy has been developed twice by the provinces, without federal involvement. The Council of the

Federation issued a statement on national energy policy in 2007 and then in 2015, as discussed in the fourth case study below, generated an updated iteration of that document in the form of the Canadian Energy Strategy.

During this period, energy policy was influenced by two trends. The first was the move to liberalization and deregulation, in which pricing and production decisions follow market trends rather than government regulation. This was seen with respect to oil and gas and also with respect to electricity in some provinces, most notably Alberta and Ontario in the 1990s. The other was greater emphasis upon the third energy policy objective: reducing associated environmental harms. Doern and Gattinger (2003) have argued this resulted in "regulatory stacking" in which new environmental protection regulatory requirements were layered over pre-existing layers of energy regulation. By the 2010s, this trend had evolved into the virtually complete integration of energy and climate policy examined here. As noted, Jim Prentice was fully aware of this integration, which he referred to as the "Triple Crown" when he called for "an integrated and pragmatic approach to energy, climate change and the environment" (Prentice 2017, 5).

Beyond these changes, there has been both continuity and further evolution in energy politics. Oil and gas have continued to be supplied domestically and also exported, while at the same time imported by eastern Canada. Newfoundland and Labrador in 1998 become an oil-producing province and in 2008 contributed 12.5 per cent of total Canadian production (Plourde 2012, 97). Provincial GDP rose quickly as a result, as did that government's dependence on oil revenues, something that posed a major problem with the oil price drop of 2014. British Columbia, which supplied 17 per cent of Canadian natural gas in 2008, under Premier Christy Clark launched a major effort to attract international capital to development of an LNG exporting facility (Plourde 2012, 97). This eventually bore fruit, after Clark's government had been replaced by the NDP, with an announcement in October 2018 of a major private-sector investment in a gas pipeline and LNG export facility at Kitimat. As discussed below, Alberta oil policy also took a turn to focus upon development of the nonconventional sources in the oil sands.

Electricity, which also is imported and exported, has remained very much a provincial matter – discussion of the possible creation of a national grid has not yet produced significant action or any involvement of the federal government. Ontario under the McGuinty and Wynne governments for a time pursued a policy of expanding renewable sources for electricity generation in a bid to make renewable technologies a motor of economic growth, but then, faced with opposition to rising electricity prices, drew back. Quebec continued to seek export opportunities for its hydroelectricity, as did Newfoundland and Nova Scotia with development of the Muskrat Falls site on the Churchill River and installation of underwater transmission (avoiding transmission through Quebec) for sale in New England. Nuclear power is used to generate electricity in Ontario and New Brunswick, but there has been no expansion to other parts of the country.

Technological change has led to two contradictory movements, one working to increase the supply of renewable energy and the other the supply of fossil fuels. The first has reduced the price of renewable sources such as wind and solar, which, combined with government policy, has started a shift to reduce the use of fossil fuels such as coal to generate electricity. At the same time, new technologies associated with hydraulic fracturing (fracking) have granted access to new, lower-cost supplies of oil and natural gas in North America. These changes in the relative prices of different fuels are bound to influence energy and climate politics, while if fossil fuels start to be extracted in considerable quantity in Quebec or the Atlantic provinces the basic difference in interest between carbon and hydro provinces may be reduced. They also have meant the US has become largely self-sufficient in oil and gas and much less reliant upon imports from Canada. These changes have not had a material impact upon the case studies examined here.

The most significant change, which most certainly has affected both the CES and PCF case studies, has been development of the western oil sands, a process of extracting oil from bitumen found in earth, clay, or sand. The bitumen is either mined, requiring removal of the top layer of earth, trees, and vegetation, or brought to the surface by underground injection of steam to allow the melted bitumen to be pumped to the surface. Bitumen had been known to Indigenous peoples and early European explorers, and the concept of using it to extract oil was being actively explored by the early twentieth century, with support from the Alberta and federal governments (Turner 2017). The first commercial plant began operations near Fort McMurray, Alberta, in 1967. The Lougheed government of Alberta, elected in 1971, increased research spending and actively encouraged the industry, including investment, with the federal government and Ontario, in the Syncrude plant, which began operations in 1978 (Turner 2017, 164). The per barrel price of extraction was still much higher than for conventional oil, and the decline in world oil prices in the 1980s hampered further development. However, by 1992, the oil sands were producing 350,000 barrels a day from the Syncrude, Suncor, and other smaller operations (Taft 2017, 156). Urquhart (2018) makes a convincing case that reductions in tax and royalties from oil sands operations made in the mid-1990s by both Alberta and the Government of Canada in response to industry lobbying played a large part in allowing increasing production. Beyond that, by the early 2000s, rising world oil prices and declining extraction costs due to technological change made the oil sands fully viable and production started to sharply increase. By 2006, production had reached one million barrels a day (Turner 2017, 172); ten years later, in 2016, production was 2.5 million barrels a day (Alberta Energy 2018). Greenhouse gas emissions from oil sands production were approximately 70 Mt that year, just under 10 per cent of Canadian total emissions (CAPP 2017).

This rapid expansion of oil sands production, the bulk of which is exported for sale in the US, has had a major impact upon both energy and climate-change politics for several reasons. The most important of those is the notoriety of the oil sands: the way in which they have become a symbol of what many see as the evil, destructive forces responsible for climate change, despite the fact that the oil sands are responsible for a relatively small portion of the world's emissions. The Canadian Association of Petroleum Producers (CAPP) points to the fact that oil sands emissions account for only 0.16 per cent of global emissions (2017). Natural Resources Canada, singing the same song, points to the fact that coal-fired electricity generation in the US generates twenty-six times the GHG emissions of the oil sands (NRCan 2016). Turner (2017 120) gives us the question on the minds of Calgary oil executives: "Why do those [oil sands] emissions make an archvillain, when the 76 megatons emitted by coal plants in Missouri or the 151 megatons generated by coal in Texas do not?" It seems likely there are two things which explain the way the oil sands have attracted opprobrium much greater than that directed at other sources. The first is the physical nature of open-pit bitumen mining, which requires ripping apart large swathes of forest, making for dramatic and appalling visual representations. Much like a clear-cut forest, the oil sands mines are a powerful picture of what environmentalists depict as Earth's open and bleeding wounds. The second is the fact that environmentalists, as discussed in chapter 8, starting in the late 2000s carried out a sophisticated, targeted campaign of vilification that has attracted world-wide attention.

Beyond construction of the oil sands as a symbol of all that is wrong with the modern world, empirical facts also help explain their political impact. They are the fastest growing source of Canadian GHG emissions. For a number of years, the Alberta government has spoken of the potential to increase present annual production three- or four-fold (something that will depend upon world oil prices and that may – or may not, depending upon technological change to reduce emissions or policy change – be influenced by a 2016 Alberta law limiting total emissions to 100 Mt). With proven reserves of 165.4 billion barrels (Alberta Energy 2018) the oil sands have the potential to continue to release greenhouse gases, both during production (the emissions referred to above) and at the point of combustion after export sale (not included in the 70 Mt referred to above) for many years to come. Perhaps environmentalists could have chosen to focus their delegitimization campaign on Missouri coal-fired electricity plants, but it does seem the oil sands represent a more potent threat if for no other reason than the fact that Missouri emissions are relatively stable while those from the oil sands are on a steep upward climb.

For whatever reasons, the expansion of oil sands production threw new shockwaves into the worlds of energy and climate-change politics. It led environmentalists to launch their "dirty oil" campaign (based on the higher per-barrel GHG emissions required to extract and process bitumen compared to liquid conventional oil), which was then countered by industry allies with claims of "ethical oil" (based on such things as the fact that Canada is more democratic than Saudi Arabia – which would you rather buy your oil from?). At the same time, the environmentalists' campaign was sufficiently effective that concern for its environmental image started to influence decision-making by the Alberta government. As discussed in the CES case below, Alberta politicians began to realize they were losing the public-relations war and had to take steps to increase Alberta's environmental legitimacy in the eyes of those outside the province. "Since the mid-2000s ... Alberta governments have felt increasingly besieged by climate change science and global calls for action to reduce GHGs, as well as by Canadian and international environmental campaigns against the oil sands" (Adkin and Stares 2016, 226). The initial response was to increase spending on public relations campaigns, centred on a discourse of sustainable development, and to increase spending on hoped for technological means of reducing emissions, such as carbon capture and storage. Former premier Jim Prentice has referred to actions his government was taking some ten years later as follows: "We had begun the climate change rebranding of Alberta and would need to fight that battle on three fronts: here in Canada; in the United States; and globally, starting in Paris at the CoP 21 meeting in December 2015" (2017, 111). His successor, Rachel Notley, carried that search for environmental legitimacy fully into provincial policy when she introduced her carbon tax, coal phase-out, and cap on total oil sands emissions. Her successor, Jason Kenney, was less interested in enhancing Alberta's environmental legitimacy as a means of influencing the thinking and behaviour of others; instead, he relied on whatever stick was handy for thumping his many enemies.

Also in the late 2000s, both environmentalists and their industry opponents shifted their attention to pipelines, albeit for very different reasons. The former hoped to mobilize local opposition to new pipelines such as Keystone XL as part of a strategy of landlocking the oil sands – if the means of transporting that oil to markets were constrained or made more expensive, capital investment in new oil sands production would become less attractive, thereby slowing the rate of expansion. Industry had also become concerned about pipeline capacity, both because additional capacity was needed to allow growth in oil sands production and because new pipelines to the coasts were needed to give access to higher-paying markets. The long-standing environmentalist-industry conflict over climate change thus took a major detour into pipeline conflicts. However, it then detoured again into the world explored in this book of national, intergovernmental energy policy as industry, allied with the Alberta government, cloaked its advocacy of new pipelines in proposals for a national (later Canadian) energy strategy. Chapter 8 dives into this bear garden of conflicts.

The Justin Trudeau Government

As set out above, after 2008 the Harper government neither acted on the climate issue itself nor made any effort to work with the provinces. Ottawa's role changed dramatically, however, with election of the Justin Trudeau Liberal government on 19 October 2015. The Liberals had run on a platform of working with the provinces to take action on the issue and of "putting a price on carbon." Once in office, the Liberals faced two challenges in doing so: first, as discussed, opposition to the oil sands on the basis of climate changed had morphed into conflicts over pipelines, meaning that question would have to be addressed as part of any new national climate change effort; and, secondly, the provinces were well advanced in their climate policies. Thus Ottawa would have to convince provinces to do more than they were currently doing while acknowledging that provincial policy was well ahead of federal policy, and would also have to approve at least one interprovincial pipeline, which, to the extent that added pipeline capacity adds to GHG emissions, would work against its climate-change objectives.

In addressing these challenges, the new government made two decisions. First, it decided it would ignore the 2020 target, neither discussing it nor taking any action intended to achieve it. Shoving the required emissions reduction well off into the future made dealing with the provinces (and industry) much easier, since it removed the need to demand immediate action. The second decision also helped relations with the provinces, as well as giving a generous dose of political reward to the new Trudeau government. It was decided that the primary objective would not be to ensure programs were in place capable of meeting the 2030 target, but instead ensuring that a carbon price was in place throughout the country. Since the big provinces with the power and motivation to push back when Ottawa asked them to do something already had pricing systems in place, conflict would only be with smaller, weaker provinces. For the first time since 1980, Ottawa would be seen as taking bold and decisive unilateral action on the energy and climate file, to the plaudits of an adoring nation still intoxicated by the fragrance of its honeymoon with a handsome young prime minister, albeit one who was careful in his choice of provincial boxing partners.

Prime Minister Trudeau convened a federal-provincial First Ministers' Meeting on 23 November 2015 prior to the Paris CoP, only the second time that first ministers had met to discuss climate change. At the Paris summit, Canadian officials strongly supported international action, in stark contrast to the role played by the previous government on the international stage. However, rather than anything more ambitious, Trudeau simply adopted the Paris target previously set by the Harper government of a 30 per cent reduction from 2005 levels by 2030. In 2016, the Trudeau government then worked with the provinces to develop the Pan-Canadian Framework agreement, centred on a federal plan to impose a minimum carbon price in any province that did not already have one by virtue of action by the provincial government. That plan was agreed to by all provinces except Saskatchewan and Manitoba. As noted, the Trudeau government announced no plans to achieve Canada's 2020 Copenhagen target and, prior to the signing of the PCF in December 2016, had not put in place all the programs needed to meet the Paris 2030 target. The Trudeau government certainly broke with the policies of its predecessor, but did not manage to shake free from the tired Canadian dynamic of making international commitments without first ensuring it would be able to achieve them. Adding to that government's troubles, during 2018 it was forced to buy a pipeline to keep Alberta happy and then saw that province and others opt out of the Pan-Canadian Framework.

Summary

Seen from a macro-scale level, during the period examined here two events, each with profound implications for the other, transformed the worlds of Canadian energy and climate change politics. The first was the emergence and evolution of the issue of climate change. A phenomenon rarely discussed outside scientific circles in 1973 was then first put on the international agenda by the Toronto conference of 1988, after which it went on to eclipse all other environmental issues and came to be seen as a global threat on a scale similar to that of nuclear war. The second, standing in direct opposition to the first, was the emergence of the oil sands as a commercially viable resource, increasing Canadian annual fossil fuel production and export and GHG emissions, and vastly increasing proven reserves. These two events – a major increase in the wealth potentially available from sale of fossil fuels and equally major concern for the implications of such a sale for both nature and human societies – were on a collision course. Due to the geographic location of the fossil fuels, that collision was not only one of differing human values and identities – capitalism versus environmentalism, in the simplest terms – but also a clashing of regions, of west versus east. The oil price shocks of the 1970s set western Canada against the east with a rancour that then easily carried over into the national climate-change politics that first emerged in the 1990s. A decade later, the oil sands and the pipelines that carry their product to market were the ground zero of what had become fully fused, high stakes energy and climate politics.

The two efforts to develop national climate-change programs in the 1990s led by the Jean Chrétien government attempted unsuccessfully to steer a path through these conflicting values and economic interests of regions. That experience demonstrated two things. The first was the way in which a motivated veto government, facing little countervailing power from Ottawa can stall a national climate program. The second is the way in which federal attempts at leadership, including unilateral action, while essential, can also damage fragile federal-provincial trust and working relationships. The search for new market access once the oil sands had started to move into full-bore production in the late 2000s led western interests, both industry and governmental, to lead the campaign to develop a new Canadian Energy Strategy and to insist that if Prime Minister Justin Trudeau wanted Alberta participation in a new national climate change program he would have to pay the price of approving new pipelines. These experiences, as discussed in the following pages, demonstrated the basic nature of the West-East divide that has always seen fully engaged and highly motivated western governments, without necessarily seeing an equivalent degree of interest on the part of Ottawa or the eastern provinces.

It is often said that politics is essentially about the distribution of cost and benefit: who gets what, when, where. Energy politics of the 1970s and early 1980s were about nothing else since the issue was simple – oil money and its distribution. To date, the basic distributive issue with respect to climate-change policy, who pays what portion of the total reduction cost, has surfaced only sporadically because this country has not yet encountered the stresses implicit in actually bringing about a significant reduction in GHG emissions. As set out above, provinces developed their climate-change plans along very different trajectories, with those in the west accommodating year-over-year emission increases and those in the east intended to bring about reductions. Clashes over distributive equity did not occur because governments felt there was really no need, despite international commitments, to cap and then reduce total Canadian emissions. Provinces significantly reducing their *own* emissions, such as Ontario or Nova Scotia, simply ignored the question of national emissions. Nor did the Pan-Canadian Framework process bring distribution of effort among the provinces into focus, since it bypassed the 2020 target and instead looked only to an objective fourteen years distant, while making no demands upon the provinces responsible for the bulk of Canadian emissions. The allocation issue must be addressed, however, along with its twin sister, the West-East divide, and the only means we have available to do so, federal-provincial relations, do not inspire confidence. We now turn to examining those three challenges in more detail.

4 The Three Underlying Challenges

As discussed at the outset of chapter 1, there are many factors that explain Canada's failure to date to put in place programs capable of fulfilling our international climate-change commitments. In particular, the inherent connection to energy issues and the associated political role of the oil industry is part of the explanation, as is the nature of the issue, leading to both scientific uncertainties and the need for extensive behaviour change on the part of so many organizations and individuals. Acid rain, with less than twenty major sources and immediate, local and long-range environmental impacts, was a comparatively easy challenge. By comparison, switching from fossil fuels to other energy sources in our buildings, motor vehicles, manufacturing, resource extraction, agriculture, and other activities found throughout Canadian society, in a fossil fuel–exporting country, is a challenge on a whole other order of magnitude. It is not assumed here that the three challenges to effective climate-change policy examined in this work are the only or necessarily the most important factors. What is claimed is that they are basic, underlying factors rooted in both our geography and constitution that have not yet received the attention they deserve. This chapter presents the nature of those three basic challenges.

The West-East Divide

The first of the three underlying challenges discussed in this chapter is referred to here as the "West-East divide" with the term "divide" referring to the gulf that exists between the interests and identities of the western fossil fuel–producing provinces, most notably Alberta and Saskatchewan, and the eastern provinces that do not contain fossil fuels, most notably Ontario and Quebec. (British Columbia generates both natural gas and coal, but has not appeared to feel as threatened by national climate-change policy as have Alberta and Saskatchewan; Newfoundland and Labrador generates offshore oil but has not played a significant role in intergovernmental energy and climate politics.) The divide exists for the most part because of the differing economic interests of west and east with respect to fossil fuel energy, differing interests that then carry forward into climate-change politics. The divide can also be attributed to non-material interests, however, in the form of the psychological factors of identity politics summed up by the term "western alienation."

As used here, the concept of the West-East divide has four component parts. The first stems from the greater existence of underground oil and natural gas resources in the west than the east. The second aspect of the divide is the way in which this produces differences in interest respecting reduction in greenhouse gas emissions. Such reduction in Canada and globally threatens sales of the western fossil fuel product and therefore provincial prosperity in a way it does not for the east (in fact, fuel switching to address climate change opens up new potential markets for the eastern energy product that Alberta and Saskatchewan do not have: hydro-electricity). At the same time, per capita reduction costs are higher in the carbon-intensive western economies than in the east, leading to difference of interest respecting any overall Canadian reduction.

The third aspect of the West-East divide, also directly related to the Canadian national reduction effort, is the difference in provincial climate-change policies – Alberta GHG emissions are growing and Alberta government policy is that they should continue to grow until they stabilize at some future date, while Ontario and Quebec emissions are declining and both provinces (although after the 2018 election the Ontario government's appetite for reduction was diminished) are putting in place policy measures intended to reduce them further. The result is that eastern reductions are effectively cancelled out by western increases.

Fourthly, as noted, the two regions are divided by differing views of Canada, of themselves, and of their respective places on the national stage. Western identity has been fashioned by a long history of what was perceived to be, quite accurately, exploitation by central Canada. This cultural factor reinforces the economic interest factors outlined above to make the West-East divide a major barrier to national policymaking.

Differing Fossil Fuel Energy Interests

While in the past coal has been mined in Nova Scotia and other parts of the country, since the post-war period oil and natural gas have been the most economically significant fossil fuels produced in Canada. They have traditionally been located almost exclusively in British Columbia, Alberta, and Saskatchewan and more recently in offshore Newfoundland and Nova Scotia. The advent of fracking as a cost-effective means of obtaining oil and natural gas is now providing potential access to supplies in eastern Canada. During the time period examined here, however, it has been the two western provinces of Alberta and Saskatchewan that have been the main exporters of oil and gas, and whose interests, therefore, with respect to both energy and climate change policy, differ markedly from those in the rest of the country. Doern and Gattinger give this picture:

> Canada has replicated within its borders some of the basic producer-consumer conflicts seen on the world stage between the Western OECD consumer countries and OPEC oil-producing countries. Canada's western producer provinces and its eastern consumer provinces frequently have fundamentally different interests. (2003, 25)

As we have seen and as will be discussed in more detail in the case study below, the inherent political conflict associated with these differing interests was vividly brought to life by Pierre Trudeau's 1980 National Energy Program, which, among other goals, was intended to give Canada a competitive advantage, flowing from the fact that it was an oil-producing nation, by ensuring that industries and consumers paid a price for oil lower than the world price. While this made sense from a national perspective, it meant that western producers were forced to forego the full benefit they would have received from world prices. At the same time, the NEP was intended to redistribute wealth through increasing the federal share of oil revenues to allow increased federal spending in other parts of the country. These federal government policy objectives locked west and east into a zero-sum game, where one could only benefit at the expense of the other. This considerably widened one of the basic fault lines of confederation, similar in terms of the threat to national unity of that other, more visible fault line related to the place in Canada of the distinct society of Quebec.

More recently, while Canadian oil prices are no longer set by Ottawa, Alberta and Saskatchewan have again been forced to forego significant financial benefit because they are able to export oil only into the American market, where prices are lower than could be received in Asian or other markets. In 2018, the Alberta government website gave this statement: "It's been more than sixty years since we last built a pipeline to Canada's west coast. Lack of access to global markets is now costing us an estimated forty million dollars every day." Consequently, during the past decade, those provinces have pursued the objective of new pipeline capacity giving access to the west or east coasts, an objective not shared by other parts of the country and, to the extent they are concerned about environmental impacts of new pipelines crossing their territory, one that some have actively opposed. Basic facts of geography that have dictated the locations of oil and gas reserves have given west and east different financial interests respecting western extraction and export of oil and gas. The dispute centred in the 1970s on the price Canadians should pay for oil, appeared again as different approaches to national climate-change policy in the 1990s, and then evolved twenty years later into disputes over pipeline siting. Throughout, the basic divide has persisted. Furthermore, this is a conflict respecting a product that has always been of central importance for all concerned, both as a source of export revenue and a vital ingredient in economic growth. The stakes are high for those in both west and east.

Differing Interests Respecting Climate-Change Policy

Dennis McConaghy, who spent his career working with TransCanada and its predecessor companies, describes how in 1990 he and his colleagues first discussed climate change, when the Alberta and federal governments asked them to provide data for the first time on greenhouse gases emitted by their operations: "Those of us assembled that morning in 1990, in the NOVA boardroom, seemingly had no sense that dealing with this climate-change risk could become antithetical to the economic interests of the hydrocarbon industry" (McConaghy 2017, 23). His choice of words is apt, since a large part of the solution to climate change involves using energy sources other than fossil fuels. The fossil fuel industries, and the jurisdictions within which they operate, to the extent the fuel-switching component of climate change policy is effective, face a shrinking of their market. This economic threat has been apparent right from the beginning, as evidenced by the oil industry campaign, starting in the early 1990s, to discredit the science and block government action, and similarly by government actions such as Alberta's effort to prevent the federal government from setting an emissions reduction target in the 1990 Green Plan (discussed in the next chapter). While their tactics and public discourse became more sophisticated in subsequent years, both the firms and governments dependent upon oil revenues know that effective action on climate change is a direct threat to their economic well-being. As such, this is a direct extension of the west-east difference in interest flowing from geographic location of the fossil fuel resource.

For the past twenty years that distributive issue has stayed in the background, since neither governments nor the societies they represent have shown any real interest in a complete transition away from fossil fuels. However, they have begun to take action to bring about emission reductions, which raises the second climate-change threat to the western provinces – the fact that their significantly higher per capita emissions and thus carbon intensity of their economies means they face higher reduction costs than do other parts of the country. Plourde describes the problem this way:

> As oil and gas production in Canada is very unevenly distributed across provinces, it has obvious implications in terms of distribution of the associated greenhouse gas (GHG) emissions ... The regional and sectoral distributions of the costs

of any national climate policy are thus matters of great concern to provincial governments. (2012, 111–12)

The western fossil fuel provinces face a cost from climate policy that does not exist in other parts of the country. Analysts agree there is a rough correspondence between per capita emissions and per capita reduction costs – the higher the former, the higher the latter (Macdonald et al. 2013, 24). What follows are annual per capita emissions in 2013 for two western and two eastern provinces (Government of Canada 2016b, 38).

Alberta   66.7 tonnes per person
Saskatchewan   67.6
Ontario   12.6
Quebec   10.1

Economic modelling done in 2009 showed that the per-capita cost of reducing emissions in Alberta and Saskatchewan is higher than in other provinces (Jaccard 2009). More recently a Conference Board study found that "clearly provinces such as Alberta and Saskatchewan face steeper [GHG mitigation] costs than others" (McCarthy 2017). Shortly before finalization of the Pan-Canadian Framework agreement (which he in fact did not sign), Saskatchewan Premier Brad Wall made the argument this way:

The federal government does not appreciate the simple reality that a revenue-neutral carbon tax is not sector-neutral. Carbon-intensive, export-sensitive industries such as agriculture and energy, the backbone of Western Canada's economy, will be hit the hardest. (Wall 2016a)

The existence of fossil fuels within their territories gives the western provinces a benefit not found in other parts of the country but it also results in a unique cost when attention turns to reducing emissions. This is less of a zero-sum game than the 1980 question of whether Canadians should pay world prices for oil, since all parts of the country pay a price for climate mitigation, even if the western price is higher, and, provided all provinces are acting unilaterally, as they did from 2006 to 2015, western refusal to mitigate does not directly impose a price on the east. However, as discussed immediately below and in the next section, once Canada begins to seriously consider and act on a given total reduction in emissions, the issue of higher western per-capita reduction prices *does* begin to shade into a zero-sum game. This is because any western refusal to reduce emissions must be compensated for by greater eastern reductions. This basic fact is what leads to the central argument made in this book, that the *cost* of those reductions must be made more equal, even while the reductions themselves may differ.

Alberta's Planned Emission Increases Undercut
Reductions Elsewhere

The claim is often made that increases in Alberta emissions, due to expansion of the oil and gas sector, will undercut reductions made in other parts of the country and make achieving Canadian targets more difficult or impossible. The former National Round Table on the Environment and Economy, writing with reference to the 2020 target of reducing total emissions to be 17 per cent below the 2005 level, had this to say: "Reducing emissions in every other province but Alberta, for example, given its growing oil and gas sector's contribution to forecasted emissions growth, will leave Canada short of achieving its stated target" (NRTEE 2012, 115). Macdonald, citing former *Globe and Mail* columnist Jeffrey Simpson, made this statement:

> Furthermore, reductions generated by some provincial policies, such as the BC carbon tax, will be undercut by future increases in emissions from the oil-producing provinces. Jeffrey Simpson, using federal government data, has noted that emissions will increase by "nearly 100 million tonnes in that province [Alberta] from 2005 to 2030. That's more than the increase for the entire country, where emissions are expected to hold steady or shrink elsewhere." (2016, 226; citing Simpson, 2014)

In 2014, the Pembina Institute published an analysis of Alberta's climate change mitigation policies, in particular its 2007 legally binding regulatory requirement that facilities emitting more than 100,000 tonnes of carbon dioxide reduce the intensity of their operations by 12 per cent (Pembina 2014, 2). The regulated facilities could comply by reducing emissions, but they also could comply by instead paying $15 a tonne into a technology fund, by purchasing offsets or by using previously acquired credits. Most facilities selected one of those options rather than the 12 per cent reduction, with the result that Alberta emissions had by 2014 only been reduced by 3.2 per cent below what they would have been absent the regulation (Pembina 2014, 8). The report says that the 2020 target set out in the 2008 Alberta climate plan was emissions of 260 Mt in that year, which represents an increase of 12 per cent over the 2005 level – while, as noted above, the 2020 target set by Ottawa for the country as a whole was 17 per cent below the 2005 level (Pembina 2014, 9). The report's characterization of Alberta's plan for emission increases as undercutting reductions made in other parts of the country is stated this way:

> The inconsistency between Canada's and Alberta's targets has never been addressed by either level of government. The implication is that Canada's national commitment will be out of reach unless other provinces collectively reduce their emissions by *more than* 17 per cent below 2005 levels, overcompensating for

the additional emissions from Alberta ... it remains unclear how Alberta's and Canada's climate targets could both be met without putting undue burden on other provinces. (Pembina 2014, 9; emphasis in original)

Writing in 2016, Adkin makes this statement: "The extraction and refinement of bitumen from the tar sands is the fastest-growing source of CO_2 emissions in Canada, and the greatest obstacle to meeting our country's obligations to reduce greenhouse gas emissions" (2016, 3). Thus, although they do not use the term, we have four claims that the government of Alberta's refusal to consider cutting emissions is undercutting the reductions that have been planned by other provinces. What does the term "undercutting" mean and what are its implications for the West-East divide? To answer those questions, it is useful to look at emissions by the major emitting provinces at two times: in 1990 when the first Canadian target was announced and then in 2017, once the Alberta increase, driven by expansion of oil sands operations, was well underway. As shown in table 2, Alberta emissions have increased by 58 per cent since 1990 and Saskatchewan emissions by 77 per cent. This compares to decreases in emissions during the same time period of 12 per cent in Ontario and 9 per cent in Quebec.

This different trend of western increases and eastern decreases is, by itself, an important component of the West-East divide. (Saskatchewan shows the greatest percentage increase, but its absolute emissions are much less significant than those of Alberta. For that reason, the focus here is upon Alberta rather than its sister carbon province.) The difference between Alberta and Ontario has been explicitly commented upon by the Government of Canada, in a surprisingly blunt comment for an entity known for its discretion when it comes to offering even the slightest criticism of performance by any given province.

Historically Alberta and Ontario have been the highest emitting provinces. Since 2005, emission patterns in these two provinces have diverged. Emissions in Alberta increased from 233 Mt in 2005 to 274 Mt in 2015 (18%), primarily as a result of the expansion of oil and gas operations ... In contrast, Ontario's have steadily decreased since 2005 (by 38 Mt or 19%), owing primarily to the closure of coal-fired electricity plants. (2017, 46)

Beyond these historical trends, there is a similar difference between west and east when it comes to their plans for future emissions.

Presumably Alberta emissions will grow approximately in keeping with that government's current climate-change planning, barring unexpected events such as a decline in oil prices so steep that oil sands production becomes no longer economically feasible. The Alberta government stated in 2017 that policies of its Climate Leadership Plan, introduced by the NDP government in 2015, combined with federal policies associated with the PCF, are expected to result in total emissions of 254 Mt in 2030 (Government of Alberta 2017, 8). As noted, unlike the other provinces, Alberta has not stated an absolute target for 2030 emissions, expressed as a percentage reduction below a given base year, and instead provides only an estimate of how much its current and planned programs will reduce emissions from the "business-as-usual" point; that is, the point they would reach in future if no policy action were taken. For that reason, the figure of 254 Mt is not an Alberta policy target but instead an estimate of remaining provincial emissions after reductions brought about by Alberta and Government of Canada policy. The 2017 document also says emissions might be 222 Mt if "innovation" (presumably referring to technological change) takes place. Since the subject here is the effect of policies, not other variables such as technology or price, the relevant figure is 254 Mt. Government of Canada data (2017) shows Alberta emissions in 2005 were 233 Mt. Using that figure, Alberta and federal policies are expected to result in a 9 per cent increase in Alberta emissions over the period 2005 to 2030, as follows:

predicted 2030 emissions	254 Mt
less 2005 emissions	− 233
increase 2005 to 2030	21 Mt = 9 per cent

This contrasts with the Canadian target of reducing emissions by 30 per cent below the 2005 level by 2030. Given this planned Alberta increase, the rest of the country will have to reduce by considerably more than 30 per cent; exactly the point made by the 2014 Pembina report. At that point, if Canada actually does achieve the 2030 target, Alberta emissions will make up 49 per cent of the Canadian total, while its population will be about 10 per cent of the total. Something will have to give – either the Canadian ability to achieve its target or the Alberta plan to continue to expand oil production and associated emissions.

How much will the rest of the country have to reduce because of the Alberta failure to reduce? Using the figures above we can do this calculation of the reduction Alberta would make if it too reduced its emissions to be 30 per cent below the 2005 level.

Alberta emissions in 2005	233 Mt
30 per cent of that figure	− 69.9
2030 emissions with a 30 per cent reduction	163.1 Mt

| 2030 emissions planned by Alberta | 254 Mt |

The difference between Alberta's planned 2030 emissions and emissions in that year if it were to reduce to be 30 per cent below the 2005 level is: 254 − 163.1 = 90.9 Mt. Writing in November 2015 shortly after the Alberta plan was announced Boothe (2015) estimated that taking the new plan into account, "we will probably miss our target by about 100 million tonnes, even with the efforts of other provinces." Thus it is fair to say the rest of the country will have to provide something like 90 or 100 Mt of reductions because of Alberta's plan to increase its emissions. That is more than total emissions from any other province except Ontario.

No other province has done its climate-change planning by factoring in the need to reduce enough to compensate for Alberta's failure to reduce and to instead increase emissions. That is, however, what they are implicitly being asked to do. That is what is meant by "undercutting" – unilateral action by one province forcing other provinces to make the reductions it is not willing to make itself. To date, Alberta's undercutting of reduction efforts elsewhere has not caused political conflict because there effectively has been no ceiling on total Canadian emissions. Targets announced by the Harper government were ignored by all concerned (including Prime Minister Harper) and target dates have been continually moved into the future. Provinces were free to act on their own and so planned increases in Alberta were of no more concern to other provinces than were planned increases in India – particularly since other provinces knew they had no ability to influence the policies of either of those sovereign and semi-sovereign entities. Nor did participation in the Pan-Canadian Framework change that perception, since the deadline was far away and provinces had not been asked to take any immediate actions beyond accepting the $50 carbon price for the year 2022. However, that will change should Canadian governments ever become serious about meeting a given target – achieving a given quantum of emission reduction – in the near future. That will make Alberta's demand that others make something like 90 Mt of emission reductions on its behalf explicit, visible, and the source of political conflict, which can only worsen the West-East divide.

Western Alienation

The factors constituting the West-East divide discussed above all relate to material interests, namely different sources of financial prosperity found in west and east and the differing costs of reducing GHG emissions. The final element to be discussed here, however, is non-material, flowing from the ways in which ideas held by those living in the west differ from those of Canadians living in other parts of the country; differences in values, symbols, and identities but above all different views of one's place in confederation. Canada has always had a concentration of wealth, population, and political power at the centre, leaving those in the surrounding regions feeling they have their noses pressed against the window of a club frequented only by the rich, gazing enviously at the world inside, a world of status and power, oysters and champagne. Gibbins defines "western alienation" as "a political ideology of regional discontent ... a sense of political, economic and, to a lesser extent, cultural estrangement from the Canadian heartland" (1992, 70). The material and non-material psychological elements of western alienation are closely bound each to the other, as is illustrated by Gibbins's presentation of the ideology's main theme, "the belief that the West is always outgunned in national politics and as a consequence has been subjected to varying degrees of economic exploitation by central Canada" (1992, 70).

Given the differences in economies, political ideologies, and cultures among the western provinces, perhaps the more accurate term is "Alberta alienation." Certainly the two provinces that have been the most ready to question federal authority over the past fifty years have been Quebec and Alberta. Each has a view of itself as a people different from other Canadians; more so, one might argue than do those living in British Columbia, Saskatchewan, or Manitoba. In terms of Alberta at least, one does not have to look far to find examples of the mindset. In a book commemorating the centenary of Alberta entering confederation as a province, Sharpe makes this comment:

> Suspicion of Ottawa remains and is quickly rekindled at the slightest hint of unilateral federal measures. The modern flashpoint is often health care, but the hostility goes back through the National Energy Program of 1980 to the resource ownership battles during the 1920s. (2005, 28)

McConaghy also points to the NEP:

> The resulting animosity [from the NEP] between Alberta and the rest of the country arguably colours, perhaps even dominates, the province's politics up to the present. Alberta's ethos has traditionally been distinguished by comparative affluence and opportunity but also by conflict and grievance with the rest of the country. (2017, 21)

Adkin suggests western alienation as it exists in Alberta has been deliberately encouraged by successive Alberta governments:

> Governments since the Social Credit years have constructed an "Albertan" identity not merely in terms of "distinctiveness" or "difference," in relation to other provincial identities, but also in terms of a fighting, feisty defence of provincial interests from the predations and insults of hostile outsiders. (2016, 583)

As Sharpe mentions above, the historic origins of western alienation are largely found in the fact that Alberta and Saskatchewan became provinces in 1905 but without the constitutional ownership of their natural resources held by the pre-existing provinces. It was only after a concerted political effort that they won that ownership in 1930. Gibbins (1992, 77) points also to the fact that in earlier times Alberta sent MPs to Ottawa representing the marginal parties of Progressives and Social Credit and thus did not hold seats at the cabinet table: "Alberta became little more than a curiosity, the freak show of the national political circus. By electing Social Credit MPs, Albertan drifted to the margins of national political life." As discussed in the next chapter, the clash with Ottawa and Ontario over oil revenues in the 1970s and early 1980s strongly reinforced the Albertan sense of being wronged by central Canada. In the years since then, and in particular once oil prices recovered from their slump in the 1980s, economic power has shifted from Montreal and Toronto to Calgary. When the Conservative party has been in power federally, as during the Mulroney and Harper administrations, a considerable quantity of political power also moved west. Nevertheless, western alienation remains a potent political force.

One of the strands in the work of scholars studying Canada dating back to the work of Harold Innis before the Second World War has been a focus upon the role of staples exports – sending resources such as fur, timber, fish, or wheat to foreign markets – in Canadian economic development and the relations between the "hinterland" (the regions in which such resources are extracted, such as Atlantic Canada or the west) and the "centre" (Ontario and Quebec) that supplied the necessary manufactured goods, private capital lent by banks, and public spending on the necessary transportation infrastructure (Careless 1954; Watkins 1963; Howlett, Netherton, and Ramesh 1999). The general assumption has been that relations between centre and hinterland have worked largely to the benefit of the former. Donald Smiley (1987, 158) has been forthright in advancing that view: "The Canadian prairies were at the first and to some considerable degree remain an economic colony of the country's central heartland." He argues that successive federal governments explicitly modelled their relations with the west upon a relationship they knew very well, that which governed relations between Canada and the United Kingdom in the British Empire, with Ottawa playing the role of imperial master and the western territories and then provinces the role of subservient colonies. Smiley lists the main characteristics of the relationship between central Canada and the west as follows: 1) the west was limited to staples export, while development of manufacturing was actively supported in the centre; 2) the west was reliant upon the centre for financial capital; 3) economic foreign policy favoured the centre over the western hinterland; and, 4) transportation, essential for staples export, was controlled by and benefitted the centre (1987, 159). Recognition of the material and nonmaterial factors giving rise to western alienation is well embedded in Canadian scholarship.

A hundred years ago, Alberta complained that rates for shipping wheat to export markets by rail punished the west. Today, Alberta complains that it is suffering from the ways in which Ottawa controls the infrastructure for shipping the new staples resources, oil and natural gas. The West-East divide in the fields of energy and climate change is in some ways simply a continuation of patterns of Canadian centre-hinterland economic and political power relations dating back to the nineteenth century, patterns that for completely understandable reasons have meant that resentment, suspicion and mistrust of the east have become permanently embedded as integral parts of the western identity. Development of effective national climate change policy in the face of the West-East divide as it has existed through more than a century of Canadian history is an enormous challenge, one that goes far beyond the specifics of climate science, emission reduction technologies or carbon pricing.

The Inherent Need to Allocate GHG Reductions

Like the West-East divide, the second challenge to effective national climate-change programs also has its roots in empirical facts respecting the physical world; in this case the nature of the climate change issue. Global climate change has come about because the release of greenhouse gases from many sources all over the world has brought about changes in the composition of the global atmosphere, most notably an increase in the quantity of carbon dioxide. This change in the atmosphere produces a variety of impacts, such as greater frequency of severe weather events, rising sea levels, geographic movement of disease-carrying vectors such as mosquitoes, changes in habitat, and others. It is not possible, however, to establish a causal link between any of these impacts, such as Hurricane Sandy, which in 2012 caused extensive flooding damage in New York City exacerbated by the higher than previous Atlantic sea levels, and greenhouse gas emissions from any one particular source, such as the Belledune coal-fired electricity generation plant in Gloucester County, New Brunswick. In this respect, climate change differs from local air pollution issues.

If residents living close to the Belledune plant are sufficiently bothered by particulate air pollution causing smog and a variety of human health effects, they can lobby the New Brunswick government to take regulatory action to force the plant to switch to natural gas. New Brunswick can solve its local air pollution problem by acting itself, with no need for action by other governments. Residents of New York City, on the other hand, wishing to avoid a repetition of hurricane-related flooding, cannot solve their problem by lobbying the New York State government. That government could shut down all the sources of greenhouse gases in the state, at the price of major economic impacts and job losses, and still not solve its climate change problem. Nor would a request from New York that New Brunswick reduce emissions from the Belledune plant give any benefit. As one source among the global millions, it too could be shut down completely without in any way making New York citizens less vulnerable to a future storm surge.

Unlike local environmental issues, climate change is a true collective action problem, defined as a problem that no one actor can solve by itself. Like Garret Hardin's mythical medieval herder, who could not solve his or her problem of disappearing commonly held pasturage by alone taking rational, self-interested action, countries of the world cannot solve their climate-change problem by acting alone (Hardin 1968). Instead, they must cooperate.

Recognizing this, countries of the world have indeed been cooperating on climate change, most notably through the vehicle of the 1992 UN Framework Convention on Climate Change. As they have done so, they have had to wrestle with the question of who should pay what portion of the cost of action. If it were possible to establish a causal connection between impact and actions of a particular source, the answer to that question would be obvious. For each impact addressed, the polluter in question would be asked to pay. However, that cannot be done and so the answer has been sought in a search for a requirement to pay that is considered "fair" – for instance, the notion that those who caused the problem over the past several centuries, and benefitted economically from those actions, have a greater responsibility to pay than others. Accordingly, the UN regime adopted the principle of "common but differentiated responsibilities," which is taken to mean that all countries have some responsibility to act (common), but some more than others (differentiated). This latter group is made up of the richer OECD nations, which have both historical responsibility and greater ability to pay than do those in the Global South. The principle was implemented at the time of the 1997 Kyoto Conference of Parties by the requirement that only OECD nations must take immediate action to reduce their emissions.

The basic logic of the Kyoto approach is to first establish an overall target, in that case a reduction of global emissions to be 5 per cent below 1990 levels by a date between 2008 and 2012, and then through some process of discussion and negotiation reach agreement on the individual country targets, such as the Canadian commitment to reduce to 6 per cent below 1990 levels, the US commitment of a 7 per cent reduction, and so on. Taken together, these commitments are expected to achieve the common target. This is referred to as a "top-down" approach. As the years went by, and countries failed to meet their targets, with global emissions going up instead of down, global policymakers became disenchanted with that approach and instead adopted a "bottom-up" method. For the 2015 Paris climate summit, no initial target was set – instead countries were asked to publicly state what commitment they would make for a reduction to be achieved by 2030. The total of those commitments, by the logic of the bottom-up approach, constitutes the target. In fact, policymakers fudged that at Paris, adopting a target of two degrees warming, while discussing an even more ambitious target of one and a half degrees, and overlooking the fact that the total of national commitments generated a target closer to three degrees of warming. The difference between that de facto target and the proclaimed two-degree target would be achieved by means of future action.

Within a given country, such as Canada, the top-down logic of the need to reach agreement on who provides what portion of the overall effort automatically applies. This is because the country, as it participates in the international process, commits to just one reduction number. Having done that, as soon as it then begins to develop policy to achieve that goal, it implicitly faces the issue of who within the country will contribute what part of the total reduction required. Within a federated state such as Canada, the question of "who" involves not only the GHG sources, such as who will pay for new transit to reduce motor vehicle use or which industrial emissions will be reduced, but also necessarily includes the question of which provinces containing those sources will pay what portion of the total cost. If sources were distributed evenly throughout the county on a per capita basis, which by and large is the case for buildings, then all sources could reduce by the same amount, such as the same 30 per cent reduction that the country as a whole is working to achieve. In that case, the price being paid by provinces would be equal on a per capita basis. However, some sources are *not* distributed evenly but instead are found in only some parts of the country, most notably oil and gas production, which is found primarily in Alberta and Saskatchewan. In those cases, the cost of meeting the national target cannot be allocated among sources and provinces on the basis of equal shares and instead some other formula must be found. How can that be done?

The starting point for policymaking, for climate change and all other issues, is usually efficiency (cost-effectiveness), which leads to one means of allocating reductions. Governments wish to achieve the policy goal at the lowest possible total cost and so, in the case of climate change, seek to have those sources with the lowest per-tonne reduction cost contribute the greatest portion of the total effort. That objective leads to adoption of cap-and-trade systems, in which trading maximizes efficiency. However, the fact that reduction costs are not equal means that an efficient allocation results in some sources, and the provinces in which they are located, paying more than others. The cost for the country as a whole is kept as low as possible by maximizing efficiency, but different regions still pay different costs. Those paying higher costs tend to object, and so in addition to the principle of efficiency, governments seek to allocate in accordance with another principle – equity. That inevitably involves, just as it does at the international level, looking for some form of allocation that is considered "fair" by those involved. It is for this reason that the prime minister and premiers at their meeting in December 1997 adopted the principle that no region would be asked to bear an "unreasonable burden."

Two points, in terms of this second challenge to national climate-change policymaking, are essential. The first is that allocation of the total reduction cost among sources and provinces is inevitable – it cannot be avoided, even if governments wish to do so. During the second national climate process, 1998–2002, the federal government stated explicitly that it did not want to discuss allocation among provinces because it believed that would lead to balkanization of the policy, with differing standards in different parts of the country. The provinces, with the exception of Quebec, agreed. Nevertheless, once a given set of policy measures is put in place there is automatically a de facto allocation of effort and cost – different sources and provinces are picking up different portions of the total cost, even if allocation has never been discussed. During the 1998–2002 NCCP, however, it *was* being discussed since modelling was continually generating data on regional impacts associated with different policy measures. Confidential interviews reveal that allocation was not discussed publicly, but was top of mind for policymakers nevertheless (Macdonald et al. 2013). The question in the minds of ministers and the governments they represented was always this: What will the set of policy options currently being considered cost my province? Allocation is inevitable and, due to the existence of modelling data, is considered by all involved, even if it is never formally part of the process.

The second essential point is that because the allocation cannot be done on the basis of equal shares, policymakers have no choice but to launch their boat upon the choppy waters of the normative dialogue of equity and fairness. The inherent need to allocate means that once Canada, or any other country or jurisdiction, comes close to putting in place effective climate policy, it finds itself engaged in distributive politics, which poses the unique challenges discussed below. One of those is the question of whether the distribution is necessarily zero sum or whether it can be win-win. The case studies reveal the importance of that point. The first, Canadian energy policy, 1973 to 1981, was purely distributive respecting division of oil revenues between Alberta and Ottawa and was zero sum: gain made by one meant loss for the other. That meant the high degree of Alberta's motivation was matched by a highly motivated Ottawa, bringing into play countervailing power and giving symmetry to the West-East divide. That was not true for the next three cases.

These two points only apply, of course, if Canada is following a top-down approach to national climate policymaking. One might think that is the only approach possible – Canada has to first set the national target, by dint of participating in the international regime, and then has no choice but to allocate as it works to achieve that goal. In fact, however, Canadian climate policy has to date been closer to a bottom-up approach, with each province deciding by itself what it would do, despite the unbroken existence of national targets since the Mulroney government in 1990 committed to stabilizing emissions by the year

2000. This is because targets have for the most part been ignored. The Harper government provides the extreme case, in which the Kyoto target was explicitly repudiated and its own Copenhagen target ignored, since there was no attempt to work with the provinces or to take significant federal action. The Chrétien government was marginally more committed to the Kyoto target, but made no significant effort to meet it and, as discussed below, was hobbled by the fact that Alberta always thought of it as Ottawa's target, which would only be pursued if examination showed it could in fact be achieved without doing major economic harm. After being elected in 2015, the Justin Trudeau government was certainly committed to its Paris target, but relied on future action to achieve it. In any case we have all conveniently agreed to ignore the 2020 target, and 2030, meanwhile, is a long way away. For these reasons, we have not seen the two points made above – that allocation in unavoidable and that it will be discussed in terms of distributive fairness as much as efficiency – in play in Canada since 1990 other than in isolated instances discussed in the case studies. They *will* become operative – unavoidably so because of the physical facts of the climate-change issue and the location of oil and gas reserves – *if* Canada begins to seriously act to achieve a given quantity of emissions reduction.

If so, Canadian national climate-change policy will be heavily marked by distributive politics, which makes up another part of this second challenge. Several points should be made respecting the nature of distributive politics. Following Stone (1988), one can think of the nature of distributive politics by using the example of the teacher bringing a cake into class and discussing with her students how it should be divided among them. They start by suggesting each should get a piece the same size as all the other pieces – equal shares. A student quickly points out, however, that one of them put in the effort and expense needed to bake the cake, and so in fairness that student should get a larger piece. Discussion moves on to the characteristics of other students that might suggest they deserve a larger piece – one is more hungry having missed lunch, one was absent the last time they enjoyed a cake in class and so on. Stone argues this shows there are two major ways used to decide a distribution: equality – "the part of a distribution that contains uniformity" – and equity – "distributions regarded as fair, even though they contain both equalities and inequalities" (1988, 33). Both are likely to be in play, but agreement can be reached much more easily on the former than the latter.

That is because of another important aspect of distributive politics: one's view of an equitable distribution is inevitably tinged (or strongly coloured) by self-interest. We tend to prefer the principle that is most favourable to ourselves when considering the means of deciding a distribution. Boothe and Boudreault put it this way: "Not surprisingly, different notions of equity [in allocating GHG reduction costs] exist and one's preferred notion is often aligned with one's own interests" (2016, 4). This influence of self-interest on perceptions of equitable distribution has been confirmed in psychology experiments (Johansson-Stenman and Konow 2010). One of the main suggestions made in the concluding chapter is that Canada abandon the worn-out dynamic of Ottawa as part of an international process setting a target for the whole country and then coming back to talk with the provinces about what should be done to meet that goal. Instead, it is suggested, we should not begin any future national effort by talking about targets at all, but instead by discussing what sharing of the cost of action might be seen as fair by all those involved. (Using a bottom-up approach, but recognizing that at the end of the day so long as we continue to participate in the international regime and so make commitments to other nations, Canada can have only one reduction target, which invokes the top-down logic of allocation.) Beginning any future national effort with a focus upon equitable sharing of cost might help bridge the West-East divide, but we must recognize that any such discussion will certainly be influenced by self-interest, as governments, industrial sectors, and others advance criteria for allocation that reduce their costs while increasing costs paid by others.

Two other points respecting distributive politics will be made quickly. The first is the widely accepted argument, which originated with Olson (1965), that those asked to bear a concentrated cost will have more incentive to mobilize for political action than do those receiving the associated, but diffused, benefit. Thus we have differing degrees of interest, as discussed in the theory section of chapter 1. Applying the concept to Canadian climate policy, which has to include significant reductions by Alberta and Saskatchewan because their emissions constitute close to half the Canadian total, but that also, as discussed, bear a greater per capita cost in doing so, we know the carbon provinces will be highly motivated to resist. Other provinces, however, will be inherently less motivated to support effective national climate policy, for two reasons. The first is that the benefits they might receive will be diffused and less visible than the costs borne by the western provinces. The benefits flowing from costs paid in Alberta and Saskatchewan are diffused not only throughout Canada, but throughout the planet, which leads to the second reason for less motivated eastern provinces. Those provinces know that Canadian national policy alone cannot solve their climate-change problem – that can only come from global action. Differing motivations associated with concentrated cost and diffused benefit is another factor making the West-East divide asymmetric, with motivated western provinces not necessarily encountering resistance from equally motivated ones in the east.

The second point is that perceived fairness of the process used to decide the distribution is as important as the perceived fairness of the distribution itself (Cropanzano and Ambrose 2001; Skogstad 2003 discusses the need for perceived legitimacy of both "input" – the process, and "output" – the decision).

Actors will accept a distribution that does not exactly coincide with their interests if they believe the decision-making process has been legitimate and fair. We accept the fact that our candidate lost the election, as long as we are confident the election was not rigged. Criteria for evaluating the fairness of the decision-making process include such things as the perception that the decision maker was unbiased, the process was marked by accountability and transparency, and was one which gave those affected an opportunity for input. As discussed, the Canadian intergovernmental relations process, marked by a high degree of secrecy and where decisions are made solely by the self-interested governments themselves, without even an advisory role provided for a neutral, unbiased party, does not meet those criteria, suggesting it needs increased transparency and accountability, if a cost allocation it generates is to be seen by Canadians as being fair.

In summary, the second challenge to effective federal-provincial climate-change policy is the fact that allocation of the cost among provinces cannot be avoided and cannot be decided on the basis of equal shares. The most cost-effective allocation will certainly be considered, but the discussion of allocation will also be couched in terms of fairness, which will involve perceptions of merit, with each actor's perception of what is fair shaped to some degree by self-interest, and with perceptions of the fairness of the process being important for perceived fairness of the distribution. Finally, those provinces asked to bear a concentrated cost will be highly motivated to defend their interests. This challenge is closely related to the first, the West-East divide, because emission reduction imposes higher per capita costs upon the carbon-intensive western economies. Because of those higher costs, in any future climate process the western provinces will be highly engaged, using the political power available to them to influence the process outcomes. To date, Canada has sidestepped the allocation issue by pushing targets off into the future so that emissions can continue to rise. If we ever want to actually *achieve* a target, however, allocation must be addressed.

The National Intergovernmental Process

The third challenge is the basic conundrum facing Canada with respect to its ability to meet the commitments it gives for a particular reduction target as it participates in the international regime: the only governance option available is national, coordinated, federal-provincial policy, and yet that option is the weakest available, far less likely to produce effective policy than if Canada were a unitary state, but also weaker than the European Union governance system and perhaps even weaker than decision making by sovereign states negotiating international regimes. The factors that make it very difficult for the intergovernmental system to generate coordinated, effective policy have been reviewed in the previous chapter. Here, discussion is limited to the fact that the intergovernmental process is the only one available.

The Only Option Available

Simply put, we have to rely on the national intergovernmental process because the provinces acting alone will not put in place effective climate-change policy and nor yet will they allow the federal government to do so – not that any federal government is likely to want to take on that chore. Why can we not simply leave it to unilateral action by each province, with no need for coordinated action? In the spring of 2015, when the Stephen Harper government was still in power and so there was no possibility of coordinated federal and provincial action, the Ecofiscal Commission published a report arguing that the best way forward was for each province to introduce a carbon pricing program by itself, with no attempt to contribute to the national target or to consider what other provinces were doing. The report said that one benefit of this approach was that: "Provincial policies can sidestep the difficult issue of burden sharing" (Ecofiscal Commission 2015, 20). However, the report went on to discuss disadvantages to this approach, saying provincial policies do need to be coordinated over time, for several reasons. One of those was the fact that "a decentralized approach can lead to insufficiently stringent policy … provinces would have an incentive to avoid using strong policies, hoping the other provinces will make the tough choices" (Ecofiscal Commission 2015, 21).

In fact, we already know that uncoordinated provincial action will lack stringency because such unilateral provincial action is essentially what we have had since governments first began to act on the issue in the early 1990s. The NCCP was never strong enough to influence provincial action (plans it produced were compilations of federal and provincial plans that by and large had been independently arrived at), the Martin government brought in some bilateral agreements, but they were too vague to influence provincial action, and of course the Harper government had no interest in coordinating federal and provincial action. During his administration, provincial governments did begin to introduce their own programs, despite the lack of Ottawa action, but each acted alone. The *targets* in those programs, presumably by coincidence, added up to approximately the national target (Ecofiscal Commission 2015; Macdonald et al. 2013). However, each year Environment Canada would report that the actual *programs* in place added up to only about half the 2020 national target (see the summary of that data provided by NRTEE 2012). A large part of the problem is the fact, set out in table 2, that during the past twenty-five years some provinces have seen their emissions increase and others decrease – an example of the free-riding referred to by the Ecofiscal Commission.

Could provinces coordinate their actions to achieve effective policy by themselves, without a role played by the federal government? Both experience to date and the basic dynamic of provincial interests and powers say that is not possible. As discussed in the fourth case study below, the provinces were successful in coordinating their actions to generate the 2015 Canadian Energy Strategy, without federal involvement. That could only be done, however, by completely sacrificing policy effectiveness; all provinces and territories signed on, but by doing so did not commitment themselves to any particular action. In terms of climate change, the provinces-only Council of the Federation attempted to reach agreement on coordinated policy in 2007, and then tried again at a special premiers' meeting in 2008. Both attempts failed to reach agreement, due largely to Alberta objections (Winfield and Macdonald 2012). Since the council, like all Canadian intergovernmental relations, operates only on consensus, any one province can block agreement; this institutional weakness is part of the reason for the provincial failure.

Other factors compound the problem of weak rules for provinces-only decision making. The first is that in most circumstances no given provincial government has a significant interest in influencing the actions of other provinces (the efforts in 2018 by Alberta to prevent British Columbia from blocking construction of the expansion of Kinder Morgan's Trans Mountain pipeline represent an exception). A provincial government only gets votes within its borders, and those voters are unlikely to be influenced by how successful their government has been in changing the behaviour of other provincial governments during an intergovernmental process. Thus time and effort spent on inter-provincial coordination produces no electoral return and so is of lower priority than issues located within the provincial borders. Alberta, at the 2007 Council of the Federation meeting referred to above, *was* motivated to influence the behaviour of others, but there was no countervailing motivation on the other side. Even provinces that are actively putting in place climate-change policy have no incentive to convince other provinces to emulate them. British Columbia has had a carbon tax in place since 2008, but has made no effort to convince others to do the same thing.

Secondly, a given province has no real *ability* to influence other provinces, even if it should want to. It does not have financial resources to encourage action by other provinces, or at least is unlikely to spend money for such a purpose, nor can it threaten to act within other provincial borders if those provinces do not themselves act. Only the federal government can do those things. The fourth case study below, of the 2015 Canadian Energy Strategy, examines a province, Alberta, taking the lead in development of a national policy effort. As a province, the only means available to Alberta to influence other provinces was persuasion. Alberta Premier Alison Redford put in considerable effort doing exactly that, and at the end of the day the strategy came into being. However, the case study shows the limits of the ability of a province to influence policy of other provinces and leads to the conclusion, discussed in the final two chapters, that a motivated and engaged federal government is essential for effective national climate policy.

Provinces may influence one another without intending to do so through such things as voter interest in an example set by another province. The result may be a policy race to the top (for an excellent case study of the way in which Canadian governments influenced one another as they engaged in policymaking respecting pulp and paper toxic pollution standards, even though they were not participating in any intergovernmental process, see Harrison 1996a). However, there has been little evidence of that to date with respect to climate policy. Provinces such as British Columbia, Ontario, Quebec, and Nova Scotia have put in place climate change programs that have reduced emissions in those jurisdictions, but Saskatchewan, for example, has not been pressured by those examples to follow suit. Thus two conclusions are drawn. First, unilateral provincial action has failed to date to achieve Canadian targets (even though some provincial targets have been achieved), and will almost certainly continue to do so. Secondly, it is safe to conclude that the provinces by themselves are unable to cobble together an effective national program. However, what about a very different approach – unilateral action by the federal government, regardless of what provinces do or do not do? Is that possible?

The federal government most likely has the constitutional jurisdiction and certainly has the financial and policy capacity to by itself bring in laws and programs that apply throughout the country and would be sufficient to meet any given target. However, a number of factors make that unrealistic. The first is the fact that the provinces – all of them, not just the carbon provinces – would certainly resist unilateral federal regulation. They own the energy resources, hold constitutional authority to regulate, and climate-change policy matters a lot to their economic well-being. They will never step off the playing field, leaving it in the sole possession of Ottawa. We know that from past experience: they objected strongly when Ottawa set aside their preferred target in December 1997; Alberta enacted law in 2002 to help ward off federal regulation; all provinces objected to the unilateral federal plan at the point the NCCP collapsed in fall 2002; and, more recently, a number of provinces have gone to court in an attempt to prevent a federal carbon tax. Provinces will resist any effort by Ottawa to meet the Canadian target all by itself.

Do provinces have the means to block any such federal action? It may well be the provinces cannot block it in the courts, since emission mitigation is almost certainly an issue of shared jurisdiction. However, they are almost certain to win the associated *political* fight. Provincial governments mobilizing their citizens to resist federal intrusion pose a major electoral threat to Ottawa. The federal government might attempt to counter that by going over the heads of provincial governments and returning carbon tax revenues directly to citizens, as has been done by the Justin Trudeau government. However, there will still be in place a federal tax, made very visible by the fact that the resisting provincial government will continually point to it.

This political problem for Ottawa is made worse by the level of tax that would be required if policy action was only being taken at the federal level. The PCF $50 tax by 2022 is intended to be complemented by other federal and provincial policies. Absent all provincial policies, the tax would have to be significantly higher (or other federal policies would have to bring about equivalent behaviour change) for the national target to be met. If the provinces were not acting, all the political and electoral cost associated with effective climate policy would be heaped upon Ottawa's shoulders alone. Leaving responsibility for climate policy completely in federal hands will never happen not only because of provincial resistance but also because any sane federal government, with a healthy interest in winning the next election, would never take on that responsibility.

As we shall see in the PCF case study, it seems clear that in the summer and fall of 2016 Ottawa decided it could live with a national program that did not include Saskatchewan; in the event, other provinces opted out as well. However, in the scenario being considered here, of unilateral federal policy action and no provincial action, Ottawa would not be engaged in this kind of conflict with some provinces. It would be facing political resistance whipped up by *all* provincial governments. No federal government would willingly enter that kind of contest. And if one did, it would almost certainly be defeated at the next election, to be replaced by a political party dedicated to making sure that Ottawa was not the sole climate policy actor being blamed by firms and citizens for the costs they are asked to pay.

Beyond this political reality is the further difficulty that a number of important climate-change policy tools lie largely in provincial hands. Switching electricity generation from fossil fuels to renewable sources must be done by provincial governments and their utilities. Land-use planning that leads to greater settlement densities and reduced transportation needs is provincial, as is regulation of building heating and cooling efficiency by means of building codes. In a purely technical sense Ottawa could pass legislation giving itself power to regulate in all such areas, although the constitutionality of that invasion of provincial jurisdiction would certainly be litigated. It is difficult, however, to imagine such a reversal of the established Canadian order, outside of war time. Moreover, doing so would increase that much more resistance by provincial governments, using all available legal and political means to resist. Ottawa can certainly play a role in these areas of provincial jurisdiction, as it is doing with PCF work in the area of electricity, but at the end of the day provinces must be the ones acting.

Finally, the nature of Canada itself dictates that we cannot leave climate-change policy solely in federal hands. As discussed, at the core of the Canadian climate-change dilemma lies the West-East divide, which is the latest expression of a long history of troubled centre-periphery relations. Western mistrust of central Canadian power is completely understandable, given the way that power was exercised in the early years. To now say that Ottawa should insist provinces vacate the policy field so it can again exercise dominant, unyielding power in the face of highly charged western resistance is to risk an irretrievable fracturing of the country and is, for that reason, unthinkable.

In all climate-change policymaking to date, Ottawa has taken on to itself a certain portion of the total reduction effort, to be achieved by use of federal policy instruments. That will certainly happen again in any future federal-provincial effort. However, it is unrealistic to think Ottawa can, by itself with no provincial involvement, bring about the entire reduction, just as it is unrealistic to think Ottawa can do nothing, leaving the whole effort in the hands of the provinces. For better or worse, coordinated action by both levels of government is the only available option.

5 Canadian National Energy Policy, 1973–1981

Case Summary

A lead government (Ottawa) and supporting governments (primarily Ontario) encountered countervailing power from veto governments (primarily Alberta, but also Saskatchewan and British Columbia), and prevailed in the contest. The interest of the lead government included both material self-interest (an increased share of oil revenues) and ideas respecting the nature of federalism (the pendulum had swung too far in the direction of provincial power). Lead government degree of interest increased after Pierre Trudeau was re-elected in 1980. The primary veto government had a high degree of interest throughout, stemming from both material (maximize oil revenues) and nonmaterial (yet again resist central Canadian domination; federalism meant the oil resource belonged only to Alberta) sources. Given equal degree of interest on both sides, the most important variable determining the balance of power between the lead and veto governments was Ottawa's skillful diplomacy that included the ability to compromise, its sources of power in both constitutional jurisdiction and central Canadian political support, and its willingness to use that power by means of unilateral action to influence provincial behaviour. Lead government predominance led to behaviour change by both governments and thus substantial policy coordination. The price paid for that coordination, however, in terms of a grievously embittered West-East divide, was much too high.

START AND END DATES: 1973–1 September 1981

MAJOR POLICY DECISIONS

unilateral
- federal government for the first time assumes the power to set Canadian oil prices, 1973
- federal government budget sets out the National Energy Program, 28 October 1980

	• Alberta government announces three retaliatory measures, 30 October 1980: 1) legal action; 2) refuse to grant two oil project approvals; 3) reduce oil shipments to eastern Canada
bilateral	• Alberta and Ottawa reach agreement, 1 September 1981
multilateral	• first ministers agree 22–3 January 1974, there would be one Canadian oil price
	• at a subsequent meeting 9–10 April 1975, first ministers are unable to agree on what that price should be, due to Ontario veto
	• First Ministers' Conference convened by the Joe Clark government, 12 November 1979; no conclusive decision on oil price

CASE OUTCOME

As of September 1981 the Trudeau government had achieved its objective of bringing about a significant change in the division of oil and gas revenues between the western producing provinces and Ottawa, with the latter's share increased and the former's decreased. Alberta had been forced to concede in the 1981 Alberta-Ottawa agreement that it could not achieve its objective of Canadian prices being fully equal to the international price (which meant Ontario to some extent achieved its objective). Ottawa also gave ground, so that the 1981 Alberta-Ottawa agreement represented a compromise. Substantial policy coordination was thus achieved. Pre-existing western alienation, with Alberta and the west feeling considerable mistrust and antagonism towards Ottawa and the eastern provinces, had been significantly deepened and entrenched.

COORDINATION CATEGORY: substantial policy coordination

While concerned only with energy policy, this case directly involves the three underlying challenges being examined here. The 1973 and 1979 sudden jumps in the world price of oil, to the extent they resulted in corresponding increases in the price of oil extracted by the western producing provinces, would result in enormous financial benefit to that region, while the eastern manufacturing provinces incurred costs due to the rising price of the imported oil on which they relied – the case is the most powerful example we have to date of the West-East divide in operation. Furthermore, the West-East divide in this case differs from the divide in the other four due to its zero-sum nature; here, motivated and engaged western oil producers were met by equally engaged countervailing power from both eastern provinces and Ottawa, a factor not found in the other cases. In terms of the second challenge, the case is all about allocation of cost and benefit (which is why it is zero sum). Thirdly, national energy policy was being made by means of the federal-provincial intergovernmental system, in a process that moved from multilateral to bilateral negotiation and was most significantly marked by federal unilateral action, first in 1973 when the Pierre Trudeau government assumed the power to set the Canadian oil price and then again in the form of the National Energy Program announced by the Trudeau government on 28 October 1980.

A central theme of this work is that effective national climate policy can only be put in place if the distributive implications of such an effort are explicitly recognized and what is seen to be a fair allocation of cost and benefit is then negotiated by the federal and provincial governments. In this first case study, distribution of cost and benefit – between the regions of west and east, between the federal and Alberta governments, and between governments as a whole and industry – was the central issue at play and was most certainly recognized and loudly debated throughout. Although the high-handed use of federal unilateral power is not something to be emulated today, this frank airing of the basic distributive issues is something that might usefully be replicated. Another lesson from the case is that unilateral federal action is an essential component of the national federal-provincial process. The 1980 NEP, which can be seen as an "act first – negotiate later" Ottawa strategy, is an extreme example of unilateral federal action used to influence provincial behaviour. The Trudeau Liberals, after being returned to power in the 18 February 1980, election, believed they had to break the logjam of stalled Ottawa-Alberta negotiations (both those with the Clark government in 1979 and their own in 1980) by decisive unilateral action after which, having demonstrated federal resolve, they could comfortably return to the negotiating table. We now know that the after-effect of the NEP, in terms of western mistrust, which carried forward to taint later efforts to develop national climate policy, was far too great a price to justify use of that tactic. The case does show, however, the effect that a determined federal government, taking unilateral action, can have upon a federal-provincial process.

Two factors are central to the federal-provincial, provincial-provincial, and government-industry conflicts that characterize the case study: 1) events outside Canada of the 1973 and 1979 oil price shocks had powerful impacts upon Canadian domestic energy politics; and, 2) the fact that at the time (strange as it may now seem) the price of oil was set not by the market but by the Government of Canada. The increase in the world price from something like $2 a barrel just before the 1973 price hike to a high point of $34 in 1981 represented huge potential windfall profits for the industry and corresponding costs for the provinces buying domestic Canadian oil – *if* Canadian domestic prices followed suit.

(Quebec and the Atlantic provinces, which relied on imported oil, were already facing those higher costs.) Whether those benefits or costs would actually be incurred depended upon decisions made by the Government of Canada, with various forms of provincial input, with respect to two questions: 1) how close should the Canadian domestic price move to the world price?; and, 2) how should oil profits be shared, both between the producing provinces and Ottawa (and indirectly, to the extent Ottawa spent those revenues in other parts of the country, between the producing and consuming regions) and between governments as a whole and industry? The enormous sums involved, combined with non-material factors such as western long-standing alienation and resentment of what it saw as exploitation by the manufacturing central provinces, meant the price and revenue-sharing issues were a recipe for intense federal-provincial conflict. With so much at stake, the relevant actors, particularly those with constitutionally guaranteed rights in the policy area (through ownership of the resource) like the government of Alberta, were not willing to accept the idea that those decisions were to be made by Ottawa alone. The federal-provincial decision-making process was most certainly put to the test.

Narrative

While there was considerable controversy over the routing of a gas pipeline in 1956, which led to defeat of the Liberal government and election of the Diefenbaker Conservatives, that government's 1961 National Oil Policy was a product of harmony and consensus. As part of a two-price system of oil pricing, it was agreed that Alberta oil would supply Ontario and all of Canada to the west (plus export to the US market), while Quebec and the Atlantic provinces would rely on imported oil, which at the time was less expensive than Alberta oil. Alberta was happy because its oil had a market, the eastern provinces were happy with the lower price, and Ontario accepted a higher price because it housed refineries to process that Alberta oil (Doern and Toner 1985, 77). More generally, consensus existed among all governments and the oil and gas firms that the policy goal should be economic development fuelled by adequate supplies of oil and gas. During this time, up to 1973, Canadian oil prices were set by the market (although all recognized that the market for oil is always significantly influenced by actions of governments).

The sharp increase in the world price of oil brought about by the 1973 OPEC embargo ended this period of harmony. The differences in economic interest between the oil-producing and oil-consuming regions of the country were not obvious during a period of stable prices. However, with the 1973 sharp price increase, those differences came to the fore. The producing provinces (Alberta, Saskatchewan, and British Columbia, with production in the latter limited to natural gas) naturally wanted to see the domestic Canadian price rise in tandem with the world price, while the consuming provinces wanted the opposite.

Even without full world prices, the western provinces were receiving significant benefit. From 1970 to 1979, the three western producing provinces moved from a total $67 million deficit to a collective $3,284 billion surplus (Milne 1986, 81). The dollars flooding into the Alberta Heritage Savings Trust Fund, established in 1976, became a symbol of this newfound wealth, very visible to the rest of the country.

An example of the power the West-East fault line had to divide Canadians, once oil prices started to skyrocket upward, is given by the inability of the federal Progressive Conservative Party to reconcile conflicting regional interests. Simpson tells us:

> Western and Ontario M.P.s clashed over issues such as energy; in fact, the party never developed a coherent response to the energy crisis of 1973 because of the differences between the western and Ontario caucuses, a failure that [then party leader Robert] Stanfield always believed was more damaging to the party in the 1974 election than the promise of a wage-and-price freeze followed by controls. (1980, 51)

Some years later, after the Clark government was defeated on a non-confidence vote in December 1979 and the political parties prepared for an election, the Liberal election platform committee suffered a similar west-east split: "The platform committee split along more or less regional lines, with the consumers of the east, led by [Marc] Lalonde, speaking for low prices, and the pro-producer western group, led by Bud Olson, recommending, at the minimum, higher 'incentive' pricing for new production" (Foster 1982, 135).

Beyond making clear the very different interests of west and east, the OPEC price increase meant that the distributive effects of the 1961 National Oil Policy two-price system were reversed. Quebec and the Atlantic provinces had been paying less than the Canadian domestic price for their imported oil, but were now paying considerably *more* than other parts of the country.

This posed a distributive equity problem for the federal government – could it allow poorer parts of the country to pay more for an essential service than was being paid by richer provinces such as Ontario and Alberta? Beyond this fairness issue, the Trudeau government was reluctant to see Quebec citizens and firms pay more for oil than did their Ontario counterparts so shortly after the May 1980 first referendum on independence, at a time when Ottawa wanted to show Quebec citizens that membership in the Canadian union was worthwhile (Doern and Toner 1985, 171–2).

Faced with these problems, the Trudeau Liberal government decided to act, and without a lot of planning or consultation with the provinces did two things. It froze the price of oil (using for the first time its powers to regulate the price under the interprovincial trade provisions of the constitution) and it imposed an export tax on Canadian natural gas sent to US markets, the revenues from which were intended to help subsidize the now expensive eastern imported oil (Doern and Toner 1985, 91–2). In a speech to the House of Commons on 6 December 1973, Prime Minister Trudeau formally announced his government was abandoning the two-price system, using a subsidy through the Oil Import Compensation Program to ensure that all Canadians paid the same price for oil (Doern and Toner 1985, 173).

The 1974 federal Petroleum Administration Act, which provided the legislative basis for federal power to set the oil price, allowed Ottawa to set prices unilaterally if there was no agreement with the provinces (Richards and Pratt 1979, 293). It was understood, however, that future pricing decisions would be made in consultation with the provinces. Those consultations were bound to be difficult, given the not surprising western reaction to the federal assumption of control over price and the fact it was horning its way into oil and gas revenues by means of the 1973 export tax. "These measures enraged Alberta and other producing provinces, since they denied them the opportunity to realize the market potential from their own resources while they offered other regions western resources at bargain basement prices" (Milne 1986, 85).

Thus one of the central issues of energy policy, the Canadian price of oil, had been formally put in the hands of Ottawa. In fact, however, it had been moved into the realm of national federal-provincial decision-making, replete with potential veto points and all the other weaknesses discussed above. How did the system cope? The answer is not well, in that after a very short period of time Ottawa proceeded to set the oil price by unilateral decision-making, with or without provincial consultation. On 22–3 January 1974, the Federal-Provincial First Ministers' Conference on Energy was held. The previous year Alberta had publicly argued it should receive the world price because oil and gas were a rapidly depleting resource. Ontario had argued prices should stay low, because increased revenues from a world price would flow largely to governments and so not contribute to additional exploration and expansion of Canadian supplies. The first ministers reached a compromise by agreeing there should be only one price throughout Canada, but did not set a specific price. That was done a few months later, after bilateral agreement between Trudeau and Alberta Premier Peter Lougheed. That agreement was endorsed by other premiers, and on 27 March 1974, the price was set at $6.50 a barrel until 1 July 1975 (Doern and Toner 1985, 175). As noted above, the world price in 1972 had been in the range of $2 per barrel, while by October 1974 the price was $10.50 a barrel (Doern and Toner 1985, 10). The federal government was willing to see price increases (which increased federal revenues) but was not willing to fully match the world price.

Another First Ministers' Conference was held on 9–10 April 1975, to decide on the price after 1 July. Ottawa by then was in favour of a further price increase to encourage conservation and increased exploration (Doern and Toner 1985,

176). Ontario, however, was strongly opposed and played a veto role at the the conference. As a result no agreement was reached. Doern and Toner refer to this as "the demise of the Federal-Provincial First Ministers' conference as a forum for oil price setting" (1985, 176). The federal government then unilaterally increased the price to $8 a barrel after 1 July 1975, and then, by May 1977 reached an agreement with the producing provinces that the Canadian price would gradually increase until it reached the world price. By 1978, it was at 80 per cent of the world price (Doern and Toner 1985, 176). Ontario, because of its refusal to compromise in 1975, had been excluded from the decision-making process. The federal government, while clearly holding the necessary jurisdiction to act unilaterally, seemed to still feel it needed to consult, at least with the fossil fuel–producing provinces.

In January 1979 the Shah of Iran went into exile and in the subsequent turmoil Iranian oil production was at least somewhat reduced. In consequence, in part because of reduced supply but also due to panic, the world price approximately doubled, re-opening the Canadian west-east conflict over how closely domestic prices should follow the world price. Doern and Toner, noting that at times the spot market was around $40 a barrel, hark back to the theme of the West-East fault line:

> The [1979] Canadian crisis was a result of the fact that Canada is both a producer and a consumer-importer of oil. The geographical and federal cleavages of the Canadian political economy, which are accentuated by the location of oil and gas reserves and markets, were once again [after the 1973 price increase] stimulated by the dramatic escalation in world price. (1985, 148)

The Joe Clark Conservative government had been elected in May 1979 although only to a minority government position, and took office on 4 June of that year. What was termed the "energy crisis" due to the second spiking of world oil prices was one of the major challenges facing the new government. During the election, Clark had made the argument that a Progressive Conservative federal government would be able to reach agreement with Progressive Conservative provincial governments, as part of his "community of communities" vision of Canada – a less aggressive role for the federal government and more support for provincial initiatives. Since they were all in the same political party, Clark and his relevant ministers and advisors believed they could readily find common ground with Peter Lougheed's Alberta government on the key issues of price and revenue sharing.

Canadian oil at the time was priced at $12.75 a barrel; since world prices had risen, that price was down from the previous year's 80 per cent to about half the world price (Simpson 1980, 180). Officials in EMR warned the government that Canada faced a pending shortage of domestic oil, which meant a need to import more high-priced oil, that the industry could not provide new supplies in the short term, and that, accordingly, price increases were needed to reduce demand and encourage conservation (Simpson 1980, 180–1). The Clark government accepted the need to move towards world prices, and during the summer of 1979 generated internal documents contemplating an increase of $18 per barrel over the next three years. An offer based on that figure, with Ottawa taking half the new revenues and provinces something less than the other half, was made to Alberta in late August (Simpson 1980, 193). The Lougheed government did not accept and negotiations continued during the fall.

Before the Ottawa-Alberta negotiations had begun, the Ontario government published a policy analysis pointing out the increased inflation and unemployment expected to accompany increasing oil prices. Ontario recommended that prices stay low and called upon the federal government to, if necessary, use its unilateral powers to ensure that end. Ontario Premier Bill Davis and Alberta Premier Lougheed met to discuss the issue at the annual premiers' conference in August, but could not reach any agreement (Simpson 1980, 192). Davis then made a series of speeches to mobilize the Ontario public against a price increase.

In November 1979 the Clark government convened another federal-provincial First Ministers' Conference to discuss energy issues. Premier Davis again spoke against price increases, but without much support from other provinces or the federal government (Simpson 1980, 199). During the conference, Alberta and the federal government moved closer towards agreement but no final deal was reached. This indicated, however, that the Clark government, like the Liberals before them, were moving from multilateral to bilateral negotiations with the Alberta government. At the end of the day, the Clark government was unable to reach agreement with Alberta due to what Doern and Toner (1985, 193) refer to as Alberta's "intransigence," which, they claim, meant that it missed an opportunity, since it next found itself negotiating with the hard line Trudeau Liberals.

The Clark government's first budget, which was deemed a confidence vote, was defeated by combined NDP and Liberal votes on 13 December 1979, causing the government to fall in the House of Commons. Clark had assumed the Liberals would never actually vote the government down, since that would mean fighting an election under their by then very unpopular leader, Pierre Trudeau, and further assumed that should they be so foolish his Conservatives could easily win, this time with a majority government (Simpson 1980). Neither assumption was correct and the federal election held on 18 February 1980, resulted in the return of the Trudeau Liberals with a majority government.

The Clark government budget that brought about its demise included a commitment to increase the gasoline tax by 18 cents a gallon in order to encourage conservation – a measure referred to by Finance Minister John Crosbie as "short term pain for long term gain." For that reason and no doubt also because of the 1979 oil price shock and the associated Alberta-Ontario public feuding, energy issues were central to the 1979–80 federal election campaign (Doern and Toner 1985, 5). In a Halifax campaign speech on 25 January 1980, Pierre Trudeau presented the Liberal energy platform, which included a "made-in-Canada" oil price (in contrast to the world price Alberta was pressing for, and so attractive to Ontario voters); energy security through expanded domestic production, plus foreign supplies and energy conservation; expansion of Petro-Canada (in contrast with the Clark government's plans to privatize it); and increased Canadian control of the energy industry (Milne 1986, 88). These ideas, which eventually became the NEP, were then developed over the spring and summer by a small group headed by Marc Lalonde, energy minister in the new Trudeau government, and bureaucrats in Energy, Mines and Resources and Finance. The prime minister was not directly involved but was supportive.

There was little discussion of these plans with the oil industry:

> Through the spring, summer and early autumn of 1980, consultation with the oil industry dropped to an all-time low. There were desultory meetings, but the industry men had the distinct impression that they were cosmetic, and the politicians and bureaucrats had objectives that were carved in stone. (Foster 1982, 143–4)

Both Strachan (1983–4) and Milne (1986) suggest that the Liberal government had become disenchanted with the oil industry after it reversed its position on proven Canadian oil supplies, saying they were substantial before 1973 and then later releasing analysis showing the reverse. For whatever reason, unlike the later national climate-change policymaking of the 1990s, when industry had considerable influence, the NEP was developed without industry input.

The Trudeau government took over from its predecessor the task of negotiating with Peter Lougheed, but with a very different mindset from that of the Conservatives. The Clark government had badly wanted a deal to show Canadians it could deliver on its promise of renewed federalism. The Trudeau government also wanted a deal, but was quite happy to take unilateral action first and to then bargain afterward. Federal energy minister Marc Lalonde met his Alberta counterpart, Merv Leitch, in April and again in June 1980, with no substantive result (Doern and Toner 1985, 45). The prime minister and premier then met at Meech Lake in July, but to no avail: "Lougheed talked energy and Trudeau talked about the Constitution" (Doern and Toner 1985, 45). The Trudeau government then prepared to unilaterally announce its program.

The "official" goals of the NEP, announced as part of the budget speech of 28 October 1980, were: 1) security of supply, with a goal of Canada producing enough oil and gas to end the need for imports by 1990; 2) opportunity for Canadians to participate in the industry, defined as 50 per cent Canadian ownership and control by 1990; and 3) fairness in pricing (not necessarily tied to world prices) and revenue sharing, the latter defined as increasing the Ottawa share relative to that of Alberta (Doern and Toner 1985, 4). Fairness was needed due to three problems pointed to in the NEP document (Doern and Toner 1985, 260). The impact of the doubling of the world oil price was not borne equally, since it benefitted the producing regions while imposing new costs on the consuming regions. Secondly, most of the new government revenues were going to Alberta – a province with 10 per cent of the Canadian population was getting 80 per cent of provincial government revenues. Finally, Alberta was already rich, having the lowest tax rate and highest disposable income rate (Doern and Toner 1985, 260). The principles of distributive justice laid out by Stone (1988) discussed above were in play: equal shares plus merit of participants.

The federal government was also motivated, as had been the Clark government before it, by the fact that very little of the newfound wealth created by the two world price increases was flowing to Ottawa. Strachan gives this picture: "Overall revenue from oil and gas had risen over the period [1978–80] by $4.8 billion; the producing provinces and the petroleum industry received all of that increase. Over the period, in real terms, the federal government actually lost ground" (1983–4, 147). Distributive fairness was a large part of the public argument made by the federal government to explain the NEP. In private, that argument was very much combined with federal self-interest.

Doern and Toner (1985) describe the NEP "unofficial" goals as being to increase the power of Ottawa relative to that of both the provinces and of industry, to make Ottawa more visible to Canadians as the government that speaks for Canada, to increase Government of Canada revenues, to ensure its ability to manage the economy, and to further the fortunes of the Liberal party. Milne (1986) presents the NEP as being in the tradition of John A. Macdonald's National Policy, a set of measures intended to contribute to the fortunes of central Canadian manufacturing interests, through tariffs on competing imports, which imposed costs on the regions. He says the "made-in-Canada" price (below world price) maintained the "metropolitis-hinterland relationship between manufacturing interests in central Canada and the resource-rich areas in the East and West" (1986, 91). (The eastern oil interest referred to is the Newfoundland offshore oil, which had been discovered in 1979 and that then became the subject of Ottawa-Newfoundland conflict over regulatory control and revenue sharing.) Beyond painting the conflict in core-periphery terms, Milne is very much in agreement with Doern and Toner's first point above, that a primary aim of the NEP was to assert federal power over the provinces.

Prime Minister Trudeau was personally more interested in constitutional issues and his plans for repatriation of the constitution, with the addition of a charter of rights, than he was in energy. Nevertheless, he was fully supportive of a bold venture that would leave its mark on history and gave his energy minister free rein. Doern and Toner point out that both Lalonde and Trudeau knew they were approaching the ends of their careers and saw this term in office as a last chance to "leave an indelible mark on Canadian history" (1985, 31). Simpson gives a similar picture, describing one factor that convinced Trudeau to run as leader in the 1979–80 election after having only weeks earlier submitted his resignation: "He could end his political career a winner and satisfy his need for history's approval by governing in a dynamic, even dramatic, fashion once returned to power" (1980, 45). The unnecessarily confrontational nature of the NEP came about primarily because it capped years of Alberta-Ottawa sparring, but also to some small extent it seems because of the personalities of the two federal leaders who were preparing to meet Peter Lougheed at the O.K. Corral. Milne (1986) points to another, more principled, aspect of Trudeau's personality to explain the NEP. Trudeau had long advocated a balancing of federal and provincial powers in confederation and had become convinced that during the past decade that pendulum had swung much too far in the direction of provincial power.

The other point to make here is that the NEP was an example of a federal government clashing with provinces over a program that had its origins in and was fully supported by top echelons of the Ottawa government. This contrasts strongly with the national climate efforts of the 1990s that received very little support from the top and in fact were several times damaged by capricious one-off interventions by Prime Minister Chrétien. The NEP shows a federal government *is* able to influence the behaviour of provinces, given sufficient motivation (which in turn depends upon leadership by a fully engaged prime minister). Of all the five cases examined here, this is the one in which the federal government was the most motivated to counter the carbon province influence on national policymaking – the variable of degree of interest, referred to in chapter 1. (Alberta, the lead government actor in development of the 2015 Canadian Energy Strategy, was no doubt equally motivated but lacked completely the constitutional powers to influence other governments that Pierre Trudeau was able to bring to bear.)

The Alberta position was laid out two days after the NEP announcement in a televised speech by Alberta Premier Peter Lougheed on 30 October 1980. Lougheed said that Alberta had already subsidized the rest of Canada by $17 billion due to the fact Alberta oil sold for less than the world price. Furthermore, during negotiations that summer his government had made concessions but none were forthcoming from the Ottawa side. He then accused the Trudeau government of wanting to fundamentally change the rules of federalism, turning Canada into a unitary state, both through the NEP and the concurrent constitutional talks. If the oil had been located in Ontario, he said Canada would already be at the world price (Doern and Toner 1985, 268–9). Ontario Premier Bill Davis responded to Lougheed's 30 October speech by saying it was "sad and of deep concern" to see Alberta imposing costs on Ontario and others by reducing the flow of oil (see below) to eastern Canada (Doern and Toner 1985, 277). He did not directly respond to the charge that Canada would have the world price if the oil came from Ontario, instead saying Ontario had historically shared its wealth through equalization payments (Doern and Toner 1985, 277). While this conflict between provinces may be seen as counter-productive and regrettable, the fact remains that regional distribution of cost and benefit – the issue central to national climate-change policy but ignored by governments as long as target dates are well in the future – was being explicitly and publicly discussed in a way it never has been during national climate efforts.

The Lougheed government's response was not limited to verbal attacks. In an attempt to wield power sufficient to influence Ottawa policy, the Alberta government took three retaliatory actions. The first was legal action, which was ultimately successful (Chalifour 2010), to challenge the new federal tax on natural gas exports. Secondly, it announced it would withhold regulatory approval for two large oil sands projects, on the assumption that would do damage to the federal self-sufficiency plan. Thirdly, the most drastic in terms of relations with eastern Canada, Lougheed announced that oil shipments to the east would be reduced in three phases of 60,000 barrels each between March and September 1981, until shipments were 85 per cent of the previous level. However, in case of emergency, Lougheed promised, shipments would not be reduced. This may have been because Alberta recognized that Ottawa likely had constitutional power to control oil extraction and shipment in time of emergency (Foster 1982, 167). Foster adds that Ottawa was aware that an emergency measure of that sort "was not an action to be toyed with lightly" – highlighting the gap between the formal constitutional power of the federal government and what public opinion, electoral calculation, and Canadian tradition realistically allow it to do (1982, 167). By cutting back eastern shipments, Alberta was also pushing up against the limits which social norms imposed on its power, as suggested by Foster's description:

> March 1, the day the first Alberta cutback of 60,000 barrels went into effect, seemed like a bleak day for Confederation. Alberta felt so alienated that it had to respond like a militant OPEC against a previous foreign oppressor. The day so long feared had come finally to pass: the oil weapon was actually being used within Canadian borders. (1982, 167)

What was the reaction of other governments to the NEP announcement? Manitoba, New Brunswick, and Prince Edward Island did not comment at all

(Doern and Toner 1985, 281). Nor yet did Quebec, which found itself in a difficult position. Doern and Toner give this description:

> The economic interests of Quebec should surely have dictated that the Parti Québécois government join with the other major consuming province, Ontario, and actively champion lower oil and gas prices as contained in the NEP ... but given its 'provincial rights' policy it was inconceivable that it could actively support the federal government's aggressively interventionist energy policy, especially since the major producing provinces took their stand against the federal government on jurisdictional grounds. (1985, 281–2)

Saskatchewan and British Columbia, both producing provinces, called for the world price, although Saskatchewan did not follow Alberta in taking retaliatory measures (Doern and Toner 1985, 282). Nova Scotia and Newfoundland, for their part, focused less on the price issue and more on what mattered to them – provincial claims that they, not Ottawa, held jurisdiction over offshore oil (Doern and Toner 1985, 283). Pollard states that whatever their position on the NEP substance, provinces were united in their dislike of the process: "All provinces, however, opposed the unilateral way in which Ottawa had introduced the NEP" (1986, 167). This resonates with the unanimous provincial opposition in the late fall of 2002 to the Chrétien government ratification of Kyoto without prior discussion, as they had requested, at a First Ministers' Meeting.

Bitter verbal sparring and the concrete actions of the NEP and Alberta's response did not prevent Alberta and Ottawa from talking to one another. In his 30 October address, Premier Lougheed had said, "We will sit down and again try to negotiate" (Doern and Toner 1985, 267). Very shortly after the NEP was announced, in November 1980, the federal and Alberta deputy energy ministers met to resume the dialogue. They met again in January 1981 and agreed that the two governments had to harmonize the basic data they were using to predict such things as future supply and price. A three-month effort by Alberta and federal staff then generated a common data base (Doern and Toner 1985, 312). Negotiation then moved up to the elected level when energy ministers Lalonde and Leitch met in Winnipeg in April 1981. Foster says that at that point the ministers had two tasks: 1) "the size of the pie had to be determined"; then 2) division between the two governments and industry had to be decided – the pie "had to be sliced up" (Foster 1982, 168). The size of the Canadian pie, of course, would be determined by the same issue that had been at the core of the dispute since 1973, how close the Canadian price would come to the world price. The NEP had kept Canadian prices below that level. Would Ottawa now bend, at least slightly?

The slicing up implicitly involved not only distribution among governments but also between governments as a whole and the producing industry. However, just as Ottawa had not consulted industry during development of the NEP over the summer of 1980, neither Ottawa nor Alberta extensively consulted with industry during their 1981 negotiations (Foster 1982, 169). Industry had much less influence upon the outcome of this case than it did for the two national climate-change processes of the 1990s or the Canadian Energy Strategy. Nevertheless, the oil industry did hold structural power at the time. Both the Alberta and federal governments amended their tax regimes in the early 1980s, once the world price began to drop, to ensure industry sufficient revenues to carry out exploration for new supplies.

The two ministers and their teams met again at the Banff Springs Hotel on 10 June, in Toronto on 19 June, and again in Montreal on 5 August (Foster 1982, 172–3). By that time, both sides were under pressure to reach agreement. "During the next month [July], officials met while political pressures began to mount; the public, premiers and the industry exhorted both sides to reach an agreement" (Dunn 1982, 127). Analysts agree that by the summer Ottawa was in the stronger bargaining position. The reductions in oil shipped east had not hurt the Canadian economy since they could be replaced by imported oil, while the reduced sales did impose costs on Alberta firms. James and Michelin (1989, 62) say that by summer the Alberta economy was "floundering," which drove Alberta back to negotiate with the federal government. Doern and Toner say that in the summer of 1981 the "balance of power now tipped decisively in favour of the federal government" (1985, 311). They attribute this to popularity of the NEP in eastern Canada, the Alberta promise that it would resume oil shipments in a case of emergency, the fact that it was very difficult for Alberta to argue against increased Canadian ownership of the industry, and, as noted, the negative impact on the Alberta economy of the shipment reductions (Doern and Toner 1985, 311).

The two sides met in Montreal in a ten-day negotiating session in late August and announced a new Ottawa-Alberta agreement on 1 September 1981. Reaching agreement had been made easier by the fact both sides expected that the revenue pie they were sharing would continue to increase with ongoing world price increases. The federal government gave some ground on price. It was agreed the price for "old" oil (discovered prior to 1 January 1981) would increase from $18.75 to $25.75 by 1 July 1982, and would then increase by $4 every six months until reaching 75 per cent of the world price. The world price would be used for "new" oil (discovered after 1 January 1981). Ottawa agreed to set its natural gas export tax (subsequently found to be unconstitutional by the Supreme Court) at zero. In return, Alberta agreed to an increase in other federal taxes. Alberta agreed to promote the start of the two oil sands projects it had delayed (which were cancelled soon after by the firms due to lowering world prices). Alberta was given control over the federal exploration incentive program within its borders, at the price of providing the necessary funding (James and Michelin 1989) – so keen to be the only one regulating the industry in Alberta, the Lougheed government was willing to pay millions to take over a federal program. Ottawa then signed bilateral agreements with British Columbia on 24 September and Saskatchewan on 26 October (Doern and Toner 1985, 503).

The agreement between Ottawa and Alberta in which both sides compromised (changed behaviour) is an example of a substantial degree of policy coordination. The power dynamic between lead and veto governments was balanced in favour of the former, but Ottawa gave ground, even as it exerted power to influence Alberta behaviour.

In a world of declining oil prices, which eliminated the central rationale for the NEP, subsequent federal-provincial agreements to modify the NEP, including actions by both Alberta and Ottawa to increase industry revenues, were signed over the next two years, after which the Mulroney Conservatives, elected in 1984, ended the program. Doern and Gattinger give this view of the effects of the program:

> Politically, however, the NEP left a bitter taste, particularly regarding relations between Central and Western Canada. It became the quintessential example, especially in Western Canada, of how not to make policy. It was seen as a combative unilateral act by an unsympathetic Eastern-dominated government. This lesson was a major contributing factor in later discussions during 1987–8 when energy free trade was secured through the Canada-U.S. Free Trade Agreement. From the Western Canadian perspective, energy free trade ensured that there could never again be "another NEP." Debates over the Kyoto treaty on climate change have also resonated with the view that Kyoto would be "another NEP," that is, another unilaterally imposed policy by Eastern governments over Western oil and gas. (2003, 31)

The case shows that lead-government power can generate policy coordination. It also shows the damage a lead government can do.

Analysis

1) What Does the Case Tell Us about the Four Subjects?

THE WEST–EAST DIVIDE

The case shows us that a strongly motivated west, fighting to protect what it sees as its legally and morally justified property rights, will have a powerful influence upon federal-provincial policy, as did Alberta between 1973 and 1980 as it nudged the Canadian oil price up towards the world-price level. The case also shows that western influence can be reduced when it encounters equally motivated countervailing power exerted by Ottawa, as happened in 1980. Finally, the case shows that the West-East divide is strongly influenced by Ottawa's actions; western alienation increased many fold due to Ottawa exercising of power and the *way* in which that power was used.

THE INHERENT NEED TO ALLOCATE REDUCTIONS

The lesson we can take from the case is that when the costs are sufficiently high, governments will address the allocation issue and negotiate some form of distribution. Climate-change policymaking has to date been able to largely ignore allocation of cost because no Canadian reduction has been imminent and because costs of policy have been small. To date, Canadian climate policy has resulted in an increase of something like five or six cents on a litre of gasoline due to a carbon tax or trading system (in general, less than a 5 per cent increase). Compare that to the ten-fold (1,000 per cent) or more increase in the price of oil seen in this case, which forced governments to the negotiating table. More effective climate-change policy that brings about a doubling or tripling of gasoline prices will catch attention comparable to what was seen in the 1970s and early 1980s. When that day comes, governments will have no choice but to negotiate sharing, as they did here.

The second lesson is that allocation can take place implicitly, even if that is not the intent of policymakers. There was an implicit allocation from the moment world prices began to rise in 1973: the importing regions were receiving a burden not borne by other parts of the country. The Trudeau government price freeze of 1973 can also be thought of as an implicit allocation, since it imposed a benefit upon the eastern importing regions and a cost upon the western regions, in terms of foregone additional revenue, regardless of whether that was the intent. Both of these reinforce the picture of the allocation issue given here – that it can exist even while governments are ignoring the issue. In this case, all involved were very aware of these implicit allocations, as noted above in terms of Alberta's "enraged" reaction to the price freeze. The allocation issue quickly became explicit and moved on to the formal policy agenda of all governments with the convening of a First Ministers' Conference in January 1974 to discuss pricing, and was explicitly negotiated until the end of the case study. Allocation existed, however, before it was thus formally addressed.

THE NATIONAL PROCESS

The most important lesson here is that a zero-sum game leads to equal motivation on both sides, which means western interests encounter eastern countervailing power. This is the major thing that differentiates this case from the next three, in which western efforts to influence national climate and energy policy were largely unchecked. Another thing we can learn about the intergovernmental process from this first case is that bilateral negotiation, which is more likely to generate agreement simply because there are fewer veto players participating than in a multilateral forum, can be a useful part of the national process.

Here, the process evolved from multilateral to bilateral negotiation after the Ontario veto in the 1975 First Ministers' Conference. Since the first ministers meet only at the call of the prime minister, it seems that Trudeau, from 1975 to 1979 and again in the 1980 to 1981 period, had decided he could accomplish his goals better by bilateral negotiation, in particular with Alberta but also with the two other western oil-producing provinces and, respecting offshore oil, with Newfoundland and Nova Scotia. The Clark government convened a multilateral First Ministers' Conference in 1979, but the bulk of its engagement with the provinces was in the form of bilateral negotiations with Alberta. It is fair to say national policy was made during this period primarily by Ottawa negotiating individually with relevant provinces. Multilateral negotiation, with Ontario and its interests so diametrically opposed to those of Alberta at the table, would certainly have taken longer and likely would again have ended in a veto and failure to agree on anything.

FEDERAL GOVERNMENT STRATEGY

The case shows us federal unilateral action is effective but, as noted above, can cause serious and lasting problems and so must be taken carefully and with restraint. It is not clear how much the NEP was simply unilateral action to achieve Ottawa's goal (reaching across the table and without a word of pardon carving itself a piece of pie) and how much it was a tactical measure intended to influence the Alberta negotiations (taking a big piece of pie, but then offering to return some of it). Given that the Trudeau government was willing to restart negotiations so soon after the NEP announcement, it seems reasonable to conclude it was in at least some part the latter – the "act first – negotiate later" strategy referred to above. As discussed, it was an effective stratagem, part of Ottawa's skill in carrying the process through to a compromise agreement with Alberta. That said, it remains an example of the damage that can be caused by Ottawa's use of power.

2) What Are the Most Important Factors Explaining the Case Outcome?

The case outcome as of the signing of the Alberta-Ottawa agreement on 1 September 1981, was substantial policy coordination. The relevant federal and provincial governments changed behaviour in terms of policy governing the division of oil revenues. Milne gives this picture of the change in allocation of revenues brought about by the NEP (1986, 85):

	1979	1982
Federal	13.1%	27.4%
Provincial	45.7%	32.3%
Industry	41.2%	40.3%

Clearly the federal government was able to achieve its objective of transferring some oil revenues from Alberta to Ottawa, while Alberta was unable to achieve its objective of preventing that from happening. Nor had Alberta been able to prevail in its fight for a Canadian oil price fully equivalent to the international price. However, Ottawa gave some ground in the 1981 agreement. The result was a compromise between those two actors. (Avoiding the full world oil price was also a partial victory for Ontario.)

This outcome of coordinated policy is explained by three factors: 1) Ottawa's high degree of interest, which meant Alberta's veto-government influence was countered by the lead government; 2) Ottawa's willingness to use unilateral action as a means of influencing behaviour of the veto government; and, 3) the skill displayed by Ottawa as it played the lead-government role. The most important factor explaining Ottawa motivation was the zero-sum nature of the case. Because Alberta and the west could only win at the expense of the east, their efforts to influence federal-provincial policy motivated countervailing power exerted by both Ontario and Ottawa. A motivated veto government met an equally motivated lead and supporting government. Ottawa motivation is also explained by another factor since, while fully engaged since 1973, Ottawa's degree of interest grew in 1980. After they unexpectedly regained power in the election that year, Trudeau and Lalonde saw this as their last chance to leave their mark on history and they made the most of it, for better or worse. In 1980–1, they played hard ball with Alberta in a way they had not during the negotiations from 1973–9. An important part of the interest of the lead government was the personal commitment and motivation of the prime minister, which only increased after his 1980 return to power.

The second factor explaining the outcome of the Alberta-Ottawa contest was the willingness of Ottawa to use available power to influence provincial behaviour. Ottawa held constitutional powers to set the oil price and to tax that were not available to a province, and also held demographic power due to its electoral base in the east and the popularity of the NEP in vote-rich Ontario and Quebec. Other than litigation, Alberta was able only to use the self-defeating strategies of delaying regulatory approvals for oil projects and cutting back oil shipments to the east, both of which over the long-term would have had the effect of reducing Alberta oil revenues.

This willingness to use federal power, however, came with a price – the unacceptable damage to national unity done by Ottawa's use of unilateral action. The case shows that unilateral federal action certainly can be effective in influencing provincial behaviour (Alberta signed an agreement after years of refusing to do so) but, if we extend the case outcome deadline past September 1981 the case also shows that Ottawa must play the unilateral action card much more carefully than was done in the case of the NEP. The price paid to accomplish the September 1981 Alberta-Ottawa agreement was far too high in terms of a widened West-East divide that poisoned subsequent federal-provincial attempts to develop coordinated climate-change policy. For that reason, the case does not provide a model for future use of federal powers.

It should be pointed out that the Trudeau government during 1980 and 1981 did not in fact use all its potential power. It made no moves towards requiring Alberta to resume full shipment of oil (presumably because there was no need to do so, given that imported oil could make up the Alberta shortfall). Its introduction of extensive new taxes in the 1980 NEP was certainly a flexing of muscle not seen since the start of the process in 1973, but it might have done far more. Alberta Premier Peter Lougheed said on 14 October 1981, after the Ottawa-Alberta agreement had been signed that throughout the conflict his government had been careful to not create a backlash in the rest of the country which the Trudeau government could use to justify "coming in under other provisions of the constitution and finishing the job" (Dunn 1982, 126). This underlines one of the central lessons taken from this case: the need for Ottawa to exercise restraint and not use all of its available powers. Even though it did use at least some restraint, Trudeau's actions caused unacceptable damage to national unity. Federal power is essential for intergovernmental coordination, but must be used with extreme caution. Ottawa must exercise restraint as it takes unilateral action; it must consciously and carefully refrain from using all the power it has available.

The other lesson concerning Ottawa's use of power has to do with the *way* that power was used. What so very much rankled Alberta was not just the exercise of federal power, but the fact that it was announced unilaterally. Pollard describes it this way:

Trudeau's "new federalism" sought to re-affirm the power of the federal government. Under the "new federalism," however, federal-provincial relations of the early 1980s became marked by suspicion and mistrust. Unilateral action replaced consultation, even though the actions of one order of government often had important consequences for the other. (1986, 164)

The unilateral nature of the NEP and its more or less surprise announcement in the 28 October 1980 budget were as much a source of the problem as was its content. There is a parallel between that surprise announcement and another surprise that also raised hackles in Edmonton: Prime Minister Chrétien's out-of-the-blue announcement on 1 September 2002 that he would ratify the Kyoto Protocol. One of the main themes of this work is that coordinated national policy is only possible if somebody, which almost has to be Ottawa, influences the behaviour of other governments. That can only be done by the use of power. However, a *skillful* use of power can at least marginally reduce provincial opposition.

That said, Pierre Trudeau's government displayed far greater skill in managing the federal-provincial process than did that of Jean Chrétien twenty years later. While the NEP bombshell may have caused provincial resentment, it also achieved its objective of forcing a new phase in the Alberta-Ottawa negotiations that had been going on since 1973. The unilateral action of the NEP and its support among central and eastern Canadian voters allowed Ottawa to negotiate from a position of strength; that, plus Ottawa's willingness to give ground and compromise, allowed the two governments to close their deal in 1981. Chrétien's 2002 ratification surprise, on the other hand, did nothing to aid negotiations. Instead, it led the way to the collapse of the negotiating process a few months later.

6 The First National Climate Change Process, 1990–1997

Case Summary

A motivated veto government (Alberta) seeking to block effective national policy did not encounter countervailing power from other provinces or the lead government (Ottawa). Ottawa had little interest in exerting countervailing power because: 1) unlike the previous case, it had no material interest respecting revenues; 2) also unlike the previous case, it had no ideological interest respecting federalism; and, 3) although a centre-left party, the Chrétien government's ideological interest respecting the need for climate action was not strong, perhaps because at the time no country was as yet taking effective action on the issue. Ottawa's lack of countervailing power was also due to two other factors: 1) a lack of skill in intergovernmental diplomacy; and 2) Ottawa's failure to take unilateral action in a way which would move provincial behaviour towards coordinated policy. Ottawa did act unilaterally, by itself setting the Kyoto target, but that only damaged the intergovernmental process. For these reasons, the balance of power favoured the veto government, which precluded effective national policy.

START AND END DATES: 1990–December 1997

MAJOR POLICY DECISIONS

unilateral
- Mulroney government announces target of stabilization at the 1990 level by 2000.
- Chrétien government sets aside federal-provincial target of stabilization at the 1990 level by 2010 in favour of unilateral federal position of 3 per cent below 1990, December 1997.
- Chrétien government agrees at 1997 Kyoto summit to target of 6 per cent below 1990 level by 2012.

bilateral	• none
multilateral	• energy and environment ministers agree to 1995 National Action Program on Climate Change
	• energy and environment ministers agree to Canadian Kyoto target of stabilization, November 1997
	• first ministers agree December 1997: 1) principle no region bears an unreasonable burden; 2) will study Kyoto target before implementing it; and, 3) provinces will fully participate

CASE OUTCOME

As of December 1997 the major policy instrument used by governments was a call for voluntary action. National policy decided by first ministers was as stated above – most significantly, rather than immediately moving to implement the Kyoto commitment, Canadian governments would study that commitment to see if it could in fact be achieved.

COORDINATION CATEGORY: minimal policy coordination

The previous case study examined explicit regional and intergovernmental conflicts over division of the costs and benefits associated with Canadian domestic and imported oil. This next case study of the first efforts to put together a coordinated federal-provincial policy for reducing greenhouse gas emissions differs in that the same west-east fault line runs through the case, but unlike the previous case neither that difference of interest or the question of allocation of cost were central to the policy discourse. Instead, discussion was largely limited to the environmental effects associated with use of fossil fuels and ways in which they could be reduced, with all involved maintaining the polite fiction that such an effort in no way involved one of the basic subject matters of the Canadian political economy that had so roiled the waters of national life a decade earlier. And, indeed, in a way they were right. This was the early days of climate change policymaking, when the issue was still struggling to get on the policy agenda, and neither Canada nor any other country was ready to consider effective use of policy instruments such as tax or law, which would bring about significant, and costly, changes in behaviour on the part of governments, firms, or citizens. The inherent challenges of differing western and eastern interests, exacerbated by the fact that climate policy inherently and unavoidably imposes regional and sectoral distributive effects, did not really impede policymaking in this case because so little was attempted in the way of effective policy. Nevertheless, the underlying challenges were present during the 1990–7 national effort, even if below the surface, and had influence on decisions made during the period, particularly in terms of a motivated and engaged veto government, Alberta, which was able to exert considerable influence on the national process. Beyond that, the case is marked by two other things: 1) significant oil industry influence upon the national process; and, 2) the way in which a national process led by ministers can so easily be set aside, first by the federal government which in late 1997 ignored an agreement just made the previous month by federal and provincial ministers, and then by first ministers.

Narrative

The case opens with the establishment in 1990 by the Mulroney government of the first Canadian emission reduction target: stabilize emissions at 1990 levels no later than the year 2000. The prime minister had earlier in 1988 stated a Canadian target of 20 per cent below the 1988 level to be achieved by 2005 (Simpson et al. 2007, 46) but that was subsequently changed as Canada participated in international meetings over the next two years, presumably to be in harmony with the stabilization position being adopted by other nations. Prime Minister Brian Mulroney, in power from 17 September 1984 to 25 June 1993, based on his policy record, is generally recognized as the greenest of the Canadian prime ministers (CBC News 2006). His government in 1985 succeeded in working with the eastern provinces to put in place an effective program for reducing acid rain emissions and some years later signed the Canada-US Air Quality Agreement. It is not clear how much Mulroney's personal inclinations led him towards environmental protection. We think of Mulroney in a suit, spreading bonhomie in a corporate boardroom, not, in the style of Pierre Elliot Trudeau, buckskin-clad, a solitary canoeist on a misty river. However, Mulroney had learned that action on environment was good politics and he carried that lesson forward, doing more on the issue than Pierre Trudeau ever did. Mulroney's government ensured that Canada played a lead role in fashioning the international Montreal Protocol on the Ozone Layer in 1987. The following year, Canada co-hosted with the United Nations Environmental Programme and the World Meteorological Organization the international conference held in Toronto 27–30 June 1988, The Changing Atmosphere: Implications for Global Security. Known as the "Toronto Conference," the event was attended by world leaders such as Gro Harlem Brundtland, who had just served as chair of the World Commission on Environment and Development (Smith 1998, 2). It was the first international conference to draw significant attention to the issue and in consequence helped to launch the international climate-change regime.

After the Toronto Conference, Mulroney's government turned to domestic action. Presumably due to provincial jurisdiction as owners of the fossil fuel resources, this meant engaging with the provinces. At their meeting in August 1988 federal and provincial energy ministers established a task force on energy and the environment, which then generated reports on the issue and possible responses in August 1989 and April 1990 (Smith 1998, 6–7). The energy ministers were then joined by environment ministers, and in November 1990, these combined federal and provincial forces released a draft national strategy for action on the issue (Smith 1998, 7). Earlier in 1990, federal environment minister Lucien Bouchard had given a "unilateral commitment" (suggesting that not all provinces had by that time agreed) that the Government of Canada would seek to stabilize Canadian emissions at the 1990 level by 2000 (Doern and Conway 1994, 98). Canadian diplomats then said Canada would work towards that target at a UN conference in May 1990 and again at the November 1990 Second World Climate Conference, held in Geneva (Commissioner of Environment and Sustainable Development 1998, 3–16).

After winning re-election on 21 November 1988, Prime Minister Mulroney had appointed Lucien Bouchard as his environment minister. Bouchard, looking to make a name for himself, led the drive for a major government-wide environmental initiative, which resulted in Canada's Green Plan, tabled in the House of Commons on 11 December 1990 (Doern and Conway 1994, 51). Referring to the international discussions of the need to stabilize greenhouse gas emissions held earlier in the year, the Green Plan set out these commitments:

> Canada confirmed its commitments to this first step through a program to stabilize emissions of CO2 and other greenhouse gases at 1990 levels by the year 2000.... the technical feasibility and the cost and trade implications of further reductions in emissions will be examined, including the 20-per-cent reduction in CO2 levels called for by the 1988 Toronto Conference. (Government of Canada 1990, 100–1)

It should be borne in mind that while "stabilization" sounds like a relatively easy task and so a less ambitious target than later ones, the 1990 target would have required not just stabilization, but also reduction. Since the goal could not be achieved immediately within the year by any politically feasible measures – a carbon tax of $200 per tonne imposed on 1 January 1990, might well have stabilized emissions by 31 December of that year; but no government could have done that and survived the next election – action taken later in the decade, for instance in 1996, by which time Canadian emissions had increased to be 9.4 per cent above the 1990 level (Macdonald and Smith 1999–2000, 112), would require not just the seemingly easy task of "stabilization" but in fact a significant *cut* in emissions.

Given that the subject of this work is federal-provincial climate-change policymaking, one important question is this: Had all the provinces given their consent to the stabilization target prior to 11 December? It is not clear they had. The Green Plan referred to a federal-provincial joint effort: "At home the Government of Canada has been working with its provincial partners to develop the National Action Strategy on Global Warming – a comprehensive framework for addressing the global warming issue in Canada" (Government of Canada 1990, 101). The document then described the basic dynamic of the federal-provincial process at that time: "Specific action programs to limit greenhouse gas emissions will be announced independently by the federal, provincial and territorial governments as they are developed" (Government of Canada 1990, 102). The Green Plan went on to say that the federal government planned to formalize these efforts in bilateral federal-provincial agreements (Government of Canada 1990, 102), which was never done. Smith states that the strategy document notes the federal government stabilization objective, but does not fully endorse it, meaning a gap had already appeared between federal and provincial positions; in her opinion the Green Plan stabilization commitment "lacked provincial support" (1998, 5).

It is fair to assume that provinces that were not major emitters of greenhouse gases and so unlikely to be strongly affected by federal or coordinated national action on the issue may well have participated in the federal-provincial process and subscribed to the stabilization objective. It is much less likely that the carbon provinces, while participating in the national effort, had given their consent to the target. Doern and Conway go much further than Smith, saying that not only did Alberta not support the target, but that it had been lobbying hard against it while Ottawa was developing the Green Plan:

> Provincial objections to a potential Green Plan in 1989–90 were closely aligned with industry, especially in Alberta's energy sector. Partly because of Lucien Bouchard's unilateral commitment earlier in 1990 to keeping Canada's carbon-dioxide emissions in the year 2000 to 1990 levels, both Alberta and the oil-and-gas industry mounted a fierce lobby against the Green Plan. Alberta interests had feared an interventionist Green Plan along the lines of the 1980 National Energy Program (NEP). Consequently, they lobbied hard, employing anti-NEP-style rhetoric, which played well in Western Canada as a whole. (Doern and Conway 1994, 98)

Despite their failure to keep the target out of the Green Plan, Alberta interests were pleased, Doern and Conway say, to find that it did not include a carbon tax and did include commitments to consultation before putting in place policy measures (1994, 98–9).

Nevertheless, it appears the Mulroney government set the stabilization objective without full prior consent of all provinces. As we shall see, the same has been true for the three subsequent national targets. Each was set by Ottawa alone, in the context of international climate change diplomacy, without first reaching agreement on the target with the provinces. As a result, each national climate-change effort has been based not on initial cooperation among governments but upon unilateral federal action.

The federal-provincial process involving energy and environment ministers did not generate any significant outcomes during 1991 or the first part of 1992, prior to the UN Conference on Environment and Development, the "Rio Conference," held 3 to 14 June 1992. The Rio Conference was the high-water mark for concern for environment, both globally and domestically within Canada and other countries. The US, under the lame-duck presidency of George H. Bush, worked against the European Union to weaken the Rio climate agreement. Prime Minister Mulroney, to his credit, did not toe the American line, but instead spoke forcefully in favour of global action to protect the environment (Mulroney 1992). Participating countries agreed at Rio to the UN Framework Convention on Climate Change, which contained the same objective of stabilization at the 1990 level by 2000. Canada ratified the UNFCCC in December 1992; the fact it was one of the first countries to do so is an indication of Prime Minister Mulroney's continuing commitment.

The somewhat ad hoc federal-provincial process for addressing climate change that had been initiated in 1988 became more institutionalized in 1993 when the Canadian Council of Ministers of Environment (CCME) and the Council of Energy Ministers (CEM) began meeting together to address climate policy at least once a year, in something referred to as the Joint Meeting of Ministers (JMM). At its first joint meeting, in November 1993, the JMM approved a Comprehensive Air Quality Management Framework for Canada. (This was not a break with tradition. See Doern and Conway 1994, for description of the Federal-Provincial Advisory Committee on Air Quality, established in the 1970s to coordinate and support provincial and federal approaches to regulating air pollution.) The commissioner of environment and sustainable development described the framework this way:

> This framework agreement provides a formal basis for, and encourages all jurisdictions to co-ordinate and co-operate in, the management of all air quality issues, including climate change, and to do so within the context of sustainable development. Thus, the JMM serves as the highest level of a national process to develop direction and statements of intent on climate change. (1998, 3–40)

Two bodies made up of federal and provincial seconded officials were created to develop policy options and recommendations to be presented to the environment and energy ministers. These were the National Air Issues Steering Committee (NAISC), made up of deputy environment and energy ministers and, reporting to it, the National Air Issues Coordinating Committee (NAICC), made up of assistant deputy ministers from environment and energy. The latter created a Climate Change Working Group (Commissioner of Environment and Sustainable Development 1998, 3–40). During the next two years, this system of committees reporting to ministers, in consultation with non-state actors such as business and environmentalists, worked to develop the first federal-provincial plan released in 1995. Although there were some modifications of the system at the start of the 1998–2002 national effort, most notably appointing the governments of Alberta and Canada as co-chairs, plus extensive use of multi-stakeholder advisory committees, essentially the same federal-provincial system continued to function until the end of the national process in late fall 2002.

The 2015–16 Pan-Canadian effort, discussed below as the fifth case study, was very different in that it opened with a meeting of first ministers, not ministers, and the agreement itself was then was adopted by first ministers. The environment commissioner is correct in saying above that the JMM was the "highest level" for development of national policy. Macdonald et al. (2013) argue that the fact that first ministers did not play an ongoing role was one of the greatest weaknesses of the federal-provincial system as it functioned from 1990 to 2002. The point is discussed in the concluding chapters.

At the 1993 JMM, as well as establishing the machinery of climate-change intergovernmental relations, the energy and environment ministers had asked their newly created committees to generate policy options (Smith 1998, 9). On 4 November 1993, Jean Chrétien's Liberal party replaced Kim Campbell's Conservatives in government. The Liberal Red Book election platform had set forth a target of reducing emissions to 20 per cent below the 1988 level by 2005 – a promise that was then ignored by the Liberal government immediately after taking office, as it was by everybody else (Macdonald and Smith 1999–2000, 110). In the same way that Justin Trudeau's government in late 2015 talked about adopting a more ambitious target than that previously set by Stephen Harper and then quietly reverted to his target, so the Chrétien government after 1993 satisfied themselves with the former Conservative target.

Policy options were presented by staff and discussed at the 8 November 1994 JMM. These included a proposal that the federal and provincial governments put in place a voluntary climate-change challenge program (Measures Working Group 1994). At that JMM, federal environment minister Sheila Copps argued in favour of use of law-based regulation to address the issue (Smith 1998; Macdonald and Smith 1999–2000). She was unable to convince her fellow ministers, due to opposition by Alberta representatives, who argued that voluntary programs could achieve the same objective at a lower cost (Smith 1998). Prior to that, in 1993, some business interests had publicly advocated the use of voluntary instruments rather than law (Macdonald and Smith 1999–2000, 111). Adding to this public debate over policy instruments, Prime Minister Chrétien had earlier ruled out use of a carbon tax. Jeffrey Simpson and his co-authors say that earlier in 1994 rumours that the Chrétien government was about to impose a new tax on fossil fuels were being fuelled by Preston Manning and his western-based Reform Party (Simpson et al. 2007, 55). These western fears (and presumably associated lobbying efforts) that the Liberals were about to impose a tax grab along the line of the 1980 NEP were sufficiently strong that Chrétien felt he had to explicitly rule out the possibility of a new federal tax on oil and gas. In May 1994, the prime minister told a Calgary audience of oil industry executives, "Relax, relax. It's not on the table, and it will not be on the table" (Corcoran 1994; Simpson et al. 2007, 55).

As noted, by the time of the November 1994 JMM a voluntary approach was the only one being considered by the federal and provincial officials developing the joint national effort. Alberta was the province most in favour of voluntarism, supported by Nova Scotia and Saskatchewan; Ontario and British Columbia remained largely silent, and there were no provinces arguing in favour of regulation (confidential interview 2007b). Within the federal government, NRCan and its minister Anne McLellan, one of the Liberal party's few representatives from Alberta, were in favour of the voluntary approach, while Environment Canada, although not opposed, was looking for some sign that regulatory action would be taken if the voluntary instrument could not produce results (confidential interview 2007b). However, the department had not developed any plans for regulation, meaning that the federal environment minister, Sheila Copps, while speaking in favour of regulation over a voluntary approach, could not put any specific proposals on the table (confidential interview 2007b). The prime minister's office and privy council office were both involved, presumably supporting NRCan in the voluntary approach (confidential interview 2007b).

In consequence, the federal-provincial plan released on 20 February 1995, the National Action Program on Climate Change (NAPCC), said nothing about use of law or tax, and instead relied only on a "challenge program" – the term used to refer to a government program that makes a formalized, codified appeal to business to "voluntarily" improve its environmental performance. (Depending upon how clearly the government in question threatens to use a more coercive instrument such as law or tax if that improvement does not take place, the term "voluntary" may not be completely accurate.) The challenge program used, the Voluntary Challenge and Registry (VCR; Quebec established its own separate program, named ÉcoGESte), consisted of these elements, according to the NAPCC: the challenge – the energy and environment ministers had sent a letter to about 250 "corporations and organizations" inviting them to participate (NAPCC 1995, 18); the registry, a public record of plans made by such bodies to reduce their GHG emissions; verifiability, the ability to check on claimed reductions; recognition, in the form of public plaudits; and evaluation, in the form of periodic review of success achieved by the program.

It seems reasonable to conclude that in those early days of climate policy, a voluntary program was the most that could have been expected of Canadian governments in terms of choice of policy instruments. As discussed, to achieve any given policy objective, the government in question must change the behaviour of other actors, be they other governments, firms, or citizens. This means governments using policy instruments are engaged in an exercise of exerting power with respect to those subject to the instrument. In 1995, environmentalists and the federal environment minister were the only ones looking for a policy instrument that involved use of government power by means of a coercive instrument such as legally binding regulation to induce behaviour change; however, they did not have anything like the political clout needed to carry the day.

While the VCR was the central element in the NAPCC, the federal-provincial plan addressed the climate issue in broad terms. It noted, but never really discussed, the basic Canadian problem when it said the plan was "based on consensus across a large number of jurisdictions with a high degree of economic, social and cultural diversity" (NAPCC 1995, 2). In the same way it noted, more or less in passing, the issue of cost allocation when it stated that one of the founding principles of the plan was "Shared Responsibility" (NAPCC 1995, 10). This was presented as meaning that action was needed by "all sectors." In addition, the NAPCC document stated that: "Shared responsibility also implies that no one region or economic sector should be unduly disadvantaged by measures intended to reduce the likelihood of climate change" (NAPCC 1995, 10). The plan provides no discussion of how that principle might be implemented. The commitment to voluntary action rather than use of any more coercive instrument is made very clear in the plan. It presents the "role of governments" as consisting of three things: 1) to lead by example, in terms of reducing their own emissions; 2) "creating appropriate conditions for actions by others;" and, 3) reducing barriers to action, such as a lack of necessary information (NAPCC 1995,: 12). In terms of the second, it makes reference to "appropriate fiscal and regulatory conditions" but neither carbon pricing nor use of law are referred to as the plan presents five things governments can do: 1) reduce barriers; 2) educate citizens and others; 3) celebrate reductions; 4) encourage renewable energy; and, 5) research and development of technology to aid in emission reductions (NAPCC 1995, 14).

A review of the NAPCC done a year after it was announced, for consideration at the 1996 JMM, gave a picture of a wide-ranging program addressing virtually all sources of greenhouse gas emissions (RFI 1996). The RFI report stated that the program contained a total of 475 federal and provincial policy measures, either already in place or planned (RFI 1996, 5–1). It gave this classification of the policy instruments being used (RFI 1996, 5–2):

government actions to reduce its own emissions	29%
voluntary measures	26%
provide information	20%
regulations/standards	14%
research and development of technologies	6%
financial incentives	5%

It seems reasonable to consider providing information as part of a voluntary approach. If we apply that here, voluntary measures accounted for 46 per cent of the total. With government actions to improve its own performance (29 per cent), making no demands on business or others for behaviour change beyond, ideally, following the government example, we have three-quarters of the policy measures being of a non-coercive nature. RFI and associates gave this summary.

> Although NAPCC includes a wide mix of measures, one of its distinguishing features is its emphasis on voluntary approaches to achieve the stabilization goal. This emphasis reflects deep differences in Canadian society regarding both the priority that should be attached to climate change as an environmental issue and the approaches that should be used to reduce GHG emissions. (1996, 1–2)

A major source of those "deep differences" was the fault line separating the western carbon provinces from the others. As noted, Alberta and the oil industry had been lobbying since the federal government began work on the Green Plan. Both favoured voluntary instruments. The Business Council on National Issues (later the Canadian Council of Chief Executives and then, after another name change, the Business Council of Canada) published a report in July 1994, arguing in favour of voluntarism as the policy instrument to be used (Business Council on National Issues 1994). We do not have data on public statements of a policy preference by the oil and gas industry, but it must have been making the same case privately to Ottawa decision-makers. On 20 January 1995, the Canadian Association of Petroleum Producers signed a memorandum of understanding with Natural Resources Canada, committing to voluntarily undertake emissions reductions. A CAPP news release that same day stated that this showed voluntary action could be effective (Macdonald and Smith 1999–2000, 111–12). A month later, on 20 February 1995, the energy and environment ministers approved and made public the VCR as the main element of the NAPCC. The fact that CAPP had been lobbying for a program such as the VCR in the NAPCC was confirmed a few months later in *Oilweek* magazine: "As CAPP sees it, its aggressive advocacy of voluntary measures to reduce CO2 emissions gave Alberta Energy Minister Pat Black the credibility needed to head off the demands for a program of regulation and taxation" (Koch 1995, 12).

In this case, there is clearly a high degree of correspondence between the industry's policy preference and the subsequent policy. It was not, however, an instance of complete domination of the policy process by the industry. The industry advocated voluntarism not as a first choice, but in order to pre-empt more coercive instruments such as taxation or law. Koch offers this quotation:

"'No politician would have supported industry if we'd offered them nothing' says Doug Bruchet, CAPP's vice-president of environment, health and safety. 'Instead we offered up one million tonnes of CO2 as part of the condition to go with the voluntary approach'" (1995, 12). This suggests the industry had followed the model presented by Layzer (2007) in which business often moves from an initial policy objective of completely blocking policy to accepting the fact it will be required by policy to internalize some cost and then negotiating the policy details to keep that cost as low as possible.

Macdonald, Houle, and Patterson (2011) concluded the VCR was selected as a policy instrument in the first instance due to lobbying by Alberta and the industry. Secondly, there was a lack of countervailing power within the federal-provincial system. Sheila Copps was arguing for regulation, but her position was weakened by the fact she was not supported by her prime minister (confidential interview 2007b). Neither the federal government, nor any provinces, were actively pressing to see the national process rely on the policy instruments of law or tax. Thirdly, and directly related to that, was the climate issue's lack of salience at the time. Industry power was greater due to the fact that in those early days public opinion was not yet galvanized.

The influence of industry is further demonstrated by subsequent evolution of the VCR. After the program had been announced, NRCan minister Anne McLellan advocated a government-industry planning process to move the VCR out of NRCan administration. The result was that in 1997 VCR Inc. was created as a stand-alone non-profit corporation, funded by both industry and government (Macdonald, Houle, and Patterson 2011). In subsequent years, something like two-thirds of the VCR Inc. budget of $850,000 was provided by industry and the remainder by the federal and provincial governments. As discussed in the next case study, by 2002 the federal government had decided to opt for a more coercive policy instrument than voluntarism and the VCR effectively stopped operations in 2004.

1996 was given over to implementation of the NAPCC. Quebec announced its version of the VCR, the ÉcoGESte program, on 10 September 1996, while the VCR itself continued to recruit participating firms and engaged in the planning necessary to transform itself into a government-industry funded and managed program (Macdonald, Houle, and Patterson, 2011). At the December 1996 JMM, ministers announced that Canada would not be able to meet the target of stabilizing emissions at the 1990 level with the programs currently in place (Macdonald and Smith 1999–2000, 112). A report prepared for that meeting by the NAICC evaluating performance of the NAPCC in its first year of operation had found that, as noted above, emissions had increased 9.4 per cent since 1990 and that the increase came from three western provinces: "On a provincial basis, total greenhouse gas emissions increased significantly in Saskatchewan,

Alberta and, to a lesser extent, in British Columbia. Emission levels in other jurisdictions have not changed significantly relative to 1990 levels" (1996, 9). The NAICC stated that Canada could not achieve the target of stabilization by the year 2000 without "significant additional actions" (NAICC 1999, ii). Ministers were told four years before the deadline that current programs would be unable to achieve that target. That did not lead them, however, to agree to put new programs in place. There was an obvious lack of commitment to achieving the national target.

In any case, by then attention was shifting from the year 2000 target and turning instead to the international effort to establish new targets for the period after 2000, targets that would be more specific than the general objective of stabilization set out in the 1992 UNFCCC. (The pattern is familiar. Canadian governments admitted they could not achieve the 2000 target and then, instead of redoubling their efforts, started planning for a new target. In 2015 the same thing happened, when the federal and provincial governments ignored the fact that current programs could not achieve the 2020 target and instead starting planning for a 2030 target.) At the first Conference of Parties (CoP) to the convention, held in 1995 in Berlin, it had been agreed that new more specific targets would be adopted by the time of the third CoP, to be held in Kyoto, Japan, in December 1997. At the time, Canada was working in alliance with Japan, the US, Australia, and New Zealand to block efforts led by the EU for a more aggressive international commitment. Within Canada, debate started over what the next Canadian target should be, with Alberta opposing any reductions (Harrison 2007, 101), environmentalists arguing in favour, and, within the federal government, ongoing differences between NRCan and Environment Canada. (Each department was working to fulfil its mandate. NRCan, like many other government departments such as industry and agriculture, worked to assist the relevant industrial sector, in this case energy industries, in order to contribute to Canadian job and wealth creation. Environment Canada's mandate was environmental protection, which meant asking industries to internalize costs of pollution; as such it, like all provincial environment departments, was often at odds with other government departments working to help those industries. See Doern and Conway [1994] for an excellent analysis of Environment Canada's struggles within the Ottawa bureaucracy.)

In late October 1997 the US announced its position going into the Kyoto summit of favouring a global goal of stabilization of emissions at the 1990 level by 2010 – thus keeping the original Rio UNFCCC goal of stabilization but providing another ten years to achieve it. The EU was calling for a target of 15 per cent below the 1990 level (Harrison 2007, 100). By that time, not long before the start of the Kyoto talks, Canadian emissions were 13 per cent above the 1990 level and the federal government was having great difficulty agreeing on what target it would propose, in part because environment minister Christine Stewart and NRCan minister Ralph Goodale were in conflict. Cabinet itself was also divided, with ministers including finance minister Paul Martin and Anne McLellan, then justice minister, arguing for "caution" in opposition to Christine Stewart, David Collinette, transport minister, and, possibly foreign affairs minister Lloyd Axworthy pressing for more ambitious policy (McIlroy and Greenspon 1997). The problem was compounded by the fact that Prime Minister Chrétien insisted the Canadian position had to be more environmentally friendly than the American stabilization goal, while at the same time wanting to be sure his government did not alienate Alberta, other provinces and the relevant industrial sectors. Fears of alienating Alberta were well-founded, since the West-East divide, fuelled by memories of the NEP, had come into view. Alberta environment minister Ty Lund had stated that his province "would reject" any binding agreement Canada might sign at Kyoto (Cohen and McIlroy 1997). A few days later he said, "It sure scares me the minute they start talking about carbon taxes. That smells very much like the National Energy Program" (Ingram 1997). At the same time, Reform Party leader Preston Manning said Ottawa was planning to "force this emissions deal down the throats of Albertans in the same way it enforced the National Energy Program" (Ingram 1997).

The other underlying challenge examined here, the issue of allocating cost, had also come into view. In a speech on climate change policy delivered 3 November 1997, Prime Minister Chrétien attempted to reassure Alberta by repeating his 1994 promise he would not impose an energy tax, and by saying that his government "would be fair to all regions, provinces and sectors" and that, "We are not interested in penalizing or singling out one region or one industry" (McIlroy 1997a). At that time, the David Suzuki Foundation had released a report saying Canadian failure on climate change was due to the fact federal and provincial ministers "have never talked seriously about how to fairly allocate responsibility for meeting the national target at a national or sectoral level" (McIlroy 1997b). A few days later a Sierra Club representative, Louise Comeau, pointed to the problem the provinces will have in agreeing on how to "split up the reductions among themselves." She said Alberta might want Ontario and other provinces that buy Alberta natural gas to take on an added share of the national burden (Laghi 1997a), presumably because they had benefitted from the emissions generated in Alberta to extract and transport the gas. Jean Charest, leader of the federal Progressive Conservative Party had also recommended addressing the allocation issue in a *Globe and Mail* opinion piece.

> It may be difficult for us to determine a final position [on the Kyoto proposal], but we could at least agree on the means of reducing greenhouse gases by: [first] Recognizing regional grievances in implementing a Canadian position. Different

regions have different economies and should not be expected to carry the same load. (Charest, 1997)

These statements show two things. The issue of allocating the total reduction among sources and provinces clearly was recognized by those engaged with national policymaking. In addition, there was sympathy with the position of the western producing provinces. The difficulty was that the issue of allocating the total reduction had at that time not been formally placed on the JMM agenda.

At a federal cabinet meeting on 4 November 1997, the government was leaning towards adopting the American position of stabilization, but decided it would not finalize the federal position until the issue had been discussed at the federal-provincial JMM the following week (Macdonald and Smith 1999–2000, 114). At that meeting, on 12 November, the energy and environment ministers gathered for the Regina JMM announced they (with the exception of Quebec) had agreed the Canadian position should be stabilization by 2010 – a news media report suggests that the federal representatives had pushed for adoption of a more ambitious goal in order to better the American position, but then settled for stabilization (Laghi 1997b). The same report says that sources inside the room said the ministers were split, not surprisingly, between the fossil fuel producers Alberta, Saskatchewan, and British Columbia, plus Ontario, concerned about its coal-fired electricity generation, and the hydro provinces "such as Quebec and Manitoba" (Laghi 1997b). Alberta, apparently, had been willing to compromise – environment minister Lund said the provinces recognized that Canada had to be part of an international consensus on global climate action (Laghi 1997b). The federal government, for its part, pointed out that as it negotiated at Kyoto it would not be legally bound by the federal-provincial agreement (Sallot 1997).

As the start date for the Kyoto summit came closer and closer, the federal cabinet continued to wrestle with its challenge of putting a square peg in a round hole – bettering the American position without alienating the western provinces. At one point it considered changing the stabilization date from 2010 to the more ambitious 2007, but backed away from that in the face of Alberta and Saskatchewan objections, and instead started to consider a target of a slight reduction below the 1990 level (*Globe and Mail* 1997a). On 1 December 1997, the day of the start of the Kyoto talks, the government announced that its position was a reduction to 3 per cent below the 1990 level. The decision was immediately criticized by Alberta and Saskatchewan. Alberta energy minister Steve West said Ottawa had "betrayed" the federal-provincial process, while his Saskatchewan counterpart said climate change was now a purely federal issue (*Globe and Mail* 1997b), implying that federal failure to stay with the JMM position meant his government no longer had a responsibility to act. As discussed in the next case study, Alberta representatives later also took the position that the Kyoto commitment was a *federal government* target, which did not necessarily bind the provinces. Ottawa's refusal to be bound by the agreement it had reached with the provinces on the stabilization target increased western mistrust, damaging the federal-provincial process. Furthermore, yet again Ottawa was unilaterally committing Canada to a reduction target without having first achieved provincial buy-in. Why should citizens of Alberta and Saskatchewan make sacrifices to achieve a target they had had no say in, set by the imperial master on the other side of the West-East divide?

Canada emerged from the Kyoto meeting having agreed in the last-minute negotiations to a target of 6 per cent below the 1990 level. The 6 per cent decision came from the highest level, having been approved by the prime minister in telephone conversation with his delegates at Kyoto (Simpson et al. 2007, 33; Hanusch 2018, 122–3). Harrison states that during the Kyoto negotiations, "while the US was preoccupied with its position relative to the EU and Japan, Canada was focused exclusively on the US position" (2007, 102). The US accepted a target of 7 per cent below the 1990 level, and Canada came in close to that mark. The question of why the Canadian prime minister and his negotiators agreed to 6 per cent rather than sticking with their original 3 per cent position is less important, for purposes of this analysis, than the question of why the Chrétien government decided it would set aside the federal-provincial Regina decision. This probably was because federal decision-makers felt they were the ones with jurisdiction to negotiate treaties, and so the federal-provincial decision had to be advisory only (although the federal government habitually consults with provinces when negotiating a treaty that will require provincial implementation).

Paul Heinbecker, the top diplomat in the Canadian delegation to the summit, which was headed by the environment and NRCan ministers, has said that the stabilization position arrived at by the ministers in November was "not tenable" because the "zero target [stabilization] was going to leave us embarrassed" and in any case did not bind the federal government (Hanusch 2018, 119). Technically, the JMM decision did not bind Ottawa but his remarks demonstrate the basic problem: federal officials and the prime minister were more focused upon the international process than the domestic one, more worried about embarrassment in front of other states than any damage they were doing to federal-provincial trust. Whatever the reason, the one thing we know is that the JMM process was not strong enough to bind the federal government. The basic weakness of intergovernmental policymaking, that any government can opt out at any time, was clearly on display with this decision by the Chrétien government to, in fact, opt out of the Regina decision.

The Kyoto summit ended on 10 December 1997, and the next day a previously scheduled Canadian First Ministers' Meeting to discuss the Social Union Framework Agreement began in Ottawa. The event started with a dinner for first ministers on the evening of 11 December, to be followed by two closed-door sessions on 12 December. Climate-change policy was not on the agenda for the FMM, but was discussed and decisions were made at the 11 December dinner, and so the subject was included in the final communiqué. The communiqué announced three decisions respecting Canadian climate change policy, plus a fourth directing the JMM to continue its work. What follows is a verbatim reproduction of the section of the final communiqué headed "Climate Change":

> First Ministers discussed the Kyoto Protocol. They agreed that climate change is an important global issue and that Canada must do its part and must do so in such a way that no region is asked to bear an unreasonable burden.
>
> They also agreed that it is important to gain a thorough understanding of the impact, the costs and the benefits of its implementation and of the various implementation options open to Canada.
>
> First Ministers agreed to establish a process, in advance of Canada's ratification of the Kyoto Protocol, that will examine the consequences of Kyoto and provide for full participation of the provincial and territorial governments with the federal government in any implementation of the protocol.
>
> First Ministers have therefore directed their Ministers of the Environment and Energy to work together to consider jointly the appropriate courses of action. (First Ministers' Meeting 1997)

As can be seen, the first decision made by the prime minister and premiers was that Canada would "do its part" as part of the global effort. There was agreement that national policy development would continue – Alberta, it is worth noting, did not opt out at this stage, suggesting the intergovernmental system does have some power to keep players at the table. The issue of allocation of cost among Canadian regions (and implicitly provinces), however, was given central place in that first section. Why was that? Roy Romanow, then Premier of Saskatchewan, has explained that government leaders at the time were still reacting to the shock of the 1995 Quebec referendum which had come very close to fracturing confederation and so were keen to find ways to pursue national interests without doing harm to provincial sensibilities, neither those of Quebec nor others. During the dinner Alberta Premier Ralph Klein made a "passionate statement" about his concerns for impacts of Kyoto in his province, saying "in no way would he proceed" with implementation of the 6 per cent reduction (Romanow 2018). The upshot was the "no unreasonable burden" principle being reiterated in the communiqué.

Secondly, the communiqué states that governments will study the question of costs and benefits. It does *not* say they agreed to implement the protocol and the Canadian commitment to achieve the 6 per cent below 1990 target. Instead, the communiqué says that first ministers agreed that they would examine the costs and benefits of implementation and implicitly says that only then, based on that examination, would they decide whether or not Canada would implement the protocol. The same point is made in the next paragraph, which says first ministers would examine the "consequences" of implementation "in advance" of the implementation decision. Finally, the communiqué commits to continuation of the federal-provincial process with, implicitly, "full participation" of the provinces and, explicitly, full participation in implementation, which must refer to use of provincial law and policy, as well as that of the federal government. Presumably premiers felt this wording closed the door to unilateral federal action; Ralph Klein had said the Kyoto commitment was "not acceptable" but his tone was "more restrained" after the dinner (Greenspon 1997). Harrison states that Alberta Premier Ralph Klein after the meeting said this gave a "provincial veto" on the question of implementation (2007, 105).

It seems clear that Prime Minister Chrétien, faced with vehement objections by the veto government Alberta and in effect having been brought up hard against the basic West-East fault line, retreated. His government had said in the international forum of the Kyoto meeting that it would do what was necessary to bring total Canadian emissions down to the level it had committed to there. A few days later, in the very different federal-provincial forum, his government said it would study the costs and benefits with its provincial partners before making any final decision on action. The federal government, with the provinces, had agreed to one target at the 12 November JMM; then unilaterally decided on a different target; then, again with the provinces, decided to defer action on the target. This federal inconsistency was to cause problems for the federal-provincial process throughout the next phase of federal-provincial climate-change policymaking.

Analysis

1) What Does the Case Tell Us about the Four Subjects?

THE WEST-EAST DIVIDE

The case shows us that the West-East divide is not necessarily symmetrical. The divide was operational here, but taking a very different form from the first case. Instead of a zero-sum game of conflict between the two regions, with Ottawa on the side of the east, this time the divide was a lopsided affair with a motivated west essentially facing no eastern resistance. Ontario did not see itself as threatened by climate change in those early days, and presumably did see some threat from the costs of policy action, given its reliance upon coal-fired electricity and the importance to the provincial economy of auto-mobile manufacturing. The ideological leaning of the Ontario government led by Mike Harris, who took power in 1995, was also in agreement with that of the Klein government, with both following the usual right-wing tendency of disinclination to take the climate issue seriously. The federal government led by Jean Chrétien after 1993 had nothing like the kind of motivation stem-ming from revenue shortfalls seen in the earlier period. Chrétien also seems to have had a strong desire, perhaps a hangover from the NEP conflict, to appease Alberta. This was displayed in the fact of his flying to Calgary in 1994 to announce his government would not impose a carbon tax, failure to support his environment minister in 1994 and early 1995 as the national program was being decided, and acquiescence to Premier Klein's demands at the 11 December 1997, first ministers' dinner. Neither Ontario nor Ottawa opposed Alberta, showing that in this case the West-East divide was asym-metrical, with respect to both degree of interest and balance of power.

THE INHERENT NEED TO ALLOCATE REDUCTIONS
The case shows that the inherent need to allocate reductions will not exert influ-ence upon policy if governments are not standing face-to-face with a significant reduction in emissions. As we have seen, the issue of differing regional impacts of climate policy was recognized and discussed but was never an item on a JMM agenda, and governments did not commission research or generate any discussion papers on how the principle of no unreasonable burden could be implemented. Those involved were aware of the allocation issue but did not see it as important enough to warrant developing policy to address it. Why not? The answer has to be that Canada was so far away from actually taking on a specific reduction quantity that there really was no burden to be shared. Canadian gov-ernments were quite willing to miss the stabilization target, opting instead for a new one ten or twelve years distant. Given that, why be concerned about who will pay what portion of a future cost that might never have to be paid at all?

THE NATIONAL PROCESS
The case illustrates the weakness of the intergovernmental process, despite its formalization in 1993. An audit done by the Environmental Commis-sioner found that "there are no clear and transparent agreements or arrange-ments between the federal government and the provinces and territories that specifically define their respective roles and responsibilities in achieving the stabilization goal" (1998, 3-20–3-21). This lack of clear rules helps to explain

the weakness of the JMM process as it was essentially cast aside, first by the prime minister and cabinet when they substituted the minus 3 per cent for the federal-provincial stabilization position, and then secondly by the FMM when they decided to study before acting. Beyond the lack of institutionalization that is common to all federal-provincial processes, this particular weakness is explained by the fact the process was led by ministers, rather than first ministers, who could not resist the takeover by the prime minister and premiers at the December 1997 FMM. The other explanation is the lack of engaged, consistent leadership by the Chrétien government (the point overlaps with the fourth subject of federal government leadership strategy but because it is so central to workings of the national process is discussed here).

How do we explain this lack of federal leadership? The explanation is found in the theoretical variables of interest and power. Prime Minister Chrétien certainly held more power than any other actor throughout. He could have convinced his cabinet to accept the JMM stabilization position, could have told his negotiators in Kyoto to stay firm on that position, regardless of the price in terms of Canadian legitimacy in the eyes of other countries (Australia, another member of the Commonwealth, and a comparable middle-power, energy-exporting nation, was apparently able to live with whatever loss of legitimacy was attached to its Kyoto commitment to *increase* emissions by 8 per cent by 2008–12), and he could also, although this time paying a much greater price in terms of Canadian national unity, have held firm on the commitment given at Kyoto to implement the 6 per cent reduction decision when sitting at the dinner table with combative premiers.

Why did he not? The answer lies in the interest of the prime minister and accordingly of his government. In the first instance, the Chrétien government simply did not have the motivation of the Trudeau government in the late 1970s as it saw oil revenues bypassing Ottawa and piling up in Alberta. Secondly, the Chrétien government had a very much on-and-off interest in environment. The 1993 election platform Red Book made many environmental promises that were not kept (Juillet and Toner 1997). The prime minister first appointed a senior Liberal politician who had contested the Liberal Party leadership that Chrétien won in 1990, Sheila Copps as environment minister, perhaps signalling the issue was a priority with his government. However, he then failed to support her in the national process and then appointed two much less senior Liberals, Sergio Marchi and Christine Stewart, neither with any previous experience, and then, blowing hot again, appointed David Anderson as environment minister in 1999, a British Columbian politician with an undoubted personal commitment to the issue (discussed in the next chapter). In the fall of 1997, however, it is clear the prime minister was motivated less by concern for environmental protection than by the influence of other actors. At the Kyoto meeting, he wanted to stay close to the US position but not get too far ahead of it, which led him to make a commitment to environmental action. In meeting with the premiers, however, it seems his main interest was in placating provincial anger, which he did by if not abandoning then certainly weakening and delaying the environmental commitment he had just made at Kyoto.

All of this shows the importance of the degree of interest of the lead government actor. When that actor's motivation is ambivalent and inconsistent the federal-provincial process cannot function effectively. The case also illustrates the way in which a multilateral process with weak leadership magnifies the power of the veto actor. To a significant extent, the absence of countervailing power meant Alberta controlled the process, ensuring it produced only the lowest-common-denominator outcomes it found acceptable.

FEDERAL GOVERNMENT STRATEGY

The case shows that federal strategy that makes use of unilateral action, something we usually think of as a sign of leadership leading to effective national policy, can in fact reduce effectiveness. (This issue is distinct from the positive damage that can be done by unilateral action like the 1980 NEP.) The Mulroney government strategy was what one would expect of a government committed to action on the issue, similar to that of the Justin Trudeau government in 2015 – unilateral action followed by efforts to induce provinces to join it in the effort. The Mulroney government also used its own unilateral action to contribute to achieving the Canadian goal when it set out in the 1990 Green Plan actions it would take itself; for instance, "Federal efforts will focus upon [such things as] … enhanced research and development of alternative energy sources" (Government of Canada 1990, 106).

The unilateral decision by the federal government to reject the policy instrument of a carbon tax in 1994 was less helpful. The real problem, however, came from the unilateral federal actions in late 1997. As discussed and as we shall see in more detail in the next case study, the setting aside of the Regina JMM stabilization position increased western mistrust of the whole national climate policy project, while the Alberta reaction to the Kyoto commitment led to the decision to delay action – the exact opposite of effective national policy. Federal unilateral action does not always contribute to policy effectiveness and in fact can reduce it.

2) What Are the Most Important Factors Explaining the Case Outcome?

The case outcome was only minimal policy coordination, since governments had not committed to significant policy change. The state of national climate change policy by the end of December 1997 was that governments had only reached agreement on the relatively ineffective policy instrument of appeals for voluntary action instead of law-based regulations. Furthermore, by decision of the first ministers, who had hijacked the ministers-led JMM process, the Kyoto commitment would be extensively studied before it was acted upon. Beyond the VCR/ÉcoGESte, some governments may have put in place some policies marginally different than those they would have adopted had they not been engaged in an intergovernmental process, but they were not significant. Nor can the main policy instrument of the VCR/ÉcoGESte be considered significant, since by definition an appeal to voluntary action is less likely to influence actions of firms or others than would a binding instrument such as law or tax. Accordingly, the case outcome was a failure to generate substantial policy coordination. Governments coordinated their actions to the extent they all participated in the same process, but they displayed only minimal behaviour change as a result of that process.

The major factors explaining that outcome are: 1) influence of the veto government (Alberta) due to the fact that it did not encounter significant countervailing power from the lead government; and, 2) the factors explaining Ottawa's failure to play an effective lead-government role – lack of motivation; erratic, unskilled diplomacy; and failure to make effective use of unilateral action to influence veto-government behaviour. Alberta influence is shown by Prime Minister Chrétien's trip to Calgary in 1994 to tell the oil industry he would not bring in a carbon tax. He presumably did that because of Alberta pressure, working in close alliance with the structural power of the oil industry as both lobbied in the drafting of the NAPCC and, subsequently, the decision that the VCR program would be co-managed by industry and government (ÉcoGESte stayed a government-run program). In terms of the 11 December 1997 FMM, we know that Alberta Premier Ralph Klein emerged from the meeting much happier than he was going into it – Alberta had been allowed to steer the ship of federal-provincial national policy.

This Alberta influence was due to the lack of countervailing power from Ottawa or the eastern provinces. Alberta was able to exert power because it was largely unopposed, due to the fact that, unlike the first case, this was not a zero-sum game. Although the topic was still fossil fuels, thus guaranteeing western attention, once oil prices and revenue were no longer on the table, a win for Alberta (warding off an effective national program) did not constitute a loss for any eastern provinces. Nor was it a loss for Ottawa, since in those early days of climate politics the government itself did not hold strong views on the need for climate action (as witnessed by Sheila Copps's isolated position within government) and it was not subjected to strong pressure from environmentalists or the public. As a result, Ottawa had little motivation to oppose Alberta influence.

Beyond lack of motivation, Ottawa's influence was also weakened by its erratic strategy, in terms of setting aside its agreement with the provinces in order to make an international commitment many of them disagreed with and then turning around and acceding to their demands. Federal strategy here is the opposite of the clear-eyed use of federal power we saw in the preceding case. In fact, there essentially was no use of Ottawa power and thus no counter-vailing power to challenge the influence of Alberta.

7 The Second National Climate Change Process, 1998–2002

Case Summary

Again, a veto government (Alberta, allied with Ontario) encountered little countervailing resistance, from provinces or the lead government, Ottawa. The veto government had the same material motivation and high degree of interest that had been present since the start of the first case in the 1970s. As in the previous case, Ottawa was not highly motivated and displayed little skill in the use of persuasion, promise, or threat to influence the provinces; it then abandoned the leadership role completely when it unilaterally decided to implement its own climate-change policy outside the federal-provincial process. Alberta too began to pursue an independent climate-change policy, also outside the federal-provincial process. For these reasons, the process generated only minimal policy coordination.

START AND END DATES: 1 January 1998–31 December 2002

MAJOR POLICY DECISIONS

unilateral
- release of federal government's own plan to accompany the federal-provincial plan, October 2000
- federal government decision to release a discussion paper on federal policy, May 2002, signalling it had started to plan for use of its own policy instruments, regardless of provincial wishes
- Alberta decision to withdraw as co-chair of the national process, subsequent to the 21 May 2002, ministers' meeting, followed by Alberta development of its own independent climate policy
- federal ratification of Kyoto Protocol in December 2002 after refusing provincial demands for a First Ministers' Meeting prior to doing so

- federal agreement with Canadian Association of
  Petroleum Producers, also in December 2002, that
  oil industry costs to comply with federal regulation
  would not exceed $15 a tonne and the total reduction
  required from the sector would not exceed 15 per cent
  below business-as-usual projections

bilateral   • none

multilateral   • implementation of the December 1997 FMM decision
                   to study feasibility of the Kyoto target, 1998–9
                 • release of federal-provincial plans, October 2000 and
                   May 2002

CASE OUTCOME

By May 2002 the federal and provincial governments had agreed on the
2000 and 2002 business plans, which did not represent coordinated policies
because they were largely compilations of actions taken by individual jurisdictions. Nor did they state that the assembly of actions would achieve the
Kyoto target. By the end of December 2002 the multilateral process had come
to an end with Ottawa's unilateral ratification of Kyoto. The federal government had in November 2002 released a plan for actions it would take by itself
to achieve the Kyoto goal. The government of Alberta had also released its
own unilateral plan, intended to achieve a target less stringent than the Kyoto
goal. That initiated the train of events that has continued since, whereby
Alberta pursues a different climate target from the rest of the country.

COORDINATION CATEGORY: minimal policy coordination

This case study of national climate-change policymaking differs significantly
from the other cases in that it is the only one to have ended in complete
failure. The other four cases all ended with signing of some kind of intergovernmental agreement, albeit not always one requiring any significant
behaviour change or policy coordination. Here, no agreement of any kind
was signed. Instead, by the end of 2002, the federal government was isolated, with no provincial support for its proposed more robust approach and
its plan for Kyoto ratification opposed by all the provinces, including even
Quebec, the province that had consistently favoured ratification. Worse yet,
by then the process itself had ceased to function. Surely the strongest indication of the failure of a decision-making process, beyond being unable to
generate a decision, is inability of the process itself to survive. If a failed
state is one that can no longer provide minimal security and services to its
citizens, then a failed intergovernmental relations process has to be one in

which government representatives no longer find themselves in the same room, discussing the same topic.

The four-year case-study period divides neatly into two halves. During 1998 and 1999, the environment and energy ministers were responding to the first ministers' December 1997 direction that they examine the feasibility of the Kyoto target by means of their own research and through a large, complex process involving government and non-government experts. Very little new policy was put in place. During the second half, governments did release action plans but until the summer of 2001 it was not at all clear that Ottawa would in fact ratify the Kyoto Protocol. After that, Ottawa began to develop its own unilateral climate policy, prompting Alberta to do the same thing. On 2 September 2002, at the opening of the World Summit on Sustainable Development in Johannesburg, the prime minister announced his government definitely would ratify Kyoto, triggering a massive lobbying effort to block that move by Canadian business, led by the oil industry and in alliance with western provinces and others such as Ontario. The JMM met for the last time in Halifax on 28 October 2002; the federal government published the final iteration of its unilateral climate action plan in November; and then in December Ottawa both ratified Kyoto and made a separate piece with the oil industry by making promises for extremely lenient federal regulatory measures. Four years of cross-country study, dialogue, debate, lobbying, and invective had produced neither effective policy nor national unity, leaving only the thin hope that Ottawa, all by itself, might be able to reduce Canadian emissions.

Narrative

In 1998, the national climate-change policymaking process shifted back from first ministers to the venue of the JMM ministers-led process supported by federal-provincial committees of officials that had been originally put in place in 1993. Changes were made, however, in consequence of the provincial anger and sense of betrayal evoked by the decision of the Chrétien government to set aside the Kyoto position, which it had previously agreed to with provincial ministers at the 12 November 1997 Regina JMM. Discussion of possible changes had begun among members of the Canadian delegation while in Kyoto and continued afterward (confidential interview 2010). The intent was to transform what had been prior to 1997 primarily a federal initiative with provincial participation into something more truly federal-provincial. The organizational vehicle for accomplishing that was a new federal-provincial body with a mandate to support the national process, co-chaired by two assistant-deputy-minister-level officials: one each from the Alberta (John Donner) and federal (David Oulton) governments. The

National Climate Change Secretariat was created not by the federal government but by the federal and provincial ministers at the first meeting of the JMM since the Regina meeting, in Toronto on 23–4 April 1998. The record of decision at that meeting reads as follows:

> Decision: The Ministers approved the creation of a national climate change secretariat, which will include representatives from the provincial, territorial and federal governments. The National Climate Change Secretariat will support the development of a national implementation strategy. Secretariat staff members will operate from their current locations, and the secretariat will have federal and provincial co-chairs. (JMM Record of Decisions 1998a)

In an interview, David Oulton, the federal co-chair, has explained why Ottawa was supportive of the shift to co-chairs. Putting Alberta at the centre of the national process was thought to be beneficial precisely because it was the province most skeptical of the Kyoto goal; if it agreed to a measure, other provinces would be likely to follow (Oulton 2010). John Donner, the Alberta co-chair, acted informally as a representative of the provinces (Oulton 2010). Total seconded staff of the secretariat, both full and part-time, was about ten, with provincial officials coming primarily from the western provinces (Oulton 2010). If the federal intent was to engage with Alberta, this revamping of the JMM structure was a success. By the fall of 1998, the Alberta government had made a deliberate decision not to stand aside but instead to fully engage with the national process (Stilborn 2003, 6). A year later, federal officials were quoted as saying Alberta was more engaged with the national process than any other province (Duffy 1999).

In addition to approving this change, at the April 1998 JMM, energy and environment ministers began to implement the directive from their political masters, the first ministers, that Canadians and their governments "gain a thorough understanding of the impact, the costs and the benefits" of achieving the Kyoto target (First Ministers' Meeting 1997). To do that, they created two types of bodies. The first was a series of sixteen Issue Tables, each made up of fifteen to thirty government and non-government experts. Seven of the tables were devoted to examination of options for reductions within a given sector (agriculture, forestry, buildings, transportation, industry, electricity, and municipalities); the remainder examined more general issues such as enhanced voluntary action, public education, and climate change science and impacts. The mandate of the tables was to provide expert analysis of a full range of policy options. It was not clear, however, if each table was to then reach consensus on preferred options; some went further in that direction than others (Hanusch 2018). In late 1998 many of the tables published their initial work plans and by the end of 1999 most had published their final reports. These reports differed, with some providing specific recommendations, while others only listed options (Hanusch 2018, 135). Not surprisingly, given the enormous diversity of views and interests among different industries, regions, environmentalists, academics, and other experts, the table reports did not provide one clear picture of the direction Canadian policy should take.

As well as reaching out to civil society for expertise in this manner, governments in the JMM process also established a number of government-only bodies to study different aspects of the Kyoto challenge. The most significant of these was the Analysis and Modelling Group (AMG), since it was the main source of information on the economic implications of policy measures being considered and the basic question the FMM had asked ministers to consider – what were the "costs and benefits" of implementing the Kyoto commitment? As shown by its November 2000 report, the AMG was at that time formally a federal-provincial body, chaired by a representative of Newfoundland and Labrador and of the Government of Canada and made up of sixteen civil servants, representing nine different governments (AMG 2000). The AMG was completely funded by the federal government alone, however, with only in-kind support in the form of seconded staff expertise provided by the provinces (McIlveen 2010). In addition to providing results of modelling of the economic impact of Kyoto policy on the country as a whole, the AMG also provided analysis of impacts upon individual provinces:

> The analysis and modelling group always broke its results out in terms of impacts per province as well as impacts per sector. So, every run that was done, every scenario was looked at in terms of relative burden to the provinces. (confidential interview 2010)

What follows is an example from the November 2000 report of analysis of differing provincial impacts associated with achieving the Kyoto target. Policy measures modelled are taken from proposals in the Issue Tables reports and assumptions are made about such things as whether or not the US is also implementing Kyoto. Impacts are for the period 2013 to 2018:

> Ontario is somewhat more vulnerable than Quebec, owing to the positive effects of Quebec's hydro electricity generation. The impact on Ontario is due to its trade-sensitive manufacturing industries. Saskatchewan and Alberta are most affected in the long term because of the dominance of resource-based industries in those provinces. (AMG 2000, 61)

While allocation of cost among provinces was never formally addressed by the national process beyond creation of a working group (discussed on the next page), ministers and officials were continually receiving information about that subject. Furthermore, provincial representatives tended to use the economic impact upon their province as an important criterion for evaluating different policy options (Macdonald et al. 2013). This meant there was an imbalance built into the national process, since information on cost distribution was being generated but the process did not provide a venue to discuss that information and then go on to reach agreement on how those costs might be shared.

The JMM met again on 19 and 20 October 1998, in Halifax without making any significant decisions, instead merely re-affirming support for primary reliance on the policy instrument of voluntary action, through the VCR and ÉcoGESte, supporting programs for public education and reviewing progress being made by the Issue Tables (JMM 1998b). The process then continued to mark time through 1999, waiting for the tables to complete their work. During that year, Quebec emerged as the one Canadian government advocating explicit allocation of the total reduction, not only among sources but also among provinces. Quebec environment minister Paul Bégin called for such an approach in a speech on 25 March 1999, and again on 8 October of that year (Ministère du Développement durable 1999a and 1999b). Then at the next JMM, held in Vancouver on 27–8 March 2000, Bégin dramatically walked out of the meeting to issue a news release that said Quebec was "totally dissatisfied" with the national approach being implemented (Ministère de l'Environnement 2000). Two reasons for discontent were given: first, the fact that governments had not yet made any effort to "enter into talks for the equitable sharing of the 6% GHG emissions reduction," and, secondly, the failure of other governments to give it credit for earlier spending on hydro-electric projects and associated "emissions avoided" (Ministère de l'Environnement 2000). The minister concluded by saying his government was planning to "implement its own action plan within its own territory and own scope as soon as possible" (Ministère de l'Environnement 2000).

Why was Quebec concerned about an equitable allocation of the total cost? It seems reasonable to think that the Quebec position was influenced in part by the fact that it was governed from 1994 to 2003 by the separatist Parti Québécois and thus was always both disinclined to participate in Canadian national programs, whatever the policy field, and also eager to stake out positions resembling those that would be taken by a sovereign state. Thus Quebec did not participate in the VCR, but instead created its own mirror program, and during this time took the position that had it been an independent country, it would have already ratified Kyoto (Bjorn et al. 2002, 67). Federal-provincial negotiation of a burden-sharing agreement, after which each province would act independently to meet its own reduction target, fit with the Quebec separatist perspective. The other reason, however, had nothing to do with ideology of the governing party and instead was based upon Quebec's view of its economic position. The analysis done by the Quebec government at the time recognized that allocation only by sector, the position favoured by the federal government and other provinces, would in the case of regionally concentrated industries, such as oil and gas, aluminum and pulp and paper, implicitly be a geographic allocation. Coupled with that was concern that since it was a fixed sum being allocated, should the oil and gas sector be given a lighter load for whatever reason, the burden for other industries in other parts of the country would be increased: "What we were afraid was that we'd have to close pulp and paper mills, you know, to favour the expansion of oil and gas production in Alberta" (confidential interview 2010).

In order to bring Quebec back into the process, governments created a new body, the Emissions Allocation and Burden Sharing Working Group (EABSWG). That body examined the way in which the European Union had reached agreement on burden sharing in 1997 and 1998 and then held a workshop on 16 October 2001, in Toronto to discuss principles that might underlie an equitable sharing of the Canadian reduction effort (Macdonald et al. 2013, 53–4). The EABSWG then continued to work throughout the remainder of 2001 and 2002, with active participation from provinces, including Alberta. By the time the National Climate Change Process ended in later 2002, however, it had still not generated a report and so never produced findings and recommendations for consideration by ministers (Macdonald et al. 2013, 54).

As discussed, the burden-sharing issue had been recognized since at least the time of the 1995 NAPCC under the principle that no region would be asked to bear an "unreasonable burden." That was one of the principles that was to have been established by a framework agreement intended to help formalize and thus strengthen the intergovernmental process. At the 27–8 March meeting, ministers agreed they would develop a "short high level framework agreement that formalizes the nature of the partnership in responding to climate change" (JMM 2000). Although not an agreement on substance, such a formalization and institutionalization of the national policy process would have helped. Gattinger (2015, 64) recommends development of a Canadian energy strategy start by entering into a framework agreement that "would have the advantage of beginning where it matters most: developing the norm of collaboration."

During the summer of 2000, federal and provincial officials came close to a final agreement on the wording of the framework agreement and expected that it would be approved by ministers as item number five on the agenda of the 16–17 October 2000 JMM in Quebec City. Section 8 of the draft agreement was headed "Burden Sharing" and stated that governments (or sectors or regions – no final decision had yet been made on that wording) would "do their fair share" and would not be asked to "bear an unreasonable share of the burden of mitigative actions" (JMM 2000). The draft went on to state that should such a burden exist, "appropriate measures" possibly including compensation would be determined (JMM 2000). The draft agreement was not approved by ministers, however, due to last-minute objections by Ontario representatives on the morning of 17 October. It is likely those objections were the result of a sudden intervention by the Ontario premier, since they surprised even the Ontario officials who had been working on the agreement and were expecting to see it adopted that day (Macdonald et al. 2013, 53). The record of decisions for the JMM stated that ministers (with the exception of Ontario) agreed the draft agreement would be sent to governments for their approval and then placed on the agenda of the next JMM. It did not appear on that agenda, however, and at the JMM held in Charlottetown on 21 May 2002, ministers agreed to "set aside" the draft agreement and to "bring [it] forward at a later date, if appropriate" (JMM Record of Decision May 21, 2002b).

The concluding chapters set out the argument that both the West-East divide and inherent need to allocate effort require that governments negotiate an equitable sharing of cost, which is likely to involve compensation. In the fall of 2000, governments came very close to formally adopting such an approach but were unable to do so due to the objections of one province. This again shows the weakness of the IGR consensual process. Why did Ontario scuttle the agreement? Earlier in the year, at the time of the 27–8 March 2000 JMM, a newspaper report stated that both business officials and environmentalists were coming to see Ontario opposition as the greatest challenge to federal-provincial action (Mickleburgh 2000). Another press report in April 2000 also identified the Ontario energy and environment ministers as those most opposed to action in closed-door discussions (Duffy 2000). Having blocked the framework agreement, Ontario then refused to sign the final meeting communiqué on the grounds that it was not sufficiently effective (Rhéal 2000), something hard to believe given the lack of climate action by Ontario to that date and the actions previously taken by the Mike Harris government to weaken Ontario environmental law. David Anderson, who had become federal environment minister in a cabinet shuffle on 3 August 1999, said (quoted in MacKinnon 2000): "Canada's plan is not together yet because Ontario is the missing piece and Ontario is a very big piece."

Thus by the time of the 16–17 October 2000 JMM we see that Alberta was fully engaged but playing a less explicitly veto role than Ontario. Quebec, on the other hand, was supportive of climate action but was concerned about the sharing of costs and focused on its own program, regardless of what other provinces did, and Ontario was working quietly on the inside to sabotage the national effort while saying very different things in public. Nor yet were any other provinces stepping up to play a lead role. As for Ottawa, Hanusch quotes David Anderson as saying that Prime Minister Chrétien insisted on "exhaustive discussion," which is why the federal government did not use its available "political force to advance things very far" (2018, 143). It is hardly surprising that the federal-provincial and federal-only plans released at the 16–17 October 2000 JMM, ostensibly the product of all the expert analysis and multi-stakeholder discussion carried out over the past two years, were so timid, vague, and ineffective.

The federal-provincial plans took two forms. The first was a general statement of the federal-provincial approach for coordinated and individual action, set out in the document *Canada's National Implementation Strategy on Climate Change* (NCCP 2000). Policy measures were to be organized by means of five themes: 1) enhanced awareness; 2) promotion of technology development; 3) governments leading by example; 4) investing in knowledge; and, 5) encouraging action (NCCP 2000, 9). The latter referred to measures intended to "catalyze immediate actions" in sectors such as agriculture, buildings, transportation, and others (NCCP 2000, 9). There was no hint that government might "catalyze" private sector emission reductions by use of legally binding regulatory requirements. Policy was to be developed in phases, with the first one going up to the time when a decision was made on Kyoto ratification. The current uncertainty respecting that event was explicitly stated: "If Canada ratifies the Kyoto Protocol" then the next phase would begin (NCCP 2000, 10). What might be done at that time was stated to be completely unpredictable in 2000, since it would depend upon "greater international certainty" respecting the Kyoto Protocol, "actions of our major trading partners," and "greater domestic clarity" respecting necessary "policy and approaches" (NCCP 2000, 10). Nowhere in the document is it stated that the Canadian goal is to reduce emissions to be 6 per cent below the 1990 level by 2008–12; instead, the picture given is one of Canada "contributing" to the global effort and "addressing" the problem by taking short-term "cost-effective" actions. Specific actions were set out in a companion document, *Canada's First National Climate Change Business Plan*. A progress report released the following year shows the actions were organized under the themes of the National Implementation Strategy, with those meant to encourage action organized by sector (NCCP 2001). There is little evidence of policy coordination, since most of the actions – such as, for instance "Program of Energy Efficiency Retrofits for Manitoba Government Buildings" (NCCP 2001, 57) – are presented as being taken by a single jurisdiction. There is no statement of the anticipated emission reductions from any or all of the current and proposed actions listed.

At the same time, the federal government released a report on actions it was taking or planning as the federal "contribution" to the First National Business Plan (Government of Canada 2000, 2). This document does provide a specific statement of the total anticipated reduction and does refer to the Kyoto goal – actions listed will generate 65 Mt of reductions, which "will take Canada one third of the way to achieving the target" (Government of Canada 2000, 2). Reductions would come from five sectors (industry, agriculture, buildings, energy, and transportation) plus action at the international level (such as funding reductions made outside the country under the Clean Development Mechanism), which were expected to generate one-quarter of the 65 Mt reduction. Policy instruments to be used were primarily subsidy and education; there was no discussion of law-based regulation or carbon pricing. Again, there was no evidence of coordination. Why was the federal government picking up one-third of the effort and leaving the remainder to the provinces? The document is silent on the issue, and a review of all the JMM news releases and records of decisions shows that decision was never discussed by ministers. One suspects that total federal spending was decided by internal Ottawa politics and that once that was decided analysis was done of the reductions that might be achieved by that amount. In short, the three documents show that actions to improve short-term energy efficiency were being taken by the fall of 2000, but there is no single marquee program, like the VCR/ÉcoGeste, which was clearly the product of coordinated planning. Nor yet had the choice of policy instruments advanced beyond that of 1995 – voluntary action was still the order of the day.

November 2000 saw the election of US president George W. Bush, who then shortly after taking office in January 2001 pulled his country out of the Kyoto Protocol. This made the challenge of Kyoto ratification that much more difficult for Canada, since it increased business concerns regarding competitiveness, given that firms in its major export market would not be taking on comparable costs. At the same time, however, US withdrawal increased Canadian leverage within the international regime since parties such as the EU, which very much wanted to see Kyoto come into force, needed Canadian ratification more than ever. At the Conference of Parties in July 2001, as noted above Canada was granted the right to count sinks as part of its reduction effort, significantly lessening the total reduction effort—an estimate at the time was that the credit for sinks represented something like 25 per cent of the reduction effort (Scoffield 2001). Prime Minister Chrétien said that "opens the way for Canada's ratification of the Protocol next year" (Varcoe and Wong 2001). At the same time, Alberta's environment minister said, "I don't believe we should be supporting the Kyoto Agreement as written." From this point until the end of the case study, the narrative is one of those two govern-ments moving increasingly apart as each of them gradually abandoned the federal-provincial process in favour of unilateral action along their own sepa-rate paths. The most visible point of conflict was the federal decision on ratifi-cation, something that clearly lay within Ottawa's own jurisdictional powers, as did the 1997 decision on the Kyoto position, but which, like that earlier decision, had enormous implications for the federal-provincial relationship. The other conflict had to do with choice of policy instrument and the ques-tion of whether governments would move away from appeals for voluntary action towards more coercive instruments such as regulation. By fall 2001, the federal environment minister and his officials in Environment Canada, with the support of the prime minister, were becoming disenchanted with the lack of results being achieved by the VCR and starting to cast around for other instruments (Anderson 2008). At the same time, during the winter of 2001–2 provincial opposition to Kyoto ratification was becoming more visible.

The JMM held in Winnipeg on 24 September 2001, did not generate any new decisions. Ministers met again on 25 February 2002, but did not issue a communiqué at the end of the meeting, something one observer sees as an indication of disagreement (Stilborn 2003, 8). The communiqué from the JMM held 21 May 2002 shows that at the 25 February meeting federal officials stated they were developing a discussion paper on policy options. As noted in chapter 3, earlier in February, at a press conference in Moscow, Alberta Premier Ralph Klein ambushed the prime minister by pulling out a letter purportedly from all premiers (several later said they did not support the let-ter) expressing concerns about the economic impacts of ratification (Bjorn et al. 2002, 61; Chrétien 2007, 386–7). In March 2002, news reports indicated Alberta was looking into possibilities of legal action to prevent federal ratifica-tion (Bjorn et al. 2002, 63). Alberta then proceeded to develop its own plan for Canadian action, outside the Kyoto framework, which would replace the abso-lute reduction represented by the Kyoto minus 6 per cent target by a 50 per cent reduction in emissions intensity, to be achieved by 2020, rather than the Kyoto date of 2012 (Government of Alberta 2002). The federal government, for its part, was also developing its own plan. In May 2002, it published the discussion paper it had referred to at the 25 February 2012 JMM. The paper set out options for use of policy instruments other than voluntary action – both emissions trading and targeted measures, which were said to include "incen-tives, regulations or, possibly, fiscal measures" and government purchase of international credits (Government of Canada 2002a, 19).

In terms of the by then increasingly fraught federal-provincial relationship, the discussion paper is a curious document, since it is not completely clear from the text which level of government Ottawa saw as being most likely to use these instruments. In a section headed "A National Partnership" the document says that "many of the measures that could be implemented would be the responsibility of provincial, territorial and municipal governments" (Government of Canada 2002a, 8). As examples, it pointed to instruments available to provincial governments, such as building codes and land-use policies respecting transportation, which are not available to the federal government, and said Ottawa was "seeking the input of provinces on how best to accomplish Canada's climate change goals" (Government of Canada 2002a, 6). On the other hand, there are repeated references to ways in which "the Government of Canada" would use the policy instrument being discussed. Another telling sign is the way in which the document relegates the provinces to the status of simply one stakeholder with whom Ottawa has an obligation to consult. For instance, it says any plan to achieve the Kyoto goal must be developed "in full consultation with provinces, territories, stakeholders and Canadians" (Government of Canada 2002a, 1). While ambiguous, the document is certainly not proposing a federal-provincial partnership, with clear discussion of the roles of each. It is much closer to a proposal for action to be taken by Ottawa, which may or may not be accompanied by provincial action. After the paper was published and immediately before it was discussed by federal and provincial ministers, David Anderson gave a much clearer indication of the federal position. Shawn McCarthy of the *Globe and Mail* reported it this way:

> Faced with opposition to the agreement among some provinces, Mr. Anderson said Ottawa may choose a plan that does not require provincial consent, although he conceded such a move would drive up the costs of implementation ... he rejected the suggestion that Ottawa could not proceed without the provinces. "We could and we may," he said. (2002)

One aspect of the federal discussion paper is relevant to both the West-East divide and the issue of allocation of cost. It is one of the few, and perhaps the only, publicly available document generated during the two 1990s climate processes to explicitly use cost allocation as the basis for decision-making. The paper says, "some approaches to achieving our climate change objectives could result in some regions of our country bearing differential burdens," goes on to refer to the "no unreasonable burden" principle, and then says "any workable plan must respect that condition" (Government of Canada 2002a, 6). In presenting the different options, the paper says that the first, a domestic emissions trading system would result in "significant economic impacts on some provinces ... [due to higher costs for] emissions-intensive industries such as oil sands and coal-fired electricity generation" (Government of Canada 2002a, 25). Although not named, obviously Alberta and Saskatchewan are the provinces in question. The paper says this violation of the "no unreasonable burden" principle must be considered when comparing the options.

Both the Alberta and federal documents were discussed at the JMM held in Charlottetown on 21 May 2002, but the Alberta request to have its paper, as well as the federal paper, included as a subject of discussion in the multi-stakeholder consultations planned for the summer was not approved. The news release issued after the meeting contained the words "Alberta does not agree with this communiqué" (JMM 2002a). While Saskatchewan, Ontario, and Nova Scotia expressed public support for the Alberta position, they signed the meeting communiqué; Quebec supported the federal position (Toulin 2002). In a press conference after the ministers' meeting, Alberta environment minister Lorne Taylor said his province was unhappy because the federal government was no longer exploring the feasibility of Kyoto, but instead moving towards its ratification, with dire consequences for his province. He said, "I think people are worried about another NEP ... well, quite frankly, if Kyoto goes through it will be" (Toulin 2002). The minister announced that Alberta was resigning as co-chair of the National Climate Change Secretariat but would continue to attend the federal-provincial meetings to press for its point of view. More significantly, he said that Alberta would develop its own climate-change plan, based on the discussion paper it had presented. Alberta did not formally opt out of the intergovernmental process, but by saying it would develop its own plan independent of the national process and so would not be bound by any future federal-provincial agreement generated by that process, it had effectively done just that. But then, the federal government was doing exactly the same thing, even though it too was not formally opting out. Without admitting it, both governments were swimming away in opposite directions from what had by then become a sinking ship.

Public consultations on the federal discussion paper were held in the summer, while on 2 August, at their annual meeting, provincial premiers requested that the prime minister convene a First Ministers' Meeting prior to ratifying Kyoto. On 24 October, after Chrétien's 2 September announcement that his government would ratify, the federal government released a draft plan for achieving the Kyoto goal. The environment and energy ministers met in Halifax on 28 October 2002. The communiqué issued after the meeting was headed "Provincial and Territorial Statement on Climate Change Policy" and contained this statement:

> The federal government has indicated that it intends to ratify the Kyoto Protocol before the end of this year. The federal framework on climate change, announced on October 28, does not as yet represent an adequate Canadian approach to reducing greenhouse gases in Canada. Provinces and Territories desire a national plan.

*The NWT reserves its position on the adequacy of the federal framework. (JMM 2002c)

The remainder of the statement reiterated the premiers' earlier request for an FMM and presented twelve principles which it was said should inform a national plan. These included the "no unreasonable burden" principle, respect for provincial and territorial jurisdiction, recognition of reductions already achieved, and ensuring that no province "bears the financial risk of federal climate change commitments" (JMM 2002c). No provinces were shown as not signing the communiqué. Nor yet is the federal government shown as not signing, but the heading makes clear it is a provinces-and-territories-only document.

On 21 November 2002, the federal government released the final iteration of its plan to achieve the Kyoto target. In the accompanying news release, the federal government said it was committed to working with the provinces and was in agreement with nine of the twelve 28 October principles (Government of Canada 2002c). Again, however, it presented the provinces as one stakeholder among others, by saying the plan is plan is built on "the best ideas to come out of ten years of consultations and collaboration with provinces, territories, industry, environmental groups, other stakeholders and Canadians" (Government of Canada 2002c). Unlike the May discussion paper, the plan clearly presented actions to be taken by the federal government alone, although it did include a "partnerships fund" by which Ottawa would contribute to the costs of provincial plans, plus actions by non-government actors (Government of Canada 2002b, 16–17). In the conclusion, the statement was made that the plan "meets our commitment that no region should bear an unreasonable burden" (Government of Canada 2002b, 55). Industrial emissions, which accounted for about half the Canadian total, would be directly regulated by Ottawa using "covenants and domestic emissions trading" (Government of Canada 2002b, 16–17). The term "covenant" was not defined, but as discussed it referred to an offer to a firm of a "voluntary" agreement, which, if the firm declined, would be replaced by a legally binding requirement to act, in the form of a law or monetary penalty. This choice of policy instrument, effectively federal regulation of firms that relied ultimately on the authority of federal law, was a form of federal unilateral action not previously seen since the national climate process began in 1990.

With full support from the Liberal backbench MPs and from environmentalists, and in the face of extremely vocal criticism from Alberta, Ontario, and other provinces, plus a concerted campaign by the oil industry and other sectors, Chrétien brought ratification to a vote in the House of Commons, even though one was not formally required, on 10 December 2002. On 17

December 2002, Canada filed its ratification papers with the United Nations. The next day in a public letter from the NRCan minister to CAPP, the federal government gave a promise to the oil industry that its reduction obligation would not be more than 15 per cent below business-as-usual projections and that its cost to comply with federal regulations would not exceed $15 a tonne. That promise was the result of private negotiations that had been going on since September between Ottawa, led by the top bureaucrat, the clerk of the privy council, with help from the Alberta minister Anne McLellan, and the industry (Munroe 2016, 61). As set out in chapter 3, over the next three years the Chrétien and Martin governments worked to negotiate covenants with the major GHG-emitting firms while, in the absence of any multilateral IGR process, negotiating bilateral agreements for shared funding of reduction projects with some provinces.

Since it was a pivotal event in the case study, we need to ask the question: Why did Prime Minister Chrétien, after leaving the question open until the summer of 2001 and not taking a definite position between that time and the 2 September 2002 announcement date, finally decide to ratify? Former *Globe and Mail* columnist Jeffrey Simpson, a shrewd observer of Ottawa politics for many years, provides with his co-authors a credible answer. Simpson points to three factors. The first is that it would again differentiate Canada from the US, something a Liberal government would desire, particularly since a Republican, George W. Bush, occupied the White House. It would be popular in his home province of Quebec. In addition, it would "form part of his legacy" in the same way as would other decisions such as making same-sex marriage legal and refusing to join the US invasion of Iraq (Simpson et al. 2007, 71).

As of the end of December 2002, what were the outcomes of the federal-provincial National Climate Change Process that had been launched at the April 1998 JMM with so much promise – with a new face, new Alberta co-chair, clear signs that province was ready to fully engage with other governments, and an implicit promise from Ottawa that it had learned from its mistake of unilaterally setting aside the Regina Kyoto position? For purposes of this discussion, three are considered most significant. The first and most important outcome, of course, was the end of the intergovernmental process. As discussed in the next section, there were many reasons for that, but at the first level of analysis it ended because the prime minister refused the provincial request to move the negotiations up from the level of ministers to first ministers. Instead, he unilaterally ratified Kyoto. Only the prime minister had the power to convene a gathering of first ministers; provincial premiers were not opting out but instead saying they wanted to continue the discussion at that higher level and the prime minister refused. Undoubtedly he saw the

request for a FMM as yet another tactic to delay ratification, as were all the
business and provincial statements that a more adequate plan had to be in
place before Kyoto could be ratified (which might have taken years and still
not have received a stamp of "adequate" from CAPP or Alberta), but the fact
remains that it was the prime minister who bears responsibility for the fact
the intergovernmental process ended rather than move into a new venue. As
for ratification, research interviews show that federal officials knew it would
effectively kill the JMM, but proceeded nevertheless (Macdonald et al. 2013,
54). The process ended because of decisions made by Ottawa.

The second case outcome was Alberta's disengagement from Canadian
climate-change policy. In October 2002, the Alberta government released its
climate-change plan, based upon its earlier discussion paper, with the target
it had proposed for Canada as a whole taken as the new Alberta target. As
discussed, that target was not a reduction of emissions to be 6 per cent below
the 1990 level by 2012, or any other fixed amount, but instead a reduction in
emissions *intensity* to be 50 per cent below the 1990 intensity level by 2020.
While an intensity target if met does generate a given quantum of reduction,
the fact remains that an intensity target can also be met while total emissions, along with total production, are rising. Thus the Alberta plan differed
from the Canadian Kyoto commitment both in terms of the absence of an
absolute target such as the Kyoto limit of 576 Mt (table 1) for total Canadian
emissions and the deadline as 2020 instead of 2012. Alberta climate policy
has continued on a separate path ever since. As discussed in chapter 4, the
Canadian Paris target is a reduction in emissions, while Alberta in 2017
forecast that its emissions would increase. The different paths being taken
by Alberta and Canada have their origins in the events that led Alberta to
resign its co-chairmanship in May 2002.

While embarking on its own policy path, Alberta also sought to shield its
industries from federal regulation. In November 2002, the Alberta government
tabled in the provincial legislature the Climate Change and Emissions Management Act. A newspaper report explained the Alberta motive.

> The Alberta government just introduced legislation to constitutionally protect
> the provincial economy ... The legislation would place greenhouse gas emissions
> within the provincial rather than federal jurisdiction, enabling industries to ignore
> federal global warming regulations. Alberta Environment spokeswoman Val
> Mellesmoen acknowledges, "This doesn't necessarily make us bullet-proof from a
> court challenge, but it might make the feds think." (Stock, 2002)

In the event, Alberta never did go to court (or at least not until many years
later), perhaps because federal attempts to regulate Alberta industries under
the Martin government never came close enough to fruition to represent

a sufficiently significant threat and were then abandoned by the Harper government when it took power in early February 2006. In 2018, both Saskatchewan and Ontario initiated court action in an attempt to prevent the federal backstop carbon tax being applied within their borders. Alberta under the Jason Kenney government joined them in taking legal action in 2019. The second case outcome is both the separate Alberta policy path and the first step towards provincial legal action to test federal climate regulation powers.

The third significant outcome of the case study was that by the end of 2002 Ottawa had decided that it would achieve the Kyoto target by itself, using its own policy instruments, regardless of what the provinces did. In its 2000 "contribution" to the federal-provincial effort, Ottawa promised to take responsibility for one-third of the reduction effort. Two years later it implicitly said it would pick up the other two-thirds if necessary: the Chrétien government had said it would only ratify if a viable plan were in place; given provincial hostility and the break-down of the federal-provincial working relationship, the only thing that could make the plan viable was a guarantee of federal policy action sufficient to achieve the Kyoto goal, even if the provinces did nothing. Thus the 21 November 2002 federal plan, despite its talk of contributions by provinces, municipalities, and others, represented that basic promise – if need be, Ottawa would do it all, alone. As set out in chapter 1, a central premise of the argument running through this book is that Canada cannot achieve its international commitment by Government of Canada action alone – the provinces, allied with industry, will never accept that and have sufficient political power to stop it. Events since 2002 do not fully confirm or refute that hypothesis, since as discussed in chapter 3, climate policymaking by the Martin government was cut short by its defeat in the House of Commons at the end of 2005. The fact remains, however, that between 2003 and 2005 we did not see a dramatic increase in the efficacy of federal policy, once it was disentangled from the federal-provincial process. As discussed in chapter 9, intense provincial hostility to the federal carbon tax in 2018 and 2019 came closer to provide support for the hypothesis.

Ottawa's decision in 2002 to abandon the federal-provincial process left Canada's ability to reduce GHG emissions badly weakened. There were two sources of weakness. First, for the next three years Ottawa was attempting the daunting task of developing individualized reduction requirements for some 800 firms and in consequence, not surprisingly, making slow progress on its central policy thrust of regulating industrial emissions. After three years, no requirements to reduce emissions had been imposed upon any firms. Had the Martin government not fallen in 2005, perhaps it might have succeeded in that task since, as noted above, by that time regulations had been published in the *Canada Gazette*. The fact that it took three years of effort just to get to the starting line without yet running down the track, however, suggests that it also might not have succeeded. We might have seen another three years of delay, or have seen regulations with no significant enforcement effort and thus little effect, while the value of that effect is lessened by the fact that industrial emissions represented only half of the policy challenge. Secondly, Ottawa no longer had available one of the most valuable instruments in its tool kit: a formal, institutionalized federal-provincial process that gave Ottawa at least some levers to influence provincial behaviour. Understandably, by the winter of 2001–2 the Chrétien government had come to see that process not as an opportunity, but as part of the problem. It saw itself as bogged down in a process that served only to help the provinces delay significant action and so felt it had to break free. The price for breaking free, however, was loss of the NCCP system to induce provincial action. As discussed in chapter 3, the Martin government did use bilateral agreements for federal financial support to influence provincial policy but not all provinces signed, whereas prior to the fall of 2002 all provinces, no matter how recalcitrant, were at least part of a formal system led by Ottawa and so susceptible to federal diplomacy exercised within that system.

Analysis

1) What Does the Case Tell Us about the Four Subjects?

THE WEST-EAST DIVIDE
The previous two cases showed that the major characteristic of the divide is that the fossil fuel provinces, and in particular Alberta, because they have so much at stake, are motivated to fully engage with national energy or climate-change processes. They also showed the divide is not necessarily symmetrical; western engagement may not be matched by that of other governments. This case reinforces the latter lesson. Quebec may have felt that policy favouring western industries would impose corresponding costs upon its industry, since it was a fixed quantity of emission reduction that had to be implemented, but Ontario apparently had no such concerns. Instead, Ontario throughout the case was largely allied with Alberta, presumably because of the ideological similarity of the Klein and Harris governments. Finally, *all* provinces, not just the western ones, opposed ratification at the 28 October 2002 JMM. The case does not show west-east conflict as was seen in the 1970s and early 1980s, but instead shows, like climate policy from 1990 to 1997, a motivated west that did not encounter equally motivated eastern opposition from provinces or Ottawa.

However, Alberta did effectively leave the process in 2002. Does that contradict the lesson respecting western engagement stated above? Two points can be made. First, Alberta did not leave the formal process; it stayed to ensure it would still have a voice there, even as it embarked on its own unilateral policy. Secondly, Alberta's effective withdrawal was more a case of being pushed out by Ottawa than a voluntary decision. Alberta did not leave in December 1997 because it was given substantial gains by the federal and other provincial premiers – as discussed at the conclusion of the previous case, confirmation by the FMM of the principle that no region would be asked to bear an unreasonable burden, the FMM decision to study rather than implement, and, third, a guaranteed provincial voice. All those served Alberta and western interests and demonstrated the considerable influence on the national process being exerted by the west. Nothing like that was on offer from Ottawa this time. Instead, Alberta saw Ottawa getting ready to ratify and start taking unilateral policy action. Thus the different Alberta decisions – stay in 1997, effectively leave in 2002 – are explained more than anything else by the different Ottawa positions and in particular by the flawed federal strategy, discussed below. Instead of engaging with Alberta, through threat and promise, Ottawa turned a cold shoulder. The case shows that in any future climate process Alberta will likely engage, as it did in 1998, and may very well stay engaged, even to the point of making some change in its climate policy, if Ottawa diplomacy is sufficiently adroit.

THE INHERENT NEED TO ALLOCATE REDUCTIONS
The case shows us that the need for perceived fairness in cost allocation is a potentially significant issue recognized by all governments, and one they will act on when pushed, as shown by the JMM decision to create the EABWG after Quebec complained. Beyond that, the Quebec action shows that the allocation issue is likely to be raised by the actor seeing itself as the victim, not the beneficiary, of an unfolding allocation and that the victim will frame the issue, not surprisingly, in a discourse of fairness. The implications of the latter point, such as the difficulty in reaching agreement among self-interested actors upon equity principles and the importance of the process for perceptions of distributive justice, have been previously discussed.

However, the issue was *not* raised by the western provinces as a principal reason for opposing ratification, despite their higher per capita reduction costs. Premier Klein simply spoke about the damage that would be done to his economy, without going on to say Alberta was receiving an unfair portion of the total damage. Like the preceding case, the lesson we can take from western silence on the issue is that the inherent need to allocate will not be a significant factor when there is no immediate plan to reduce total emissions by a given quantity – until 2 September 2002, it was not even clear whether Canada would ratify Kyoto. After that, Alberta worked with the oil industry in a last-ditch fight to prevent ratification while preparing court action to fend off federal regulation. Alberta was fighting to prevent *any* reduction of its emissions, not a reduction that it saw as an unfair portion of the total. It seems likely, though, that should Canada ever get to the point of implementing a total reduction in the short-term, provinces with greater carbon intensity and higher per capita costs will raise the allocation issue.

THE NATIONAL PROCESS

The lesson to be taken from this case is that the intergovernmental process used from 1998 to 2002 is not a model for any future national effort. Ministers should not be the ones asked to lead any future federal-provincial climate-change policymaking and nor should any future effort be based on uncertain and conflicting ideas respecting the objective. In this case, some such as Alberta believed the objective was only to study, while others such as Environment Canada believed it was to study and then implement. In future, all must agree upon the objective at the outset. Finally, this case shows us that a national process requires consistent, committed federal leadership if it is not to end in failure.

FEDERAL GOVERNMENT STRATEGY

As stated above, the lesson here is in what the federal government should not do. Ottawa made a good decision by agreeing to make Alberta co-chair of the National Secretariat, since this seemed to indicate the federal government was ready to fully engage with its major opponent. However, that engagement never materialized. Most particularly, the Chrétien government failed to use its planned unilateral action as a threat to increase its bargaining power. There is no indication in the public record or confidential interviews that it ever said, during the winter of 2001–2, that it wanted to move to more coercive policy instruments than the voluntary action of the VCR, hoped provinces would begin to consider use of such instruments, and, if they did not, would start to use them itself. Instead, it seems federal officials simply gave up on both the VCR and the national process and decided they would act themselves. Surely that represents a wasted opportunity. If you are willing to alienate the provinces by talking about use of federal law, why not first use that talk to try to get them to budge a bit?

The larger failure of federal strategy related to its use of unilateral action has to do with the ratification decision. Here, the problem is not only failure to use that possible action as a threat to gain something from the provinces, but also failure to delay as long as possible action it knew had the potential to cause irreparable damage to the intergovernmental process and then, when it could not be delayed any longer, to take steps to reduce the collateral damage. Former prime minister

Chrétien has stated that by the summer of 2002 "precious time was passing and the [Kyoto] target deadline was drawing nearer" (2007, 387). For that reason, he implies, the decision had to be made then and he decided to ratify while flying to the Johannesburg summit, where he made the announcement on 2 September 2002 (Chrétien 2007, 388). He may have felt an urgency at the time, but, at least with the advantage of hindsight, it seems there was no absolute need to ratify in 2002. At that point, the Kyoto target was still ten years away. Furthermore, Russia did not ratify until November 2004, which provided the necessary fifty-five countries representing 55 per cent of global emissions that allowed the protocol to come into legal effect in February 2005. Canada could have waited at least until the summer of 2004 to ratify without impairing the viability of the international regime. Throughout the case study period, it was the ratification decision, which was still very much up in the air until mid-2001, that was the potentially explosive event. A federal government working to achieve the goals of both ratification and a viable national process generating effective policy would have done everything necessary to prepare the provinces, industry, and the Canadian public for ratification, bringing them along step by step and giving itself the time needed to do that. At the end of the day, it is unlikely the Alberta government would have ever embraced ratification. But with more careful preparation, including bargaining, which gave Alberta something in exchange for its acquiescence, ratification might not have been the final nail in the coffin of the NCCP.

The counter-argument to the claim made above is that while the international situation may not have required Kyoto ratification before the end of 2002, the prime minister personally did require it, since he was being forced out of office by the Paul Martin Liberals. He was the only one who could make the decision and he personally wanted ratification to embellish his legacy. Knowing he had only limited time left, the counter-argument goes, it is unrealistic to say Canada could have ratified in late 2003 or 2004. Two points can be made in response. The first is the fact that on 22 August 2002, Chrétien announced he would retire at the end of the current term, in February 2004. That date might have seemed to him less viable by December, but he did have at least some time available. The second, stronger, point is that Chrétien had available the option of *not* ratifying before he left office, leaving the decision to Martin and foregoing the legacy gain, in order to avoid doing damage to the federal-provincial process. The personal desires of the prime minister may explain why ratification happened when it did, but they do not mean that was the only option available to the Government of Canada.

By sending signals in the winter of 2001–2 that it was moving towards both ratification and unilateral policymaking, and then doing both in a very short time period and in an abrupt manner, the Chrétien government drove Alberta out of the NCCP and started the process for dissolution of the national effort. Had it done more to lay the groundwork for ratification, while delaying setting off that particular explosion for as long as possible, while at the same time only talking about unilateral policy in terms of a last resort threat, to be used only if provinces absolutely refused to consider use of more coercive instruments, we might have seen very different case study outcomes. That would only have been possible, however, if Ottawa strategy had been more consistently managed throughout by the PMO and the prime minister himself.

One of the problems with the Chrétien government's climate-change policy was the erratic behaviour of the prime minister. As was his management style, for the most part he left the issue in the hand of his ministers, to the point of tolerating the considerable discord between Environment Canada and NRCan (Simpson et al. 2007, 75). When required to do so by events such as the pending third UNFCCC conference of parties in Kyoto, he naturally enough, and rightly, reached into the process and took personal charge. Perhaps because of his previous benign neglect, when he did so, however, the result was sudden jumps in decisions made, as witnessed in December 1997 when he moved from the stabilization goal to minus 3 per cent and then to 6 per cent and from a commitment to act, honourably given to other countries, to instead agreeing to study that commitment to see if in fact it would be kept. The decision to move to unilateral federal policy, first signalled at the 25 February 2002 JMM, was a less abrupt change but far more could have been done both to prepare the provinces for it and, more important, to use the threat of such action to move the national process towards more effective policy. Another sudden jump was the ratification announcement on 2 September 2002, because it surprised everybody.

> Chrétien's closest advisors did not know his intentions when the prime minister departed ... for Johannesburg ... The Prime Minister's Office even issued a statement that no announcement would be made at Johannesburg. There, however, Chretién announced that Canada would indeed ratify Kyoto. (Simpson et al. 2007, 71–2)

Making a sudden jump from the position that ratification is likely but not yet decided to a done deal, without advance warning, is not a good means of minimizing the effects of the decision. A phone call the day before to Premier Klein and some other key premiers would have helped. Beyond that, more consistent engagement of the prime minister throughout might have produced more consistent, predictable federal policy. Simpson and his co-authors (2007, 77), noting that Chrétien "intervened intermittently on the file" and devoted little political capital to the issue make essentially the same point.

What this case tells us about federal leadership is that three things are needed from Ottawa: motivation, giving the issue higher priority than was done here; the prime minister's engagement throughout, rather than jumping in and out of the issue as was done here; and consistency – no surprises!

2) What Are the Most Important Factors Explaining the Case Outcome?

As stated above, the three case outcomes were collapse of the federal-provincial process, the Alberta decision to pursue a separate policy path while shielding itself from federal regulation, and the decision by the Government of Canada to take the whole reduction challenge onto its own shoulders. Since the IGR process did function for five years and generated two joint action plans, it cannot be said there was absolutely no coordination among governments (as was the case in the Harper years). However, there was no significant coordination. Accordingly, the case is placed in the "minimal coordination" category.

How do we explain these outcomes? Like the previous case, the explanation lies in the fact that Alberta veto-government influence went unchecked by Ottawa. As we have seen, Alberta was fully engaged with the process from 1998, not playing a full veto role as long as activity was limited to study and then, after that, to developing plans based primarily upon voluntary action. (During this time, Ontario was the major veto government.) It was only when Ottawa started to send signals in the winter of 2001–2 that it was considering use of more effective policy instruments that Alberta began to exert veto influence, seeking to block that federal initiative. When that failed, Alberta quietly slipped away from the process to follow its own path, even while formally staying a member of the NCCP.

Ottawa was unable to exert countervailing power due to its faulty strategy (or lack of strategy). The process collapsed because Ottawa developed plans to play a unilateral regulatory role, but did so in an inept way. In particular, the federal government made a mistake by moving to develop its own regulatory regime, which was first expressed in the discussion paper issued in May 2002, without any attempt to first gain benefit from it in the form of a threat used to influence provincial behaviour. There may have been private discussions with provincial officials, but there certainly were no public statements that unless the provinces took certain actions Ottawa would itself begin to directly regulate their sources. Since Ottawa was moving in that direction anyway, it would have been very easy to at least send that signal prior to making the final decision. In the same way, Kyoto ratification simply happened, surprising everybody, with no prior attempt to use it as a threat to influence provincial behaviour. At the end, Ottawa abandoned its lead-government role, effectively leaving the federal-provincial process and embarking on its own unilateral regulation.

Like the previous case, the national climate effort from 1998 to 2002 was able to generate only minimal policy coordination because the influence of veto governments, Ontario and Alberta, went unchecked. That was because Ottawa was not consistently motivated and engaged, did not engage in skillful diplomacy, and did not attempt to exercise power by using unilateral action as a means of influencing provincial behaviour.

8 The Canadian Energy Strategy, 2005–2015

Case Summary

A lead government (Alberta) was strongly motivated by material interest and by a desire for legitimacy in the eyes of Canadians and others. The oil industry had the same interests. The only veto-government resistance, from British Columbia, was overcome by lead-government persuasion and the promise of possible industry money. However, while encountering little resistance, as a province the lead government had limited power to influence the behaviour of other governments; it could not use promise or threat to induce other provincial governments to commit to specific policy changes, or the federal government to participate. The result was minimal policy coordination.

START AND END DATES: 2005–17 July 2015

MAJOR POLICY DECISIONS

unilateral	• after being briefly involved, the federal government opts out of the process in 2012
	• the federal government amends a number of its laws in ways which favour industry regulatory approvals and reduce environmental protection, March 2012
	• British Columbia decides it will not participate in the CES process, summer 2012
bilateral	• British Columbia and Alberta sign an agreement on pipelines going from Alberta to the west coast on 5 November 2013, leading British Columbia to join the CES process

multilateral	• provinces and territories, other than British Columbia and Quebec, at the Council of the Federation meeting 26–7 July 2012, formally launch the CES process
	• provinces and territories release the CES at the Council of the Federation meeting 17 July 2015

CASE OUTCOME

By signing the CES document, provinces and territories agreed on a set of actions they *could* take together to increase economic return from Canadian energy and to reduce associated environmental impacts, but no provincial or territorial government had made a commitment to do anything specific.

COORDINATION CATEGORY: minimal coordination

The Canadian Energy Strategy (CES) was developed by the provinces and territories, working through the Council of the Federation, over the ten-year period of 2005 to 2015. Between 2005 and 2007, the Council developed the document *A Shared Vision for Energy in Canada* (Council of the Federation 2007). The same year it was released, non-state actors started to advocate a national energy strategy, and in 2012 the council decided it would generate a second iteration of that document, which was finalized and released in 2015, titled *Canadian Energy Strategy* (Council of the Federation 2015a). The CES is unique among the five cases examined. Like the NEP case, the subject is again national energy policy (this time with a heavy dose of climate-change politics) but while in the first energy case the federal government was the instigator and lead actor, Ottawa played almost no direct role in the CES (but did unilaterally take significant related action by responding to what the oil industry claimed had to be a significant part of any national energy strategy – "regulatory reform" – when in 2012 it amended the Fisheries Act, the Canadian Environmental Assessment Act, and other federal laws to ease the path of regulatory approvals for resource development). Beyond this differing federal role, the NEP process was almost all bilateral, principally in terms of Ottawa-Alberta negotiations, while the CES was multilateral throughout, at least in terms of the provinces and territories, with the significant exception of the bilateral Alberta-British Columbia negotiations, which led the latter province to join the CES process that it had initially boycotted. Another difference from the earlier energy case is that while the oil industry was a marginal actor in the NEP, it was very much at the centre of the action in the CES, both in the early stages of putting the perceived need for a national energy strategy on the public policy agenda and by successfully lobbying for the federal deregulatory action referred to above.

This case also differs from the others in that each of those started with a clear understanding of the problem being addressed for which coordinated federal-provincial policy would provide a solution – spiking world oil prices imposing escalating costs on eastern imported oil and, in the other three cases, climate change. Even when that understanding was at its weakest, in the early 1990s when the climate science was still being disputed, everybody knew the national effort existed because of the prior existence of a claimed environmental problem. In the case of the CES, however, it is difficult to know what problem was being addressed. The CES document repeatedly claims benefits will flow from improved coordination of energy policies but never once says specifically how a current *lack* of coordination is causing problems that must be addressed by an agreed national strategy (Council of the Federation 2015a).

As can be seen from the intertwining story lines of the narrative which follows, instead of addressing one overriding problem, the CES seems to address a number of different problems, each of them a problem for a different participating actor. Most prominent was the problem shared by both the oil industry and the governments of the producing provinces, most notably Alberta – the need for new pipelines. Two things were required. The first, discussed briefly on pages 86 and 92, was a simple increase in total pipeline capacity available to take oil sands bitumen to markets, because government and industry believed that without it lack of capacity would become a constraining factor on future oil sands development. The second, also discussed on those pages, was the need for "market diversification," the term used to refer to additional pipeline access to the Canadian west or east coasts, since oil shipped by pipeline to the US and sold in markets there was receiving a lower price than it would if it were transported from one or other coast by ship to Asian or other markets. Part and parcel of the pipeline problem was the fact that the existing approvals regime was seen by industry as one that took too long, imposed far too many uncertainties and whose standards were tilted far too much towards the side of environmental protection. For reasons that are not completely clear, but likely had to do with fears that naked self-interest would be too glaringly revealed, the industry and government actors pointing to these problems did not simply call for new pipelines and deregulation. Instead, they called for a new national energy strategy (the term "national" was eventually dropped, both because it evoked Alberta memories of the dreaded NEP and perhaps also because of long-standing Quebec aversion to use of the term for anything other than its own institutions and buildings), which would not only apply to fossil fuels, but to *all* energy sources and would not only be about the west but about *all* parts of the country. All parts of the country would benefit and so all should participate.

If the industry and Alberta motivations were clear, what led the other, non-fossil-fuel provinces to participate? Presumably it was in part because they saw increased coordination as helping them gain economic benefit from their own energy sources, be it export of hydro-electricity or Ontario's interest in developing a new renewable energy industry. Another motivating factor, particularly for Ontario and Quebec, was in part a genuine desire to see increased Canadian action on climate change. The Alberta push for a national energy strategy gave them bargaining leverage that they could use to be sure such a strategy included action on the climate problem (which led to compromise bargaining as the CES was finalized in the summer of 2015). Such a strategy had been made possible by a new attitude on the part of the Alberta government, particularly under Premiers Redford (2011 to 2014) and Prentice (fall 2014 to May 2015; Rachel Notley was premier at the time of the finalization and release of the CES in early August 2015). As has been seen, under Ralph Klein's leadership Alberta questioned the need for any climate action and resisted national policy. Redford and Prentice, on the other hand, had lived through the campaign by environmentalists to portray the product of the oil sands as "dirty oil" – a stain on the Canadian self-image. They knew that if their province wanted to continue to reap the oil sands benefit, they had to counter that image, in the first instance by adopting a less confrontational stance and accepting the need to discuss both energy and climate as part of the same policy package. (As discussed in the next case study, it was NDP Premier Notley who then carried that process of legitimation into the realm of action by putting a price on carbon).

And the environmentalists – what problem did they have for which such a strategy might be a solution and so induced them to participate as partners with industry in the October 2009 Winnipeg and April 2010 Banff declarations calling for a new national strategy? It should immediately be pointed out that many of the front-line Canadian ENGOs, such as Greenpeace and the David Suzuki Foundation, were not participants. (However, they, with their allies in the US environmental movement, played a crucial role in bringing the CES into being, both through the "dirty oil" campaign and the efforts to landlock oil sands oil by mobilizing local opposition to new pipeline capacity, most notably Keystone XL but also new pipelines to the British Columbia coast. To some extent, it was the environmentalists who created the problems for which, in the eyes of industry and Alberta, a national energy strategy was the solution.) Some environmentalists, on the other hand, did directly participate, at least in the early stages. Three of the eleven think tanks that participated in the October 2009 Winnipeg meeting were more on the side of environmental protection than of economic development – the International Institute for Sustainable Development (IISD), the National Round Table on the Environment and Economy (NRTEE), and the Pembina Institute (Winnipeg Consensus n.d.). Their motivation can be inferred from the explanation of the purpose of the Winnipeg meeting set out in the document there generated:

> The intent of the Winnipeg meeting was never to craft detailed positions or to claim an exclusive role in energy policy leadership. Rather it was to explore ways to overcome policy fragmentation and pursue the opportunities that are emerging at the intersection of clean technology, infrastructure, climate change and investment in a "green" economy. (Winnipeg Consensus n.d., 2)

Four things were said to be intersecting. One, infrastructure, might refer to new pipelines and so favour wealth creation over environment. The other three, however, were on the side of the angels. It seems reasonable to suppose the three think tanks saw an opportunity to advance the environmental agenda – business was willing to engage in a dialogue and by the 2000s any such dialogue could not be solely about economic return from energy sales, but had to include measures to reduce environmental impacts. When the concept of sustainable development had emerged in the late 1980s and was being enthusiastically adopted by business, the more radical ENGOs had stayed well away. The mainstream environmental movement, however, sensing an opportunity because of that business acceptance, had readily entered into dialogue with business and government on how the concept could be implemented (Macdonald 2010). In the same way, it is likely these mainstream environmental think tanks also saw in the concept of a national energy strategy a strategic opportunity to advance the cause of Canadian action on climate change.

And the federal government – what problem did it see which led it to participate, through the federal-provincial body the Energy and Mines Ministers' Conference (EMMC) in 2010 and 2011? More importantly, how did that perception evolve so that by the following year it was pouring cold water on the idea, saying that if the provinces wanted to waste their time and effort they should go ahead but it planned to stick to its watertight compartment (which included unilateral action on one of industry's main proposals)? Given what we know about the economic agenda of the Harper government, including its Responsible Resource Development policy and its unabashed support for Northern Gateway long before the National Energy Board could rule on the application, it is clear that government's view was closely aligned with that of the oil industry and western provinces. It seems however, that after putting a toe in the water it decided it could achieve the goal shared by those governments and industry by means of its own unilateral actions, with no need for the messy, entangling business of working with provinces and their conflicting interests.

What Is the Canadian Energy Strategy?

Before telling the story of the coming into being of the CES, there is value in explaining exactly what it is and, just as important, what it is not. The 2015 Canadian Energy Strategy is set out in a document (Council of the Federation 2015a) of thirty-six pages, written in a non-technical style, making it clear that the audience is the Canadian public and not policy or energy technology experts. The document provides introductory discussion and then sets out visions, objectives, and principles. The bulk of the document is then organized by means of the three subject areas listed in table 7: 1) sustainability and conservation; 2) technology and innovation; and, 3) delivering energy to people.

7 Canadian Energy Strategy subjects and areas of focus

Sustainability and conservation

1. *Promote energy efficiency and conservation.*
2. Transition to a lower carbon economy.
3. Enhance energy information and awareness.

Technology and innovation

4. *Accelerate the development and deployment of energy research and technologies that advance more efficient production, transmission, and use of clean and conventional energy sources.*
5. *Develop and implement strategies that meet energy sector human resource needs now and well into the twenty-first century.*
6. *Facilitate the development of renewable, green and/or cleaner energy sources to meet future demand and contribute to environmental goals and priorities.*

Delivering energy to people

7. *Develop and enhance a modern, reliable, environmentally safe and efficient series of transmission and transportation networks for domestic and export/ import sources of energy.*
8. *Improve the timeliness and certainty of regulatory approval decision-making processes while maintaining rigorous protection of the environment and public interest.*
9. Promote market diversification.
10. *Pursue formalized participation of provinces and territories in international discussions and negotiations on energy.*

Source: Council of the Federation 2015a, 9. All words in table 7 are identical to those in the CES document. The seven areas of focus in italics are identical to the seven "action points" in the 2007 document *A Shared Vision for Energy in Canada* (Council of the Federation 2007).

Each of those three subjects is subdivided into three or four sub-topics, labelled "areas of focus." The ten areas of focus in the document are listed in table 7. Within the CES document, under each area of focus three or four goals are listed and under each goal is listed one or more actions that if taken would help achieve that goal. A total of fifty possible actions are listed. An example of one such action is provided below.

Sustainability and Conservation
　Area of focus #1 Promote energy efficiency and conservation
　　Goal 1.1 Strengthen Canadians' understanding of the benefits of energy efficiency and conservation.

Action 1.1.1 Expand consumer access to reliable and meaningful energy use information that supports informed decision-making, influences behavioral [sic] change, and builds awareness of the benefits of energy conservation.

The 2007 document was based on three themes of security of energy supply, maximizing economic benefit and reducing environmental harms (Council of the Federation 2007). The same three are referred to in the 2015 strategy: "The strategy is based on collaboration among provinces and territories to shape an energy future that provides energy security, contributes to economic growth and prosperity, and embodies a high standard of environmental and social responsibility" (Council of the Federation 2015a, 4). However, as can be seen in table 7, three different themes (subjects) are used to organize the 2015 document. What stands out is the addition of "delivering energy to people." The two main goals of the oil industry and Alberta, changes to the regulatory approvals process and market diversification, are listed as areas of focus eight and nine under that heading.

While the subject matter was thus changed significantly, in other respects the 2015 document remains remarkably true to the 2007 original. Seven of the ten "areas of focus" (the ones shown in italics in table 7) are verbatim, word for word identical with the seven "action points" in the 2007 document (Council of the Federation 2015a; Council of the Federation 2007). What are we to make of the three new areas of focus that have been added? With respect to the third ("Enhance energy information and awareness") it is not clear what had changed between 2007 and 2015 to warrant adding that new area of focus. The reasons for adding the other two, however, are much clearer. The second addition is number two, "Transition to a lower carbon economy." Two of the actions listed under that heading are relatively benign (review emissions reporting requirements and increase use of market instruments) and, as is the case for many of the possible actions listed, unlikely to raise any eyebrows. The third, Action 2.3.1, is, however, in a different category and as such is worth reproducing in full.

Collaborate on the development of options for an integrated pan-Canadian and North American approach to greenhouse gas reductions. Any such approach should be built on initiatives introduced by governments and aimed to enhance jurisdictions' ability to flexibly implement ambitious measures for reducing greenhouse gas emissions. The approach should also take into account possible impacts on competitiveness. (Council of the Federation 2015a, 17)

Remarkably enough, the provinces are saying here they are willing to consider entering into another national climate-change policy process, possibly including US or Mexican participation, despite the failure of the 1998–2002 NCCP and despite the fact that the current federal government, led by Prime Minister Harper, had made it abundantly clear it would not be leading any such effort. Nobody from Ottawa was pushing them to make this commitment. As discussed later in this chapter, this wording did not appear in a leaked draft of the document and so must have been added in the final negotiations over the text, presumably at the behest of Ontario and Quebec. By then, Rachel Notley's NDP government was in power in Alberta and signalling that it was going to take action such as pricing carbon, which presumably meant Alberta opposition to participation in another national effort had been reduced. In Saskatchewan, however, Brad Wall's right-wing government was still in power and a year later Premier Wall refused to sign on to the Pan-Canadian program. Why, then, did he sign this document? Perhaps in part it was because the agreement to participate was immediately hedged with caveats. The provinces did not quite say they would participate in a national effort, but instead develop options for doing so. The national effort would be "built upon" (which can be read as "consist only of") actions taken by the provinces, with nothing imposed by Ottawa. Provinces were guaranteed flexibility, a term which can be read as maximizing provincial autonomy within a national effort. And, as always, the national effort would be balanced, since it would give due regard to economic costs associated with competitiveness. Finally, as is the case for all other action items listed in the CES, this is a *possible* action only, something provinces might do, not something they had committed to do.

While these qualifications of the commitment may help to explain its inclusion in the document, another factor is almost certainly responsible for the third new area of focus, number nine, "Promote market diversification." The second goal under that heading is to "build social license to support the efficient movement of energy products, technologies, and services across Canada" (Council of the Federation 2015a, 31). In effect, all the provinces, including Quebec, in which by the summer of 2015 local opposition to the Energy East proposal was in evidence, had signed up to mobilize public opinion in support of new pipelines. Market diversification was what the industry and Alberta had always wanted to see in any new national energy strategy, and lo and behold, there it was, speaking in guarded, coded language (as discussed below an earlier draft spoke more directly about the need for new pipelines) but there nevertheless. These two changes to the 2007 document reflect the two changes in the political dialogue during the subsequent eight years – an increased interest in acting on climate change and an increased demand to build new pipelines.

Moving from the specific subject matter of the 2015 document to its general tenor, three things stand out. The first is that it reads as a very odd document indeed because it provides almost no discussion of the problems being addressed. This means the solutions – actions Canadian provinces might take together – seem to appear out of thin air. As noted, there is no discussion of the nature of the problem posed by a lack of coordination. Nor is there discussion of the problems that led the provinces to adoption of particular goals and possible actions to achieve them. For instance, one goal, set out above, is to "build social license." However, the lack of social license, in terms of the many campaigns against Northern Gateway and other pipeline proposals, litigation by Aboriginal and other actors, or the intense questioning of the role of the National Energy Board, is never mentioned. More broadly, the post-2007 energy problems that gave rise to the new themes, and in particular money lost each year because oil could only be sold in the US, are not mentioned at all. Secondly, there is a high level of generalization and lack of precision throughout. The goals listed are reasonably specific, but in the actions there is no discussion of *how* such things might be done – who might take which particular steps, by when, and in which order of sequence. Of course, as discussed in chapter 2, that kind of ambiguity is the norm in Canadian intergovernmental agreements. Governments wishing to be sure they were not committed to any particular action by signing the CES would stay well away from such specifics.

All of this leads to the question posed above: What is the CES and, just as important, what is it not? It is, first, by means of its subject headings and actions a picture of the way the provinces saw the integrated policy fields of energy and climate in 2015, with at its heart the basic contradiction between reducing emissions and building new pipelines. Secondly, as noted, it is a list of possible actions governments might take together if so motivated. What it is not is a list of commitments to action made by the signing governments.

A province such as Saskatchewan, deciding whether to stay in the process or bail out, has its choice made easier by the fact that staying in does not actually require it to do anything at all. Perhaps that has to be seen as a necessary price paid in order to reach agreement, similar to the 1995 NAPCC, which relied completely upon voluntary action. Does that mean the document is meaningless? Far from it, because by signing it provinces *were* acting. They were sending a message to their voters and other Canadians respecting what they saw as legitimate goals for Canadian energy and climate policy. Each province was saying that the western producing provinces had a right to work to expand their fossil fuel export markets, with all that means for domestic emissions within Canada and global emissions once those exported fuels are burned. However, each province, including those exporting fossil fuels, was also saying that national action to reduce emissions was a legitimate Canadian goal. Thus the document straddled the West-East divide, just as the Trudeau Liberal government did the next year as it led the Pan-Canadian process. Rather than seeing the 2015 Canadian Energy Strategy as meaningless, we need to see it as a significant achievement simply because it exists all – multilateral agreement is possible, albeit at the price of effective policy. We now turn to the story of how it came into existence.

Narrative

The 2015 Canadian Energy Strategy came into being because a number of actors in the late 2000s, most notably business associations and think tanks working in the area of environment, were calling upon governments to develop a national energy strategy. In November 2007 the Canada West Foundation released the report *Getting It Right: A Canadian Energy Strategy for a Carbon-Constrained Future*, which started with this premise: "The emerging Canadian policy debate on climate change will inevitably and quickly slide into a debate on national energy strategy, for energy and climate change are two sides of the same public policy coin" (Gibbins 2007, 1). Prof. Roger Gibbins, head of the Foundation and author of the report, argued that western Canadian actors should play a leading role in shaping this inevitable energy and climate policy debate, since they are the ones with the most at stake in any discussion of energy. The report noted the basic problem of differing regional interests respecting energy and also the issue of the need to allocate the cost of GHG emissions reduction. The latter, however, was addressed from a distinctly western perspective when the report warned against any efforts to let wealth redistribution enter the energy and climate policy debate by means of a national climate-change policy in which Albertans "bear the bulk of the cost" because they are responsible for a "disproportionate share" of total emissions and are also a rich province that "can afford the remediation" (Gibbins 2007, 3). Instead, the report argued, as it set out a number of principles which it felt should guide the upcoming debate, the cost should be spread across sectors and regions and include both upstream producers of energy and downstream users.

One of the western actors responding to this call was the oil industry. The strategy used was creation of a new business association, the Energy Policy Institute of Canada (EPIC), which held its founding meeting on 13 August 2009, and then ended operations in July 2014 (Taft 2017, 29). EPIC members were both industry trade associations, such as CAPP, and individual oil and pipeline firms, such as Suncor, Enbridge, TransCanada, and Imperial Oil, who paid substantial annual fees of $50,000 to $100,000 to fund the institute's activities (Taft 2017, 25). The budget presented at the first meeting was for $2.9 million (Taft 2017, 29). Taft quotes Thomas D'Aquino, former president of the Canadian Council of Chief Executives and the first chair of EPIC as saying, "EPIC's goal was to develop an Energy Strategy for Canada" (Taft 2017, 29). D'Aquino said that the plan was to be accomplished by taking four steps; first, to get the relevant private firms on board; secondly, to draw in academics working on energy; thirdly, to do outreach to the Canadian public through newspapers and magazines; and then, fourthly, to take their ideas to governments (Taft 2017, 30). A similar picture of the EPIC strategy of first stimulating discussion among non-state actors and then drawing in and making recommendations to governments is given by Daniel Gagnier, a former Alcan executive who had worked in the offices of both Quebec Premier Jean Charest and Ontario Premier David Peterson and then served for a time as president of EPIC (Gagnier 2014).

Why was the oil industry putting in this degree of time, effort, and financial resources to see Canadian governments reach agreement on a national energy strategy? Some hints of the answer to that question can be found in the January 2011 EPIC document *A Strategy for Canada's Global Energy Leadership: Framework Document* (EPIC 2011). The document begins by explaining that development of a national energy strategy is EPIC's raison d'être:

> The sole purpose and unique interest of the Energy Policy Institute of Canada ("EPIC") is to provide a broad, cross-sectoral full value chain perspective on a Canadian energy framework and strategy. (EPIC 2011, 3)

The statement of the mission repeats this theme: to work with governments and others to create a "common sense energy strategy" covering both energy production and consumption that will lead to economic benefit and environmental protection (EPIC 2011, 3). The document then lists five goals: 1) "Maximize economic and social value of Canada's energy system;" 2) "Support action that will help Canada reduce greenhouse gas emissions;" 3) "Enhance Canada's ... international energy trade and development of new markets;" 4) Encourage greater government transparency; and, 5) Engage energy "producers and consumers" in order to achieve the first four goals (EPIC 2011, 3).

The executive summary then explains the benefits to be derived from creation of a Canadian energy strategy. First among these are changes to the regulatory system:

> A comprehensive Canadian energy strategy will enhance regulatory efficiency, quicken the time-to-market for major energy projects, and strike the right balance among economic, social and environmental considerations. (EPIC 2011, 5)

That focus carries forward into the five recommendations, the first of which includes "providing a regulatory framework that ends overlap and duplication" (EPIC 2011, 6). The second is a recommended set of actions to improve energy security, including electricity transmission and "a new pipeline infrastructure to the West Coast to open up export markets around the Pacific Rim" (EPIC 2011, 6). Other recommendations include ensuring good trade relations with the US, again diversifying markets by means of new pipeline infrastucture to the west coast, protecting the environment, technology innovation, workforce training, ensuring energy investment, and increasing Canadian public aware-ness of the need for energy conservation and more generally an increase in "energy literacy" (EPIC 2011, 7).

The same framing of the proposed national energy strategy as being focused on new markets and changes to the regulatory context was provided by Lor-raine Mitchelmore, president of Shell Canada, in December 2011. A *Globe and Mail* "information feature" (text developed by its advertising department rather than reporters) referred to Shell Canada as "leading the oil and gas industry charge since it called for a national energy framework in March" (National Energy Strategy 2011). Ms. Mitchelmore is quoted as saying, "Government can enable two key elements of a national energy framework – market access and regulatory efficiency" (National Energy Strategy 2011). Clearly while indus-try was arguing a national energy strategy would help in many areas, includ-ing environmental protection, it saw the strategy as a means of achieving two priorities – changes to regulation that would make approval of new energy projects more likely and less time consuming, and construction of new pipe-lines to give Canadian oil access to markets other than American.

Others were also calling for discussion of a national energy strategy. In June 2009 the Senate Standing Committee on Energy, the Environment and Natural Resources began examining the concept of a national energy strategy. Having heard from organizations such as EPIC, the Canada West Foundation, and others, the committee issued an interim report in June 2010 that called for "a common energy framework in order that federal, provincial and territo-rial governments and other stakeholders work together to better co-ordinate Canada's future energy" (Senate Standing Committee 2010, 3). As noted, in October 2009, representatives of eleven think tanks gathered in Winnipeg to address the same topic. The group reached consensus on the need to "help spark national dialogue on the difficult and increasingly significant role of energy in Canada's environmental and economic future" (Winnipeg Consensus n.d., 2). Gibbins then prepared a background paper (2010a), which was dis-cussed at a meeting in Banff of some sixty representatives of industry and envi-ronmental organizations, but still with no government involvement, in April 2010 (winnipegconsensus.org). That meeting issued a call for a "Canadian Clean Energy Strategy" based on four principles: 1) economic opportunity; 2) social responsibility; 3) environmental stewardship; and, 4) that favourite of the oil industry, "international strategy in relation to trade and development of new markets" (Banff Clean Energy Dialogue 2010, 6).

The basic goal of the Winnipeg and Banff meetings, of course, was to involve governments, since without their powers of regulation and funding, any national strategy could only exist on paper. In May 2010, Roger Gibbins published an article advocating a "build it and they will come" strategy; argu-ing the way to induce government involvement, and particularly that of the federal government, was for the non-state actors to continue to develop the process until it gained enough momentum that governments had no choice but to hop on the bus (Gibbins 2010a). The first sign of success on that front was discussion of the concept at the August 2010 meeting of the Council of the Federation, although without being mentioned in the final meeting communiqué (Macdonald and Lesch 2013). In September 2010, a meeting of the federal-provincial body, the Energy and Mines Ministers' Conference (EMMC) did not specifically discuss the concept of a national energy strategy, but did instruct officials to look for opportunities for "greater pan-Canadian collaboration" (NRCan 2010).

In December 2010 the premiers of British Columbia, Alberta, and Saskatchewan, coming together under the aegis of the New West Partnership that they had created in the spring of that year, signed a memorandum of understanding setting out their agreement to work together to increase access to Asian markets for Canadian energy exports (Saskatchewan 2010). In January 2011 EPIC released its report calling for a national energy strategy, referred to above. In March 2011 the Canada West Foundation published a report titled *Finding Common Ground: The Next Step in Developing a Canadian Energy Strategy*. The report reviewed steps taken toward a national energy strategy since 2009 and made further suggestions for principles that should guide further development, including both pricing carbon and gaining access to Asian markets.

The industry voice calling for deregulation and a new pipeline to the west coast was not the only one heard at this point in the evolving dialogue. It was, however, the one that resonated in the ear of the Harper government. On 2 May 2011, the Harper Conservatives were re-elected, this time to a majority position, thus freeing their hand to act in Parliament more in keeping with their ideological instincts. On 15 July 2011, Harper's newly appointed NRCan minister, Joe Oliver, delivered a speech in Calgary that must have been music to the ears of its audience, since it played on all the themes being advanced by EPIC: the importance of energy to the Canadian economy; more specifically, the economic value of the oil sands; the need for new markets; the need for "regulatory reform;" and a commitment that the federal government would participate fully in development of a national energy strategy:

> At the upcoming Energy and Mines Ministers Conference, or EMMC, our goal will be to find ways to harness our energy potential in a responsible manner. Over the last few years, provinces and territories, industry, think tanks and stakeholders across Canada have been coming to a consensus that a pan-Canadian approach to energy is needed. At the last EMMC, Ministers tasked officials to look into how we can move forward. At our upcoming conference, I will work together with my provincial and territorial colleagues on a shared vision. (Oliver 2011, 4)

This federal role was what the Alberta government had been hoping for. A newspaper report from July 2011 gave this picture:

> The Alberta government has urged Ottawa to lead the effort for a national energy strategy ... Alberta Energy Minister Ron Liepert has been leading the charge for a national energy strategy ... in an interview ... the Alberta minister clearly has some concerns about hurdles faced by the oil industry in getting approvals for new pipelines. (McCarthy, 2011)

Prior to the EMMC on 18–19 July 2011, other stakeholders weighed in with advice for the ministers. The Canadian Council of Chief Executives, speaking for business as a whole rather than the narrower interests of the oil industry, focused on "cleaner energy" with less environmental impact, including both renewable energy sources and changes to fossil fuel energy technologies (Canadian Council of Chief Executives 2011). Their shopping list of suggestions included the industry staples of market diversification and regulatory reform, but also carbon pricing and a national climate-change policy.

At the 18–19 July 2011 EMMC meeting, after hearing submissions from a number of the relevant actors discussed above, ministers agreed on an "Action Plan" with three main headings: 1) "Economic Prosperity and Responsible Energy Supply;" 2) "Efficient Energy Use;" and, 3) "Knowledge and Innovation (Canadian Intergovernmental Conference Secretariat, 2011)." Channelling EPIC, the first two items under the first heading were "Intensify efforts to streamline regulatory project reviews" and "Collaborate and focus efforts on capturing new markets" (Canadian Intergovernmental Conference Secretariat 2011). The West-East fault line, however, was in evidence at the meeting. The Ontario government, represented by its energy minister, although it supported the action plan, objected to wording in the meeting news release calling the oil sands "a responsible and major supplier of energy to the world." The Ontario minister said his government was not comfortable with that wording when "his government was working to phase out coal by increased use of solar and wind energy" (Vanderklippe 2011).

Three months after that federal-provincial meeting, Alison Redford won the race for leadership of the Alberta Progressive Conservative Party and on 7 October 2011, replaced Ed Stelmach as premier. As discussed, Redford represented a strong contrast to Alberta leadership during the failed 1990s attempt to develop national climate-change policy. While Alberta Premier Ralph Klein (premier from 1992 to 2006), was a much beloved, hard-drinking former newspaperman who famously suggested climate change had come from dinosaur farts, Redford was a capable, cosmopolitan lawyer with experience overseas, at the international level and in Ottawa in Brian Mulroney's PMO. Judging from her public statements, it appears she instinctively understood that for Alberta to get what it wanted – increased pipeline capacity and access to Asian markets – it had to do far more to engage with its critics, acknowledge the reality of climate change and the need to act upon it, and actively seek good relations with the other provinces. The concept of a national energy strategy, having gained significant momentum by fall of 2011, was the ideal vehicle for such a new approach. She threw herself into that effort with a vengeance.

In November 2011 Premier Redford met with the premiers of British Columbia and Saskatchewan to discuss the national energy strategy. Both expressed their support (Walton 2012). On 16 November 2011, Redford met with Ontario Premier Dalton McGuinty and later in the day delivered a speech to a Toronto business audience, saying the west must reach out to other provinces to develop a united approach to energy, encompassing the oil sands, hydro-electricity in British Columbia and new renewable sources in Ontario (CBC News 2011). The next day, she met with Prime Minister Harper to discuss federal health spending and the national energy strategy, likely advocating federal leadership for the latter. After the meeting Harper said he was not entirely clear what was meant by a national energy strategy and gave a clear sign he had not committed to federal leadership (Walton 2012). On 11 January 2012, Redford met with Quebec Premier Jean Charest to discuss the NES. Charest was open to the idea, but questioned the need for federal participation (CBC News 2012). The Council of the Federation met on 16–17 January 2012 in Victoria, but did not include the national energy strategy on its agenda.

In March 2012 the Harper government went a long way to providing the regulatory reform called for by EPIC as part of any national energy strategy. A number of federal laws, including the Canadian Environmental Assessment Act, were amended with little debate as part of two budget omnibus bills, in ways intended to speed up approvals of resource development projects. Valiante describes the effect of those changes this way:

> Part of achieving that goal [of faster approvals] has been through reducing the types of projects that are subject to EA review and reducing the time that reviews take. Reducing the time for reviews has been achieved, in part, by limiting the number of participants to those directly affected and, in part, by limiting the types of issues which can be raised and to which proponents must respond. (2016, 69–70)

After meeting with Premier Redford (whose party had been re-elected the previous month) on 25 May 2012, federal minister Joe Oliver said his government was "entirely supportive of the collaborative approach to energy development, involving the federal government and all the provinces" (Wingrove 2012) and noted that they had already acted on the regulatory reform part of the national energy strategy agenda – the deregulatory changes to federal laws referred to above. A newspaper report at the time suggests Oliver was more interested in the low-key EMMC federal-provincial collaboration managed by ministers than the more visible first ministers' process being advocated by Premier Redford

(Wingrove 2012). In any case, Stephen Harper's preference for a federalism of watertight compartments and dislike of collaborative federal-provincial programs made federal participation in Premier Redford's project unlikely. The 10–11 September 2012 Energy and Mines Ministers' Conference released a progress report on "Pan-Canadian Collaboration" (Energy and Mines Ministers' Conference 2012) but did not thereafter attempt to develop something akin to a national energy strategy.

In the event, it was the provinces-only body of the Council of the Federation, rather than the federal-provincial energy and mines ministers' secretariat, which developed the 2015 Canadian Energy Strategy. At the council meeting on 26–7 July 2012, a working group consisting of Premier Redford, Newfoundland and Labrador Premier Kathy Dundale, and Manitoba Premier Greg Salinger was created to develop a new plan, building on the original 2007 iteration. The government of British Columbia, however, refused to participate in the CES effort. A few days earlier, on 23 July 2012, the British Columbia government had announced that it would only accept heavy oil pipelines crossing its territory to the coast if five conditions were met (BC 2012). Those were: 1) that the pipeline had received a positive recommendation from the NEB; 2) that a "world-class" marine spill prevention and clean-up program was in place, which would require federal action; 3) that programs for dealing with spills on land were also in place; 4) that Aboriginal peoples had been consulted and given opportunity to participate in the project; and, 5) that British Columbia receive a "fair share" of the financial returns from the project. The British Columbia government had prepared a detailed study of the five conditions, which noted with respect to the last that the Northern Gateway project, which at the time was the subject of an NEB hearing, would provide $81 billion in additional government revenues over 30 years, of which a considerable portion would go to the federal and Alberta governments, but only $6.7 billion or 8 per cent to British Columbia; conversely, that province would bear 100 per cent of the risk from spills on its land or coast (BC 2012).

By means of this fifth condition, British Columbia was raising the issue of allocation of cost. While the subject was allocation of cost and benefit associated with oil leaking from a pipeline, the concept of equity in energy and climate-change policy was exactly the same as in the principle that no region would be asked to bear an "unreasonable burden" as the result of national climate policy, or the demand made by Quebec in October 2000 that the total GHG emission reduction effort be shared in a fair manner among the provinces. This time, however, the way to achieve such equity was explicitly stated – financial compensation. What was not clearly stated was the answer to this question: Who should pay that compensation?

Premier Redford was quick to respond that it certainly would not be her province. The day that British Columbia announced its five conditions, Premier Redford said Alberta already shared its oil royalties with the rest of the country through the equalization program; that her province had lived through the days of the National Energy Program; and that, in consequence, she would "protect the royalty revenue that Albertans are entitled to" (Kleiss 2012). On 29 September 2012, British Columbia Premier Christy Clark sent a letter to Premier Redford explaining the British Columbia position, again listing the five conditions and clarifying that British Columbia had never requested a share of Alberta royalties; the source of the British Columbia compensation, the premier said, was something to be discussed by "our governments" (Clark 2012). That discussion took place at a "frosty" twenty-minute meeting of the two premiers in Calgary a few days later, on 1 October 2012. Apparently providing compensation from Alberta royalties was discussed, which Redford said was what made the meeting "a little bit frosty" (Krugel 2012). Although no progress was made at that meeting, the two premiers met again the next year, on 13 June 2013, and without discussing pipelines agreed their governments would work together to examine joint efforts in areas of skills training and immigration (Neissner 2013). Clark and Redford then met again, on 15 October 2013, and announced they had agreed to establish a joint working group, chaired by deputy ministers from both governments, to examine the five British Columbia conditions, on the understanding that any compensation to British Columbia would not come from Alberta royalties. On 5 November 2013, the governments announced that agreement had been reached: essentially, Alberta accepted the five British Columbia conditions, with the fifth clarified to exclude Alberta payments from oil royalties. In consequence, British Columbia agreed to participate in the Alberta-led effort to develop a Canadian energy strategy. With respect to compensation, the Alberta news release provided this statement: "On condition five, Alberta agrees that B.C. has a right to negotiate with industry on appropriate economic benefits." Both governments agree "it is not for" both Alberta and British Columbia to negotiate those benefits with industry, and both agree that "Alberta's royalties are not on the table for negotiation" (Government of Alberta 2013).

Apparently British Columbia then proceeded to enter into negotiations with industry for financial compensation in exchange for a guarantee the provincial government would not oppose that company's pipeline crossing its territory. Any discussions with Enbridge concerning the Northern Gateway pipeline were made moot by the court decision overturning the previous Harper government approval and the Trudeau government's November 2016 decision to reject the project. Kinder Morgan, on the other hand, agreed to make annual payments to British Columbia of a minimum of $25 million and maximum of $50 million, depending on volume shipped, over a period of twenty years. That agreement was announced on the same day that Premier Clark announced her approval of the pipeline, 10 January 2017 (Hunter 2017). (In 2018, of course, that same pipeline became a point of major contention between the two provinces – the NDP government led by Premier John Horgan was not interested in allowing the pipeline in exchange for compensation. His government wanted it stopped, period. The story is told in the next case study.)

Returning to the narrative of the CES, in July 2013 the Council of the Federation published a "progress report" (Council of the Federation 2013) on activity to date; the three areas used to structure the 2015 CES had been decided at that time (set out in table 7, page 184: sustainability, technology, and delivering energy to people) and ten working groups created to develop the sub-areas in each of the three (the ten "areas of focus" in the 2015 CES, discussed above – the wording for the ten is identical between the 2013 progress report and 2015 final report). The report indicated that British Columbia was not participating and Quebec was participating on specific initiatives, but was not part of the formal effort (Council of the Federation 2013, 3). Most of the report was taken up with examples of actions being taken in different provinces in each of the three areas; reference was made to a "stakeholder engagement workshop" that had been held on 24–5 June 2013 (Council of the Federation 2013, 18). It was stated the final report would be released in 2014.

In April 2014 the Quebec Liberals defeated the Parti Québécois and the new government announced it would fully participate in the CES. A press report suggests that at the Council of the Federation meeting on 28–9 August 2014, the Ontario and Quebec premiers argued the CES had to include more specific commitments on climate change (Taber and Morrow 2015). In April 2015, shortly after the Ontario government had announced it would link its cap-and-trade program with that of Quebec and California, the premiers of Quebec and Ontario issued a joint statement on climate change, pledging, in non-specific terms, to continue to work together on the issue (Joint Statement 2015). It seems likely this alliance was also carried into the negotiations for finalizing the CES, turning that process into another forum for the West-East divide. We do know that a few days before the 2015 premiers' meeting, Saskatchewan premier Brad Wall was complaining publicly about the way in which the Ontario and Quebec premiers denigrated the western oil industry, despite, he said, receiving equalization payments from western government revenues contributed by the industry (CBC News 2015b). (Canadian equalization payments are not made directly by one province to another. They are payments by the federal government to receiving provinces. Federal revenues, of course, include tax paid by oil firms operating in a province such as Saskatchewan.)

The CES was released by the premiers on 17 July 2015, after negotiations over the central tension in the document, which corresponded to tensions between west and east – the extent to which the document would specifically call for new pipelines versus the extent to which it would specifically call for action on climate change. In terms of the first, a news report based on the reporter's viewing of an earlier draft of the document said the draft wording was the "country must have the necessary pipelines" (Morrow 2015). That wording does not appear in the final document; instead there is reference to a need to "identify the energy infrastructure required" (Council of the Federation 2015a, 26). Wording in the draft on the need for "market diversification" and action on "international export opportunities" remains, however, in the final document (Morrow 2015; Council of the Federation 2015a). With respect to climate-change action, in some ways the wording was strengthened but in other ways weakened. The draft referred to the need to "transition to a lower-carbon economy" but gave no specifics (Morrow 2015). The final CES, by contrast, as discussed above, does refer to collaboration on "options for an integrated pan-Canadian and North American approach to greenhouse gas reductions" (Council of the Federation 2015a, 17). On the other hand, wording in the draft committing all provinces to "absolute" cuts in emissions, was dropped (Taber and Morrow 2015). At the time, Alberta was the only province with an intensity rather than absolute reduction target. Presumably it was the Alberta premier who insisted the reference to absolute cuts be eliminated; Premier Notley was quoted after the document was released as saying that her main role had been to keep language *out* of the CES document (Henton 2015).

Analysis

1) What Does the Case Tell Us about the Four Subjects?

THE WEST–EAST DIVIDE
Like the previous three cases, the CES shows that western governments, and in particular that of Alberta are highly motivated and able to influence a national energy or climate process. The 2015 CES would not have existed had not western interests diverged from those of the rest of the country. By around 2010, it had become clear to the industry and Alberta governments that they had a problem that did not exist for energy generators in other parts of the country and that they could not solve by themselves, since new pipeline capacity required both federal approvals and, in terms of coastal access, acquiescence of other provinces. The initial push came in the form of meetings held in the western cities of Winnipeg and Banff, not eastern cities such as Montreal and Halifax. The industry push came from the western oil and gas firms, not other energy sectors, such as electricity, renewable energies or nuclear. Finally, of course, it was Premier Redford's campaign starting in fall 2011 that more than anything else brought the CES into being. The CES truly was a national initiative, speaking to issues of importance to all parts of the country and with all

parts participating. At its core, however, it was a western initiative, intended to help achieve western ends. Thus the case shows us, yet again, engaged and motivated western governments working to influence national energy and climate politics in their own self-interest – a phenomenon we have already seen in the first three cases and that, at the risk of spoiling the ending, we will see again in the case that follows.

The case also shows, however, that the motivation of western provinces to influence national energy and climate-change policy will not necessarily be matched by similar motivation in the eastern provinces. In the first case, Ontario actively opposed Alberta. In the two climate cases of the 1990s, however, there was no countervailing power coming from the eastern provinces. In this instance, to at least some degree, eastern provinces opposed Alberta at the end of the case, when Ontario and Quebec demanded the CES pay more attention to climate change. However, it seems their motivation was weak, since they were willing to sign the document even though they had not achieved their goal of having it refer to absolute emission cuts by all provinces (something opposed by Alberta). The findings contribute to the view of the West-East divide as a phenomenon in which western provinces are always motivated and seeking to influence national energy or climate policy, but in which countervailing power has to come from Ottawa, since there is no inherent reason for it to come from eastern provinces.

THE INHERENT NEED TO ALLOCATE REDUCTIONS

The Alberta-British Columbia negotiations of 2012–13 were an example of allocation of risk and benefit, including compensation for the party bearing the risk. As such, although it is only one case, they suggest a few things about this challenge. Like Quebec in the previous case, the allocation issue was raised by a government that saw itself as the victim, using the language of fairness. Secondly, compensation was seen by the victim as an adequate means of addressing its complaint, which is important for the set of suggestions made in chapter 11. There, compensation is suggested as a means of arriving at roughly comparable per capita reduction costs throughout the country. (Subsequent events, however, show the limits of compensation. The NDP government that in 2017 took power in British Columbia with support from the Green Party was more ideologically opposed to the Trans Mountain expansion than was the previous Liberal government and presumably for that reason took a different position from the latter, opposing the pipeline without expressing any interest in compensation.)

Aside from the Alberta-British Columbia negotiations, however, the case tells us nothing about the allocation issue. A fixed quantum of cost or benefit was never the subject of discussion, so there was nothing to allocate. Beyond that, the CES document never referred to cost, but instead sketched a rose-tinted world in which only potential benefit existed, freely available to all in equal measure. The document suggests that Prince Edward Island, for example, will benefit as much as Alberta if the proposed collaborative actions are taken. Since the benefit is the same for all, there is no allocation but instead receipt of equal portions. In this regard, the unique nature of the CES means that the allocation issue which is central to the other four cases, even though only explicitly addressed in the first, was absent here.

THE NATIONAL PROCESS

Despite the absence of the federal government, the process used was similar to that for development of all national coordinated policies. Working groups of provincial officials developed policy options and reported up to ministers and premiers. Presumably a sub-group of the latter, the original committee of premiers (Alberta, Manitoba, and Newfoundland and Labrador, augmented by New Brunswick) reached decisions that were then recommended to the other premiers. The process would have received some predictability and order from the regular twice-yearly meetings of the Council of the Federation. As always, the work was largely done in secret with no direct participation by non-stake actors. (As noted, one stakeholder consultation session was held.)

What does the CES case tell us about any future climate or energy effort that is almost certain to use approximately the same procedures? The lesson is obvious: multilateral agreement with no governments opting out is possible, provided one is willing to pretty much completely sacrifice policy effectiveness. This means that in any future national effort, citizens and other non-state actors must beware of agreement reached for agreement's sake. Governments want to reach agreement because, as discussed, they want to appear to be taking effective action. However, the CES case shows us that the simple fact of agreement by no means guarantees efficacy.

STRATEGY OF THE LEAD GOVERNMENT

Alberta happily played the lead role, both within the Council of the Federation, through its membership in the premiers' working group, and outside that forum, by means of the series of bilateral meetings arranged by Premier Redford. As discussed, the only real strategy available to Alberta, given that unlike a federal government it could not threaten to regulate inside the borders of other provinces and nor yet offer financial promises, was persuasion. Alberta sought to show other provinces that their own self-interest could best be served by participating in development of the CES, as framed by Alberta with a focus on "delivering energy to people." Lead-actor persuasion was sufficient to accomplish that goal, but not what was presumably the Alberta goal of having other provinces explicitly endorse the need for new pipelines.

The lesson the case gives us is that the lead role has to be played by Ottawa. We have seen that the provinces by themselves cannot generate effective national climate-change policy. Here, by extension we see that a province cannot lead a national effort, be it of provinces only or of both levels of government. If Ottawa is not the lead actor, coordinated policy, defined as governments changing behaviour, is not possible. The corollary to that lesson, derived from other cases, is that simple leadership by Ottawa is not enough – that leadership must be both motivated and adroit.

2) What Are the Most Important Factors Explaining the Case Outcome?

The outcome of the case comes in two parts. The good news is that all participating governments were able to reach agreement on the same one document. The bad news is that no government committed to any specific action by virtue of signing, and the most important government with respect to national policy, the Government of Canada, was not a party to the agreement. The first part of the outcome suggests we might see this as a successful example of multilateral policymaking. It is not as though governments did not care what they were signing. At least some, probably Alberta, Ontario, and Quebec, had taken it seriously enough to negotiate wording with respect to both pipelines and climate change in the final days of the process. However, the *nature* of the agreement reached – the second part of the outcome – is far more important than the mere fact of reaching comprehensive agreement. Since the agreement imposed no obligations to act it completely fails the test for coordinated policy set out in chapter 1; the agreement by itself is unlikely to generate significant behaviour change. For that reason, the CES cannot be seen to have generated substantial coordination.

The most important factor explaining the ineffective policy generated by the CES process is the fact that it was led by a provincial government. As discussed, the government of Alberta simply did not have available the means of influencing other governments we saw used so effectively by Ottawa in the first case (albeit at an unacceptable price). It seems fair to assume Alberta would have preferred an agreement containing positive commitments by other governments to accept pipelines crossing their territory, but knew it could not achieve that goal. Persuasion, the only instrument Alberta could use, unaccompanied by the other means of exercising power, threat and promise, can only go so far. Premier Redford and her successors did a very good job playing the cards they had been dealt, and were aided by the automatic desire of governments to be seen as agreeing and thus accomplishing something, but the end result was of less value for national policy than something like the voluntary instrument of the 1995 Voluntary Challenge and Registry.

One other factor should be mentioned, which is the significant role played by industry in getting the project off the ground. Although not examined here, it seems safe to assume the Canada West Foundation – which as far as we know was the first mover – did not have the same elite contacts, financial resources, and non-overt structural power as did the oil industry, which also demonstrated agency power based on financial resources when it was able to assemble a budget for EPIC of close to three million dollars on what seems like relatively short notice. Industry wanted a national energy strategy and got what it wanted. We can also assume that the Harper government deregulatory actions of March 2012, although not formally a part of the CES process, came about due to industry lobbying. Certainly industry had said publicly many times that was what they wanted to see done, and it would be surprising indeed if CEOs and other business leaders were not saying the same things to the Harper government in private. This case and creation of the VCR are the two most significant examples of the ability of industry to influence a national process. Although it could not stop ratification, the oil industry also displayed considerable political power in the fall of 2002 when it cut a deal with the Chrétien government severely limiting costs it would bear from federal regulation. In chapter 11, the suggestion is made that since the oil industry is bound to be working to exert private influence in any future federal-provincial climate-change process it be given a formal public role, so that all may be fully aware of the advice it is providing.

9 The Pan-Canadian Framework, 2015–2019

Case Summary

During the process leading up to signing of the agreement on 9 December 2016, a lead government (Ottawa) led by a highly motivated prime minister faced relatively little veto-government resistance for two reasons: 1) this time Alberta played a swing role (prior to the election of the Jason Kenney government on 16 April 2019), supporting the program in exchange for a pipeline; and, 2) little behaviour change was asked of the large, powerful provinces. Accordingly, despite less than fully skillful diplomacy, Ottawa was able to conclude an agreement with eleven provinces and territories, which represented substantial policy coordination. In part due to election of new provincial governments, in the years following policy coordination was significantly weakened by provincial defections and a corresponding increase in veto-government resistance.

START AND END DATES: 6 February 2015–9 December 2016; implementation to 16 April 2019

MAJOR POLICY DECISIONS

unilateral
- federal approval of the British Columbia Petronus LNG pipeline, 28 September 2016 (the companies involved announced in July 2017 they would not proceed with the project)
- federal government decision to adopt a federal backstop carbon price as the centrepiece of its approach to leading a national climate change policy effort, formally announced 3 October 2016
- federal decisions on three other pipelines, 29 November 2016: rejection of Northern Gateway, approval of Kinder Morgan's Trans Mountain expansion approval of Enbridge Line 3

- Saskatchewan and Manitoba refuse to sign the PCF agreement, 9 December 2016
- Manitoba joins the PCF in February 2018, then effectively withdraws 3 October 2018
- Ontario effectively withdraws from the PCF in summer 2018
- Alberta withdraws from the PCF until a pipeline is built, 30 August 2018
- federal government announces its backstop price will be imposed in four provinces, 23 October 2018
- newly elected Alberta government repeals Alberta carbon tax, May 2019

bilateral

- Ottawa-Nova Scotia agreement, 21 November 2016 that Nova Scotia coal-fired electricity could continue to operate past the Ottawa 2030 regulatory deadline and that Nova Scotia would introduce a cap-and-trade system
- Ottawa-Saskatchewan agreement, 28 November 2016, that Saskatchewan can keep coal-fired electricity plants in operation past 2030 if it makes equivalent emission reductions elsewhere; not related to Saskatchewan's refusal to participate in the PCF

multilateral

- all Canadian governments agree to the Vancouver Declaration, 3 March 2016
- all Canadian governments except Saskatchewan and Manitoba agree to the Pan-Canadian Framework on Clean Growth and Climate Change, 9 December 2016

CASE OUTCOMES

With signing of the Pan-Canadian Framework agreement governments representing 87 per cent of total GHG emissions had agreed to a program of coordinated federal-provincial action, using more effective policy instruments than had been agreed upon in the 1990s. The PCF was, however, largely a federal undertaking with provincial acquiescence, particularly since it did not require major behaviour change on the part of the big four emitters representing 80 per cent of emissions. Although not treated as outcomes for analytical purposes, other aspects of the program were these: the 2020 target had been ignored, programs sufficient to achieve the 2030 target were not yet in place, the allocation issue had been ignored, and, finally, the program was a missed opportunity – more might have been done.

By the time of the Alberta election in spring 2019, the case outcomes were very different. Five provinces, representing over half the Canadian population and three-quarters of total Canadian emissions, were actively hostile and playing a veto role. The degree of policy coordination achieved by the program had been sharply reduced. The Trudeau government's goal of a minimum carbon price in all parts of the country had been achieved, but only because a federal tax, strongly resisted by relevant provincial governments, was in place in a number of provinces. The second outcome, that the program was largely a federal effort with some provincial participation, was even more true than it had been at the point of signing.

COORDINATION CATEGORY
Substantial policy coordination at the date of signing; subsequently, significantly less policy coordination

When Prime Minister Brian Mulroney's Conservative government put climate change on the agenda of Canadian governments from 1988 to 1990, his government had an open field in front of it. While the phenomenon of climate change had been understood by scientists for many years, it had not yet been the subject of policy action by governments anywhere. Accordingly, Canadian provincial governments were at their most vulnerable to strong federal action, since they had not yet started to accumulate data on the issue, let alone develop policy options for addressing it. Mulroney's government was able to announce a national target, ratify the UNFCCC, and start the federal-provincial process that generated the 1995 National Action Program on Climate Change with provincial resistance limited to private lobbying by Alberta. In fall 2015, when Justin Trudeau's Liberal government was elected on a platform of developing another national climate change effort, the playing field had changed considerably. The space for open-field running available to Mulroney had become constricted, owing to the fact that virtually all Canadian provinces had in place some sort of climate-change policy and at least two of the large ones, British Columbia and Quebec, some years before had started to implement sophisticated programs using effective policy instruments, with broad public support within the province, which by late 2015 were fully operational. The other two powerful provinces, Alberta and Ontario, were in the process of putting in place equally sophisticated programs. None of those provinces were likely to happily scrap or make major modifications to their programs just because of the arrival in Ottawa of a new federal government with thoughts on what a national program should look like. This basic fact of pre-existing provincial programs goes a long way towards explaining the nature of federal leadership provided by the Justin Trudeau government – most notably the clear desire to avoid conflict with those four provinces – as it successfully cobbled together the December 2016 Pan-Canadian federal-provincial program.

The other difference from the Mulroney era was that by 2015 energy and climate-change policy had become fully integrated. It was impossible for any federal government to consider leading a climate policy effort without being very aware that the question of federal regulation of interprovincial pipelines was going to be significant. Even though it was something falling solely within federal jurisdiction, provincial interest in new pipelines (both for and against) influenced federal decisions and the nature of the program.

From the time he first announced his party's climate-change election platform in a speech at the Calgary Petroleum Club on 6 February 2015, through to the PCF signing in December 2016, Trudeau took great care to accommodate prickly provincial sensitivities (with the exception of his clumsy announcement of the federal backstop tax on 3 October 2016). One of his main policy instruments was something hard for provinces to disagree with: promises of federal funding. On the other hand, the federal threat to impose backstop carbon pricing in any province that had not already done so itself was at the outer end of the spectrum of legitimate unilateral federal action. Obviously aware of this, Ottawa designed the instrument so as to minimize provincial opposition. At the 3 March 2016 Vancouver meeting of first ministers, the prime minister quickly acceded to provincial demands that provincial climate pricing action would be defined by the term "carbon pricing mechanisms" (First Ministers' Meeting 2016a), which all knew could be interpreted as including such things as Saskatchewan's carbon sequestration program and Nova Scotia's law-based regulation, rather than the more narrow and specific definition of a carbon tax or trading system. The prime minister later reneged on that agreement, reverting to his preferred narrow definition, but the flexibility he showed on 3 March had helped him get past the potential veto point of that FMM. In addition, from the outset, Ottawa gave a commitment that any revenues generated by the federal backstop price would be returned to the province in question (without precisely specifying they would be returned to the provincial *government*). The territories were effectively exempted from requirements to act, while Ottawa accepted fairly vague promises of future carbon pricing from provinces such as New Brunswick and Newfoundland. Despite some inept diplomacy, Ottawa managed to keep its eye on what it considered (mistakenly, as this chapter argues) the main prize – the same minimum carbon price in all parts of the country – and to bring all but two governments to the point of signing.

Program implementation over the next two years, however, proved to be more challenging. A number of federal-provincial programs for shared cost actions to reduce emissions were signed and federal legislation to enact the backstop price was enacted. Progress there was countered, however, by pitfalls associated with the bargain made with Alberta. That province had agreed to participate in and support the Pan-Canadian program in exchange for federal approval of a new pipeline. In the result, Ottawa became owner of the Trans Mountain expansion line but with no certainty it could be given regulatory approval in a way that would withstand yet another court challenge. Just as difficult, the backstop threat that ideally would have influenced provincial policies without ever being actually used, thereby staying largely invisible, became the highly visible focus of partisan conflict. Right-wing provincial governments attacked it repeatedly and the federal Conservative opposition made it the central point in its line of attack on the sitting government. In defence, the Trudeau Liberals promised citizens in the relevant provinces they would receive more than they had paid (because carbon taxes paid by business were returned not to them but to citizens) and the money would come directly in the mail from Ottawa, not through their provincial government. By the time the prime minister announced the backstop price would be applied in four provinces, on 23 October 2018, the future of the Pan-Canadian Framework program had become unclear; there was little doubt, however, that this right-wing versus centre-left partisan battle over carbon pricing and associated election outcomes would play a major role in the program's destiny.

Narrative

The story begins with a speech given by Liberal leader Justin Trudeau at the Calgary Petroleum Club on 6 February 2015, in which he said: "I'm the Leader of the Liberal Party of Canada, my last name is Trudeau, and I'm standing here at the Petroleum Club of Calgary. I understand how energy issues can divide the country" (Trudeau 2015). Trudeau started by calling for action on both the environment and economy, the former to come through carbon pricing that was in place or being introduced in the four large provinces, representing 80 per cent of emissions. He then pointed to the need for a federal role: "The problem is that the provincial approaches are uncoordinated and limited by a lack of federal leadership. There is no way to ensure all regions of the country are doing their part" (Trudeau 2015).

He went on to say that if elected his party would introduce a climate program based on the model of Medicare, with provinces delivering the service and the federal government establishing minimum standards and providing assistance with funding. The program would "set a national standard in partnership with provinces and territories," ensure that the latter had flexibility, "including their own carbon pricing policies," and provide federal "targeted funding" as needed (Trudeau 2015). The term "national standard" was not defined and the speech did not make any reference to the need for a minimum carbon price in all provinces. Although not included in the speech, a newspaper interview Trudeau gave that day makes it clear that by that date Trudeau also planned, if elected, to lead the Canadian delegation to the Paris summit that fall, to meet with the premiers within 90 days of that event to develop a national plan, and was hoping to reach agreement with the provinces on a "national floor price for carbon" (McCarthy 2015).

The Liberal climate-change platform as it was revealed over the following months repeated the two major themes of putting a price on carbon and working with the provinces. The official Liberal platform, released in final form on 6 October 2015, was more specific, saying provinces would be invited to attend the Paris summit with the federal government and then, within 90 days, all Canadian governments would establish a "pan-Canadian framework" to address climate change (Liberal Party of Canada 2015, 39). The federal government would not establish the national reduction target by itself, but instead with the provinces. The pledge of targeted funding for the provinces was repeated, as was the promise provinces would be guaranteed "flexibility to design their own policies ... including their own carbon pricing policies" (Liberal Party of Canada 2015, 40). This was a double message, saying provinces would be free to establish their own policies but such policies would have to include pricing, presumably by a tax or trading system. Although Trudeau had discussed it publicly, no mention was made of federal action to ensure a minimum price in each province.

After winning the 19 October 2015 election and taking office on 4 November, the new prime minister, true to his word, immediately began to start working with the provinces by inviting premiers to a First Ministers' Meeting, held 23 November 2015. The premiers and territorial leaders, absent the Newfoundland premier, who was engaged with an election, met by themselves that morning for a "brief, informal meeting" (Council of the Federation, 2015b). At the FMM itself, the prime minister said he hoped to set a more ambitious national target than that of the previous Harper administration, and there was general agreement that the country should send a message at the Paris talks that it was ready to work with other countries to address the issue. The one dissenting voice came from Saskatchewan premier Brad Wall, who said that thirty thousand jobs had been lost in the energy sector and for that reason he hoped Canadian policy would do "no further harm" to the industry (CBC News 2015a).

The prime minister and his newly appointed environment minister, Catherine McKenna, accompanied by a number of premiers and provincial environment ministers then attended the Paris Conference of Parties, which opened on 30 November 2015. The federal minister presented the Harper government's 2030 target of a reduction by 30 per cent below the 2005 level as a "floor" and suggested that a more ambitious target might be adopted after discussions with the provinces. In his address to the conference, the prime minister again said he would work with the provinces to develop a "pan-Canadian framework," which would include "national emissions-reduction targets" and, among other policy options, "carbon pricing" (Canada's National Statement 2015).

On 29 January 2016, the federal environment minister hosted a meeting in Ottawa of her provincial counterparts, which she described as a prelude to a meeting of first ministers to be held in the first week of March. At that point, it appeared that all governments were committed to development of a new national program. In a joint statement issued after the meeting, ministers said they had discussed a range of policy options and that the discussion brought them "one step closer to development of a pan-Canadian framework for combating climate change" (Federal-Provincial Territorial Meeting 2016). According to press reports, the federal minister may at that meeting have floated the idea of a federal backstop carbon price. Minister McKenna was quoted as saying it was "too early" to say whether Ottawa would set a minimum price that all provinces must meet (McCarthy 2016a). Herb Cox, the Saskatchewan environment minister, was quoted as saying his province rejects the concept of a federally-imposed carbon price (Cheadle 2016a). A few weeks later, the press was reporting that the prime minister wanted to see a federal backstop minimum carbon price as part of the national program being developed, a move supported by environmentalists (McCarthy 2016b).

By mid-February the process for federal-provincial policymaking that Ottawa was proposing had also started to become public knowledge. Intergovernmental affairs officials from all governments met in Toronto on 19 February to review the federal proposal, which would then be discussed at a First Ministers' Meeting in Vancouver in early March. CBC News reported on that day that Ottawa had earlier sent to the provinces a proposal for creation of four federal-provincial working groups – on carbon pricing, other reduction policies, innovation and clean growth, and adaptation – which would then report to a meeting of first ministers in the fall (CBC News 2016a). Given that many of them already had climate programs in place and the federal government was now coming into the policy field afresh, after ten years of the Harper government hands-off policy, not surprisingly provincial officials told the CBC they were nervous about Ottawa invading their jurisdiction; for their part, federal officials said a national carbon price would be part of the discussion but no specific price was being proposed and, in a comment that says something about the challenge facing Ottawa, they were simply glad that all provinces had agreed to show up in Vancouver (CBC News 2016a). By the end of February, the basic elements of both the process being suggested by Ottawa and the federal plan for a backstop price – a required minimum price, rising each year, with revenues from any federal price being returned to the province in which they were applied – were public knowledge and two provinces, Manitoba and Saskatchewan, had registered public objections (McCarthy and Bailey 2016a).

On 2 March 2016, premiers met in Vancouver under the aegis of the Council of the Federation. After the meeting, Premier Dwight Ball of Newfoundland, current chair of the Federation, reported that premiers were "united against the idea of one carbon price strategy for the entire country" and wanted to have "flexibility" to design their own climate policies (CBC News 2016b). Premier

Ball also said that the provinces wanted Ottawa to consider "carbon pricing mechanisms," which would include things like carbon capture and storage and programs to promote renewable energy as part of its national carbon price plan (McCarthy and Bailey 2016b). British Columbia Premier Christy Clark was less categorical, saying there was "no consensus" among provinces on the federal proposal; she went on to say governments should focus on other things, such as federal funding for green infrastructure (McCarthy and Bailey 2016b). Ontario Premier Kathleen Wynne urged her colleagues to work together, while Alberta Premier Rachel Notley was quoted as saying she would "leave the gun in the holster until we are actually at the gunfight, and we are not there right now" (CBC News 2016b)." Saskatchewan Premier Brad Wall had said earlier in February that "a carbon tax was not right for his province or the country right now" and that he wanted to see an economic impact analysis done before anything like that was agreed to (CBC News 2016a). On 2 March Premier Wall made it clear that his government would not accept a federal price imposed on greenhouse gas sources in Saskatchewan (McCarthy and Bailey 2016b).

The first hours of the meeting the next day of premiers and the prime minister were "frosty" (McCarthy and Bailey 2016c) as the provinces resisted the federal proposal for a mandatory minimum price. The prime minister backed down and agreed to compromise wording in the meeting communiqué, which stated that first ministers committed to act on the transition to a low-carbon economy "by adopting a broad range of domestic measures, including carbon pricing mechanisms, adapted to each province's and territory's specific circumstances" (First Ministers' Meeting 2016a). In a move reminiscent of Prime Minister Chrétien's refusal in December 1997 to be bound by the Kyoto target agreement his government had just reached with the provinces, a few months later Prime Minister Trudeau clearly did not feel he was bound by that compromise wording. However, he did agree to the wording in Vancouver. Nor yet did the Vancouver Declaration, the communiqué issued at the end of the meeting, make any reference to a minimum carbon price or to federal backstop action to impose such a price if any given province did not. Since that proposal had earlier been discussed with the provinces, its absence from the formal communiqué was a victory for provinces like Saskatchewan and Nova Scotia, which argued at the meeting that their climate programs were equivalent to carbon pricing in the form of tax or a trading system (McCarthy and Bailey 2016c).

At the end of the day, all the premiers and territorial leaders, including Brad Wall, signed on to the Vancouver Declaration. Wall said he was able to sign because the broad language agreed to around "carbon mechanisms" would include measures already being taken in Saskatchewan, such as carbon capture and storage, but he said there would be a "fight" if there was any kind of "notion" that he had agreed to carbon taxes (Cheadle 2016b). What had the premiers and prime minister agreed to? The Vancouver Declaration (First Ministers' Meeting

2016a) is a cumbersome, repetitive, lengthy document, clocking in at 2,718 words. It is divided into five sections devoted to the following topics: 1) increasing ambition; 2) promoting green jobs; 3) delivering emission reductions; 4) action on adaptation; and, 5) enhancing cooperation, which includes a list of proposed federal actions, the process agreed to, centred on the four working groups that would report to ministers, who would then report to first ministers, and then a final grab-bag of items such as building on the Canadian Energy Strategy and engaging with Indigenous peoples and the Canadian public (First Ministers' Meeting 2016a). The document makes no reference to the 2020 target – that inconvenient fact had been airbrushed out of the picture ever since the Liberal government was elected on 19 October 2015. The main things the fourteen signing governments agreed to are as follows: to meet the 2030 target and perhaps even do better ("increase the level of ambition"); foster and encourage investment in clean technology; use carbon pricing mechanisms; develop carbon sinks and work together on a pan-Canadian offsets system and carbon credits, which could be traded internationally; put in place adaptation and climate resilience policies; cooperate on science, public communication, and other things; and create the four working groups (First Ministers' Meeting 2016a). In addition, the federal government committed to six specific actions such as green infrastructure spending, the Low Carbon Economy Fund, promised in the Liberal election platform and intended to contribute to the cost of provincial climate actions, and programs to reduce use of diesel in northern communities.

The working groups were devoted to the subjects that had been earlier reported in the press. Each would be co-chaired by a federal and provincial or territorial official and they would be made up of only government officials, with no non-state expert participation, but they would "include Indigenous peoples in their work" (First Ministers' Meeting 2016a, 6). The working group on clean technology and jobs would report to federal and provincial ministers of innovation and economic development. The group examining carbon pricing would report to finance ministers and environment ministers in the form of CCME. The other two groups, on reduction measures beyond the price policy instrument and adaptation, would also report to CCME. The document concluded by saying first ministers would meet in the fall of 2016 to finalize the Pan-Canadian Framework and, with wording presumably inserted at the behest of one or more provinces, to "review progress on the Canadian Energy Strategy" (First Ministers' Meeting 2016a). Thus after the Harper government had pulled out of the CES in 2012, the Trudeau Liberal government came back in, at least at the level of lip service. If such a review was done at the 9 December 2016 First Ministers' Meeting, it was done privately since there is no reference to the CES in the communiqué and PCF document that issued from that meeting.

Presumably the machinery thus created by first ministers started to hum, although, as is the norm in intergovernmental relations at the level of officials, it did so in private, making no waves, or even ripples, in the daily news media. The next event in the story being told here has to do with a very different, although closely related topic. On 30 June 2016, the Federal Court of Appeal overturned the approval of the Northern Gateway pipeline previously given by the Stephen Harper government, on the basis that the federal government had failed to adequately consult Aboriginal bands; consultation had been adequate during the NEB process, but the federal government had a responsibility to consult on other matters after that decision, which the court deemed not to have been properly done. In the previous case study, the intense desire of the oil industry and government of Alberta for both expansion of pipeline capacity from the oil sands in general and, more particularly, expansion or creation of new capacity to take oil sands bitumen to a Canadian coast was a central factor in the process that generated the 2015 Canadian Energy Strategy. Since that pipeline capacity had not appeared a year later, when governments were putting in motion a new national climate-change process, that business and government interest was certain to be a factor there as well.

As noted above, once pipeline approvals had become politicized by opposition of US environmentalists and local citizens to Keystone XL, around 2010, energy and climate-change politics had become fully fused. That certainly applied in Canada by 2016, during the Pan-Canadian intergovernmental process, which added another layer of complexity, since the negotiations were multilateral, but regulatory approval of an international or interprovincial pipeline clearly lay within the domain of the federal government alone. (That said, provincial and municipal regulation of such a pipeline became an issue in British Columbia in 2018. The courts transferred jurisdiction from the City of Burnaby to the National Energy Board because the city seemed to be stalling on approvals. The British Columbia government asked for a court ruling on its authority to regulate bitumen carried through the province in a pipeline approved by the federal government. In 2019, the British Columbia Court of Appeal ruled it did not have that authority, prompting the provincial government to announce it would appeal the decision to the Supreme Court.)

The Pan-Canadian negotiating dynamic had become clear by the time of the court decision on Northern Gateway: both the federal government and the western provinces wanted something that only the other could provide, which laid the groundwork for bargaining. To understand events in the Pan-Canadian process as they unfolded over the summer and early fall 2016, it is important to understand what each wanted of the other.

The federal government wanted something the provinces were free to give or withhold: provincial participation in a national program centred on a federal backstop minimum carbon price. This gave the provinces some degree of power and bargaining leverage. However, the three western provinces were not negotiating together as one bloc, and nor yet were federal desires the same for all three. It is likely that Ottawa had decided by the summer of 2016 that its Pan-Canadian process could survive without Saskatchewan participation, given that its emissions were only 10 per cent of the Canadian total. However, it could not survive if *both* Alberta and Saskatchewan declined to participate, since Alberta emissions were 38 per cent of the total – if both of them opted out, any federal-provincial agreement would apply to barely half of total Canadian emissions and so could not be considered viable. That meant Alberta's desire for federal approval of a coastal pipeline application, either expansion by twinning of Kinder Morgan's Trans Mountain pipeline from Alberta to the west coast or Energy East to the east coast, was of central importance. As set out below, on 3 October, when Prime Minister Trudeau unilaterally announced the federal carbon price backstop plan, Alberta Premier Rachel Notley responded within hours, saying her province would only participate in the national program if Ottawa approved a coastal pipeline. It seems almost certain she would have given that message privately to Ottawa many months before. If so, by the summer of 2016, Ottawa would have badly wanted Alberta participation and would have known it had to provide Kinder Morgan approval (the Energy East approval process was just starting and final federal approval in order to get it was several years in the future – the private sector proponent cancelled plans for Energy East in the fall of 2017).

At the same time, British Columbia and Ottawa each wanted something of the other. Since using it as part of her winning strategy in the 2013 provincial election, British Columbia Premier Christy Clark had made LNG export the centrepiece of her economic development strategy. By 2016, the project closest to coming into being was a proposal by the Malaysian energy firm Petronas to build at Prince Rupert a massive plant for export of LNG to Asia (in July 2017 the company cancelled those plans due to poor market conditions; in 2018, a group of private sector firms operating as LNG Canada announced they would proceed with a different British Columbia LNG project located at Kitimat). For the 2016 planning of the Petronus project, natural gas would be provided by pipeline from the British Columbia interior. Approvals had been given by the province, but federal approval was still needed because the project would be largely built on "federal lands and waters administered by the Prince Rupert Port Authority" (McKenna 2016). That federal approval, of course, was something Premier Clark very much wanted.

For its part, Ottawa wanted British Columbia to participate in the Pan-Canadian process but also wanted something more – first, to see British Columbia increase its carbon tax beyond the current level of $30 a tonne and, secondly, to be sure that British Columbia would not block the Kinder Morgan pipeline that Alberta so badly wanted. An advisory panel had recommended that British Columbia increase the tax, but on 19 August 2016, Premier Clark had said the tax would remain at $30 a tonne. It is likely that by that time federal officials had already decided on the backstop price system announced on 3 October; $10 a tonne in 2018, rising by $10 each year until it arrived at $50 in 2022. If British Columbia could be convinced to increase its tax to $50 there would be no need for the federal backstop in that province and other provinces could be told they were only being asked to match the level of effort shown by a sister province.

On 27 September 2016, environment minister McKenna and NRCan minister Jim Carr flew to British Columbia to announce federal approval of the Petronus LNG project. Minister McKenna suggested that a British Columbia-Ottawa deal on the carbon tax had been reached when she said, "With the legally binding conditions we are putting in place and with British Columbia's commitment to increase its price on carbon in line with the Pan-Canadian Framework, I am confident we will minimize the environmental impacts of the project" (O'Neill et al. 2016). Gary Mason, writing in the *Globe and Mail* said: "In return [for the federal LNG approval], Ms. Clark had to offer her backing of a national carbon strategy, and agree to raise her province's own carbon tax accordingly" (2016). Premier Clark announced in January 2017 that the Kinder Morgan pipeline had met her province's five conditions, once the company agreed to provide British Columbia with twenty-five to fifty million dollars a year over twenty years, depending on the quantity of oil shipped. It is not clear if dropping British Columbia opposition to Kinder Morgan was discussed with federal officials prior to the September 2016 federal LNG approval. The next step in this approvals-participation-tax dynamic, federal approval of Kinder Morgan on 29 November, just prior to the 9 December FMM, is discussed below.

Returning to the narrative of the federal-provincial process, the premiers met by themselves, as the Council of the Federation, in Whitehorse on 20–2 July 2016. It was apparent that the two provinces most opposed to the federal carbon pricing plan were Saskatchewan and Nova Scotia. Premier Brad Wall complained that the federal government was pre-empting the federal-provincial process by apparently having decided on its pricing plan before the federal-provincial working group on that topic had finished its deliberations and said his government was exploring options to block federal regulation of a crown corporation such as SaskPower (CBC News 2016c). Premier Stephen McNeill of Nova Scotia also expressed his opposition to the federal plan, saying his government by use of law rather than a carbon tax had already reduced that province's emissions to be 10 per cent below the 1990 level and that the resulting increase in electricity rates constituted a form of carbon pricing (CBC News 2016c). The three territorial leaders also took a position in opposition to the federal plan.

On 18 September 2016, federal minister Catherine McKenna confirmed that her government no longer considered the Harper target of minus 30 per cent as a "floor" and that instead it was now being treated as the Canadian target (Payton 2016). A few days later, on 21 September, the minister stated that acceptable provincial carbon pricing had to be either a tax or a trading system and that the price would be higher than British Columbia's current $30 a tonne (CBC News 2016d). With those two announcements, the Trudeau government had broken two of its commitments to the provinces – the commitment made in the Liberal election platform and repeated by the new minister after the Liberals had formed government to include the provinces in decision-making on Canada's national target and the Vancouver Declaration agreement that carbon pricing "mechanisms" were acceptable. A few weeks later, the federal government did far greater damage to the federal-provincial process.

On 3 October 2016, CCME held its annual meeting of federal and provincial environment ministers. On the agenda were reports from three of the working groups. Federal representatives circulated a document titled *Pan-Canadian Approach to Pricing Carbon Pollution* (Government of Canada 2016a), which set out the elements of the federal program, including the narrow definition of pricing as only a tax or trading system and the annual price increases to $50 a tonne, and informed the provincial ministers that the prime minister at that moment was publicly announcing the program in the House of Commons (Nunavut Environment Department 2016). With those words, according to the Yukon minister, "The air was sucked out of the room" (CBC News 2016e). Ministers from three of the provinces without a tax or trading system and so potentially subject to the federal backstop price left the meeting. Ontario and Quebec supported the federal plan. Alberta Premier Rachel Notley said her province would only participate if there was "concurrent progress" on pipelines (CBC News 2016e). The Saskatchewan premier made the obvious point that publicly announcing unilateral federal action at the same time as engaging in federal-provincial talks on the same subject puts considerable stress on the federal-provincial relationship: "The level of disrespect shown by the prime minister and his government today is amazing. This is a betrayal of the statements made by the prime minister in Vancouver this March" (CBC News 2016e).

The prime minister's 3 October speech in the House of Commons contained no surprises in terms of the design of the unilateral federal program: pricing was mandatory, in that the federal government itself would impose a price in any province that did not have a price meeting the "federal benchmark" (set out in the 9 December PCF document; a means of ensuring the price was sufficient and that trading systems resulted in the same emission reductions as would be achieved by a tax); provincial programs had to be a carbon tax or trading system; pricing would start at $10 a tonne in 2018 and rise by ten dollars a year until reaching $50 in 2022; cap-and-trade provinces had to reduce emissions by the same amount as would have been achieved by those tax levels; and any federal pricing would not increase federal revenues, since those funds would "stay in" the relevant province or territory, although it was not stated whether funds would be returned to the provincial or territorial government or to those paying the federal price, such as firms or citizens (Trudeau 2016). The speech also contained this sentence: "As we are talking today, the minister of the environment and climate change is discussing the details of this plan with our provincial and territorial partners" (Trudeau 2016). More accurate than "discussing" would have been the phrase "explaining to our partners exactly what it is they will have to do." While the details were not a surprise, the announcement on the same day as a federal-provincial environment ministers' meeting certainly was, eliciting the reactions outlined above. In terms of damage to federal-provincial trust and thus the working of the intergovernmental process, this was a clumsy move, comparable to the strategic errors previously made by Prime Minister Chrétien's government. It could not have helped any efforts Ottawa might have been privately making at that time to keep Saskatchewan on board.

How likely was it, in the days after the prime minister staked out this non-negotiable position, that a multilateral agreement could be reached before the end of the year? A review of provincial positions helps answer that question. Ontario and Quebec, with combined emissions representing about a third of the Canadian total, were supportive, although Quebec representatives were regularly expressing concern, mild by Quebec standards, concerning federal encroachment on provincial jurisdiction. Saskatchewan was still adamantly opposed, threatening legal action and unlikely to budge from that position. Alberta would participate, if a pipeline were approved. The territories were also opposed, but had succeeded at the 3 October ministers meeting in having wording inserted into the draft plan saying their circumstances would be taken into account (Nunavut Environment Department 2016). British Columbia, having already secured its pipeline approval, was supportive. The newly elected Manitoba government, on the other hand, said it was "reviewing its options" (McCarthy 2016c). Three Atlantic provinces that did not have pricing in place, Newfoundland, Prince Edward Island, and New Brunswick, were not actively opposing the federal plan and were reviewing options for ways in which they could comply. The fourth, Nova Scotia, which had publicly opposed the federal plan, was taking the position that since it had done more than any other province to reduce emissions, it should not be asked to do more now. However, it was not actively opposing the federal plan in the manner of Saskatchewan, but instead saying it wanted to negotiate an agreement with Ottawa that would take into account those earlier actions. The four Atlantic provinces together accounted for only about 5 per cent of Canadian emissions and so a national plan without their participation would be viable based on coverage alone. However, they represent 40 per cent of Canadian provinces, and a plan without the participation of four provinces would certainly not be viable in terms of legitimacy. In early October it seemed quite likely that any national program would not include Saskatchewan, Manitoba, and Nova Scotia and, though less likely, possibly also be missing Newfoundland, Prince Edward Island, and New Brunswick.

Presumably motivated by that calculation, Ottawa proceeded to negotiate a bilateral agreement with Nova Scotia. On 21 November 2016, the federal environment minister made two announcements, first that it had amended the Harper government's regulatory requirements respecting coal-fired electricity plants, replacing the open-ended requirement that they significantly reduce GHG emissions or close down once they had reached the end of their useful life with a specific deadline of 2030. The second, after the minister met with Premier McNeill in Halifax, was that Ottawa would allow Nova Scotia coal-fired plants to continue operations past 2030, in exchange for the premier's commitment that Nova Scotia would introduce a cap-and-trade system and negotiate a new equivalency agreement (McCarthy 2016d). Ottawa thus ensured that its major opponent among the Atlantic provinces would sign on to the national program at the upcoming meeting of first ministers. (Saskatchewan and Ottawa signed an agreement on 28 November 2016, allowing coal-fired electricity plants to continue to operate after 2030, providing offsetting reductions were made elsewhere in the province; unlike the Nova Scotia agreement, however, Saskatchewan agreement to participate in the PCF was not part of the deal.)

The Ottawa-Nova Scotia agreement illustrates the basic problem with the primary objective of the Trudeau government's plan. The main goal sought by Ottawa was to ensure that a minimum carbon price was in place in all parts of the country, rather than to ensure that *programs* were in place in all parts of the country sufficient to achieve the 2030 goal. This is illustrated by the fact that the Trudeau government accepted the Pan-Canadian agreement signed 9 December 2016, even though it fell short of the Paris target by 44 Mt and that another 86 Mt of reduction would only come from programs referred to in the document, but not yet designed and announced by governments (Pan-Canadian Framework 2016, 44). A year later the shortfall was estimated to be 66 Mt (Government of Canada 2017, 129); in 2019, the shortfall was estimated to be 79 Mt (ECCC 2019a, 5).

Ottawa's fixation with carbon price rather than reductions, regardless of the policy instrument used, produced the bizarre result of the Nova Scotia cap-and-trade promise. The province that had already reduced its emissions more than any other, and was well on track to itself achieve the Paris target, which it did the next year (Environment and Climate Change Canada 2019b), was asked to introduce a whole new reduction program, while Alberta, whose emissions had always been rising and were projected to continue that increase right through to 2030, was asked only to make a minor change to its carbon tax program, by adding to it the federally mandated increase to fifty dollars by 2022. Clearly, equity among provinces was not part of the Ottawa calculation. Nor yet was efficacy. Nova Scotia accounted for some 2 per cent of total Canadian emissions. Wringing yet another emissions reduction program out of that government would do little to help meet the Canadian goal. Alberta accounted for 38 per cent and Ontario 22 per cent, for a total of 60 per cent of Canadian emissions. Convincing those two provinces to introduce new programs would contribute significantly to reaching the Canadian goal, but perhaps because that was not Ottawa's primary objective, no such request was made of them. The analysis section below recognizes the significant achievement of the Trudeau government in putting in place the first coordinated federal-provincial program to use policy instruments more effective than voluntary action, but also necessarily discusses this central weakness of the program.

29 November 2016 was the date of the penultimate, and pretty much inevitable, event in the negotiation of the Pan-Canadian agreement. On that day, Prime Minister Trudeau announced that his government had rejected the Northern Gateway pipeline but approved both Kinder Morgan and Enbridge Line 3, the former providing increased access to the west coast and the latter to the US market, for a total of one million barrels a day increased pipeline capacity for Alberta oil (McCarthy and Lewis 2016). Alberta Premier Rachel Notley met with Trudeau after his announcement and congratulated the prime minister on "showing some extraordinary leadership today" (McCarthy and Lewis 2016). Environmentalists and some British Columbian politicians screamed blue murder and press reports noted that Justin Trudeau had met his first big political test, making a decision that alienated a considerable number of voters, to the point that it had the potential to lose seats in British Columbia. Willing to pay that price, the prime minister had delivered on his part of the implicit deal with Alberta. A few days later, that government returned the favour.

The premiers and territorial leaders convened a brief Council of the Federation meeting in Ottawa on the morning of 9 December 2016, without issuing a press statement, and then went into the First Ministers' Meeting. After the day's discussion, the first ministers released the Pan-Canadian Framework document and a separate communiqué which, of course, described the former document in glowing terms (Pan-Canadian Framework 2016; First Ministers' Meeting 2016b). As expected, Saskatchewan refused to participate. Manitoba said it might participate later, but only if additional federal health care funding was provided. By temporarily walking out of the meeting in the afternoon and telling the press she could not sign, British Columbia Premier Clark won a concession to the effect that British Columbia alone would decide in 2020, the point at which the federal backstop price would reach $30, if the British Columbia tax would increase the next year to $40. This was guaranteed by adding the following sentence to the PCF document: "B.C. will assess the interim study [not mentioned in the remainder of the document, but presumably referring to a verbal commitment to a study to determine if the cap-and-trade provinces have an effective price of $30 in 2020] in 2020 and determine a path forward to meet climate change objectives" (Pan-Canadian Framework 2016, 53). All other provinces and territories agreed to participate. (The British Columbia

NDP government elected in 2017 has since reversed that position and committed to matching the federal price up to $50 in 2022.)

What were the case study outcomes, as of the evening of 9 December 2016? The first, and most significant for purposes of this analysis of federal-provincial energy and climate programs, is that all but two Canadian governments reached agreement on a national program centred on effective policy instruments. The 1980 NEP also made use of law, but without the same degree of provincial acceptance. All governments had agreed on the 1995 NAPCC, but that was easier to do since it imposed nothing on the private firms emitting greenhouse gases within provincial borders except to consider joining a voluntary program; by the same token, all governments had agreed to the 2015 CES, but that too was made easy by the voluntary nature of the program. In this case, eight provinces agreed that even if nothing else were done they would have a carbon price of $50 a tonne in place within their borders by 2022. For that reason alone, the PCF is a remarkable achievement in the history of Canadian national federal-provincial energy and climate-change programs, even taking into account the difficulties it ran into in subsequent years.

The other major outcome, which perhaps also serves to help explain the success of the PCF, is that a process tightly managed by Ottawa over a remarkably short time frame produced a national program that is best characterized as a Government of Canada program with provincial participation. The PCF document (2016) sets out actions the federal government had committed to in specific detail. Actions to be taken by provinces are less precise. By and large, it seems the more specific commitments in the PCF document are the ones beginning with the words "The federal government will …" Annex I of the document lists specific actions Ottawa will take and funding provided in the 2016 federal budget. Annex II, devoted to provincial and territorial actions, lists actions previously taken or sets out in vague terms action the individual jurisdiction and Ottawa will take together (Pan-Canadian Framework 2016, 47–77).

General guiding principles are stated, such as the need to "recognize flexibility for regional differences" (Pan-Canadian Framework 2016, 9) but a lot of the text is devoted to describing actions already taken, while future actions are described only in very general terms. An example is this statement: "Connecting clean power across Canada through stronger transmission-line interconnections will help reduce emissions" (Pan-Canadian Framework 2016, 11); and this: "Federal, provincial, and territorial governments will work together to help build new and enhanced transmission lines between and within provinces and territories" (Pan-Canadian Framework 2016, 13). Like the CES, the general goal, or opportunity, is described but no specifics as to exactly who will do what, by when, are provided. Some are more specific, such as this: "Federal, provincial, and territorial governments will work with industry and other stakeholders to develop a Canada-wide strategy for zero-emission vehicles by 2018" (Pan-Canadian Framework 2016, 18). But the only specific action committed to is development of a plan. We then return to vague language with this: "Federal, provincial and territorial governments will work together to protect and enhance carbon sinks" (Pan-Canadian Framework 2016, 22).

The document contains no commitments by any province to change its existing climate change plan or to achieve a provincial reduction target different from the one it had in place before entering into the national process. Since there are no mechanisms in place to monitor implementation of federal-provincial agreements in Canada, there is wide scope for provinces to simply not take the kinds of actions referred to, although the document does say progress would be reviewed in 2022. Only the federal government, because it is more visible and has made more specific commitments, is likely to be held to account. It is impossible to escape the feeling this is a federal plan to which provinces have acceded. The roughly nine months between the two meetings of the PM and premiers was enough to get consent from most provinces, but was not enough – there simply were not enough meetings of ministers – to put together a true multilateral plan, with buy-in from all governments.

Thus the two outcomes of the Pan-Canadian process as of the date of signing were: 1) a substantial degree of policy coordination involving meaningful policy change in order to use instruments more effective than voluntary action; and, 2) a program largely designed by Ottawa and consisting of federal action. Other attributes of the PCF are discussed in the next few paragraphs.

The Pan-Canadian program takes for granted that Canada cannot meet the 2020 target (by not making a single reference to it in the PCF document). The 2017 report of the commissioner of environment and sustainable development found that "Environment and Climate Change Canada was no longer working to meet the 2020 target for reducing greenhouse gas emissions set out in 2010 under the Copenhagen Accord" (section 1.41). Once again, Canadian governments refused to make the effort of meeting a pending target but saved face by promising to meet a new target, safely removed by at least a decade.

Beyond that, the PCF provides no guarantees it can meet the 2030 target. A single page is devoted to the latter subject, headed "Pathway to meeting Canada's 2030 target" (Pan-Canadian Framework 2016, 44). Projected 2030 emissions are said to be 742 Mt, while the target is said to be 523 Mt (later changed to 513 Mt, as shown in table 1) by that date – leaving a gap of 219 Mt. Of that amount, it is said 89 Mt will come from policy measures in place as of 1 November 2016. No specifics are given, other than some examples such as "regulations (e.g. HFCs, heavy duty vehicles, methane)" and examples from two provincial climate plans, and the statement "international cap-and-trade credits" (Pan-Canadian Framework 2016, 44). Another 86 Mt is said to be expected from "measures in the Pan-Canadian Framework" including two specific measures, "coal phase-out by 2030" and "federal clean fuel standard," followed by vague references to "buildings" and "industry" (Pan-Canadian Framework 2016, 44). Thirdly, we are told the remaining 44 Mt needed will come from "additional measures such as public transit and green infrastructure, technology and innovation, and stored carbon (forests, soils, wetlands)" (Pan-Canadian Framework 2016, 44). No other information on anticipated reductions brought about by particular policy measures is given. It is fair to say that if Canada had in place policies and programs, with anticipated emission reductions for each, which added up to the 219 Mt gap, they would have been listed. Since they are not, it is fair to say first ministers signed the 2016 PCF document knowing it gave no guarantee Canada would reach the 2030 target: just as Prime Minister Mulroney was unable to give a guarantee in 1990 that Canada would reach his 2000 target; and just as Prime Ministers Chrétien and Harper were unable to give guarantees we would reach their targets. The PCF has honourable antecedents.

Two other aspects of the PCF should be mentioned briefly. The first is that the national process generated a plan that in no way considers the distribution of emission reductions among sources, regions, or provinces. It completely ignores the West-East divide and the fact that other provinces will have to reduce by an additional 90 Mt because Alberta chose to increase rather than decrease its emissions. There is a very strong possibility those other provinces will balk and refuse to do that. If so, either Ottawa will have to use federal law to bring about that reduction somewhere in the country or, the more likely outcome given our reluctance to date to talk about this inconvenient truth, Canada will miss the 2030 target by 90 Mt. The PCF also ignores the fact that, with the same certainty we ascribe to death and taxes, the necessary 219 Mt reduction, if it is achieved, will have been allocated among sources and provinces, generating political heat, resistance, and conflict while that is done. The principle that no region will be asked to bear an "unreasonable burden," which appeared repeatedly throughout the 1990s documents has been dropped and no reference to provincial equity in reduction distribution has taken its place. Nor is there any mechanism in the plan to decide on allocation, and to thereby provide a safety valve for the inevitable conflict. The PCF sidesteps two of the main challenges to effective national policy by pretending they do not exist. Everything we know about Canadian climate-change policy to date, however, tells us they will only continue to not exist if Canada uses the same stratagem it has in the past – failing to miss the Paris target by a wide mark, thereby ensuring there will be no need to deal with the messy question of who pays for which reductions.

The concept of the same carbon price throughout the country is in basic contradiction to the concept of equity in sharing the total reduction effort, given the fact that carbon intensity of provincial economies, and with that costs of reduction, vary considerably. It is the same problem found with any use of tax to influence behaviour – the same tax level imposes a greater burden on the poor than the rich. This point is discussed in the report of the working group on carbon pricing, both in terms of differing household incomes and, in terms of geographic distributive impacts, with respect to greater impacts borne by "Northern, remote and Indigenous communities" with the suggestion these problems might be addressed through use of pricing revenues (Working Group on Carbon Pricing Mechanisms n.d., 28). The report suggests principles to guide the use of pan-Canadian carbon pricing, including the need to avoid a "disproportionate burden on vulnerable groups," defined as trade exposed industries, northern and remote communities, and the poor (Working Group on Carbon Pricing Mechanisms n.d., 43). No reference is made to differences in impacts on regions or provinces.

Finally, it has to be said that the Pan-Canadian process represents a missed opportunity. After nine years of a federal government motivated by both ideology and electoral self-interest to take no action on the issue, on 19 October 2015, the clouds parted and Canada was bathed in sunlight. By then the science was largely believed, other countries were acting and most provinces, the most important actors, had also shown their willingness to act. The Justin Trudeau government had a unique opportunity to put in place a national program that added up to coordinated actions actually able to achieve the 219 Mt reduction in a verifiable and credible manner. However, the basic logic that flowed from the decision to adopt a minimum carbon price in all parts of the country as the central federal objective made taking full advantage of that opportunity unlikely. As the Trudeau government continually pointed out, before it started the national process some 80 per cent of Canadians lived in jurisdictions with some form of pricing. The federal objective, accordingly, was to spread that system over the remaining 20 per cent in the Atlantic provinces, Manitoba and Saskatchewan. But that meant the federal objective was to change behaviour of provinces that, taken together, contributed only one-fifth of Canadian emissions while by and large leaving the big four emitting provinces alone (Government of Canada 2016b). For that reason, even if fully effective, the one mandatory requirement imposed upon provinces would not have achieved a lot. The Justin Trudeau government should certainly get credit for what it did do – far more than any other federal government before it. But in passing we shed a small tear for what more it might have done.

Implementation to 16 April 2019

Successful implementation of the Pan-Canadian program after its signing on 9 December 2016 depended upon the same series of interlocking commitments that had allowed it to come into being in the first place. The Justin Trudeau government would provide both emission reductions and at least one new pipeline. British Columbia would accept a new pipeline running through its territory to the west coast because it had an agreement with Alberta and compensation from Kinder Morgan. Alberta would participate in the national program in exchange for federal approval of such a pipeline. The other big-emission provinces, Ontario and Quebec, would accept an increase in their effective price on carbon, to be achieved through their trading systems, because nothing else was asked of them. By spring 2019, however, due to elections and changes of government in British Columbia, Ontario, and Alberta and a court ruling quashing approval of the Trans Mountain expansion, the mortar holding those interlocking commitments together had become sufficiently fractured that it had become difficult to characterize the PCF as truly being a "national program." We now recount the trials and tribulations of the PCF in the days of its implementation.

On 28 July 2017, the NDP came to power in British Columbia, reliant on support from the Green Party. As centre-left parties, both were in favour of action on climate change through participation in the PCF, and Premier Horgan proceeded to implement a plan to increase the British Columbia carbon tax by stages, bringing it to the $50 backstop level by 2022. This pro-environment position meant, however, that both parties were strongly opposed to the Trans Mountain expansion, and on taking office the NDP promised to do whatever they could to stop it. The previous British Columbia-Alberta agreement whereby the Clark Liberals accepted the pipeline had come undone by virtue of an election result.

While some had expected that British Columbia would stall the issuance of its own regulatory approvals for the pipeline, that did not occur. Instead, it announced plans to itself regulate heavy oil in pipelines and then, after Alberta and federal opposition, agreed to refer that plan to the courts for a ruling on whether it had constitutional jurisdiction to do so. On 8 April 2018, Kinder Morgan, threatening capital flight, announced it was suspending work on the new pipeline construction, due to political risk caused by the British Columbia action, and demanded that all such risk be removed by 31 May. If not, the company said, it would not proceed with the project. The federal government, making no effort to resist corporate power, accepted that deadline and began negotiations with the company on ways in which it could insure against any such financial loss. In April, the Alberta government sought to threaten British Columbia by introducing legislation giving it authority to halt gasoline shipments to that province. On 29 May 2018, the federal government announced that rather than insuring, it had purchased the existing pipeline and all things associated with the proposed expansion. This federal purchase, however, did nothing to reduce the level of conflict between Alberta and British Columbia, nor to produce any real warming in the Alberta-Ottawa relationship.

The next election that had an impact on the fortunes of the PCF took place on 7 June 2018, when the Doug Ford Progressive Conservative government was elected in Ontario, defeating the Kathleen Wynne Liberals. Ford had promised to end the Ontario cap-and-trade program and challenge in court the ability of Ottawa to impose its backstop price in that province. The new government proceeded to act on both campaign promises. The Ontario premier never said he was withdrawing from the Pan-Canadian program but that was essentially what his government did – even though, oddly enough, it was still formally a member of the program as of 11 December 2018 (Julie Bertrand, Environment and Climate Change Canada, email to the author 11 December 2018). Beyond ending its cap-and-trade program and challenging in court the federal tax that replaced it, the Ontario government embarked on plans to develop a new, unilateral climate-change program; there were virtually no meetings between leaders or ministers of the two governments but considerable public acrimony; and the Ontario government cancelled the PCF shared-cost programs previously agreed to with Ottawa by the former Liberal government. In response, Ottawa said it would still seek to spend that money on energy-efficiency programs in Ontario even without provincial government participation (Environment and Climate Change Canada 2018).

On 29 November 2018, the Ontario Ford government announced its climate action plan, with a 2030 target less ambitious than the preceding Ontario plan and a lack of detail on how it would achieve reductions, absent the cap-and-trade program. As noted in chapter 1, this was justified on the grounds that Ontario had already contributed its fair share to the national effort, which evoked discussion of whether other provinces would have to do more to make up for the reduced Ontario effort.

By then, the new Ontario government had both turned away from Ottawa and also from Kathleen Wynne's climate-change ally, the Quebec Liberal government. The Ford government replaced that alliance with one more to its ideological liking, a partnership with Scott Moe's right-wing Saskatchewan government (Moe had replaced the retiring Brad Wall as premier); the two governments vowed they would fight together against Justin Trudeau's backstop carbon tax, each taking legal action in an attempt to have it declared unconstitutional. Earlier in the year, Moe's government had been informed in a letter from federal minister McKenna that because of its refusal to participate in the PCF it had lost its share of funding from the PCF Low Carbon Economy Fund and that the federal backstop price would be applied in that province.

McKenna said the Saskatchewan share of funding would still be spent in that province, but by working with municipalities, non-governmental organizations or others, rather than jointly with the provincial government (Huffington Post 2018). At the Council of the Federation meeting 19–20 July 2018, Ford and Moe worked to convince other premiers to join their battle against Ottawa, but without immediate success.

At the beginning of August, the Trudeau government announced that it planned to reduce the carbon price that its backstop system would impose upon large industrial emitters. As it had evolved, the backstop price consisted of two elements: a tax on fuels, to be paid by distributors, and a tax on emissions from large-emitting firms. Presumably driven by competitiveness concerns related to the lack of climate policy at the federal level in the US, and "months of lobbying by industries" (McCarthy 2018), the tax on large-emitting firms was reduced, with a greater reduction for those in trade-exposed industries such as cement and steel.

On 30 August 2018, the Federal Court of Appeal overturned the regulatory approval given to Trans Mountain by the Trudeau government on 29 November 2016. It did so on two grounds: 1) failure to adequately consult with Aboriginal peoples; and, 2) the fact the NEB review did not include environmental impacts of increased tanker traffic, including effects on endangered southern resident killer whales. In response, that same day Alberta Premier Rachel Notley announced her government was leaving the PCF. Alberta would keep its carbon tax, but it would stay at $30 a tonne once it reached that level in 2020 rather than increasing by steps to the federal level of $50 in 2022. Nor did she rescind any other Alberta climate-change policies; in fact, in 2018 the government of Alberta continued to work with the Government of Canada on PCF programs (Bertrand 2018). Notley also left the door open for a return to the PCF, saying, "until the federal government gets its act together, Alberta is pulling out of the federal climate plan, and let's be clear, without Alberta that plan is not worth the paper it is written on" (Dangerfield 2018). Given that Alberta is the largest emitter, the second part of her statement is true in one sense; on the other hand, given that the PCF plan allows her government to increase emissions right through to 2030, Alberta participation was never a guarantee that the PCF could meet the 2030 target.

In subsequent weeks, the Trudeau government made clear its plans to comply with the court ruling, rather than to appeal it, to undertake new consultation with affected Aboriginal peoples, and to ask the NEB to consider marine effects in preparation for a new decision on the pipeline. The NEB did so and again recommended project approval on 22 February 2019. Consultations continued through spring 2019. In June, the Trudeau government again approved the Trans Mountain expansion. Further court challenges were then filed on the basis of inadequate consultation, leaving the future of the pipeline still uncertain.

Prior to that, by the fall of 2018, it was becoming clear that the federal carbon tax would not only be imposed in Saskatchewan. In early 2018, Manitoba introduced plans for a carbon tax, but one capped at $25, saying it would not comply with the PCF requirement to raise carbon prices above that level. In early October, after failing to convince Prime Minister Trudeau to give a commitment to refrain from imposing the federal tax in 2020, when the price is scheduled to be $30 in all provinces, Manitoba Premier Brian Pallister announced he had changed his mind. The Manitoba government would not impose its own carbon tax and would oppose application of the federal tax in that province. This volte-face happened immediately after a personal meeting between the prime minister and the Manitoba premier; it seems Justin Trudeau lacked the necessary personal touch needed to keep a rebellious player on the team.

For its part, New Brunswick had never been happy about the need to bring in carbon pricing particularly since, like Nova Scotia, it was on track to meet the 2030 target. In December 2017 the Liberal government of Brian Gallant announced it would dedicate a portion of its provincial transportation fuel tax for climate programs but did not bring in a new pricing mechanism. Not surprisingly, Ottawa deemed the province to be out of compliance with the federal pricing requirement. The 24 September 2018 election produced a minority Liberal government that was then defeated on a non-confidence vote, and on 9 November 2018, the Progressive Conservative government of Blaine Higgs took power. Once that happened, like the other provinces led by conservative governments, New Brunswick became a vocal critic of the federal tax and moved to intervene in the Saskatchewan and Ontario court cases to argue against the federal tax.

On 23 October 2018, Prime Minister Trudeau announced that four provinces – Saskatchewan, Manitoba, Ontario, and New Brunswick – were out of compliance with the PCF pricing requirement and that the federal tax would in 2019 be imposed in those four. (Because it still had a carbon tax, the backstop price was not applied at that time in Alberta.) Revenues raised in the four provinces would not be returned to the provincial governments. Instead, 90 per cent would be returned to citizens and the remainder to institutions and small businesses. Carbon tax revenue paid by business firms (distinct from large-emitting firms, which were subject to a different federal tax) would not be returned to them but instead to citizens, meaning most families would receive more in rebates than they paid in carbon tax. The Trudeau government did a masterful job of framing the announcement as one of giving money away, rather than imposing a new tax. Conservative premiers and Andrew Scheer, leader of the federal Conservative Party, spat and snarled. Battle had been joined on what was certain to be one of the major issues in the fall 2019 federal election.

On 3 May 2019, the Saskatchewan Court of Appeal issued its decision in the case against the federal carbon tax brought by the Saskatchewan government.

In a split three-two decision, the court found the tax to be constitutional, giving Justin Trudeau a badly needed win to shore up the central element in the faltering PCF program. The Saskatchewan premier announced his government would appeal to the Supreme Court. In late June 2019, the Ontario Court of Appeal found the tax to be constitutional and the Ford government announced that it too would appeal to the Supreme Court

A few weeks before the Saskatchewan court decision, on 16 April 2019, Alberta voters soundly defeated the Notley NDP government and gave Jason Kenney's United Conservative Party (which was a combination of the two previous right-wing parties, the Progressive Conservatives and Wild Rose) a majority government. Throughout Notley's tenure, the Alberta economy had suffered, both from the 2014 drop in oil prices and restrictions on pipeline capacity which limited exports to the US and to more lucrative Asian markets. Not surprisingly, inability to build the Trans Mountain expansion line had become a major irritant for Alberta voters, seeming to symbolize the way in which the province was misunderstood and ignored by the rest of Canada. Building on that discontent, Kenney's election platform consisted of a staunch defence of the oil industry and promises to come out swinging against its perceived enemies – British Columbia, environmentalists, Indigenous groups on the wrong side of the pipeline issue, and Ottawa. His stance signalled a return to the combative approach of Ralph Klein and a jettisoning of the more sophisticated approach introduced by Premiers Redford, Prentice, and Notley, which recognized that Alberta needed allies, ones it could only find by publicly recognizing the reality of climate change and the need to reduce (or at least slow down the rate of increase) the province's GHG emissions. Like Doug Ford before him, Kenney promised that his first legislative action would be repeal of the Alberta carbon tax, to be followed by political and legal action intended to thwart imposition of the federal tax within Alberta borders.

As discussed, as of the date of signing on 9 December 2016, the major outcomes of the PCF were: 1) coordinated federal-provincial action covering 87 per cent of Canadian emissions, using more effective policy tools than those of the 1990s national programs; and, 2) a program in which the bulk of the policy action was being taken by Ottawa. How had those outcomes changed by the time of the Alberta election? The most significant was the sharp reduction in federal-provincial coordination. Once Kenney had replaced Notley and moved into alliance with Saskatchewan, Manitoba, Ontario, and New Brunswick in the fight against the PCF, the portion of Canadian GHG emissions coming from provinces fully cooperating with the program had declined to just 24 per cent. Furthermore, those participating provinces represented a minority (44 per cent) of the Canadian population. While the PCF was technically still a national, federal-provincial coordinated effort, because five provinces were actively hostile to the program, there was far less coordination of government activity than there had been at the point of signing – to the point, as noted, that the term "national" might be considered a misnomer.

The second outcome by the spring of 2019, flowing directly from the first, was that the PCF had become even more a unilateral Ottawa program. Prime Minister Trudeau's government had made slow but steady progress in taking its own PCF policy action. Beyond the backstop carbon price, progress had been made in developing its other main unilateral action: the clean fuel standard. The term refers to a system of federal regulation of all fuel use, both mobile and stationary, in which legally binding standards would mandate reductions in the carbon intensity of different fuels. Technical design and consultations were continuing, with regulations for different fuels planned to take effect in 2020 and 2021 (Government of Canada 2018a). Ottawa had also used federal law to regulate HFCs and to impose a 2030 end date (with exemptions given to Saskatchewan and Nova Scotia) for generation of electricity in Canada by means of coal-fired plants. Federal regulations to reduce methane emissions from the oil and gas industry, with provision for provincial equivalent action, had been put in place in 2018. Jointly funded projects to reduce emissions had been initiated in a number of provinces (Government of Canada 2018b) and, as noted, in the case of non-participating provinces such as Saskatchewan and Ontario, federal money was being given directly to others located within the province. From 2015 to 2019, the Government of Canada took more effective action to reduce GHG emissions than it ever had before. Almost all of that action, however, was being taken by Ottawa alone, with only minimal coordination with provincial partners.

In summary, by spring 2019 the major outcomes of the PCF program were: 1) significantly reduced policy coordination; and, 2) more than ever, it had become a Government of Canada program with some provincial participation. Furthermore, it was a program whose future had become uncertain. Should a Conservative government take power in Ottawa it would be ended; if not, a re-elected Liberal government would be under strong pressure to in some way revise the program in an effort to bring the enemy provinces back into the fold.

One of the basic arguments advanced in this work is that Canada can only achieve an international emission reduction commitment through coordinated federal-provincial action, because the provinces will never cede the policy field completely to Ottawa. The evolution of the PCF since its signing supports that argument. By 2019, far from leaving Ottawa free to act, Conservative governments in the hostile provinces were litigating, attacking (such as the Ontario plan to require gas-pump stickers highlighting the cost, but not the rebates, of the federal tax) and using opposition to a carbon tax for partisan ends to help the federal Conservatives win the October 2019 election. While doing so, provinces like Ontario and Alberta were reducing their climate policy effort. It is difficult to imagine how the PCF can survive, let alone generate effective, emission-reducing policy, in such an environment.

Analysis

1) What Does the Case Tell Us about the Four Subjects?

THE WEST-EAST DIVIDE

The case shows us, again, that the western provinces are the ones most engaged with national energy and climate policy and the most likely sources of resistance. As in the other cases, differing regional interests were very much in evidence during the period leading to the 9 December 2016 signing. Ontario and Quebec were already acting on the issue and, since nothing significant was asked of them, supported the federal initiative. The Atlantic provinces were asked to change behaviour but seemed to feel they could find ways to live with the federal demand. The three most westerly provinces, on the other hand, worked to weaken the federal-led effort: Saskatchewan by opting out, Alberta by demanding increased pipeline capacity that would help to avoid limiting oil sands production and associated emissions, and British Columbia by getting federal approval for an LNG plant that would have significantly added to that province's emissions had the project gone ahead, and by a last-minute refusal to accept the tax increase to fifty dollars.

Events during the implementation period, from signing to 16 April 2018, show that the West-East divide is capable of adding another dimension when provincial governments in other parts of the country ally themselves with carbon provinces for ideological reasons. We saw that during the 1990s, when the Klein government of Alberta worked with the Harris government of Ontario to play a joint veto role, even though their energy interests were convergent. The same thing happened in 2018, when the Ontario Ford government allied itself with Scott Moe's Saskatchewan government in a veto effort to defeat the federal backstop price in court. Earlier cases showed that the West-East divide is not necessarily symmetrical: western motivation is not necessarily matched by countervailing motivation on the part of Ottawa or central and eastern provinces. To that, we add the lesson that western motivation may be matched by eastern *similar* motivation, moving in the same veto direction.

THE INHERENT NEED TO ALLOCATE EMISSION REDUCTIONS

The case shows us the same things we have seen in previous cases. When the target is some years distant and no immediate overall reduction is being imposed, equity in distribution of associated costs is not a major concern. As noted, the "no unreasonable burden" principle did not appear in the two main documents which listed principles guiding the national process, the Vancouver Declaration and PCF. The only actor to make any reference to cost allocation or equity was the Saskatchewan premier. Premier Wall made the same point respecting fairness in a special debate in the provincial legislature on 24 October 2016, which resulted in a resolution, supported by the opposition, condemning the federal plan:

> Make no mistake, Mr. Speaker: this tax [the federal backstop tax] may be revenue neutral I guess in principle but it is not sector neutral [Wall had argued the tax imposed higher costs on more carbon-intensive industrial sectors]. And it is not neutral as to the regions of this country. There are two provinces that will pay mightily with jobs that Saskatchewan and Alberta families depend on if this tax goes ahead. (Wall 2016b)

The fairness of cost allocation was not a major part of his argument, however. Wall's basic message was, first, that the carbon pricing was not needed, since his province was doing other things to reduce emissions, and, secondly, that the federal carbon price would cause significant economic damage in his province. Nevertheless, he did raise the allocation issue on at least two occasions prior to his refusal to sign on. As noted, the allocation issue was also discussed after Ontario announced its new climate plan on 29 November 2018. As we have seen in the previous cases, the allocation issue may not be explicitly addressed, but is never completely absent.

THE NATIONAL PROCESS

The case shows us that a multilateral intergovernmental process, supplemented as needed by a bilateral agreement, led by a motivated and engaged prime minister and with direct involvement of first ministers can produce a substantial degree of policy coordination. It also shows that the roadway of implementation, in the years after the intergovernmental agreement is signed, does not always run smoothly.

FEDERAL GOVERNMENT STRATEGY

The case shows the importance of the degree of interest displayed by the lead government, Ottawa. For whatever reasons, perhaps mostly the change in values and examples offered by other governments acting on the issue between the 1990s and 2010s, the government of Prime Minister Justin Trudeau was far more motivated, engaged and willing to confront the provinces than had been that of Prime Minister Chrétien. Although making diplomatic errors, lack of negotiating skill was far less significant in the Justin Trudeau case than in the two Chrétien cases. To complete that comparison, the Trudeau government was willing to use unilateral action to influence provincial behaviour, while Chrétien was not. The case strongly suggests that such federal action is a necessary component of national coordinated energy or climate-change policy.

2) What Are the Most Important Factors Explaining the Case Outcome?

As discussed, the case outcomes at the date of signing were a substantial degree of policy coordination, albeit in a largely federal program. As of spring 2019, coordination had diminished and the program was even more federal, with some provincial participation. Those outcomes are explained by these factors: 1) an initial absence of veto-government resistance up to the point of signing, followed by a subsequent increase in veto resistance due to election of conservative provincial governments; 2) a high degree of lead-government interest throughout; and, 3) willingness on the part of that lead government to use unilateral action as a threat to influence provincial behaviour. Each factor is discussed.

The fact that Ottawa faced less veto-government resistance during negotiation of the program than it had during the two climate programs of the 1990s is explained by two factors. The first was Justin Trudeau's decision to take carbon pricing as his main objective, which as discussed meant he was not required to ask a lot of the big emitting provinces that already had pricing in place. Since they were asked so little, they initially at least offered little veto resistance. Related to that was the second reason for less veto-government resistance: the Alberta swing-government role. This was due perhaps to the unexpected outcome of the 5 May 2015 Alberta election. In the 1990s, Prime Minister Chrétien had faced right-wing Alberta governments with no interest in acting on climate change. That changed with the elections of Premiers Redford and Prentice, who had different views on the issue itself but more important had seen a need for Alberta to gain environmental legitimacy by taking action. Possibly if the Alberta Conservatives led by Jim Prentice had won in 2015 they would have subsequently cooperated with the Trudeau program for that reason, but that cooperation was made that much more certain by election of an NDP centre-left government that not only sought environmental legitimacy but also believed action should be taken on the issue regardless of other considerations. The carbon tax introduced by the Notley government put it in the same camp as British Columbia, Ontario, and Quebec, a camp largely unaffected by Ottawa's backstop carbon price. The result was that instead of facing a powerful veto alliance of Alberta and Saskatchewan, representing close to half of total Canadian emissions, Ottawa needed only to engage in a stare-down with Saskatchewan, a province that contributed only

10 per cent of emissions and so could more easily be left out of the program. (After election of the Jason Kenney government in April 2019 Alberta reverted to the confrontational stance of the Klein days; barring re-election of an NDP government, any future national effort is likely to see Alberta again playing its traditional veto role.)

Things changed, of course, with the June 2018 Ontario election and creation of a new Saskatchewan-Ontario alliance working to counter the federal back-stop price by means of court action and mobilization of their electorates in resistance. It was the election of the Ontario Doug Ford government that had the greatest effect upon evolution of the PCF. The Manitoba government had shown a willingness to act on the issue and was in any case a less important player by virtue of providing only 3 per cent of Canadian emissions. Alberta stayed allied with Ottawa (until the Notley NDP government was defeated), since federal action was its only hope of gaining a new pipeline, even after it formally left the program (with the implicit swing-government promise that it would rejoin should the pipeline be built and if Premier Notley were still in power). Neither actions by Manitoba, Alberta nor New Brunswick (2 per cent of emissions) which had not put in place carbon pricing meeting Ottawa's standard affected the program the way the Ontario defection did. Ford's election ended the Ontario-Quebec alliance, which we saw in 2015 pushing the CES towards inclusion of statements on climate action. It ended the supporting role Ontario under the Wynne government had played during development of the PCF. That was replaced by a particularly vitriolic opposition to Ottawa, right from the start, not only on climate change but also other issues such as immigration. In the days of John Robarts and Bill Davis during the constitutional and energy conflicts of the 1970s, Ontario, with its large population and economic importance, had been Ottawa's loyal and powerful lieutenant. That was certainly not the case after Ford's election, as the province reverted back to the opposition role the Harris government had played during the 1998–2002 climate program, with this time the opposition being much more brazen and visible.

How do we explain the Ontario change in role? Certainly the explanation does not lie in enduring economic interest, as it does for the western carbon provinces which, even with the switch to NDP governments in Alberta and British Columbia, kept their eye on the main prize of expanding fossil fuel exports, be they bitumen or liquefied natural gas. Nor is it explained solely by the right-wing ideology of the governing party. The centre-right Coalition Ave-nir Québec elected on 1 October 2018 did not cancel that province's cap-and-trade program or participation in the PCF. Patrick Brown, Ford's predecessor as Ontario Progressive Conservative leader, had convinced his party to support an election platform that endorsed carbon pricing. Instead, the answer lies in the particular nature of Ford's right-wing ideology – populist, pro-car, skeptical of elites and therefore of the scientists and others calling for action on climate change. The Ontario change in role, happening at about the time that France was forced to cancel a carbon tax due to populist rebellion, confirms Rabe's argument (2018) that pricing carbon is only the first political challenge, while *keeping* those programs in existence is another.

The second factor explaining the case outcomes is the high degree of motivation of the federal government led by Justin Trudeau. Situated on the centre-left, the Liberals were open to action on climate due to party ideology. By the time the party took power in 2015, Canadian attitudes towards the issue were very different from those of the 1990s and examples abounded, both in Canada (for instance, the British Columbia and Quebec tax and trading programs) and in other jurisdictions, such as California, the UK, and Germany, of governments moving to take more effective action. Just as important was the personal commitment of the prime minister. As he did with other issues such as feminism and reconciliation with Indigenous peoples, Justin Trudeau made very clear he was determined to loudly proclaim his personal values and to see them translated into government policy. For better or worse, he stayed personally engaged throughout, determined to both build a pipeline and to price carbon over the head of loudly resisting provincial governments.

The outcomes of initial substantial coordination followed by a significant reduction in that coordination and evolution of the PCF to be largely an Ottawa program also flowed from the willingness of the Trudeau government to use unilateral action as a means of influencing provincial behaviour. It is likely that in early 2016, when Ottawa's plans for a federal backstop price were first publicly discussed, the Trudeau government hoped it would not in fact have to impose the tax anywhere. By spring 2019, when it became clear the tax would in fact be imposed in five provinces, the instrument had become a mixture of a threat that had in fact influenced the behaviour of some provinces and unilateral action. As such, the federal backstop price, as an example of unilateral action by Ottawa, is in the same league as Pierre Trudeau's National Energy Program. The lead-government actor did not do anything similar in the other three cases examined, since Alberta lacked the constitutional power and the Chrétien government lacked the motivation of the two Trudeau governments. Passage of time has shown that the unilateral action of the NEP, while inducing Ottawa-Alberta compromise, generated more damage than benefit. Given the degree of rancour and opposition displayed by right-wing premiers and political parties, there is a strong possibility that same may hold for the backstop price. Nevertheless, it does show that federal unilateral action, falling somewhere between threat and declared fact of *force majeure*, can assist in generating policy coordination.

In closing, a few words can be said about the other aspects of the PCF. The complete ignoring of the 2020 target illustrates the power of the Canadian dynamic of policy failure set out in chapter 1. Disguising the lack of will and effort needed to achieve an international commitment by focusing on a new target, some years distant, was done in 1997, in 2010 and again in 2015. It provides the government in question with environmental legitimacy by allowing it to appear committed to policy action while avoiding the conflicts and costs that must be borne to actually achieve a target. Unless things change, there is a very real chance it will be done again in the years leading up to 2030, regardless of which government is in power. Because we are so willing to push action off into the future, we are able to avoid the regional conflict inherent to the allocation issue. The Justin Trudeau government's focus on the easy challenge (which, as events turned out, has not been so easy) of ensuring carbon pricing throughout Canada when the big four emitting provinces already had pricing in place, rather than the much more difficult task of convincing those four to do more than they had already themselves decided on, is a continuation of the dynamic first seen with the easy challenge of the 1995 voluntary program. At that time, as discussed, a voluntary program was all that could realistically have been hoped for. In 2015, however, with very different public attitudes, foreign and domestic examples, and a majority government eager to act, the PCF was a missed opportunity. Taking advantage of that opportunity would have required facing the challenges that are the subject of this book, in particular vastly different western and eastern energy interests. That was not done because the Canadian dynamic of favouring peaceful relations over effective policy was exerting its usual force.

As of the spring of 2019, the Pan-Canadian Framework program, so completely a product of this dynamic that has brought only policy failure since 1990, was providing the worst of both worlds. It did not have programs in place capable of meeting the stated goal, while a major element of the program, federal construction of a pipeline, will if implemented increase emissions. While providing no guarantees of achieving its goal, the PCF was causing considerable damage to national unity and the possibilities of constructive federal-provincial engagement. The outcome of the 2019 Alberta election made that situation even worse since by then a supposedly national program was opposed by half the provinces, representing more than half the population, and three-quarters of total emissions.

A new approach is needed.

10 Drawing Lessons

Writing in 2010, Weibust noted that the federal-provincial body CCME was inactive on the file and that the Council of the Federation had placed climate change on its agenda two years previously, but had been unable to reach agreement. She made this comment:

> This should not surprise us. Given the very substantial discrepancies of interests between the provinces, it would be remarkable if they could reach agreement on reducing greenhouse gas emissions. Both Alberta and Saskatchewan contain oil sands, which are the fastest growing source of Canadian greenhouse gas emissions. On the other side of the dispute are Quebec and Manitoba, with comparatively low per capita emissions and a wealth of hydroelectric resources. (Weibust 2010, 231)

Indeed, Canadian failure to date should not surprise us. It is much harder for this country to successfully act on the issue than it is for many others for all the reasons previously discussed. Canada has cold winters, hot summers, long distances, and a politically active oil industry, to say nothing of the underlying challenges reviewed in the preceding pages and referred to here by Weibust. Those living in the fossil fuel–producing provinces undoubtedly care for the global environment and their grandchildren's future just as much as those living in other regions, but they face very different motivations. Continuing to increase emissions translates for them far more directly into increased provincial wealth and jobs than do emission increases elsewhere, while the per capita cost of reducing emissions is much higher. Is it any wonder they hesitate to act? To add to the difficulty – or perhaps more accurately, to make the difficulty all but insurmountable – the only governance system we have available for reconciling those differences is a rickety, jury-rigged contraption which can barely stay afloat, let alone navigate to a safe harbour.

To suggest that Canada can in fact use the contraption of its intergovernmental policymaking system to put in place national climate-change policy capable of meeting our international commitments, without significant modification such as a move to qualified majority voting or significantly increased federal powers, might seem foolhardy in the extreme. Nevertheless, that is the task of these two concluding chapters. To do that, this chapter looks back to the five case studies in order to see what lessons can be learned from our experience to date. The first part of the chapter sets out lessons from the five cases respecting the four subjects examined. The second discusses factors that contribute to the ability of the energy and climate intergovernmental relations process to generate a substantial degree of policy coordination.

The Three Challenges and Federal Strategy

This section aggregates and summarizes the lessons respecting each of the four subjects which have been presented in the case studies. Table 8 at the end of the section provides a concise overview.

The West-East Divide

Three lessons can be taken from the case studies respecting the West-East divide. The first is that the divide was present in all five cases, with highly motivated western governments, in particular Alberta, fully engaged with the relevant national process and seeking to influence, with some degree of success, its outcome. The lesson we take from this is that those governments will certainly again be engaged and seeking to influence any future national climate-change policy effort. The second lesson is that the divide is not necessarily symmetrical with respect to government motivation; the keen interest in the national process displayed by a western carbon province like Alberta was rarely matched by that of other provincial governments. If countervailing power is to come from anywhere, it will have to be from the Government of Canada. The third lesson is that while Ottawa is better positioned than any other Canadian government to bridge the divide, it also, through clumsiness, can make the divide wider. Each of the three is discussed in order to show how the cases lead to that particular lesson.

The West-East divide was most clearly visible in and was also made significantly worse by the case of Canadian energy policy from 1973 to 1981. That is hardly surprising, since the case centred on the differing interests of the oil-producing and oil-consuming provinces respecting the oil price and the conflict between Ottawa and Alberta respecting the sharing of oil revenues. The issue was not possible future environmental damage but instead financial winners and losers in the here and now. We also find the West-East divide in all the other cases. It was evident right from the beginning of the first national climate effort, when Alberta lobbied to keep a reduction target out of the federal

Green Plan, through to Premier Klein's vociferous objections to the national target Ottawa accepted at Kyoto. We find it also in the second climate effort in the form of Alberta's continual skepticism and eventual effective withdrawal from the process. As noted, the Canadian Energy Strategy only came into being because of lobbying by the oil industry and subsequent Alberta government leadership; in the closing days, there was a clear conflict of interest between that government on one hand and Ontario and Quebec on the other. Finally, it was a western carbon province, Saskatchewan, that refused to sign on to the Pan-Canadian Framework in December 2016, while two other western provinces, British Columbia and Alberta, used the leverage they enjoyed by virtue of the PCF process to gain LNG and federal pipeline approvals (and Alberta then moved from a swing to a quasi-veto position when it failed to get the latter, before moving to a fully entrenched veto position with election of the Jason Kenney government). In each of the five cases, the western carbon provinces were highly motivated and pursuing interests that differed from those found in other parts of the country.

Beyond being marked by active western involvement, each of the cases was also marked by influence exerted by those provinces. Alberta was lobbying in favour of the world price at the outset of the first case study and through eventual compromise with Ottawa achieved at least part of its objective. In the second case, Alberta succeeded in ensuring that the main policy instrument used was a call for voluntary action and then, in 1997, convinced other governments that the Kyoto commitment should be studied for two years before any action was taken. In the case of the NCCP, Alberta could not convince other governments to adopt its alternative national reduction target but it did manage to take on that target for itself, instead of adhering to the Kyoto target, without paying any price. Alberta succeeded in ensuring that the CES included a call for new infrastructure to transport oil and gas. During negotiation of the PCF, the mantle of western resistance shifted to Saskatchewan. That province refused to participate, but far from playing a passive role then went to court to block the federal backstop tax. Alberta exerted a major influence by ensuring that the program would include a new pipeline.

Given the importance of fossil fuels to the economies of Alberta and Saskatchewan, this influence is hardly surprising. In all five cases, those carbon-intensive economics were under some form of threat – in terms of energy, from Ottawa's demand for tax revenues and then years later by the price discount dictated by pipeline infrastructure; in terms of climate change, from potential national policy that would require them to impose expensive emission reductions. In each case, that threat spurred active involvement with the national process, which in turn led to ability to influence the process.

From this, it seems reasonable to conclude that the divide will be a significant factor, perhaps the most significant, in any future national climate-change process that comes close to effective action – defined as action that analysts predict will achieve the stated target on the basis of programs announced at time of signing. This is because such an agreement will *have* to include significant reductions by Alberta and Saskatchewan, simply because together they account for almost half of total Canadian emissions. Achieving a total reduction on the order of 30, 40, or 50 per cent with no action by those provinces and the reduction thus coming from only half the Canadian sources is neither physically nor politically possible. The West-East financial interest divide, with all of its accompanying psychological baggage of identity, differing values, and remembered insults and injuries, will certainly be a major challenge in any future national climate effort.

Secondly, the cases show us there is no inherent reason the divide should be symmetrical, with equally motivated actors in both regions, each working to counter the power of the other as both work to influence intergovernmental decision-making. Active engagement on the part of the western provinces has seldom been matched by those in the centre and east. The one instance of symmetry in provincial motivation was the zero-sum game of national energy policy in the 1973 to 1981 period, in which Ontario, seeking the benefit of low oil prices, was fully engaged, as was Alberta, seeking the benefit of the high world price. That led Ontario to ally itself in a support-government role with Ottawa, increasing the political power of the latter.

In the three climate-change processes, however, there was no inherent reason why the other provinces should have been as motivated as were the carbon provinces. The latter had far more at stake than did the hydro provinces. If Alberta and the other western provinces were successful in beating back effective climate policy there was no immediate cost paid by Ontario or other provinces – in fact, quite the opposite since it saved them the costs of climate action. In terms of the CES national process, opposition to a coastal pipeline, the central issue for Alberta, was significant in British Columbia, Quebec, and elsewhere, and the Ontario and Quebec governments were motivated by their centre-left ideologies to press for inclusion of climate action in the document. In none of these cases, however, was the degree of motivation found in Alberta matched in the central or eastern provinces. (And in at least two cases, those of the Harris and Ford Ontario governments, not only was there a lack of countervailing motivation and power, but governing party ideology led to an *alliance* with western governments.)

This lack of symmetry in degree of motivation also exists between Alberta and Saskatchewan on one hand and Ottawa on the other. Again, the climate-change issue is simply less important for any federal government than it is for the governments of the carbon provinces. Here too the exception is provided by the first case, in which Ottawa was motivated by a material interest in oil revenues (as well as other factors) and so displayed a degree of interest comparable to that of the veto governments. By and large, however, Ottawa's concern to maintain national unity, interest in obtaining for the Canadian economy the benefits flowing from fossil fuel exports, and, as just mentioned, the lower priority it gives the issue, all mean that Ottawa will be less motivated than Alberta and Saskatchewan (although we must recognize Justin Trudeau's high degree of interest both to implement carbon pricing and to get a pipeline built).

This asymmetrical nature of the divide is important because it helps to explain the extent to which western interests have been able to influence energy and climate-change national processes to date, as just discussed. Alberta could not prevail in the fight with Ottawa in 1980–1 because the latter was equally motivated and armed with bigger cannon. Since then, however, with the exception of new pipeline capacity, things have largely gone Alberta's way – it was able to ensure that none of the three climate processes threatened its ability to generate wealth by requiring it to switch to a path of declining emissions, and it got what it wanted, or at least could reasonably expect, from the CES. The lesson drawn from this is that in any future national climate process we are likely to find one or more strongly motivated western veto provinces, with little likelihood they will be met by countervailing power from eastern provinces. The degree of motivation of the federal government, for that reason, will be critical, but a highly motivated Ottawa cannot be guaranteed.

The third lesson begins with the fact that the West-East divide is not an inevitable product of geography or differing societal histories, values, and identities. History has meant that Canada could not avoid the two solitudes of French or English, or the gap that separates the Indigenous world from the rest of the country. Western mistrust, however, was to a large degree created by specific actions of the federal government, going back to John A. Macdonald's National Policy, which favoured Ontario and Quebec industrial interests over the Atlantic and prairie hinterlands and carrying through to the initial refusal, in 1905, to grant full ownership of their resources to the new provinces of Alberta and Saskatchewan. Pierre Trudeau's NEP fuelled a firestorm of western anger precisely because it was seen as yet another in a string of Ottawa betrayals. In any future national climate-change program, leadership from Ottawa in bridging the West-East divide will be essential. No province can play the same role. However, there is a very real risk that Ottawa, if it is not careful, could by its actions turn the divide into an even greater challenge. Saskatchewan refusal to participate in the PCF, followed by Alberta cancellation of its carbon tax in 2019, is a warning of potential west-east difficulties that lie ahead. In meeting those difficulties, Ottawa must practice careful, skilled diplomacy (a lesson given later in this chapter) that does not add to regional animosity.

The Inherent Need to Allocate

Three lessons are taken respecting this subject. First, as was seen from the cases, governments feel free to ignore the issue of allocation of cost and benefit associated with climate change policy when a total national emissions reduction is not imminent. Secondly, the issue is most likely to be raised by a government seeing itself as the victim of an unfair distribution of cost. Pretty much by definition, that government will raise the issue using the language of distributive fairness and the issue will have to be addressed in those terms, which means both the actual distribution and the process used to decide it must be seen as fair. Thirdly, as noted in discussion of the inherent need to allocate in chapter 4, if and when the issue does present itself it will have the effect of moving the intergovernmental process towards a zero-sum negotiation, which is likely to have the effect of motivating eastern governments, thus providing countervailing power to western influence. That countervailing power, of course, also provides a significant potential for counterproductive conflict.

The issue was certainly present in the first case, in terms of distribution of benefit between Alberta and the rest of the country and more specifically of tax revenues between the Alberta and federal governments. As noted, an implicit change in distribution of cost and benefit was made both by the first oil price hike and by Ottawa's action of freezing the price. Unlike the climate cases, what was implicit quickly became explicit and the subject of negotiation. The issue was completely absent from the CES, since the framing provided by those advocating the strategy was one of unlimited benefit, available to all those who chose to participate, and thus with nothing to allocate. The one important exception in that case was the British Columbia-Alberta negotiations, which were very much involved with allocation of environmental risk and associated benefit: British Columbia demanded that it receive a "fair share" of pipeline economic benefits that "reflects the level and nature of the risk being borne by the province, the environment and taxpayers" (Clark 2012).

The allocation issue was implicitly present in the three climate cases, since all were intended to reach agreement on a fixed quantity of emissions reduction. In the two climate-change processes of the 1990s, the issue was recognized as one principle among others and was taken into account in the May 2002 federal discussion paper. The issue made the transition from being implicitly present, a background condition all were aware of but not focused on, to being explicitly raised by some actors, requiring discussion by all, on two occasions during the 1990s climate processes. The first was the adoption by first ministers at their meeting in early December 1997 of the principle that no region would be asked to bear an "unreasonable burden" as part of the national effort. The second was the action by Quebec at the 27–8 March 2000 Vancouver JMM, when the Quebec environment minister expressed his regret that other governments refused to discuss the "equitable sharing" of the cost of the total national effort. Conversely, it was not recognized at all in the Pan-Canadian Framework process other than as references by the Saskatchewan premier to the greater costs his province was being asked to bear. Presumably this was because governments were discussing a target fourteen years removed in a process that required little of the four large provinces.

Thus the first lesson is that without an imminent deadline, governments by and large will ignore the issue. That does not mean, however, it will not be present later on, when a deadline is near and modelling data is readily available showing the costs to be paid by different sectors and provinces. Addressing it then, when passions are running high, may be more difficult than addressing it earlier. In the next chapter, the suggestion is made that discussion of cost allocation might be one way of drawing reluctant provinces in to a new national process.

In the cases of Quebec in 2000, British Columbia in 2012, and Saskatchewan in 2016, it was the actor who saw itself as suffering from a proposed allocation who raised the issue. This is hardly surprising, since the perceived victim is the one with the most powerful motives for putting the issue on the table, but it is important for how the issue is likely to play out in future, when a total proposed reduction is sitting squarely on the table and economic modelling will have shown the allocation resulting from currently proposed policies. Given higher western per capita reduction costs, the allocation issue is likely to become tightly connected to the West-East divide, exacerbating the western feeling that it is being unfairly treated in national politics. That, of course, raises the possibility of such a government opting out of the national process – how Ottawa can address that danger is discussed in the next chapter.

Judging by the language used by Quebec and British Columbia, and the 1990s principle of no unreasonable burden, it seems fair to predict that once the issue is raised in future it will have to be addressed within the norms of distributive justice, as discussed in chapter 4. Arguments related to both equality (likes should be treated alike) and merit of the recipients (for instance, "my province deserves a lower reduction effort because our industries are highly exposed to trade competitiveness") will be in play; fairness of the process used to decide, as well as the resulting distribution, will be discussed; and the views of all actors will be influenced by self-interest. All of those pose considerable difficulties. However, governments distribute cost and benefit every day as they make and implement policy, and one way or another they find a way to muddle through. Beyond muddling, as noted chapter 11 discusses the possibility of using the allocation issue as a means of broaching a future intergovernmental dialogue.

The third lesson, that explicit discussion of allocation of the total reduction among sources and provinces moves the process in a zero-sum direction, is directly related to the asymmetrical nature of the West-East divide. As discussed, the carbon provinces are motivated by material interest while other provinces, with the possible exception of Quebec interest in additional revenue from hydroelectricity export to jurisdictions wishing to reduce their GHG emissions, are motivated primarily by their views on the importance of the climate-change issue. To date, that motivation has been weaker than the financial motivation of a province like Alberta and so they have been less engaged than has Alberta. That would change, however, if a total reduction were imminent and provinces were bargaining over who contributes what share of that total. By definition, since the reduction quantity is fixed, that discussion is zero sum. If one province wins by reducing less, another province must lose by making a greater reduction. At present, Alberta is free-riding on the efforts of other provinces, implicitly asking them to cover for its failure to act. If that discussion were made explicit, motivation of those other provinces would change and we would start to hear demands for Alberta to contribute its fair share. Greater countervailing motivation might well be useful, but it also has considerable potential to stall the process in unresolved conflict. Chapter 11 discusses the way in which the allocation issue presents potential benefit, but must be handled with extreme care.

The National Process

Four lessons are provided. The first and most important lesson respecting the process has been stated at the conclusion of the CES case: a national process cannot be led by a provincial government. Another lesson is that to come anywhere close to being effective, any future national program should be led by first ministers, rather than ministers. The third lesson is that the process used to date of unilateral action by all governments to establish the national and provincial emission reduction targets builds a lack of coordination directly into the federal-provincial system. Fourthly, the cases show that the oil industry is an attentive actor who has sought to influence the national process in the past and likely will do so again.

There is no need to say a lot about the first lesson. Alberta was certainly motivated as it led the CES process, but it had one arm tied behind its back. It could persuade, but it could not make credible promises or threats. It might have used the promise of royalty-sharing to get Premier Clark's British Columbia government to accept a pipeline, but that would have been unprecedented in provincial relations, and presumably because such a thing was so unthinkable, it chose not to. At the end of the day it turned out that promise was not needed, since the firm was willing to pay. A few years later Alberta attempted to use threat to force the British Columbia NDP government to accept a pipeline. It stopped selling British Columbia wines and threatened to stop gasoline exports to that province, just as Premier Lougheed had reduced oil shipments to the east. Neither posed a threat of sufficient damage to influence behaviour of the British Columbia government. The first lesson is clear. The lead-government role can only be played by Ottawa.

A comparison of the PCF with the two climate change efforts of the 1990s tells us something about the role of first ministers. In the former, first ministers were an integral part of the process, with an initial meeting prior to the Paris summit, the Vancouver meeting in early March to decide the process, and then the final meeting to agree to the national program. This involvement meant that the national effort was fully endorsed at the highest level and a clear message was sent to ministers that this was a priority issue. In the 1990s processes, on the other hand, first ministers had no formal role and were only involved one time, more or less by accident, because a prescheduled FMM took place right after the Kyoto summit. That one involvement, however, took the national process off onto the different track of study rather than implementation and laid the seed of the differing Ottawa and Alberta views of the purpose of the NCCP. When a First Ministers' Meeting might have been useful, in late 2002 prior to ratification, it was refused by the prime minister. The lesson we can draw from this is that the climate issue is of sufficient importance that government leaders are certain to be involved, one way or another. Given that, it is far better to have them play a predetermined role in an orderly process being managed from the top.

The PCF process also offers a sidebar to this lesson. There, the prime minister and premiers did not meet again after signing the agreement on 9 December 2016. One cannot help but wonder if there might have been benefit from continuing those meetings, to review implementation, after that date. Regularly scheduled First Ministers' Meetings could not have prevented something like the Ontario 2018 and Alberta 2019 withdrawals, due to changes in government. However, they might have made the Manitoba and New Brunswick defections less likely, particularly if all governments had made an initial commitment to only withdraw after first giving a specified period of time's notice and after at least one discussion at a regularly scheduled FMM.

The third lesson relates to the fact that to date all four national targets have been set by means of unilateral action by Ottawa as it engages with other countries at the international level. Since they have no voice in setting the target (or worse yet, when their voice in the form of a target agreed at a federal-provincial meeting is rejected by Ottawa, as was the case prior to the Kyoto summit) there is no reason to expect they will feel fully committed to achieving the national target.

The process of setting national and provincial targets used to date builds a lack of coordination directly into national climate-change politics. All of the four national targets to date have been set unilaterally by Ottawa, as part of an international process, with either none or only peripheral consultation with provinces, and influenced more by US-Canada relations or what is happening at the international level than by what is happening within the country. They should more accurately be termed "Ottawa" targets, a term that explains why many provinces have not seen them as something they must immediately stand up and salute. At the same time, as shown in chapter 3, all of the provincial targets have also been set by provincial governments unilaterally, for the most part without any regard to the national target or to what other Canadian governments are doing. The problem is perfectly illustrated by the fact, discussed in chapter 3, that Quebec, Ontario, and British Columbia could introduce new climate-change action plans, with new provincial targets in each, while participating in a national policymaking process. Obviously each government believed it could do both at the same time – work with other governments to decide how to achieve the Paris goal and at the same time set their own separate goals. Those beliefs suggest the three governments did not see themselves as fully engaged in an intergovernmental process that required behaviour change, in the form of targets coordinated with those of other governments. This is a powerful lesson from the climate case studies: each government setting its own target all by itself seriously detracts from coordinated and therefore effective national policy.

The fourth lesson is that of all the non-state actors, it is the oil industry, for whom energy and climate policy are of considerable importance and which has the necessary resources, that is the most likely to seek to influence any future national climate-change process. Industry was largely frozen out of the NEP government-to-government talks, but both Alberta and Ottawa felt obligated shortly afterward to revise the tax system in favour of the oil firms. Industry, led by the oil and gas sector, played a major role in co-management of the VCR and then a few years later was unable to stop Prime Minister Chrétien from ratifying Kyoto but was able to cut a very favourable deal with his government. Industry was also one of the major actors pushing for a Canadian Energy Strategy that would endorse the concept of market diversification through new pipeline construction and pushing for the "regulatory reform" enacted by the Harper government in the spring of 2012. Conversely, industry does not seem to have been heavily involved in the PCF process, which may be explained by the fact that a number of the firms had previously made a separate peace with the new Alberta government as it prepared its November 2015 climate policy. The lesson to be taken from this is that the oil industry, and very likely other sectors, are almost certain to play an active, self-interested role in seeking to influence any future national climate-change effort, likely in alliance with Alberta and other oil-producing provinces.

The structural power of business means it has guaranteed access to communicate with government in private. One possible way of reducing the extent to which such secret communication skews any future national effort away from policy effectiveness is to build into the process opportunities for open, public dialogue. If the lobbying positions of industrial sectors were made public in that way, those holding contrary views such as environmentalists, Indigenous groups, churches, or others would be more likely to mobilize and provide their advice to government. The case studies show that in any future process, the oil industry will be seeking to exert influence. Opening the door to other actors with different views can only help.

Federal Strategy

Given the lesson that a province cannot lead a national process, the Alberta lead-government role in the case of the CES is set aside and discussion is limited to what the cases show us about Ottawa's strategy as it plays that role. For that, three lessons can be taken from the case studies. The first is that the federal government must have a high degree of interest, very much wanting to see an effective national program put in place. The second lesson is that a federal government so motivated must display skill as it engages in federal-provincial diplomacy. The third lesson is that Ottawa must use some of its available power to influence provincial behaviour, but must do so carefully, with restraint.

As it leads any future national climate effort, Ottawa must be motivated. Alberta and Saskatchewan, as they play a veto role, are highly motivated because the energy and climate issues are so important for their economies. As we have seen, it is unlikely a provincial government will be equally motivated, exerting countervailing power – that has to come from the federal level. To counter the influence of the western carbon provinces, Ottawa must be equally motivated. That can only happen if the prime minister is personally engaged throughout.

The second lesson is that Ottawa must use skillful, consistent diplomacy. In terms of skill, an example of what Ottawa should *not* do is offered by Prime Minister Chrétien's government. As discussed, his hands-off style, punctuated by clumsy interventions, caused considerable harm to the federal-provincial process. The erratic jumps in the federal position displayed by the Chrétien government not only made life difficult for the provincial partners but also precluded the use of potential changes in the federal position as a form of threat. The move to unilateral federal regulation in the spring of 2002 was simply done, without prior discussion with the provinces. The opportunity of using such a possible change before the fact as a means of influencing, and thereby coordinating, provincial behaviour was lost.

The third lesson is that in addition to persuasion and promise, Ottawa must exercise power by taking unilateral action to influence provincial behaviour. In doing so, however, it must exercise restraint. An example comes from Prime Minister Chrétien's administration, when that government set aside the Kyoto target it had previously agreed to with the provinces and instead set a different

target. Since it holds jurisdiction for foreign affairs, clearly Ottawa was acting within its rights in using its available power to do so. However, the fact of
holding a given power does not mean that power should be fully used, since in
this instance it damaged federal-provincial trust and made future cooperation
more difficult to achieve. The lesson is the need for Ottawa to restrain its use
of power. The federal government should use unilateral actions to move the
process forward, but should be very careful when doing so. Canada was created
in 1867 with the conscious intent that it be a highly centralized state, and so
considerable constitutional power was given to the federal government relative
to the provinces. Since then, social norms respecting that power balance have
been almost completely reversed and we live now in an era of collaborative
federalism, in which the two levels of government have become close to equal
powers. To be in compliance with those social norms, Ottawa now cannot use
all of the power provided to it by the Canadian constitution.

More important than the Chrétien example is the negative lesson respecting Ottawa's use of power provided by Pierre Elliott Trudeau's overly forceful
approach, which is still ringing in the ears of westerners. The lesson is that effective federal leadership can sometimes come at a price too high to be worth paying. Prime Minister Justin Trudeau's unilateral imposition of a backstop carbon
tax in the face of determined resistance by provincial governments comes dangerously close to being in the same category. We will only know in future the
price to be paid for that unilateral action in terms of damage to national unity.
Some federal power must be used to influence provincial behaviour and so
achieve coordinated policy, but that must be done carefully and with restraint.
All of the lessons set out in this chapter are displayed in table 8, on the next page.

Factors Leading to Coordinated Policy

The concluding analysis for each case study included a listing of factors that
explain the case outcome. How can we now analyse those factors and use them
to draw lessons for design of any future national climate-change program? In
an ideal world, we would simply rank the case outcomes from most to least
"effective" or "successful" and then look for the differences in the explanatory
factors associated with each. If a factor is present in the most effective case but
not in the least, we could with some confidence say that factor leads to effective national policy. Unfortunately, that cannot be done because it is difficult
to say that any of the cases generated effective national policy, defined as that
which achieves the stated policy goal and successfully addresses the problem.
The first case did meet at least one of the goals stated by Ottawa (recognizing other governments had different objectives), changing the balance of oil
revenues. That was done in a form eventually agreed to by both Ottawa and
Alberta, but at an unacceptably high price for national unity. The first two

8 Lessons respecting the four subjects

West-East divide

1) Alberta and Saskatchewan will almost certainly be motivated and engaged in any future national climate-change effort, seeking to influence the outcome by playing a veto-government role.

2) Lacking their material self-interest in wealth creation by oil and gas sales, there is no inherent reason Alberta and Saskatchewan motivation will be matched by other provinces. Accordingly, the lead-government role will almost certainly have to be played by Ottawa.

3) The West-East divide exists in large part because of past federal government actions. In future, Ottawa's actions can easily make the divide worse.

Allocation

1) How the reduction is divided among sources and provinces will only be an issue when a total reduction is imminent.

2) If the issue is raised, it will be by a government seeing itself as suffering from the implicit allocation of the reduction effort. That government will use the language of distributive fairness.

3) If the issue becomes dominant, the national process will be shifted in the direction of a zero-sum game, which will increase the motivation of eastern provinces to fully engage with the process and perhaps to exert influence countervailing that of Alberta and Saskatchewan. However, such a process is fraught with dangers.

National process

1) A provincial government lacks the ability to use persuasion, promise and threat to influence other governments in the direction of coordinated policy. That lead-government role must be played by Ottawa.

2) Any future process should be led by first ministers, not ministers.

3) The process of setting the national and provincial targets used to date is the exact opposite of coordinated policy.

4) The oil industry will likely be engaged and seeking to protect its economic self-interest by influencing the outcome of any future national climate-change process.

Federal strategy

1) Ottawa must be motivated.

2) Ottawa must use consistent, skillful diplomacy.

3) Ottawa must use some but not all of its available power as it seeks to influence provincial behaviour in order to achieve coordinated national policy.

national climate-change programs failed to meet the 2000 and 2012 goals, and the 2020 goal has simply been ignored, with no national program intended to achieve it ever put in place. The jury is still out on the 2030 goal, but we do know the Pan-Canadian process has been seriously weakened by provincial defections and resistance and even before those governments left did not have in place programs capable of achieving the objective. The CES never stated the problem to be solved, and simply listed possible actions rather than specific commitments to act, and so cannot be considered effective.

For these reasons, it is not possible to differentiate the five cases in any meaningful way in terms of success or effectiveness. We can see differences, however, using the criterion of policy coordination, identified by government changes in behaviour as a result of participation in the intergovernmental process. Just as none of the cases were fully effective, nor did any achieve fully coordinated policy. It is fair to say that the two 1990s climate-change processes achieved only minimal coordination. In the first, all governments did sign on to the 1995 program, centred on the Voluntary Challenge and Registry (in Quebec Éco-GESte); however, since it was a voluntary program, no substantial new policies were required. In the second program, the coordinated programs announced by all governments in 2000 and 2002 were for the most part listings of unilateral actions. The process then collapsed in fall 2002, which by definition meant coordination was no longer possible. A further sign of only minimal coordination is the fact that during that process Alberta started down the separate policy track that it is still following today while Ottawa started down its own unilateral policy track, which continued until a federal government willing to work with the provinces took power: the Justin Trudeau government in October 2015. Nor yet does the CES case display more than minimal policy coordination; governments were engaged in the same process and signed the same document but gave no specific commitments. Beyond that, the federal government was not a participant. Accordingly, for analytical purposes, these three cases are placed in the category "minimal coordination."

The remaining two cases, on the other hand, are placed in a second category labelled "substantial coordination." By means of the Ottawa-Alberta bilateral agreement signed on 1 September 1981, modifying the 1980 National Energy Program, both parties changed their behaviour respecting revenue sharing and thus achieved a substantial degree of policy coordination. Negotiation of the Pan-Canadian Framework process resulted in eight provinces representing 87 per cent of total emissions signing an agreement with Ottawa, committing to collective policy efforts and agreeing to use of a more effective policy instrument than any used in the 1990s; each agreed to impose or accept a carbon price of $50 by 2022 and to work with Ottawa on a variety of other initiatives. At that point, the process had generated substantial policy coordination. Two years later, when Ottawa announced it would unilaterally impose its backstop carbon price in four resisting provinces (which became five after the 2019 Alberta election) the degree of coordination had been significantly reduced. The case is put in the substantial coordination category, but the discussion below includes that subsequent significant decrease in coordination.

As a result, we have these two categories:

Minimal policy coordination:
  The first national climate change process 1990–1997
  The second national climate change process 1998–2002
  The Canadian Energy Strategy 2005–2015

Substantial policy coordination:
  Canadian national energy policy 1973–1981
  The Pan-Canadian Framework at point of signing (with subsequent decline in coordination)

How do we explain these two different degrees of policy coordination? For that, we look to differences in the factors that explain the different case outcomes, presented in the concluding analysis in the case-study chapters. We now draw upon that analysis to identify the differing factors that led to either minimal or substantial policy coordination. In doing so, analysis is guided by the approach to understanding coordination (or its absence) in Canadian energy and climate intergovernmental relations set out in chapter 2. As noted there, the key is the balance of power between the lead and veto governments. Factors influencing that balance of power include such things as government's degree of interest, diplomatic skill, willingness to take unilateral action, and, more generally, the degree of countervailing power each encounters. Constitutional jurisdiction is also a source of power, but because current norms prevent the federal government from using powers technically available, such as disallowance of provincial legislation, jurisdiction is a less significant factor. Table 9 provides a summary picture of the factors leading to minimal or substantial coordination in the five cases. That comparison is then discussed in the text that follows.

*Comparing Factors Leading to Minimal and Substantial
Policy Coordination*

A review of table 9 shows these differences between the two categories. First, in the CES case in the minimal coordination category, the lead-government role was played by a province, while the Government of Canada played that role in the two cases in the substantial coordination category. Given the fact that

9 Factors explaining the difference between minimal and substantial policy coordination

---

Minimal policy coordination

Case #2: The first national climate change process 1990–1997
- veto-government (Alberta) did not encounter significant lead-government (Ottawa) countervailing power due to:
  - lack of lead-government motivation
  - lack of lead-government skill in using persuasion and promise
  - failure of lead government to use unilateral action to influence provincial behaviour

Case #3: The second national climate change process 1998–2002
- veto-government (Alberta) did not encounter significant lead-government (Ottawa) countervailing power due to:
  - lack of lead-government motivation
  - lack of lead-government skill in using persuasion and promise
  - failure of lead government to use unilateral action to influence provincial behaviour

Case #4: The Canadian Energy Strategy 2005–2015
- lead-government (Alberta) encountered no significant veto-government resistance
- however, lacking ability to use promise and threat and so using only persuasion, lead government was unable to induce significant behaviour change on the part of other provinces

Substantial policy coordination (with decline in PCF case)

Case #1: Canadian national energy policy 1973–1981
- lead government (Ottawa) encountered substantial veto-government (Alberta) countervailing power but was able to prevail due to:
  - high lead-government motivation
  - lead-government skill in persuasion and promise
  - lead-government willingness to use unilateral action to influence provincial behaviour

Case #5: The Pan-Canadian Framework on 9 December 2016, plus subsequent implementation
- initial substantial coordination at point of signing explained by fact that the lead government (Ottawa) faced less veto-government countervailing power because Alberta played a swing-government role also explained by:
  - high lead-government motivation
  - lead government willingness to use unilateral action to influence provincial behaviour
- during implementation, coordination subsequently declined, due to increase in veto-government countervailing power as hostile governments were elected in some provinces

provincial capabilities to use persuasion, promise, and threat to play a lead-government role are so much less than those of the federal government, it is not possible to make a meaningful comparison between the lead-government role played by Alberta in the minimal coordination CES case and the lead-government role played by Ottawa in the two substantial coordination cases. Accordingly, the CES case is set aside and the discussion that follows compares the remaining two cases in the minimal coordination category with the two in the substantial coordination category.

As can be seen from table 9, the major difference between the two categories is in the balance of power between the lead and veto governments. In the two remaining cases in the minimal coordination category (Cases #2 and #3) the balance of power favoured the veto government over the lead government. In neither case did the veto government encounter significant countervailing power exercised by the lead government. Put simply, during the national climate-change processes of the 1990s, the Chrétien government was never sufficiently motivated to play an effective lead-government role. As a result, the Alberta veto influence went largely unchecked.

In the two cases in the substantial-coordination category (Cases #1 and #5), that balance of power was reversed. In those cases, the lead government exercised more power than did the veto government (at least at the point of signing the agreement). In Case #1, that was because Ottawa was motivated, skilled, and willing to use unilateral action to influence provincial behaviour. In Case #2, it was because Alberta was playing a swing-government role, with only Saskatchewan playing a significant veto-government role. Here too Ottawa was motivated and willing to take unilateral action to influence provincial behaviour. The lead-veto balance of power changed in the implementation phase of Case #5, of course, as new governments were elected and provinces like Ontario and Alberta moved from supporting or swing roles to veto roles.

In keeping with the approach used here to understand energy and climate intergovernmental coordination, the key factor explaining the difference between minimal and substantial coordination is the balance of power between the lead and veto government. While that is not surprising, what is significant is the major factor influencing that balance. Rather than factors influencing the balance of power such as financial and staffing resources deployed by governments, legitimacy or constitutional jurisdiction, the most important factor – shown by the difference between the two categories – is the way in which Ottawa played its hand. Action taken, or not taken, by Ottawa is the most important factor explaining the differences in the lead-veto balance of power which led to minimal or substantial policy coordination. (The one other factor is the fact that Alberta played a swing rather than veto role in Case #5.)

10 Explaining the difference between minimal and substantial coordination

	Minimal coordination	Substantial coordination
	Case #2 Climate 1990–1997	Case #1 Energy, 1973–1981
	Case #3 Climate 1998–2002	Case #5 PCF 2015, 9 December 2016
Lead-veto balance of power	favoured **veto**, due to:	favoured **lead**, due to:
	• Ottawa low motivation	• Ottawa high motivation
	• Ottawa not skilled	• Ottawa skilled (less so in Case #5)
	• no useful Ottawa unilateral action	• Ottawa unilateral action
		• Case #5 no veto role by Alberta

The Chrétien government in the two 1990s cases was not highly motivated, as indicated by the fact that for most of the time the prime minister left the file in the hands of his ministers. The Chrétien government displayed inept diplomacy, failed to exercise power in the form of unilateral action intended to influence provincial behavior, and when it did eventually take unilateral action failed to get benefit from first using it as a threat. Instead, Ottawa's unilateral action meant it effectively left the process. As a result, from 1990 to 2002 veto government Alberta was able to ensure the process did not generate coordinated action.

By contrast, in both the energy policy 1973–81 and PCF case, Ottawa was highly motivated, had personal engagement and leadership of the prime minister, and was willing to use unilateral action to influence provincial behaviour. Ottawa displayed less skill in the PCF case prior to signing the agreement, most notably by announcing the unilateral introduction of the backstop price at the same time the federal and provincial ministers were, in theory, meeting to design the coordinated program. However, this inept diplomacy was compensated for by the fact that during negotiation of the agreement it faced less veto-government resistance due to the Alberta swing role. Although for different reasons, in both cases, the balance of power favoured the lead government over the veto government.

This explanation is summarized in table 10. For the reasons set out above, the CES case is not included in the table. The PCF case is shown at the point of signing. The subsequent decline in PCF coordination is discussed below.

The most important factor influencing the lead-veto balance of power is Government of Canada strategy. This finding augurs well for future success in developing an effective national climate-change program since, unlike immutable factors such as the geographic location of fossil fuel resources or the IGR decision-making process, it can be influenced by future federal governments.

The Subsequent Decline in PCF Coordination

The lead-veto balance of power also explains the decline in degree of coordination in the period after the agreement was signed. The most significant events changing that balance of power were the movements of Ontario and Alberta from support and swing to veto roles due to the election of conservative governments. This factor of government change is exogenous to the federal-provincial process. The election of the Doug Ford government in Ontario came about because of circumstances unique to Ontario politics (had Patrick Brown stayed on as PC leader he likely would have won the election and kept Ontario in the program), not because of any actions by Ottawa. The same can be said for the election of Jason Kenney in Alberta. Movement of new governments into veto roles is simply an example of the risk inherent to federal-provincial programs extending over a period of years; as was the case with the failure of Meech Lake, there is always the chance that provincial elections may result in a government happy to participate being replaced by one with different views.

The second factor, however, is directly related to lead-government lack of skill. As shown in the case study, the Justin Trudeau government needlessly antagonized provinces during the negotiation period and was unable to keep Saskatchewan in the program at the time the agreement was signed, even though earlier in 2016 it had signed the Vancouver Declaration. Another failing was the inability in 2018 to keep Manitoba and New Brunswick in the program on the basis of their own carbon pricing, even though both had shown signs of willingness to cooperate. The defection of Rachel Notley's Alberta government can also be laid at Ottawa's door, both because of the original willingness to agree to the bargain of a pipeline in exchange for participation and a lack of skill in its own regulatory process, in which it failed to protect the Trans Mountain expansion from a successful court challenge. Although unlikely, the April 2019 Alberta election might have had a different outcome if the expansion were under construction at the time. Lead-government lack of skill helps to explain the fact that the program does not display substantial policy coordination.

Lessons

The first lesson drawn from this comparison, of course, is that a province cannot lead an energy or climate intergovernmental process through to a point of substantial policy coordination. This is the same as the lesson set out in table 8.

The second lesson is that policy coordination depends upon the balance of power between lead and veto governments. Only when that balance favours the lead government (Ottawa) can coordination be achieved. That lead-veto balance of power is determined in the first instance by the presence or absence of active resistance by veto governments. None were substantially present in the CES case, but the lead government, a province, was so lacking in power it could not take advantage of that fact. Had Ottawa acceded to Alberta's request and played the lead role in that case, the absence of veto influence might have allowed increased policy coordination. (Although an Ottawa push for provinces to formally declare they would accept new pipelines crossing their territory might well have engendered more veto resistance.) The absence of Alberta as a veto actor in the PCF case helps to explain the initial substantial policy coordination. The second factor determining the lead-veto balance of power is action by the lead government, Ottawa. When Ottawa is motivated, skilled, and willing to take unilateral action as a means of exercising power to influence provincial behavior, it can successfully counter veto-government influence. These are the same lessons as those provided in table 8.

The same caveat provided in the preceding section respecting Ottawa's use of power bears repeating. The power exerted by Ottawa by means of the National Energy Program, while not drawing on the full constitutional powers it had available, was nevertheless closer than in any of the other cases to the kind of top-down authority found in formal organizations, where coordination is always found. The Canadian intergovernmental system, however, is *not* a formal organization. The simple fact of being a federated state, with consent of subnational units being required before basic rules can be changed, moves Canada and all other federations into a very different category from that of an army or business corporation. Beyond that, the norms of Canadian federalism evolved considerably between 1867 and 1980, with the result that Pierre Trudeau's actions were seen by the aggrieved western parties as lacking legitimacy. Since 1980, those norms have moved even further in the direction of collaborative federalism, marked by equality between the two levels of government rather than domination. It is too early to say whether Justin Trudeau's backstop tax will come to be seen as a similar transgression of norms and exacerbation of the basic Canadian problem of the West-East divide. There is a real possibility it will.

Using the example of the Chrétien government setting aside the November 1997 federal-provincial agreement on the Kyoto target, it was pointed out that unilateral action by the federal government can be counterproductive, working *against* policy coordination. Beyond that, two other lessons respecting use of unilateral action by the Government of Canada are drawn from the comparison of categories. First, Ottawa exertion of power in the form of unilateral action can achieve policy coordination by influencing provincial behaviour. Secondly, the price paid to achieve that coordination in terms of damage to the Canadian confederation may be too high. Ottawa must not in future use the kind of power it did in the NEP case. Certainly, Ottawa must exert power as well as diplomatic skill in order to influence provincial behaviour and thus achieve some degree of policy coordination. That power, however, must be exercised with care and restraint.

The third lesson drawn from this comparison is that federal-provincial energy and climate programs have a limited shelf life. Elections and the coming into power of new governments can drastically alter the program dynamic. Election of the Brian Mulroney government in 1984 led to the ending of the substantial policy coordination achieved by the Pierre Trudeau government. Elections in Ontario, New Brunswick, and Alberta significantly reduced Pan-Canadian policy coordination. To maintain policy coordination, even a successful program will likely have to be renegotiated every five years or so.

11 Putting in Place an Effective National Climate-Change Program

What is Canada's most important achievement over the past 150 years? Some will look to military success, in the death and valour of Vimy Ridge, or on Juno Beach, where men of the 3rd Canadian Infantry Division suffered heavy casualties as they waded ashore on 6 June 1944, or, more recently, the contributions of Canadian soldiers, both men and women, in Afghanistan. Others, wishing to stress Canadian values of humanity and generosity, will look to a proud tradition of international engagement, honouring Lester B. Pearson and his 1957 Nobel Prize and Canadian contributions to peacekeeping. Others might point to science and the invention of insulin, or to sport and the famous 1972 victory over the Soviet Union, that blessed moment when Canadians across the time zones were all doing the same thing at the same time – madly honking their car horns to celebrate Paul Henderson's winning goal. These are all valid achievements, as are many others, certainly worthy of celebration. Another way of answering the question, however, is not to look to positive action by individual Canadians or the country as a whole, but instead to look at what Canada has *not* done – it has not allowed conflict stemming from differences in identity, race, or regional economic interest to degenerate, Oka notwithstanding, into civil unrest, armed conflict, or secession by one part of the country. Perhaps Canada's greatest achievement is simply the fact, against difficult odds, of its continued existence.

Small, homogenous societies such as Sweden have existed as nation and state for centuries without facing the threat of small-scale internal armed conflict or full-blown civil war. Many other societies have not been so lucky. The United States paid an enormous price in terms of lives lost and blighted during its civil war of 1861 to 1865. More recently, Lebanon, Northern Ireland, the former Yugoslavia, Rwanda, and Democratic Republic of the Congo are all examples of groups of people unable to live together in harmony in one state and who are instead driven by hatred of the other to kill and maim. Canada might well have been a member of that unhappy group, given the challenges it has always faced as a small population living in very distinct economic regions divided by long distances, language, and identity and containing what was originally thought of as two nations, or solitudes, and what is now accepted to be three – Indigenous, Québécois, and, that inelegant term used to bundle together everybody else, the "Rest of Canada." As someone once said – perhaps Goldwin Smith? – Canada cannot be thought of as the Roman fasces, rods bound tightly together to form one stout, larger rod, but instead should be seen as a string of fishing poles, bound together only at the ends to form a series of weak links, draped across the northern border of the United States. How can such an entity survive?

The greatest threat to Canadian survival, of course, has been the Quiet Revolution of the 1960s and the conviction of a significant portion of Québécois that their destiny lay with creation of their own independent country. Immediately prior to the 1980 Quebec referendum, Prime Minister Pierre Trudeau promised Quebec a new constitutional arrangement if they were to vote no, but then, after the fact, devoted his energies instead to his cherished Charter of Rights and Freedoms and, by means of the Night of the Long Knives, repatriated the constitution without Quebec consent. To his credit, Prime Minister Mulroney tried to make good on Trudeau's promise but was met with the failures of Meech Lake and Charlottetown and Quebec then came within a whisker of separating in the referendum of 1995. Prime Minister Chrétien then took various steps, including in the environmental arena the 1998 federal-provincial Harmonization Accord, intended to show Québécois that confederation could work to their advantage. By and large, however, since 1995 the Rest of Canada has addressed the threat of Quebec separation not by overt action but instead by an unwritten, and perhaps largely unspoken policy of benign neglect, based on the conviction that the constitution must never again be opened up for possible amendment in our lifetimes. This is perhaps a realistic recognition of the fact that there is little Canadians outside Quebec can do to influence the decision of those within the province on what for them is a question fundamental to their national life. Whatever the source, this approach has worked for more than twenty years – Quebec is still part of Canada, albeit very much a distinct society, and while separatist sentiment is still alive the chances of Quebec separation in the immediate future seem to be slim. Canada, so far at least, has survived.

In this instance, turning a blind eye to a major Canadian problem has worked, at least until now. That does not mean the same strategy will work for another major Canadian problem examined here: our inability to keep our international commitments to reduced GHG emissions. That is because of the basic difference in the two problems. For the first, the goal of the Rest of Canada and federalists living within Quebec is that no action be taken, that the status quo prevail and that the Canadian state thus survive within its existing borders. For the second, however, the status quo *is* the problem, since it represents continually rising emissions other than at times of economic recession. Benign neglect, or no action, is not an option with respect to climate change.

So, what should be done? How can Canadians and their governments use the experience gained from previous national energy and climate-change programs as they plan future action? What follows are suggestions for doing exactly that. For the most part, they are based specifically upon the lessons drawn respecting the four subjects examined and those from the comparison of national processes that have achieved substantial and minimal degrees of policy coordination. Some, however, and most specifically the recommendation made to all Canadians that they initiate a new national dialogue, are based upon our entire energy and climate history to date. Since it is the actor who must lead, most of the recommendations are made to a future Government of Canada. The chapter concludes with discussion of possible objections to the suggestions made and four further, minor key suggestions.

A New National Dialogue between West and East

As we have seen, to date Canada has pursued a strategy of turning a blind eye to the fact that the formally stated climate policies of the western carbon provinces makes achieving any Canadian reduction target very difficult indeed, combined with a refusal to publicly discuss the fact that achieving such a target will impose much higher costs on those provinces than upon others. The history of Canadian emission increases since 1990 shows that strategy has failed. We cannot continue to ignore our two different emission pathways, with emissions steadily rising since 1990 and projected to continue to rise until 2030 in one part of the country and declining in other parts. We must break out of our polite Canadian shell and start talking to one another about our greatest barrier to effective climate-change policy – the West-East divide.

Jim Prentice called for a national dialogue and national vision, but warned that such efforts might "quickly boil into a divisive national disagreement" (Prentice 2017, 164). We must start talking across the abyss running through the centre of the country, but it must be a very different kind of conversation than the one to date. There, one side is shouting out, "We don't want your pipelines!" The other side is shouting back, "We send you equalization money produced by pipelines!" Recrimination and insult can only produce a hardening of attitudes on either side of the divide and will certainly not lead to compromise and shared effort. The new national conversation that is so badly needed might usefully start with each side admitting something to itself that so far it has avoided thinking about. First, Canadians outside Alberta and Saskatchewan must get clearly in their minds that they themselves cannot reduce western emissions, that they cannot *force* the carbon provinces to do anything.

It is all too easy to fall into the trap of saying that Alberta got rich by contributing disproportionally to global climate change and is rich enough now that it can afford to swallow the cost of emission reductions and thus atone for past sins. That discourse can have only one effect – prickly Alberta retreats behind its firewall and litigates and politics continually until Ottawa, the only government that actually could force western reductions, gets tired and gives up, after which both sides get on with their lives, but in a badly fractured country. Instead, the new national conversation must begin with recognition of the fact that the Quebec and Alberta issues differ in terms of the question of inaction or action, but in another respect are very similar. At the end of the day, it is only Quebec citizens who can decide their question of possible statehood. Although not so literally true, in the same way it is only Alberta citizens and their duly elected government who can decide Alberta climate-change policy. This is true for two reasons – political reality and the norms of regional fairness that keep Canadian federalism functioning.

The federal government almost certainly has constitutional jurisdiction to regulate GHG emissions within Alberta borders. That fact carries some weight in any given federal-provincial climate policy process, as did the fact that Ottawa could likely have reversed the 1980 Alberta decision to reduce oil shipments to eastern Canada. As an unspoken threat of federal unilateral action, it seems to have contributed to Premier Lougheed's promise he would resume shipments in case of real need (although one would like to think his position also stemmed from a basic sense of fairness in dealing with fellow Canadians). However, all the realities of Canadian social and political life dictated that Ottawa not take such action in 1980 and today dictate that Ottawa not use the Canadian Environmental Protection Act to reduce Alberta emissions to a point 30 per cent below their 2005 level by 2030.

As discussed, electoral self-interest means no federal government is likely to do that. It would lose too many votes, not only on the prairies but also in Quebec, whose citizens are hyper-sensitive to federal bullying of any province, and likely elsewhere as well. More importantly, it would not do so because it would be such an egregious violation of the unwritten norms that govern Canadian political life. A federal backstop price rising to $50 a tonne imposed in five provinces whose governments have said they want no such tax comes dangerously close to crossing the line of acceptable federal behaviour. Full-bore action by Ottawa, acting unilaterally and in the face of heated provincial government resistance, might well achieve the Paris target within western borders, but would go far beyond that line. At the end of the day, only Albertans and their government can decide whether their emissions will fall in keeping with the national target.

The second necessary starting point for the new national conversation is for the citizens of the carbon provinces to fully admit to themselves what they are asking the rest of the country to do on their behalf. In 2015, the government of Alberta announced its new climate-change policy. Such things as the new carbon tax were significant actions that would have reduced Alberta emissions had they been kept in place, and the Notley government is to be congratulated for taking them. Any such reductions, however, would have been overwhelmed by increasing emissions caused by expansion of oils sand production. Premier Notley's implicit policy was that Alberta emissions should increase, not decrease. In the following year, Alberta participated with other governments in the Pan-Canadian plan intended to decrease total Canadian emissions. As the price for signing on to the latter, it insisted that the federal government approve new pipelines. After taking those actions, Alberta was subscribed to two contradictory policy goals: first, to increase its emissions, albeit not as much as they would have grown absent things such as the coal phase-out, and, secondly, to work with other governments to decrease total Canadian emissions. The contradiction comes from the fact that the Alberta goal to increase emissions works *against* the goal adopted by Alberta and all but two other Canadian governments to decrease emissions. This means Alberta has implicitly adopted a third policy goal – to ask Canadians to pick up the 90 or so Mt of Alberta emissions, which result from the fact it plans to increase its emissions by 9 per cent rather than reducing them by 30 per cent. (The Jason Kenney government, of course, by scrapping Notley's measures, is planning on even bigger increases, requiring even more offsetting action by other provinces.)

This third policy goal, however, did not appear anywhere. It was not explicitly referred to in the Alberta plan, the PCF plan, or any of the other provincial plans, although the facts provided in those documents made it plain to see for anybody who cared to look. It was not talked about by governments; the federal environment minister repeatedly congratulated Alberta on the reductions it was making (as so she should) but never referred to the fact that Alberta emission increases were overwhelming reductions made elsewhere (as she also should). As we saw in chapter 4, the lack of the emperor's clothing is only referred to by commentators such as the Pembina Institute. As a result, the Alberta policy (with a lineage running unbroken from Klein to Kenney) of asking others to make reductions on its behalf is not clearly visible, either to other Canadians or to Albertans themselves. The second starting point for the national dialogue has to be recognition by Albertans that they are shifting costs from their shoulders onto those of their fellow Canadians. Albertans are free-riding and they need to admit that to themselves.

Beyond these two starting points, the focus of such a new national conversation must be the search for a fair sharing of the costs of climate-change action. We must reverse our existing posture of see no evil, speak no evil, turning our faces away from the West-East divide and the implacable need for cost allocation, and instead open up a frank, courteous discussion of burden sharing. That dialogue has been going on at the international level for years. There, the need for distributive equity, in particular between the Global North and South, has long been recognized by governments in the formula of "common but differentiated responsibilities" and given institutional form by creation of such things as the Global Environmental Facility, which channels financial assistance from the industrialized nations to those in the Global South who are acting on climate change. Twenty years ago, it was also recognized by Canadian governments under the formula that no region would be asked to bear an "unreasonable burden." However, in this country we never moved beyond the level of rhetoric. We never asked ourselves how we would define "unreasonable" and we never got to the point of seriously discussing what portion of the total burden would be borne by each province. With election of the Harper government in 2006 and an end to any meaningful federal role within Canada or any constructive Canadian international role, followed by unilateral action by provinces, there was no need or opportunity for such discussion. In 2016, the PCF carbon pricing working group did discuss distributive equity in terms of the need to assist "vulnerable communities" but never really defined such communities, beyond references to rural and northern, and never discussed how that might be done (Working Group on Carbon Pricing Mechanisms, n.d.). The concept of "no unreasonable burden" was abandoned by the Justin Trudeau government and never appeared in the PCF policy dialogue, even at the level of pious rhetoric. The principle must be resurrected and then the national conversation must wrestle with the difficult question of how to put it into practice.

This new national conversation on equity in sharing reduction costs must be informed by expert analysis. As we know from the case study histories provided, for many years economic modelling has been able to provide pictures of cost distribution associated with different policy options. At the same time, economists have for many years examined the distribution of environmental impacts (for instance, the well-known phenomenon, which underlies the environmental justice movement, that poverty-stricken communities suffer greater environmental harms than do the affluent) and distribution of costs associated with environmental policies (Raymond 2003; Serret and Johnstone 2006). We have available to us both the results of many years of philosophical inquiry into what constitutes fairness in distribution (Fleishacker 2004) and also, with respect to environmental policy, the technical means of translating different approaches to that subject into specific policy options (Cory et al. 2012). With respect to Canadian climate-change policy, outside such things as creation in 2000 of the Emissions Allocation and Burden Sharing Working Group, which as discussed had no influence upon policy, the subject has been treated only sparingly (for examples of some Canadian work on the subject see: Mowat Centre 2017; Boothe and Boudreault 2016; Trebilcock 2014; Macdonald 2014;

Macdonald et al. 2013; Rivers 2010). Instead, the focus has been upon policy options that maximize efficiency, the basic interest of think tanks such as the Ecofiscal Commission. We need to keep that focus upon efficiency, but combine it with another focus upon equity. Technical studies that used modelling to examine ways in which efficiency could be combined with equity were a prelude to the EU burden-sharing agreements of 1997 and 1998 (Haug and Jordan 2010). We can learn from the European example, as the EABWG set out to do and as has been advocated by others (Macdonald et al. 2013; Mowat Centre 2017).

Ottawa Must Start and Lead Another National
Climate-Change Process

While the preceding suggestion was made to all Canadians, this and subsequent suggestions are provided to whichever political party finds itself in power in Ottawa in the near future. Before he died, Jim Prentice issued this call for action: "It is now time for strong national leadership in energy and environmental policy. It is time for an overarching national policy, driven by the national government as the arbiter of the national interest" (2017, 163). Prentice said that his discussions with premiers showed him that the provinces were committed to action and recognized the need for national policy, but they wanted one that would "recognize the differing circumstances of each province, including basic economic realities" (Prentice 2017, 167). In recognition of these differing circumstances, Prentice made this statement: "What we need is an agreed-on and strongly articulated national vision, coupled with the recognition of 'common but differentiated responsibilities'" (2017, 167).

As noted, the term "common but differentiated responsibilities" comes from the international regime and refers to the search for equity in the distribution of the total reduction effort. Prentice made apt use of the term when he applied it to Canada. The phrase encapsulates exactly what is called for here: a federal-provincial plan of action that takes fully into account differing provincial reduction costs by means of explicit agreement on an equitable sharing of those costs.

We saw in the preceding chapter that such a plan of action cannot be developed by means of provincial leadership. Ottawa must lead. We also saw in the comparison of previous national processes that achieved more policy coordination than others that one explanation for that difference is federal degree of interest. Ottawa was far more motivated in the first and the fifth case studies than it was in the two from the 1990s. Similar motivation will be a necessary condition in future. Where can it come from? Experience to date shows it must have two sources – first, personal leadership by the prime minister and, secondly, a government formed by a centre-left party with electoral support in central Canada.

As shown by the examples of both Pierre Trudeau and his son, and perhaps also to some extent by that of Alberta Premier Alison Redford, whose personal convictions led her to devote considerable energies to pushing forward the Canadian Energy Strategy, the starting point for federal motivation has to come from the personal belief of the prime minister. The lesson offered by those three first ministers is that effective government action happens when the leader believes the issue is important enough to warrant personal expenditure of time, effort and a considerable portion of available political capital. After that, the necessary motivation has to come from the ideology of the governing party and support from backbench MPs, the phenomenon we saw pushing Prime Minister Chrétien towards Kyoto ratification in 2002.

Finally, however, beliefs and principles must align with electoral calculation. In an ideal world, just as Nixon went to China, a national party with its electoral base in the west headed by a prime minister committed to acting on the climate issue would be best positioned to bridge the West-East divide. However, it is difficult to imagine such a prime minister getting sufficient western votes in the first place, let alone being re-elected after leading another national climate effort. For that reason – sad to say in this wicked world – we likely must settle for a party drawing electoral support more from the east than the west. We also must recognize that unless conservative ideology on the climate file undergoes a massive change, that party must be on the centre-left. If so, such a leader and party strategists must be able to see clearly that a national effort that inevitably will involve some friction with the western carbon provinces will play well enough among other Canadian voters to compensate for a loss of votes in the west. The best example to date of this combination of passionate personal commitment by the leader with cold-blooded strategizing comes from British Columbia. There, Premier Gordon Campbell introduced his 2008 carbon tax, which stole wind from the sails of his green-friendly NDP opposition, and also did something he personally very much wanted to do.

Use Ju-jitsu: Lead with the Allocation Issue

Based on experience to date, we can expect Saskatchewan and Alberta (and perhaps other provinces) to resist any attempt by Ottawa to develop another national program. Together, those two provinces provide almost half the total Canadian emissions and so their participation will be essential, which gives them considerable leverage at the bargaining table. They may well use the threat of dropping out of a future national effort to strengthen their attempt to bargain it down to a lowest-common-denominator result. Given the asymmetry of the divide, some other provinces will support Ottawa but will not be strongly motivated to oppose the western provinces, and Quebec in particular may share their concerns about federal intrusion into provincial jurisdiction. In such a scenario, the necessary countervailing power can only come from Ottawa, but as discussed that government faces a difficult task. Ottawa must somehow convince the western provinces, and perhaps others such as an Ontario led by a right-wing government, to do more than they are doing now, but not threaten them to the point that they refuse to participate in a new national effort. How can that be done?

One possibility is to use ju-jitsu tactics, which take advantage of the strength of the opponent to gain superiority. As presented throughout the preceding pages, Ottawa will face two related challenges: the West-East divide and the fact that the closer it gets to effective national policy, the more the issue of who pays what portion of the total reduction cost will become salient. By use of ju-jitsu, Ottawa might be able to take advantage of the strength of the latter challenge, which will work to increase western resistance given the higher per capita reduction costs in those carbon-intensive economies, to help overcome the first challenge, the basic fact of highly motivated western engagement with a subject so important to them. In the normal course of events, governments would do as they have in the past by starting to discuss national policy when the target date is still far away, and for that reason nobody is focusing on cost distribution. A ju-jitsu move would reverse that order to start talking about distributive equity before talking about anything else. Ottawa might be able to use the allocation issue to help overcome western resistance by reframing the national dialogue. To date, that dialogue has been: "What should be done to achieve the target Ottawa just unilaterally adopted (and which poses significant harm to the western provincial economies)?" Using ju-jitsu, Ottawa could shift the dialogue to: "How can we share the reduction cost most fairly, and what target results from doing that?" Rather than leading with the issue that is a *threat* to Alberta and the other fossil fuel provinces, Ottawa can first play the card that represents the exact opposite: an offer to *help* those provinces with their reduction costs. (Admittedly, this strategy does not address the challenge of veto resistance from provincial governments motivated by right-wing ideology, rather than material energy interests. That challenge is discussed in the next section.)

The federal government could take advantage of its prerogative to establish the national process by inviting the provinces to join it in a process to examine cost allocation: given existing policies, what is the current allocation among sectors and provinces?; what do we think about that?; what principles of distributive equity might be used to guide allocation?; what decision-making process might be seen as fair?; for a variety of different principles, what allocations of cost associated with the existing or a more ambitious target might result? How could such things as differing provincial reductions and compensation be used to achieve at least an approximate parity of per capita cost? The basic theme, mawkish as it might sound, would be "working together" – just as Canadians worked together at Vimy Ridge or on the ice in 1972 – and that is exactly what it would be; rather than shouting at or ignoring each other, Canadians and their governments would be engaged in a conversation all would find inviting. How can we help one another to achieve our common goal?

Opening a new national dialogue and federal-provincial process on the ground of cost sharing rather than means of achieving the latest target Ottawa set all by itself has the advantage of moving the process towards zero sum and thus a more equal balancing of western and eastern interest in influencing the national outcome. Also, as discussed, zero sum is for Canada a minefield that must be traversed with extreme caution. There is benefit, though, in discussing zero sum at the outset, in more abstract terms, rather than at the end when time is short and tempers are frayed. More importantly, as shown in chapter 4, allocation will take place, either explicitly or implicitly, and policymakers will have data on allocation throughout. To avoid having one of those mines explode in our face, better to use it as part of the solution and to cast it in the most positive terms possible – helping one another by a fair sharing of the load.

Several things make it likely the provinces will respond positively, even if grudgingly, to an invitation from Ottawa to engage in such a process. First, as discussed more fully below, the starting point would not be the one seen in all previous national climate processes to date, in which Ottawa returns from international negotiations to tell the provinces what they must now do. Instead, the starting point would be a discussion of how we go about fairly sharing the cost of action. Secondly, we can safely assume the provinces cannot be seen to stay away at the outset of any given national process. As shown by the five cases, all provinces have participated at the outset in all the previous energy and climate federal-provincial processes. Opting out is a serious measure and to date has only been done after first engaging with the process, as did Alberta in 2002 after participating for a dozen years (and which technically did not opt out); Saskatchewan in 2016, after initially signing on to the 3 March 2016 Vancouver Declaration; and Ontario and Alberta after change of governments in 2018 and 2019. Thirdly, we can expect the key players, the western provinces, will participate since experience has shown they are the governments that have always been most engaged with national energy and climate discussions. They have to be because the subject is so important to them. The threat of opting out can be used to influence behaviour of other governments; the fact of having opted out means one no longer has a seat at the table and therefore no ability to influence others. Finally, we come back to the point made above. The initial topic of discussion would not be actual reductions at all, but instead principles of fairness to be used once the dialogue gets to the point of discussing reductions. What Canadian does not want to talk about fairness?

What principle should be used to achieve equity in allocation of the reduction cost among sources and provinces? The answer is not straightforward, since many are available. As discussed, there is no agreement on principles of distributive justice in general. Nor is there for allocation of climate-change action costs. Boothe and Boudreault note that there is agreement on how to achieve climate-policy efficiency, by pricing carbon, but no such agreement on how to achieve equity. They review three options:

> In contrast [to agreement on efficiency], there is no single textbook approach to establishing equity in allocating the emissions reduction burden. Approaches include egalitarian notions of fairness, i.e. all citizens having equal claims on allowable emissions, or consideration of relative ability-to-pay, as is the case with income taxes, or historical shares of emissions per jurisdiction. (2016, 5)

The first, "egalitarian" has the benefit of being grounded in the widely-accepted distributive justice norm that likes should be treated alike (see chapter 4's discussion of Stone 1988). Ability to pay underlies the international norm of "common but differentiated responsibilities" and was the principle used by the EU for allocation in its 2008 policy package (Macdonald et al. 2013). Historical responsibility for the problem also underlies the international norm; the reverse side of that coin is "credit for early action," which means an allocation today should take into account actions previously taken to reduce. As noted in the 1998–2002 case study, Quebec in 2000 claimed it should be given credit for its earlier investments in hydroelectric power.

No firm recommendation is possible here, since the subject has not been considered in depth in the preceding pages and nor yet can we draw upon Canadian experience to date in allocating emission-reduction cost. Instead, a very tentative suggestion is offered, based on the political viability of different approaches. That is to, first, rule out ability to pay since that would see Alberta, the richest per capita province, being asked to reduce more on a per capita basis than anyone else. Since the political challenge is to convince Alberta to participate in a new national program, and since that province already has higher per capita reduction costs (discussed in chapter 4), ability to pay is a non-starter. Instead, the suggestion is to use the egalitarian approach, but not to guarantee every citizen the same right to emissions. As noted in chapter 4 above, per capita emissions are something like five times higher in Alberta and Saskatchewan than Ontario and Quebec, meaning such an approach would require major reductions in the former provinces and leave considerable room for growth in the latter. Instead of per capita equity in *emissions*, we should seek per capita equity in *costs*. Per capita reduction costs can be kept roughly equal among the provinces, even though per capita emissions would still vary widely.

Use of this principle of approximately equal per capita reduction costs meets the "likes treated alike" criterion. It would also be in keeping with the principle that underlies the Canadian equalization program, that provinces should be able to offer comparable levels of government services, even though their ability to generate revenue by means of taxation varies (because the same tax level generates more revenue in a rich province than a poor one). In the same way, provinces would ask their citizens and factories to bear comparable reduction costs, even though, due to higher per capita reduction costs in the carbon-intensive provinces, resulting per capita reductions would vary. (A dollar spent on reduction in Ontario buys more reduction than does the same dollar spent in Alberta; what is proposed is that each spend the same dollar and we simply accept the fact that the resulting Alberta reduction is less.) Surely, promising Alberta and Saskatchewan that their per capita costs would not be greater than those borne by other Canadians can only help.

Whatever principle is used, the allocation among provinces will inevitably be the result of self-interested negotiation. The purpose here is not to recommend any particular way of allocating, but instead to suggest that the allocation process might offer a useful starting point for the next federal-provincial process.

Change Provincial Self-Interest: Set All the Targets Together

Discussion in the preceding pages has focused upon ways in which Ottawa can convince provincial governments to adopt new policies that, taken as a whole and combined with federal action, can achieve an international commitment. However, the theoretical approach used for understanding intergovernmental coordination suggested provinces might change behaviour not only because of external pressure, but also because their view of their own self-interest might change once they began to participate in an intergovernmental process. Like states faced with collective-action problems they cannot solve on their own and who accordingly for self-interested reasons coordinate policies by means of an international agreement, the possibility exists that Canadian governments might cooperate because they saw it as being in their interest to do so. The ongoing difficulties in reducing barriers to internal trade, which all are motivated to do because they recognize associated benefits to the Canadian economy, shows how difficult collective-action cooperation is in the Canadian context. Self-interest may provide a generalized push towards cooperation, but a particular cost will blunt that desire. In the realm of energy and climate policy, governments have never been significantly motivated by perceived benefits of cooperation (although that was certainly the rhetoric employed by the Canadian Energy Strategy.) Perhaps it cannot be achieved there, but the method used to date to set the international target certainly makes it impossible.

As we have seen, to date all of the national and provincial targets have been set unilaterally, thus guaranteeing a lack of coordination. How can we possibly have coordinated policy when the most basic step, setting the policy objective, has not been coordinated? The problem has two sources. The first is the fact that successive federal governments have set the national target by themselves, not on the basis of any prior agreement with provincial governments, but instead on the basis of what other states, most notably the US, are presenting in the international arena as their own national targets. The other source of the problem is the fact that provincial governments, even while participating in an ostensibly coordinated national process, have set their own targets without consultation with other Canadian governments.

To address this problem, the Ottawa-led federal-provincial process suggested here, beyond an initial focus on equity in cost sharing, should be centred on one simple mechanism. Ottawa should propose that the next iteration of national and provincial targets be the product of coordinated intergovernmental discussion and agreement within the framework of this new national process. To do that, Ottawa should re-open the Paris 2030 target, telling our international partners and Canadian citizens that it will be replaced by a new target, one for the first time set at home and one to which all Canadian governments, having themselves set the target, will feel committed. At the same time, Ottawa should invite all provincial governments to re-open their provincial target (something they have done many times before) and to replace it with a new target that, for the first time, has been set through consultation and collaboration with other Canadian governments.

As discussed below, the process cannot simply be one of provincial governments going to Ottawa to put a take-it-or-leave-it position on the table, with those positions then summed to arrive at the national target. Instead, Ottawa must itself put on the table a proposal for actions it will take using federal policy instruments to achieve a given portion of the total reduction. Ottawa must then use all the tools it has available, including both promises of financial assistance and threats of unilateral action, to nudge the national target up to a more ambitious level than that represented by the initial provincial positions, while at the same time ensuring that veto governments do not bail out. In doing that, the federal government would be aided considerably by the fact that the negotiations would be guided by the need to achieve equity in burden sharing. New provincial targets would emerge from that process of negotiation. The provincial targets would sum to the national target and each would be based on what that province had come to see as its fair share of the total reduction cost represented by the national target. Each provincial government would have, for the first time, a sense of ownership in the national target. Ideally, that would be accompanied by recognition that a self-interested desire to achieve the target could only be achieved through policy coordination. Ideally, they would work to meet or exceed their own target as a way of achieving the national target. For the first time, they would *want* to see Canada achieve its goal, rather than simply seeing that as Ottawa's problem.

The 2015 Liberal election platform had the right idea when it promised to include the provinces in setting the next national target, but unfortunately that was not done. It must be done next time, with the concept extended to include the setting of all the next provincial targets as part of the same process. If so, after what is likely to be a protracted process of haggling and horse-trading, the next generation of targets would all be decided at the same time, in the same room, one littered with empty coffee cups and pizza boxes, occupied by sleep-starved negotiators, and with the flags of all fourteen jurisdictions, plus perhaps those of one or more Indigenous peoples, proudly displayed at the back, all the same size and height, none standing above the others.

Ottawa Must Use Skillful Diplomacy

We have learned from the case studies that the provinces, always jealous of their autonomy, and the two western fossil fuel provinces in particular, wishing to avoid a too-stringent cap on their own emissions, will almost certainly resist the lead-government role envisaged here for Ottawa. Alberta in particular would have to be willing to move from an intensity to an absolute target, one that sees a reduction in that province's emissions rather than an increase. Whichever party is in power in Edmonton, NDP or United Conservative Party, Alberta resistance will be similar. Inducing that province and others to change tack will be a major challenge for the federal government. For that reason, Ottawa must not make its task even harder by making errors as it leads the federal-provincial dance.

As seen from the cases, the federal effort, which must be led personally by the prime minister, must be consistent. Ottawa must move steadily towards its goal of bringing the sum of the collective effort up to a higher level than was represented by the opening provincial positions. There must be no surprises. Premiers must be kept fully informed of what Ottawa plans to do next, in private, at each step along the way. Only in that way can Ottawa use threatened action as a means of influencing provincial behaviour. Prime Minister Chrétien's surprise announcement of Kyoto ratification must not be repeated; but not yet must Ottawa repeat Prime Minister Justin Trudeau's announcement of the federal backstop price on the same day that ministers are meeting.

Ottawa Must Use Some Power, but Not All the Power It Has Available

With any luck, the provinces will participate in the new federal-provincial process suggested here, at least at the outset, for the reasons given above. It will then be up to Ottawa to keep them there, using adroit diplomacy that makes full use of threat, promise, and persuasion, but also using available power, based in the federal government's financial resources, constitutional jurisdiction, and legitimacy. The federal government must be very mindful, however, that its power is a two-edged sword. It can help to move provinces towards cooperation but also, as we have seen in the example of the Chrétien government alienating provinces by using its rightful jurisdictional powers to set aside the Kyoto target they had agreed to, can make cooperation more difficult. Beyond that, as noted many times in the preceding pages, flexing of muscle by Pierre Trudeau caused lasting damage.

Accept a Target Less Ambitious Than the Current Minus 30 Per Cent

It must be admitted that the process suggested here might well result in a target considerably less ambitious than 30 per cent below the 2005 level. Despite all of Ottawa's skill and willingness to use restrained power, a collaborative process from which any province can opt out will be inevitably driven towards the lowest common denominator. The lesson of the CES certainly supports this view, as do the lessons of the two 1990s climate efforts, plus, to a lesser extent, that of the PCF. And that denominator will be whatever national and provincial targets the veto provinces are willing to accept. It is hoped that such things as equity in burden sharing, a voice in setting the national target that might bring about a change in provincial interest from purely parochial to more broadly national, plus Ottawa's use of skilled, muscular diplomacy, can raise the bar somewhat. However, it is unlikely to take it all the way up to the current Paris target of reducing emissions down to a total of 513 Mt in 2030.

Settling for a weaker target than the current one might be seen as a retrograde step. That view would be mistaken, however, since as it sits the Paris target is essentially meaningless. In the first instance, it was not based upon any analysis by the Harper government of how it might be achieved. Secondly, when the PCF was signed in December 2016, programs were not in place to meet it and that program has since been weakened by provincial defections. Most importantly, it had not been agreed to by any province, since none were consulted. It must also be borne in mind that both Alberta and Saskatchewan have effectively refused to merge their climate-change policymaking into a larger national process, the former by setting out on its own path in 2002 and then opting out of the PCF in 2019 and the latter by opting out of the PCF in 2016. If those two provinces sign on to a national program and for the first time begin to work towards achieving a national target to which they are committed, even one less ambitious than minus 30 per cent, we will have made considerable progress. For many years, Canada has been following two climate policy paths of increasing and decreasing emissions with the former cancelling out gains made in the latter path. Bringing all provinces on to the same path of decreasing emissions is well worth the price of a less ambitious target. Better a less ambitious target that is actually achieved than yet another policy failure.

Objections

One possible objection to the process suggested here, in which, no matter how much the accent is placed upon fairness, the thorny issues of differing economic interests and identities will be central, is that it runs counter to the process often followed in negotiations of starting with the less difficult issues on which agreement can more readily be reached. The theory is that such a step-by-step process that first accomplishes the easy agreements allows a reservoir of trust to be established, which can then be drawn on later when the hard issues are on the table. It is a valid point, but it is not suggested here because of the well-known tendency of Canadian governments in energy and climate processes to reach agreement for agreement's sake, sacrificing effectiveness in order to give the appearance of coordinated action. If we start with the easy issues, governments are likely to agree on those and then stop there, avoiding the hard issue of allocation in favour of the much more pleasant task of writing the meeting communiqué in the most glowing terms possible, showing that because governments have agreed on something, no matter what, nothing more need be done. Using ju-jitsu for bridging the west-east divide by starting with cost sharing is the proposed strategy and for that reason the difficult issues must be met head-on at the outset – in both societal discussion, the first suggestion made above, and government negotiation.

The second response is that this is why we need a motivated federal government. Ottawa can do two things to nudge the agreement in the direction of greater stringency. First, it can unilaterally decide what portion of any overall target it will itself achieve using federal law and spending powers. The October 2000 federal commitment to itself provide one-third of the total effort provides an example. That commitment would be made public prior to the negotiations with the challenge then thrown to the provinces, implicitly or explicitly, to make up the rest. Having used federal unilateral action as a contribution to the overall effort, Ottawa can then use such action as threat. Whether referring to federal pricing or law-based regulation, Ottawa can make it clear that any province not contributing a sufficient portion of the overall reduction will find the Government of Canada using its constitutionally provided powers, and with the support of enough voters to matter, regulating emissions in that province's backyard. Justin Trudeau's backstop carbon price is the model here, but with one significant difference. Such unilateral action would not simply be decided upon by Ottawa ahead of time. Instead, it would emerge from the discussions, with the provinces having considerable opportunity to comment (and with, ideally, the prior federal threat having significantly influenced their behaviour).

Any such threat, however, must be real but also must be made with the utmost of delicacy and restraint, not using anything like the full power available, to avoid the province in question deciding it is better off outside the process, litigating to hold off federal regulation. This is where combining target setting and cost allocation in the same process might provide benefit. Ottawa can make its threat of unilateral action while at the same time offering to reduce the required provincial reduction, the difference made up by offering inducements to other provinces to increase theirs or by Ottawa picking up the difference in its own program.

Beyond that, any such threat must be combined with promise. That can come in the form of the two promises Ottawa used to negotiate the PCF. Revenues from federal pricing, if Ottawa does in fact regulate in somebody's backyard, will be returned to the province in question and federal spending will help the province defray the cost of action. In addition to that federal funding, a cost-sharing agreement might also involve financial transfers from one province to another. In 2012, Alberta rejected the idea of giving British Columbia a portion of its oil royalties in exchange for the latter accepting a pipeline through its territory. However, in the process envisaged here we might well see such an arrangement. At the international level, the Clean Development Mechanism allows countries to meet part of their reduction target by funding emission reductions made in other countries at a lower per-tonne cost than they could achieve themselves. The purchase of carbon offsets is also now an established practice. By the same token, cost savings through the larger cap-and-trade market represented by the California-Quebec system is also now established and need not be discontinued. There is no reason that such flexibility mechanisms might not also be used to facilitate coordinated action in Canada, with provinces facing high reduction costs purchasing lower-cost reductions in other parts of the country.

Finally, as discussed, a promise might also be made respecting provincial targets. The EU Kyoto burden-sharing agreement was achieved by means of differing member state targets, from a reduction effort of minus 21 per cent by Germany to an increase in emissions of 27 per cent granted to Portugal, with the total of reductions and increases adding up to the internationally promised 8 per cent reduction (Haug and Jordan 2010, 86). The same thing could be done here, with provinces facing higher per-tonne reduction costs not required to reduce as much as others, provided that their per capita reduction costs were comparable. By a combination of all these means – differing provincial targets, federal spending to defray provincial costs, and flexibility mechanisms involving province-to-province financial transfers – agreement might be reached whereby reduction efforts measured in per capita GHG megatonnes might not be comparable, but per capita dollar costs would be.

Yet another possible objection lies in the fact that there is a problem in borrowing from the EU experience in the use of financial compensation and differing targets. There, the major reductions were being made by richer countries and those less well off, such as Portugal, were asked to do less. This reflects the notion that capacity to pay should be one factor used in deciding an equitable cost allocation, just as in the international regime the richer OECD nations have been asked to do more than has the Global South. Here, however, in the case of a province such as Alberta the notion that those with higher per-unit reduction costs will be asked to do less conflicts with the principle of capacity to pay. As the richest per capita province, the latter principle would lead to seeing a province such as Alberta doing the most to reduce. There also might well be objections to financial assistance provided by Ottawa to Alberta, given the wealth of the latter.

These are valid objections, but they are countered to at least some extent by the goal that per capita *costs* should be comparable, even if actual reductions are not. Ideally, citizens of wealthy Alberta would be paying roughly the same amount as other Canadians. Beyond that, realpolitik dictates that it is essential to keep at the bargaining table the province that emits the largest share of Canadian emissions and is currently planning to increase those emissions even further. Everything we know about western alienation and Albertan suspicions of Ottawa lead us to believe that threat alone (although that instrument certainly should be used) will not by itself bring about Alberta behaviour change. The rest of Canada must offer Alberta understanding of its particular position, goodwill and promises of assistance. If at the end of the day Alberta gets a slightly easier ride than other provinces, the rest of the country will still be much further ahead than it is now, when it is being implicitly asked to pick up 90 Mt of Alberta emissions in order to meet the Paris target.

This is where a bilateral agreement might be used to supplement an overall multilateral agreement. Both the Joe Clark and Pierre Elliott Trudeau governments moved from multilateral to bilateral strategies to address the very difficult, because so clearly zero-sum, challenge of rapidly increasing world oil prices. Presumably that was because it is easier to find common ground with only one other actor in the room. It is not known if during the 2015–16 PCF process Ottawa and Saskatchewan ever discussed a possible bilateral arrangement (other than the one governing the province's coal-fired electricity plants), but it seems possible they will eventually end up in one as did Nova Scotia and Ottawa. If bilateral agreements help facilitate the national process, there seems no reason not to use them, and it also seems most likely Ottawa would sign one or more of them with western, carbon provinces.

A final possible objection is that there is a contradiction between the recommendation made above that Ottawa engage in collaborative federalism, treating the provinces as equals in setting the national target, and the recommendation that Ottawa use some of its available power to influence the behaviour of provinces. Seeing the two recommendations as contradictory is understandable, and so needs to be explained. The provinces must be treated as equals, for the first time, in setting national targets in order to change their view of their self-interest, to help them lift their gaze from their parochial interest to share, to at least some extent, the national interest. Provinces will only cooperate in the national climate effort if they have bought in to that effort, even at the expense of a target less ambitious than the current minus 30 per cent. As discussed, that changed self-interest is essential for coordination, in a symphony orchestra or a federation. However, external pressure from the lead government is also essential. Leadership in any organizational venue involves both empowering subordinates and also nudging their behaviour. For Ottawa to engage in both – to function as first among equals – is not a contradiction.

Final Suggestions

Four final suggestions are offered. First, the process should be designed so as to give industry and other actors beyond provinces and territories, in particular ENGOs and Indigenous peoples, a voice. As discussed, this public dialogue on what non-state actors want governments to do might somewhat mute the influence of the oil industry, which will certainly be working to reduce climate policy effectiveness. To the extent it is transparent and accessible for those outside government, the process is more likely to be seen as fair and therefore a distribution of cost arrived at is more likely to be seen as fair. Secondly, it is essential that first ministers be involved at the outset, to ensure agreement on the process to be used and to send the message that this is something taken seriously by all governments, and, at the end, to conclude the final agreement. Leaving things in the hands of ministers, particularly the energy and environment ministers, whose differing mandates guaranteed conflict, did not serve the 1990s processes well. The PCF, initiated by Ottawa and with first ministers playing the central role, is the model to follow. Thirdly, it must be recognized and accepted that any multilateral agreement on targets and allocation, perhaps supplemented by one or more bilateral agreements, will inevitably be asymmetrical. Targets and financial compensation flows are certain to vary. The principle of uniformity that underlay the federal approach to the PCF – the same minimum price is to be found in all parts of the country – should not be brought forward into the future effort proposed here. There, uniformity should be sought in terms of rough comparability of per capita cost, thus providing rough equity. Beyond that, however, uniformity should not be treated as a desirable characteristic. The big emitters must be kept at the bargaining table – whatever is needed to do that, including particular concessions and bilateral side deals leading to asymmetry, is completely acceptable. The final suggestion flows from the fact of PCF defections in 2018 and 2019. Governments must recognize that circumstances, and elected governments, change and so any program will require renegotiation on a regular basis.

♦

Canada is not a unitary state, either in its formal constitutional or its societal form. Whether we use Joe Clark's term of a "community of communities" or any other, there is no denying that our country contains within it many distinct societies – located on either side of *le fleuve Saint-Laurent*; on the Rock of Newfoundland; on Indigenous lands scattered throughout the country; in big-city and suburban diaspora communities with roots in India, Hong Kong, Italy, and so many other parts of the world; on the cattle ranches of Alberta. Our national genius is that all those distinct societies can live together, in relative peace and harmony. Sometimes, however, that gets a little difficult.

In 1914, Canada faced the national challenge of coming to the aid of the mother country in a European war. That challenge was viewed very differently, however, by those whose families had lived for generations in the province of Quebec and those who had only recently immigrated from Great Britain to Ontario. As was shown by the anti-conscription riots in Quebec City in the spring of 1918, meeting that challenge put a considerable strain on the national fabric.

For some time now, we have faced a national challenge of similar magnitude in the form of the need to both make and keep promises to the international community as the states of the world attempt to work together to address the collective-action problem of climate change. To date, we have avoided a similar strain by letting down our international partners and failing to take our commitments seriously as we kept on pushing the deadline further and further into the future. We have taken the easy way out and thereby avoided meeting head-on the challenge posed by differing western and eastern interests respecting fossil fuel energy and climate change. Canadian governments have given greater priority to avoiding a strain on the national fabric than they have to acting effectively on one of the greatest challenges facing humanity today. That must change.

Given the realities of geography, history, and regional interest and identity, meeting the challenge of climate change will almost certainly cause regional conflict. It will make it more difficult for all of us to live and work together, thinking of ourselves as both citizens of the country and of a particular part of the country. In particular, meeting the climate challenge has enormous potential to make unbridgeable the already enormous gulf separating the western carbon provinces from the rest of the country.

However, we have gone through such challenges before and we can do so again. More specifically in terms of environmental challenges, one previous experience that parallels our present climate-change dynamic is the 1992 collapse of the Newfoundland cod fishery. A natural resource of considerable economic value suddenly disappeared, despite the best intentions of policymakers, industry, and local fishers. Today, we face the need to make a considerable portion of the oil and natural gas resource disappear by agreeing it will be left in the ground, rather than exported and sold. In 1992, the rest of the country, represented by Ottawa, came to the aid of the province facing such a problem of shrinking resource-extraction revenues. The same thing must be done now. The environmental challenge of climate change, which, like the cod fishery collapse, imposes a much higher cost upon one region than others, must be met with the same generous response. The rest of the country must do all it can to help Alberta and Saskatchewan pay the cost of abandoning some portion of their available fossil fuel wealth. At a minimum, the rest of the country must provide a guarantee that citizens in those two provinces will not be asked to pay a higher per capita reduction cost than is being borne by Canadians everywhere else.

Achieving a national climate-change target for the first time will let us regain our rightful place in the international climate-change community, a community that, thanks to Brian Mulroney, we once led. If done with care, tact, and respect, doing so will help us come together rather than drive us apart.

The challenge is before us and with it the opportunity to forge a stronger, more united Canada.

References

Adkin, Laurie E. 2016. "Ecology and Governance in a First World Petro-State." In *First World Petro-Politics: The Political Ecology and Governance of Alberta*, edited by Laurie E. Adkin. Toronto: University of Toronto Press.

– "Democracy and the Albertan Petro-State." In *First World Petro-Politics: The Political Ecology and Governance of Alberta*, edited by Laurie E. Adkin. Toronto: University of Toronto Press.

Adkin, Laurie E., and Brittany J. Stares. 2016. "Turning up the Heat: Hegemonic Politics in a First World Petro-State." In *First World Petro-Politics: The Political Ecology and Governance of Alberta*, edited by Laurie E. Adkin. Toronto: University of Toronto Press.

Alberta Energy. 2018. "Facts and Statistics." www.energy.alberta.ca/OilSands/791.asp.

Analysis and Modelling Group. 2000. *An Assessment of the Economic and Environmental Implications for Canada of the Kyoto Protocol.*

Anderson, David. February 7, 2008. Interview communication to Douglas Macdonald.

Anderson, George. 2012. "Introduction." In *Oil and Gas in Federal Systems*, edited by George Anderson. Don Mills: Oxford University Press.

Bakvis, Herman, Gerald Baier, and Douglas Brown. 2009. *Contested Federalism: Certainty and Ambiguity in the Canadian Federation*. Don Mills: Oxford University Press.

Bakvis, Herman and Grace Skogstad. 2012a. "Canadian Federalism: Performance, Effectiveness and Legitimacy." In *Canadian Federalism: Performance, Effectiveness and Legitimacy*, edited by Herman Bakvis and Grace Skogstad. Don Mills: Oxford University Press.

– 2012b. "Conclusion: Taking Stock of Canadian Federalism." In *Canadian Federalism: Performance, Effectiveness and Legitimacy*, edited by Herman Bakvis and Grace Skogstad. Don Mills: Oxford University Press.

Banff Clean Energy Dialogue. 2010. *Towards a Canadian Clean Energy Strategy: Summary of the Banff Clean Energy Dialogue, April 8–10, 2010.* http://www.winnipegconsensus.org/downloads/banff_final_report_en.pdf.

BC Government News. 2012. "British Columbia outlines requirements for heavy oil pipeline consideration." https://news.gov.bc.ca/stories/british-columbia-outlines-requirements-for-heavy-oil-pipeline-consideration.

Beetham, David. 1991. *The Legitimation of Power.* London: Macmillan.

Bjorn, Andrew, et al. 2002. *Ratification of the Kyoto Protocol: A Citizen's Guide to the Canadian Climate Change Policy Process.* Sustainable Toronto.

Blue, Ian. 2009. "Off the Grid: Jurisdiction and the Canadian Electricity Sector." *Dalhousie Law Journal* 32: 339–66.

Bolleyer, Nicole. 2009. *Intergovernmental Cooperation: Rational Choices in Federal Systems and Beyond.* Oxford: Oxford University Press.

Bonner, Susan. 2006. "No realistic option to reduce energy consumption by one-third over next few years: PM Harper." *The Hill Times,* July 10, 2006.

Boothe, Paul. 2015. "Alberta's greenhouse gas plan: a glass half full or half empty." *Maclean's,* November 24, 2015. www.macleans.ca/economy/economicanalysis/albertas-greenhouse-gas-plan-a-glass-half-full-or-half-empty/.

Boothe, Paul, and Félix-A. Boudreault. 2016. *Sharing the Burden: Canadian GHG Emissions.* Ivey: Lawrence National Centre for Policy and Management. www.ivey.uwo.ca/cmsmedia/2169603/ghg-emissions-report-sharing-the-burden.pdf.

Brownsey, Keith. 2008. "The New Oil Order: The Staples Paradigm and the Canadian Upstream Oil and Gas Industry." In *Canada's Resource Economy in Transition,* edited by Michael Howlett and Keith Brownsey. Toronto: Emond Montgomery.

Business Council on National Issues. 1994. *Climate Change: A Strategy for Voluntary Business Action.* Ottawa: Business Council on National Issues.

Cameron, D. and R. Simeon. 2002. "Intergovernmental Relations in Canada: The Emergence of Collaborative Federalism." *Publius,* 32 (2): 49–71.

Canada Gazette. 2006. "Notice of intent to develop and implement regulations and other measures to reduce air emissions." Vol. 140, no. 42.

Canada West Foundation. 2011. *Finding Common Ground: The Next Step in Developing a Canadian Energy Strategy.* http://cwf.ca/wp-content/uploads/2015/11/CWF_FindingCommonGround_Report_APR2011.pdf.

"Canada's National Statement at CoP 21." 2015. https://pm.gc.ca/eng/news/2015/11/30/canadas-national-statement-cop21.

Canadian Association of Petroleum Producers. 2017. "Greenhouse gas emissions." www.capp.ca/responsible-development/air-and-climate/greenhouse-gas-emissions.

Canadian Council of Chief Executives. 2011. "Kananaskis 2011: Building an agenda for a sound energy future." http://thebusinesscouncil.ca/wp-content/uploads/archives/Kananaskis_2011_Building_an_Agenda_for_a_Sound_Energy_Future_Final_July2011.pdf.

Canadian Intergovernmental Conference Secretariat. 2011. "2011 Energy and Mines Ministers Conference: Action Plan – A Collaborative Approach to Energy." www.scics.ca/en/product-produit/action-plan-collaborative-approach-to -energy/.

Careless, J.M.S. 1954. "Frontierism, Metropolitanism, and Canadian History." *Canadian Historical Review*, 35 (1): 1–21.

CBC News. 2006. "Mulroney honoured for environmental record." April 20, 2006. www.cbc.ca/news/canada/mulroney-honoured-for-environmental-record -1.616580.

– 2011. "Alberta premier urges united energy front for Canada." November 16, 2011. www.cbc.ca/news/canada/edmonton/alberta-premier-urges-united -energy-front-for-canada-1.1110404.

– 2012. "Redford meets with Quebec Premier Jean Charest." January 11, 2012. www.cbc.ca/news/canada/edmonton/redford-meets-with-quebec-premier-jean -charest-1.1149274.

– 2015a. "Justin Trudeau promises 'Canadian approach' to climate change." November 23, 2015. www.cbc.ca/news/politics/trudeau-first-ministers-meet -climate-change-1.3331290.

– 2015b. "Premiers conference could see clash over pipelines and emissions." July 16, 2015. www.cbc.ca/news/politics/premiers-conference-could-see-clash -over-pipelines-and-emissions-1.3154166.

– 2016a. "Ottawa wants provinces to form 'working groups' on climate change." February 19, 2016. https://www.cbc.ca/news/politics/ottawa-four-groups-climate -change-1.3455603.

– 2016b. "Trudeau, premiers meet in Vancouver as views on climate change diverge." March 2, 2016. www.cbc.ca/news/politics/first-ministers-climate-plan-vancouver -1.3472189.

– 2016c. "Brad Wall finds allies among premiers opposed to forced carbon tax." July 21, 2016. www.cbc.ca/news/politics/premiers-thursday-carbon -tax-1.3689855.

– 2016d. "A carbon tax or cap-and-trade: Liberals suggest every province must choose." September 21, 2016. www.cbc.ca/news/politics/cap-trade-carbon-tax -provinces-1.3773285.

– 2016e. "Sask., N.S and N.L. ministers walk out of climate talks after Trudeau announces carbon price." October 3, 2016. www.cbc.ca/news/politics/federal -provincial-environment-ministers-meeting-1.3789134.

– 2018. "Nearly a third of Canadians don't believe humans, industry 'mostly' cause climate change: poll." April 4, 2018. www.cbc.ca/news/politics /poll-abacus-carbon-tax-1.4603824.

Chalifour, Nathalie J. 2010. "The Constitutional Authority to Levy Carbon Taxes." In *Canada: The State of the Federation 2009: Carbon Pricing and Environmental Federalism*, edited by Thomas J. Courchene and John R. Allan. Montreal and Kingston: McGill-Queen's University Press.

Charest, Jean. 1997. "Kyoto summit: Will Canada clean up its act?" *The Globe and Mail*, November 27, 1997.

Chasek, Pamela S., David L. Downie and Janet Welsh Brown. 2010. *Global Environmental Politics*. Boulder: Westview Press.

Cheadle, Bruce. 2016a. "Environment ministers confront Canada's carbon-cutting realities." *Canadian Press*, January 29, 2016. www.news1130.com/2016/01/29 /environment-ministers-meet-in-ottawa-to-discuss-carbon-cutting-strategies/.

– 2016b. "Premiers agree carbon pricing to be part of overall carbon plan." *Maclean's*, March 4, 2016. www.macleans.ca/news/canada/premiers-agree-carbon-pricing-to -be-part-of-overall-climate-plan/.

Chrétien, Jean. 2007. *My Years as Prime Minister*. Toronto: Alfred A. Knopf.

Clark, Campbell. 2018. "Scheer is dangerously eager to please." *The Globe and Mail*, November 5, 2018.

Clark, Campbell and Brian Laghi. 2007. "PM charts a greener course." *The Globe and Mail*, January 5, 2007.

Clark, Christy. 2012. "Premier Christy Clark's letter to Alberta Premier Alison Redford." Office of the Premier. https://news.gov.bc.ca/stories/premier-christy-clarks-letter -to-alberta-premier-alison-redford.

Clegg, Stewart R. and Mark Haugaard, eds. 2009. *The SAGE Handbook of Power*. Los Angeles: Sage.

Cohen, Andrew and Anne McIlroy. 1997. "U.S. proposes gradual reduction of greenhouse gases." *The Globe and Mail*, October 23, 1997.

Commissioner of Environment and Sustainable Development. 1998. *Report of the Commissioner of Environment and Sustainable Development to the House of Commons: Global Challenges*. Minister of Public Works and Government Services Canada.

– 2017. *Report 1 Progress on Reducing Greenhouse Gases – Environment and Climate Change Canada*. www.oag-bvg.gc.ca/internet/English/parl_cesd_201710_01_e _42489.html.

Confidential interviews. 2007a. Thirteen interviews with government and other officials working in the area of federal climate change policy. Interviews by Stephanie Birk-Parish and May Jeong, under the direction of Douglas Macdonald.

– 2007b. Interviews with individuals from government and industry knowledgeable respecting origins of the VCR and NAPCC. Interviews by Douglas Macdonald, David Houle, or Caitlin Patterson.

Confidential interviews. 2010. Interviews with individuals who had been involved with the 1990–2002 national processes, done in connection with the 2013 Allocating Emission Reductions report. Interviews by Douglas Macdonald or David Gordon.

Corcoran, Terence. 1994. "Goodbye carbon tax, hello sanity." *The Globe and Mail*, June 1, 1994.

Cory, Dennis C. and Tauhidor Rahman, et al. 2012. *Environmental Justice and Federalism.* Cheltenham: Edward Elgar.

Council of the Federation. 2007. *A Shared Vision for Energy in Canada.* www .pmprovincesterritoires.ca/phocadownload/publications/energystrategy_en.pdf.

– 2013. *Canadian Energy Strategy: Progress Report to the Council of the Federation.*

– 2015a. *Canadian Energy Strategy.* www.canadaspremiers.ca/phocadownload /publications/canadian_energy_strategy_eng_fnl.pdf.

– 2015b. "Meeting of Canada's Premiers." www.canadaspremiers.ca/meeting -of-canada-s-premiers-november-23-2015-ottawa-ontario/.

Cropanzano, R., & Ambrose, M.L. 2001. "Procedural and Distributive Justice Are More Similar Than You Think: A Monistic Perspective and Research Agenda." In *Advances in Organizational Justice*, edited by J. Greenberg & R. Cropanzano. Stanford: Stanford University Press.

Dangerfield, Katie. 2018. "Canada's climate change plan – Alberta is out, so is it dead on the table?" *Global News*, August 31, 2018. https://globalnews.ca/news/4420844 /alberta-climate-change-plan-federal-justin-trudeau/

Dion, Stéphane. November 30, 2010. Interview by Douglas Macdonald.

Doern, G. Bruce. 2005. "Canadian Energy Policy and the Struggle for Sustainable Development: Political-Economic Context." In *Canadian Energy Policy and the Struggle for Sustainable Development*, edited by G. Bruce Doern. Toronto: University of Toronto Press.

Doern, G. Bruce and Glen Toner. 1985. *The Politics of Energy: The Development and Implementation of the NEP.* Toronto: Methuen.

Doern, G. Bruce and Monica Gattinger. 2003. *Power Switch: Energy Regulatory Governance in the Twenty-First Century.* Toronto, ON: University of Toronto Press.

Doern, G. Bruce and T. Conway. 1994. *The Greening of Canada: Federal Institutions and Decisions.* Toronto: University of Toronto Press.

Doyle, Simon. 2006. "Conservative 'strategy of delay' on climate change, critics say." *The Hill Times*, October 9, 2006.

Duffy, Andrew. 1999. "Tough Emission Standards will put Alberta at forefront: surprise reversal." *National Post*, October 18, 1999

– 2000. "Ministers backed away from taking action to reduce emissions." *National Edition*, April 3, 2000.

Dunn, Sheilagh M. 1982. *Intergovernmental Relations in Canada: The Year in Review 1981: Volume One: Policy and Politics.* Kingston: Institute of Intergovernmental Relations, Queen's University.

Ecofiscal Commission. 2015. *The Way Forward: A Practical Approach to Reducing Canada's Greenhouse Gas Emissions.* http://ecofiscal.ca/wp-content/uploads /2015/04/Ecofiscal-Commission-Report-The-Way-Forward-April-2015.pdf.

Energy and Mines Ministers' Conference. 2012. *Canada as a Global Energy Leader: Toward Greater Pan-Canadian Collaboration: A Progress Report.*

Energy Policy Institute of Canada. 2011. *A Strategy for Canada's Global Energy Leadership: Framework Document.* No longer available online, in author's possession.

Environics. 2006. "Dataset: Environics Focus Canada 2006–1." http://odesi1 .scholarsportal.info/webview/index.jsp?object=http://142.150.190.11:80%2Fobj %2FStudy%2Fcora-efc2006-E-2006-4&mode=documentation&v=2&top=yes.

– 2007. "Dataset: Environics Focus Canada 2007–2." http://odesi1.scholarsportal .info/webview/index.jsp?object=http://142.150.190.11:80%2Fobj%2FStudy%2Fc ora-efc2007-E-2007-2&mode=documentation&v=2&top=yes.

– 2009. "Datasets: Environics Focus Canada 2009–1; Environics Focus Canada 2009–2; Environics Focus Canada 2009–3; Environics Focus Canada 2009–4." https://search1.odesi.ca/#/search/_term_term=environics&type:0;&fromDate:20 09&toDate:2010&refineColl_all:false&cora:false&icpsr:false&dlimf:false;&refin eOdesi_all:true&statCaMicro:true&statCaAgg:true&pop:true&other:true;&add Terms@;&page:1?uri=%2Fodesi%2Fcora-efc2010-E-2010.xml.

Environics, The Institute and David Suzuki Foundation. 2015. *Focus Canada 2015: Canadian Public Opinion about Climate Change.* www.environicsinstitute.org /docs/default-source/project-documents/focus-canada-2015-canadian-public -opinion-on-climate-change/final-report-english.pdf?sfvrsn=2dd8c6ae_2.

Environment Canada. 2007. "News Release: Turning the corner: An action plan to reduce greenhouse gases and air pollution."

Environment and Climate Change Canada. 2017. "National Inventory Report 1990– 2015: Greenhouse Gas Sources and Sinks in Canada – Executive Summary." www .ec.gc.ca/ges-ghg/default.asp?lang=En&n=662F9C56-1#es-5.

– 2018. "News Release: Government of Canada to support energy efficiency and climate action in Ontario." www.canada.ca/en/environment-climate-change /news/2018/11/government-of-canada-to-support-energy-efficiency-and-climate -action-in-ontario.html

– 2019a. *Progress towards Canada's greenhouse gas emission reduction target.* www .canada.ca/content/dam/eccc/documents/pdf/cesindicators/progress-towards -canada-greenhouse-gas-reduction-target/2019 /progress-towards-ghg-emissions-target-en.pdf.

– 2019b. *National Inventory Report 1990–2017: Greenhouse Gas Sources and Sinks in Canada. Executive Summary.* http://publications.gc.ca/collections/collection _2019/eccc/En81-4-1-2017-eng.pdf.

– 2019c. *Canadian Environmental Sustainability Indicators: Greenhouse gas emissions.* https://www.canada.ca/content/dam/eccc/documents/pdf /cesindicators/ghg-emissions/2019/national-GHG-emissions-en.pdf.

Fafard, Patrick C. 2000. "Groups, Governments and the Environment: Some Evidence from the Harmonization Initiative." In *Managing the Environmental Union: Intergovernmental Relations and Environmental Policy in Canada,* edited by Patrick C. Fafard and Kathryn Harrison. Montreal: McGill-Queen's University Press.

Falkner, Robert. 2008. *Business Power and Conflict in International Environmental Politics*. New York: Palgrave Macmillan.

Federal-Provincial Territorial Meeting of Ministers of the Environment. 2016. "Joint Statement." www.scics.ca/en/product-produit/joint-statement-federal-provincial-and-territorial-governments-working-together-on-first-steps-towards-a-pan-canadian-framework-to-address-climate-change/.

First Ministers' Meeting. 1997. "News Release – Joint Communiqué December 12, 1997" www.scics.ca/en/product-produit/news-release-joint-communique-first-ministers-meeting-ottawa-december-12-1997/.

– 2016a. *Vancouver Declaration on Clean Growth and Climate Change*. www.scics.ca/en/product-produit/vancouver-declaration-on-clean-growth-and-climate-change/.

– 2016b. Communiqué of Canada's First Ministers.

Fleishacker, S. 2004. *A Short History of Distributive Justice*. Cambridge: Harvard University Press.

Foster, Peter. 1982. *The Sorcerer's Apprentices: Canada's Super-Bureaucrats and the Energy Mess*. Toronto: HarperCollins.

Froschauer, Karl. 2000. *White Gold: Hydroelectric Power in Canada*. Vancouver: UBC Press.

Gagnier, Daniel. 2014. "Canada's Economy-Energy Conundrum: EPIC's Contribution to a National Discussion." *Policy Magazine*. http://policymagazine.ca/pdf/9/PolicyMagazineSeptember-October-14-Gagnier.pdf.

Galbraith, John. 1983. *The Anatomy of Power*. Boston: Houghton Mifflin.

Gattinger, Monica. 2015. "Golden Age or Golden Cage of Energy Federalism?" In *Canada: State of the Federation, 2012: Regions, Resources and Resiliency*, edited by Loleen Berdahl, André Juneau, and Carolyn Hughes Tuohy. Montreal: McGill-Queen's University Press.

Gibbins, Roger. 1992. "Alberta and the National Community." In *Government and Politics in Alberta*, edited by Allan Tupper and Roger Gibbins. Edmonton: University of Alberta Press.

– 2007. *Getting It Right: A Canadian Energy Strategy for a Carbon-Constrained Future*. Calgary: Canada West Foundation.

– 2010a. "Creating a Canadian Energy Framework." www.winnipegconsensus.org/downloads/research_energy_framework.pdf

– 2010b. "Creating a Canadian energy framework: if you build it, they will come." *Policy Options*, 31 (5): 61–3.

Globe and Mail. 1997. "Ottawa cancels global-warming announcement." November 29, 1997.

– 1997. "Ottawa changes gas target." December 2, 1997.

– 2007. Front page headline. January 5, 2007.

Government of Alberta. 2002. "Albertans & Climate Change: A Plan for Action." www.alberta.ca/release.cfm?xID=12378.

– 2008. *Climate Change Strategy: Responsibility/Leadership/Action.* https://open
.alberta.ca/dataset/e86a9861-aa19-400e-bb7a-909ef8ccfe46/resource/ad5754f4
-cc7f-40bf-a2ad-0775bd83ba7e/download/4063885-2008-albertas-2008-climate
-change-strategy.pdf.

– 2013. "Alberta and British Columbia reach agreement on opening new markets."

– 2017. *Climate Leadership Plan: Progress Report.* https://open.alberta.ca
/publications/climate-leadership-plan-progress-report-2016-17.

– 2019. *Climate Leadership Plan Progress Report.* https://open.alberta.ca
/dataset/83285ecd-dbbe-4b6f-a1a2-ceaebf289fa3/resource/f6b4da5f-76d7-4ed2
-9fd7-9a133c323440/download/clp-progress-report-2017-18-final.pdf.

Government of British Columbia. 2016. *Climate Leadership Plan.* https://www2
.gov.bc.ca/assets/gov/environment/climate-change/action/clp/clp_booklet
_web.pdf#page=14.

– 2018. *clean BC. our nature. our power. our future.* https://www2.gov.bc.ca/assets
/gov/environment/climate-change/action/cleanbc/cleanbc_2018-bc-climate
-strategy.pdf.

Government of Canada. 1990. *Canada's Green Plan: Canada's Green Plan for a
Healthy Environment.* http://cfs.nrcan.gc.ca/pubwarehouse/pdfs/24604.pdf.

– 2000. *Government of Canada Action Plan 2000.*

– 2002a. *A Discussion Paper on Canada's Contribution to Addressing Climate Change.*

– 2002b. *Climate Change Plan for Canada.*

– 2002c. "News Release: Government of Canada Releases Climate Change Plan for
Canada."

– 2005. *Project Green: Moving Forward on Climate Change: A Plan for Honouring
Our Kyoto Commitment.*

– 2006. "News Release: Canada's Clean Air Act Delivered to Canadians." October 19,
2006.

– 2016a. "Pan-Canadian Approach to Pricing Carbon Pollution." October 3, 2016.

– 2016b. *Canada's Second Biennial Report on Climate Change.* www.canada.ca
/content/dam/eccc/migration/main/ges-ghg/02d095cb-bab0-40d6-b7f0
-828145249af5/3001-20unfccc-202nd-20biennial-20report_e_v7_lowres.pdf.

– 2017. *Canada's Seventh National Communication on Climate Change and
Third Biennial Report.* http://unfccc.int/files/national_reports/national
_communications_and_biennial_reports/application/pdf/82051493
_canada-nc7-br3-1-5108_eccc_can7thncomm3rdbi-report_en_04_web.pdfn.

– 2018a. "Clean Fuel Standard: Timelines, approach and next steps." www.canada
.ca/en/environment-climate-change/services/managing-pollution/energy
-production/fuel-regulations/clean-fuel-standard/timelines-approach-next
-steps.html.

– 2018b. "The Low Carbon Economy Fund." www.canada.ca/en/environment
-climate-change/services/climate-change/low-carbon-economy-fund.html.

Government of New Brunswick. (Undated, released in 2016). *Transitioning to a Low Carbon Economy: New Brunswick Climate Change Action Plan*. https://www2 .gnb.ca/content/dam/gnb/Departments/env/pdf/Climate-Climatiques /TransitioningToALowCarbonEconomy.pdf.

Government of Ontario. 2007. *Go Green: Ontario's Action Plan on Climate Change*. http://www.climateontario.ca/doc/workshop/2011LakeSimcoe/Ontarios%20 Go%20Green%20Action%20Plan%20on%20Climate%20Change.pdf.

– 2016. *Ontario's Five Year Climate Change Action Plan 2016–2020*. www .applications.ene.gov.on.ca/ccap/products/CCAP_ENGLISH.pdf.

Government of Quebec. 2015. "Communiqué de presse: Québec adopte la cible de reduction de gaz à effet serre la plus ambitieuse au Canada." www.mddelcc.gouv .qc.ca/infuseur/communique.asp?no=3353.

Government of Saskatchewan. 2017. *Prairie Resilience: A Made-in-Saskatchewan Climate Change Strategy*. https://www.saskatchewan.ca/business/environmental -protection-and-sustainability/a-made-in-saskatchewan-climate-change-strategy /prairie-resilience.

Greenspon, Edward. 1997. "Provinces let down at Kyoto, Klein says." *The Globe and Mail*, December 12, 1997.

Hanusch, Frederic. 2018. *Democracy and Climate Change*. London: Routledge.

Hardin, Garett. 1968. "The Tragedy of the Commons." *Science*, 162: 1243–8.

Harrison, Kathryn. 1996a. "The Regulator's Dilemma: Regulation of Pulp Mill Effluents in the Canadian Federal State." *Canadian Journal of Political Science*, XXIX (3): 469–96.

– 1996b. *Passing the Buck: Federalism and Canadian Environmental Policy*. Vancouver: UBC Press.

– 2002. "Federal-Provincial Relations on the Environment: Unilateralism, Collaboration, and Rationalization." In *Canadian Environmental Policy: Context and Cases*, edited by Debora L. VanNinjatten and Robert Boardman. Don Mills: Oxford University Press.

– 2007. "The Road Not Taken: Climate Change Policy in Canada and the United States." *Global Environmental Politics*, 7 (4): 92–117.

– 2012. "A Tale of Two Taxes: The Fate of Environmental Tax Reform in Canada." *Review of Policy Research*, 29 (3): 383–407.

– 2015. "International Carbon Trade and Domestic Climate Politics." *Global Environmental Politics*, 15 (3): 27–48.

Harrison, Kathryn and Tyler Bryant. 2016. "The Provinces and Climate Policy." In *Provinces: Canadian provincial politics* (third ed.) edited by Christopher Dunn. Toronto: University of Toronto Press.

Haug, Constanze and Andrew Jordan. 2010. "Sharing burdens or distributing efforts? Negotiating emission reduction commitments in the European Union." In *Climate Change Policy in the European Union: Confronting the Dilemmas of Adaptation and Mitigation?*, edited by Andrew Jordan, Dave Huitema, Harro vanAsselt, Tim Rayner, and Frans Berkhout. Cambridge: Cambridge University Press.

Heclo, Hugh. 1994. "Ideas, Interests and Institutions." In *The Dynamics of American Politics: Approaches and Interpretations*, edited by Lawrence C. Dodd and Calvin Jillson. Boulder: West View Press.

Henton, Darcy. 2015. "Notley: National energy strategy 'a good start' but not licence to build pipelines." *Calgary Herald*, July 17, 2015. http://calgaryherald.com/news /politics/premier-notley-calls-national-energy-strategy-a-good-start-but-not -licence-to-build-pipelines.

Herle, David. 2007. "Poll-Driven Politics – The Role of Public Opinion in Canada." *Policy Options*, 28 (5).

Houle, David. 2015. "Carbon Pricing in Canadian Provinces: from Early Experiments to Adoption (1995–2014)." PhD Diss., Department of Political Science, University of Toronto.

Howlett, Michael, Alex Netherton and M. Ramesh. 1999. *The Political Economy of Canada: An Introduction*. Oxford: Oxford University Press.

Huffington Post. 2018. "Catherine McKenna to Saskatchewan: You Are Pricing Carbon, One Way or Another." March 3, 2018. www.huffingtonpost .ca/2018/03/12/catherine-mckenna-saskatchewan-carbon-tax_a_23383633/.

Hughes, David. 2018. *Canada's Energy Outlook: Current realities and implications for a carbon-restrained future: Executive Summary*. Ottawa: Canadian Centre for Policy Alternatives. https://ccpabc2018.files.wordpress.com/2018/05/cmp _canadas-energy-outlook-2018_summary1.pdf.

Hunter, Justin. 2017. "B.C. approves Kinder Morgan pipeline expansion." *The Globe and Mail*, January 11, 2017. www.theglobeandmail.com/news/british-columbia /bc-gives-kinder-morgan-environmental-green-light/article33588586/.

Ingram, Matthew. 1997. "Carbon tax hysteria mounts." *Commentary: The Globe and Mail*, October 30, 1997.

Jaccard, M.K. and Associates. 2009. *Exploration of two Canadian greenhouse gas emission targets: 25% below 1990 and 20% below 2006 levels by 2020*. Vancouver: M.K. Jaccard and Associates. www.pembina.org/pub/1910.

James, Patrick and Robert Michelin. 1989. "The Canadian National Energy Program and Its Aftermath: Perspectives on an Era of Confrontation." *American Review of Canadian Studies*, 19: 59–81.

JMM. 1998a. "Record of Decisions" April 24, 1998.

– 1998b. "News Release." October 19–20, 1998.

– 2000. "National Briefing Note: Federal-Provincial-Territorial Framework Agreement on Climate Change, Agenda Item 5: Draft Federal-Provincial-Territorial Framework Agreement on Climate Change." Unpublished, in possession of the author.

– 2002a. "News Release." May 21, 2002.

– 2002b. "Record of Decision." May 21, 2002.

– 2002c. "Provincial and Territorial Statement on Climate Change Policy." October 28, 2002.

Johansson-Stenman, Olof and James Konow. 2010. "Fair Air: Distributive Justice and Environmental Economics." *Environment and Resource Economics*, 46: 147–66.

Joint Statement on Climate Change from the Premiers of Ontario and Québec. 2015. https://news.ontario.ca/opo/en/2015/04/joint-statement-on-climate-change-from -the-premiers-of-ontario-and-quebec.html.

Juillet, Luc and Glen Toner. 1997. "From Great Leaps to Baby Steps: Environment and Sustainable Development Policy under the Liberals." In *How Ottawa Spends 1997–98*, edited by Gene Swimmer. Ottawa: Carleton University Press.

Kleiss, Karen. 2012. "Redford Rejects B.C. Demand for "Fair Share" of Royalties." *The Edmonton Journal*, July 24, 2012. www.edmontonjournal.com/technology /Redford+rejects+demand+fair+share+Northern+Gateway/6976173/story.html.

Koch, George. 1995. "Averting Catastrophe: Anything, except imposed solutions." *Oilweek*, May 15, 1995.

Krugel, Lauren. 2012. "Christy Clark, Alison Redford Pipeline Meeting Impasses." *Canadian Press*, October 1, 2012.

Laghi, Brian. 1997a. "Greenhouse-gas plan vital, Ottawa told." *The Globe and Mail*, November 12, 1997.

– 1997b. "Provinces in accord on gas emissions." *The Globe and Mail*, November 13, 1997.

Lambrecht, Kirk N. 2013. *Aboriginal Consultation, Environmental Assessment, and Regulatory Review in Canada*. Regina: University of Regina Press.

Lauber, Volkmar, ed. 2005. *Switching to Renewable Power: A Framework for the 21st Century*. London: Earthscan.

Layzer, Judith A. 2007. "Deep Freeze: How Business Has Shaped the Global Warming Debate in Congress." In *Business and Environmental Policy: Corporate Interests in the American Political System*, edited by Michael E. Kraft and Sheldon Kamieniecki. Cambridge: MIT Press.

Liberal Party of Canada. 2015. *Real Change: A New Plan for a Strong Middle Class*. www.liberal.ca/wp-content/uploads/2015/10/New-plan-for-a-strong-middle -class.pdf

Luger, Stan. 2000. *Corporate Power, American Democracy and the Automobile Industry*. Cambridge: Cambridge University Press.

Lukes, Stephen. 2005. *Power: A Radical View*. New York: Palgrave Macmillan.

Macdonald, Douglas. 2007. *Business and Environmental Politics in Canada*. Peterborough: Broadview Press.

– 2010. "Charles Caccia and the Construction of Environmental Legitimacy." *Journal of Environmental Law and Practice*, 22: 41–58.

– 2011. "Harper Energy and Climate Policy: Failing to Address the Key Challenges." In *How Ottawa Spends 2011–12*, edited by G. Bruce Doern and Christopher Stoney. Montreal: McGill-Queen's University Press.

– 2014. "Allocating greenhouse gas emission reductions amongst sectors and jurisdictions in federated systems: the European Union, Germany and Canada." In *Multilevel Environmental Governance: Managing Water and Climate Change in Europe and North America*, edited by Inger Weibust and James Meadowcroft. Chelthenham: Edward Elgar.

– 2016. "Climate Change Policy." In *Canadian Environmental Policy and Politics: The Challenge of Austerity and Ambivalence*, edited by Debora L. VanNijnatten. Don Mills: Oxford University Press.

Macdonald, Douglas, David Houle and Caitlin Patterson. 2011. "L'utilisation du volontarisme afin de contrôler les émissions de gaz à effet de serre du secteur industriel." In *Politiques environnementales et accords volontaires: le volontarisme comme instrument de politiques environnementales au Québec*, edited by Jean Crête. Quebec City: Presses de l'Université Laval.

Macdonald, Douglas, David Gordon, Asya Bidordinova, Jochen Monstadt, Stefan Scheiner, Kristine Kern, Alexey Pristupa and Anders Hayden. 2013. *Allocating Canadian Greenhouse Gas Emission Reductions amongst Canadian Sources and Provinces: Learning from the EU, Australia and Germany*. www.environment .utoronto.ca/allocating-canadian-greenhouse-gas-emission-reductions-amongst -sources-and-provinces-learning-from-the-european-union-australia-and -germany/.

Macdonald, Douglas and Heather A. Smith. 1999–2000. "Promises made, promises broken: Questioning Canada's commitments to climate change." *International Journal*, Winter: 107–24.

Macdonald, Douglas and Matthew Lesch. 2013. "Competing Visions and Inequitable Costs: the National Energy Strategy and Regional Distributive Conflicts." *Journal of Environmental Law and Practice*, 25: 1–17.

– 2015. "Management of Distributive Impacts Impeding Expansion of Interprovincial Hydro-electricity Transmission." *Journal of Canadian Studies*, 49 (2): 191–221.

MacKinnon, Mark. 2000. "Ontario May Doom Climate Change Deal." *The Globe and Mail*, October 18, 2000.

Mansbridge, Jane H., ed. 1990. *Beyond Self-Interest*. Chicago: The University of Chicago Press.

Mason, Gary. 2016. "The politics behind the LNG go-ahead." *The Globe and Mail*, September 30, 2016

McCarthy, Shawn. 2002. "Ottawa may shun provinces to implement Kyoto." *The Globe and Mail*, May 20, 2002.

– 2011. "National energy strategy gains clout." *The Globe and Mail*, July 11, 2011

– 2015. "Trudeau announces carbon-pricing plan in Calgary: Liberals would convene first ministers' conference to hash out a plan and leave it up to the provinces to decide how to achieve principles." *The Globe and Mail*, February 7, 2015.

– 2016a. "Aggressive action urged to reach climate goal." *The Globe and Mail*, January 30, 2016.

– 2016b. "Ottawa seeks to set national minimum on carbon pricing." *The Globe and Mail*, February 17, 2016.

– 2016c. "Premiers draw battle lines over carbon." *The Globe and Mail*, October 5, 2016

– 2016d. "Provinces fall in line with Ottawa's carbon plan." *The Globe and Mail*, November 22, 2016.

– 2017. "UN gives leaders 10 years to curb CO2." *The Globe and Mail*, April 12, 2017.

– 2018. "Ottawa cuts carbon tax to ease competitiveness concerns." *The Globe and Mail*, August 1, 2018.

McCarthy, Shawn and Ian Bailey. 2016a. "Prime Minister intent on seizing momentum to forge national climate plan." *The Globe and Mail*, February 29, 2016.

– 2016b. "Provinces oppose carbon floor-price proposal." *The Globe and Mail*, March 3, 2016.

– 2016c. "Premiers balk at PM's carbon-pricing plan: Agreement reached on need for additional action to address global commitment on emissions, but stops short of unified strategy." *The Globe and Mail*, March 4, 2016.

McCarthy, Shawn and Jeff Lewis. 2016. "Trudeau hedges energy bets: Move gives Alberta a boost, but upsets environmentalists." *The Globe and Mail*, November 30, 2016.

McConaghy, Dennis. 2017. *Dysfunction: Canada after Keystone XL*. Toronto: Dundurn.

McDougall, John N. 1982. *Fuels and the National Policy*. Toronto: Butterworths.

McIlroy, Anne. 1997a. "Action on global warming for the long term, PM says." *The Globe and Mail*, November 4, 1997.

– 1997b. "Global-warming decision on hold." *The Globe and Mail*, November 5, 1997.

McIlroy, Anne and Edward Greenspon. 1997. "Slash emissions, PM urges." *The Globe and Mail*, October 28, 1997.

McIlveen, Neil (2010). Interview by Douglas Macdonald.

McKenna, Catherine. 2016. "Decision Statement to Pacific Northwest LNG Limited Parternship." www.ceaa.gc.ca/050/documents/p80032/115669E.pdf.

Meadowcroft, James. 2012. "Greening the State?" In *Comparative Environmental Politics: Theory, Practice and Prospects*, edited by Paul F. Steinberg and Stacy D. VanDeveer. Cambridge: MIT Press.

Measures Working Group. 1994. *Measures for Canada's National Action Program on Climate Change: Final Report*. Prepared for the Climate Change Task Group of the National Air Issues Co-ordinating Committee.

Meisner, Dirk. 2018. "B.C. sets new targets to dramatically reduce emissions by 2014." *The Globe and Mail*, May 7, 2018. www.theglobeandmail.com/canada

/british-columbia/article-bc-sets-new-targets-to-dramatically-reduce-greenhouse
-gas-emissions/.

Mickleburgh, Rod. 2000. "Ontario's Emissions an Issue as Ministers Meet in
Vancouver." *The Globe and Mail*, March 27, 2000.

Milne, David. 1986. *Tug of War: Ottawa and the Provinces under Trudeau and
Mulroney*. Toronto: James Lorimer and Co.

Ministère de l'Environnement. 2000. "Communiqué."

Ministère de l'Environnement et Lutte contre les changements climatiques, Québec.
2015. "Communiqué de presse: Québec adopte la cible de réduction de gaz à effet
serre la plus ambitieuse au Canada." http://www.mddelcc.gouv.qc.ca/infuseur
/communique.asp?no=3353.

Ministère du Développement durable, de l'Environnement, de la Faune et des Parcs.
1999a. "Communiqués de presse Mars 25, 1999." www.mddefp.gouv.qc.ca
/communiques/1999/c990325c.htm.

– 1999b. "Communiqués de presse October 8, 1999." www.mddefp.gouv.qc.ca
/communiques/1999/c991008a.htm.

Morrow, Adrian. 2015. "What you need to know about the Canadian Energy
Strategy." *The Globe and Mail*, July 16, 2015.

Mowat Centre. 2017. *The Road to Paris: Navigating the intergovernmental path
to our climate commitments*. https://mowatcentre.ca/wp-content/uploads
/publications/158_the_road_to-paris.pdf.

Mulroney, Brian. 1992. "Notes for an address: Earth Summit, Rio de Janeiro, Brazil."

Munroe, Kaija Belfrey. 2016. *Business in a Changing Climate: Explaining Industry
Support for Carbon Pricing*. Toronto: University of Toronto Press.

NAPCC. 1995. *Canada's National Action Program on Climate Change*.

National Air Issues Coordinating Committee. 1996. *Review of Canada's National
Action Program on Climate Change*.

National Climate Change Process. 2000. *Canada's National Implementation Strategy
on Climate Change*.

– 2001. *Progress Report: Canada's First National Climate Change Business Plan*.

National Energy Strategy. 2011. "Business, environmentalists and energy players
call for a national energy strategy." *The Globe and Mail*, December 15, 2011.
Information feature.

Natural Resources Canada. 2010. "Canadian Energy Ministers Commit to
Innovation and Further Collaboration." www.nrcan.gc.ca/media-room
/news-release/74/2010-09/2797.

– 2016. "Oil Sands GHG emissions – US." www.nrcan.gc.ca/energy/publications
/18731.

National Round Table on the Environment and the Economy. 2012. *Reality Check:
The State of Climate Progress in Canada*. www.collectionscanada.gc.ca
/web archives2/20130322165455/http:/nrtee-trnee.ca/reality-check-the
-state-of-climate-progress-in-canada.

Negru, John. 1990. *The Electric Century: An illustrated history of electricity in Canada: The Canadian Electrical Association*. Montreal, QC: The Canadian Electrical Association.

Neisnner, Dirk. 2013. "Premiers Clark and Redford talk joint energy export plan." *Canadian Press*, October 15, 2013.

Nunavut Environment Department. 2016. *FPT Ministerial Meeting Report*. www .assembly.nu.ca/sites/default/files/TD-289-4(3)-EN-FPT-Ministerial-Report-on -the-Canadian-Council-of-Ministers-of-Environment,-Ocotber-3,-2016.pdf.

Oliver, Joe. 2011. "Notes for a Speech: Energy and the Road to Canada's Prosperity." www.nrcan.gc.ca/media-room/speeches/2011/3397.

Olson, Mancur. 1965. *The Logic of Collective Action: Public Goods and the Theory of Groups*. Cambridge: Harvard University Press.

O'Neill, Peter, Gordon Hoekstra and Brian Morton. 2016. "Federal government approves $11.4 billion LNG project in B.C." *The Vancouver Sun*, September 28, 2016. http://vancouversun.com/news/local-news/feds -flying-to-vancouver-for-historic-lng-decision-expected-to-ok-megaproject.

Ontario. 2016. *Ontario's Five Year Climate Change Action Plan 2016–2020*. www .applications.ene.gov.on.ca/ccap/products/CCAP_ENGLISH.pdf.

Ontario Ministry of the Environment, Conservation and Parks. 2018. *Preserving and Protecting Our Environment for Future Generations: A Made-in-Ontario Environment Plan*. https://prod-environmental-registry.s3.amazonaws.com /2018-11/EnvironmentPlan.pdf.

Oulton, David. 2010. Interview by Douglas Macdonald.

Oxford English Dictionary, The New Shorter. 1993. Edited by Leslie Brown. Oxford: Clarendon Press.

Page, Christopher. 2006. *The Roles of Public Opinion Research in Canadian Government*. Toronto: University of Toronto Press.

Pallister, Brian. 2018. "Letter to the editor." *The Globe and Mail*, October 27, 2018.

Pan-Canadian Framework on Clean Growth and Climate Change. 2016. "Pan-Canadian Framework on Clean Growth and Climate Change." www.canada.ca/content/dam/themes/environment/documents/weather1 /20170113-1-en.pdf.

Papillon, Martin and Richard Simeon. 2004. "The Weakest Link? First Ministers' Conferences in Canadian Intergovernmental Relations." In *Canada: The State of the Federation 2002*, edited by Peter J. Meekison, Hamish Telford, and Harvey Lazar. Montreal: McGill-Queen's University Press.

Parker, Jeffrey. 2015. *Comparative Federalism and Intergovernmental Agreements: Anaylyzing Australia, Canada, Australia, Germany, South Africa, Switzerland and the United States*. London: Routledge.

Payton, Laura. 2016. "Liberals back away from setting tougher carbon targets." CTV News, September 18, 2016. www.ctvnews.ca/politics /liberals-back-away-from-setting-tougher-carbon-targets-1.3075857.

Pembina Institute. 2007. "Analysis of the Government of Canada's April 2007 Greenhouse Gas Policy Announcement."

– 2014. *Backgrounder: Climate Change Policy in Alberta*. www.pembina.org/reports /sger-climate-policy-backgrounder.pdf.

Plourde, André. 2012. "Canada." In *Oil and Gas in Federal Systems*, edited by George Andeson. Don Mills: Oxford University Press.

Podobnik, Bruce. 2006. *Global Energy Shifts: Fostering Sustainability in a Turbulent Age*. Philadephia: Temple University Press.

Pollard, Bruce G. 1986. "Canadian Energy Policy in 1985: Toward a renewed federalism?" *Publius*, 16 (3): 163–74.

Prentice, Jim with Jean-Sébatien Rioux. 2017. *Triple Crown: Winning Canada's Energy Future*. Toronto: HarperCollins.

Rabe, Barry. 2018. *Can We Price Carbon?* Cambridge, MA: MIT Press.

Raymond, Leigh. 2003. *Private Rights in Public Resources: Equity and Property Allocation in Market-Based Environmental Policy*. Washington, DC: Resources for the Future.

Resource Futures International Torrie Smith Associates and Policy Assessment Corp. 1996. *Reviewing the Progress Made under Canada's National Action Program on Climate Change: Final Report*.

Rhéal, Segun. 2000. "Ontario Calls for Emission Standards." *The Globe and Mail*, October 17, 2000.

Richards, John and Larry Pratt. 1979. *Prairie Capitalism: Power and Influence in the New West*. Toronto: McClelland and Stewart.

Rivers, Nic. 2010. *Distributional Incidence of Climate Change Policy in Canada*. Sustainable Prosperity. http://institute.smartprosperity.ca/sites/default/files /publications/files/Distributional%20incidence%20of%20climate%20change%20 policy%20in%20Canada.pdf.

Romanow, Roy. March 7, 2018. Interview by Douglas Macdonald.

Sallot, Jeff. 1997. "Pollution pact doesn't need provinces, Ottawa says." *The Globe and Mail*, November 14, 1997.

Saskatchewan. 2010. "Western provinces unite to improve access to Asian markets." www.saskatchewan.ca/government/news-and-media/2010/december/16 /western-provinces-unite-to-improve-access-to-asian-markets.

Sawyer, Dave and Chris Bataille. 2017. "Taking Stock: Opportunities for Collaborative Climate Action to 2030. Policy Brief 2: The Pan-Canadian Framework on Clean Growth and Climate Change." Decarbonization Pathways Canada, Climate Action Network Canada, Environmental Defence, Équiterre and the Pembina Institute.

Schlozman, Kay Lehman and John T. Tierney. 1986. "Interests in Politics." In *Organized Interests and American Democracy*. New York: Harper and Row.

Scoffield, Heather. 2001. "Thanks to Luck, Alliance and Concessions, Canada Left Kyoto with More Than Expected." *The Globe and Mail*, July 25, 2001.

Scotti, Monique. 2018. "How Ottawa might try to save the Trans Mountain pipeline." *Global News*, April 9, 2018. https://globalnews.ca/news/4132850/trans-mountain-kinder-morgan-ottawa-save/.

Senate Standing Committee on Energy, the Environment and Natural Resources. June 2010. *Towards a Canadian Sustainable Energy Strategy: A Discussion Paper.*

Serret, Ysé and Nick Johnstone, eds. 2006. *The Distributional Effects of Environmental Policy*. Cheltenham: Edward Elgar, OECD.

Sharpe, Sydney. 2005. "Alberta and Its Politics – From Prophesy to Progress." In *Alberta: A State of Mind*, edited by Sydney Sharpe, Roger Gibbins, James H. Marsh, and Heather Bala Edwards. Toronto: Key Porter Books.

Simeon, Richard. 2006. *Federal Provincial Diplomacy: The Making of Recent Policy in Canada: with a New Preface and Postscript*. Toronto: University of Toronto Press.

Simeon, Richard and Amy Nugent. 2008. "Parliamentary Canada and Intergovernmental Canada: Exploring the Tensions." In *Canadian Federalism: Performance, Effectiveness and Legitimacy*, edited by Herman Bakvis and Grace Skogstad. Don Mills: Oxford University Press.

Simeon, Richard and Ian Robinson. 1990. *State, Society, and the Development of Canadian Federalism*. Toronto: University of Toronto Press.

Simmons, Julie M. 2004. "Securing the Threads of Co-operation in the Tapestry of Intergovernmental Relations: Does the Institutionalization of Ministerial Conferences Matter?" In *Canada: The State of the Federation 2002: Reconsidering the Institutions of Canadian Federalism*, edited by Peter J. Meekison, Hamish Telford, and Harvey Lazar. Montreal: McGill-Queen's University Press.

– 2016. "Federalism, Intergovernmental Relations and the Environment." In *Canadian Environmental Policy and Politics: The Challenge of Austerity and Ambivalence*, edited by Debora L. VanNijnatten. Don Mills: Oxford University Press.

Simpson, Jeffrey. 1980. *Discipline of Power: The Conservative Interlude and the Liberal Restoration*. Toronto: Personal Library, Publishers.

– 2014. "Don't Buy the Spin on Our Emissions Cutting." *The Globe and Mail*, February 7, 2014.

Simpson, Jeffrey, Mark Jaccard and Nic Rivers. 2007. *Hot Air: Meeting Canada's Climate Change Challenge*. Toronto: McClelland and Stewart.

Skogstad, Grace. 2003. "Who Governs? Who Should Govern? Political Authority and Legitimacy in Canada in the Twenty-First Century." *Canadian Journal of Political Science*, 36 (5): 955–73.

Smil, Vaclav. 2008. *Energy in Nature and Society: General Energetics of Complex Systems*. Cambridge: MIT Press.

Smiley, Donald V. 1979. "An Outsider's Observations of Federal-Provincial Relations among Consenting Adults." In *Confrontation and Collaboration – Intergovernmental Relations in Canada Today*, edited by Richard Simeon. Toronto: The Institute of Public Administration of Canada.

– 1980. *Canada in Question: Federalism in the Eighties*. Toronto: McGraw-Hill Ryerson.

– 1987. *The Federal Condition in Canada*. Toronto: McGraw-Hill Ryerson.

Smith, Heather. 1998. "Canadian Federalism and International Environmental Policy Making: The Case of Climate Change," Working Paper, Institute for Intergovernmental Relations, Queen's University. www.queensu.ca/iigr/sites /webpublish.queensu.ca.iigrwww/files/files/WorkingPapers/Archive/1998/1998 -5HeatherSmith.pdf.

Smith, Jennifer. 2004. *Federalism*. Vancouver: UBC Press.

Snoddon, Tracey and Debora VanNijnatten. 2016. "Carbon pricing and intergovernmental relations in Canada." *IRPP Insight*, November (12). http://irpp .org/wp-content/uploads/2016/11/insight-no12.pdf.

Sprinz, Detlef and Tapani Vaahtanoranta. 1994. "The Interest-Based Explanation of International Environmental Policy." *International Organization*, 48 (1): 77–105.

Stevenson, Garth. 2009. *Unfulfilled Union: Canadian Federalism and National Unity*. Montreal: McGill-Queen's University Press.

– 2012. "The Political Economy of Regionalism and Federalism." In *Canadian Federalism: Performance, Effectiveness and Legitimacy*, edited by Herman Bakvis and Grace Skogstad. Don Mills: Oxford University Press.

Stilborn, Jack. 2003. "Canadian Intergovernmental Relations and the Kyoto Protocol: What Happened, What Didn't." Paper delivered at the Canadian Political Science Association annual conference, May 30, 2003.

Stock, Peter. 2002. "Kyoto's teeth: Alberta and B.C. prepare to protect their economies from federal climate controls." *The Report Newsmagazine*, December 16, 2002.

Stone, Deborah A. 1988. *Policy Paradox and Political Reason*. Glenview, Illinois: Scott, Forseman.

Strachan, W.R. 1983–4. "The Development of Canadian Energy Policy 1970–1982 – One Man's View." *Journal of Business Administration*, 14: 143–62.

Taber, Jane and Adrian Morrow. 2015. "Premiers agree on energy strategy with weakened climate pledges." *The Globe and Mail*, July 17, 2015. https://beta .theglobeandmail.com/news/national/premiers-making-progress -on-national-energy-strategy-deal-could-be-signed-today/article25545448.

Taft, Kevin. 2017. *Oil's deep state: How the petroleum industry undermines democracy and stops action on global warming – in Alberta and in Ottawa*. Toronto: James Lorimer and Co.

Toke, David. 2011. *Ecological Modernization and Renewable Energy*. New York: Palgrave Macmillan.

Tomasello, Michael, et al. 2009. *Why We Cooperate*. Cambridge: MIT Press.

Tombe, Trevor. 2016. "Policy, not pipelines, will determine if we meet our goals." *Maclean's*, December 2, 2016. www.macleans.ca/economy/economicanalysis /policy-not-pipelines-will-determine-if-we-meet-our-goals/.

Toulin, Alan. 2002. "Alberta quits Kyoto negotiation: All other provinces sign session's final communiqué; Minister warns of 'another National Energy Program' if climate treaty is implemented." *National Post*, May 22, 2002.

Trebilcock, Michael J. 2014. *Dealing with Losers: The Political Economy of Policy Transitions.* Oxford: Oxford University Press.

Trudeau, Justin. 2015. "Justin Trudeau Pitches a Medicare Approach to Fighting Climate Change." www.liberal.ca/justin-trudeau-pitches-medicare-approach -to-fight-climate-change-in-canada/.

– 2016. "Prime Minister Justin Trudeau Delivers a Speech on Carbon Pricing." https://pm.gc.ca/eng/news/2016/10/03/prime-minister-trudeau-delivers-speech -pricing-carbon-pollution.

Turner, Chris. 2017. *The Patch: The People, Pipelines and Politics of the Oil Sands.* New York: Simon and Schuster.

Urquhart, Ian. 2018. *Costly Fix: Power, Politics, and Nature in the Tar Sands.* Toronto: University of Toronto Press.

Valiante, Marcia. 2002. "Legal Foundations of Canadian Environmental Policy: Underlining Our Values in a Shifting Landscape." In *Canadian Environmental Policy and Politics: Context and Cases,* edited by Debora L. VanNijnatten and Robert Boardman. Don Mills: Oxford University Press.

– 2016. "Environmental Law in the Time of Austerity." In *Canadian Environmental Policy and Politics: The Challenges of Austerity and Ambivalence,* edited by Debora L. VanNijnatten. Don Mills: Oxford University Press.

Vanderklippe, Nathan. 2011. "Ontario refuses to call Alberta's oil sands 'responsible.'" *The Globe and Mail,* July 20, 2011.

Varcoe, Chris and Sandee Wong. 2001. "Alberta Condemns Kyoto Demands." *Calgary Herald,* July 24, 2001.

Wall, Brad. 2016a. "The simple, seductive logic of a revenue-neutral carbon tax." *The Globe and Mail,* October 14, 2016.

– 2016b. Saskatchewan, Legislative Assembly. *Hansard* 58(29A). 28th Legislature, 1st Session, page 805. http://docs.legassembly.sk.ca/legdocs/Legislative% 20Assembly/Hansard/28L1S/161024Debates.pdf.

Walton, Dawn. 2012. "Redford has a national energy plan – but don't call it the NEP." *The Globe and Mail,* January 9, 2012.

Watkins. M.H. 1963. "A Staple Theory of Economic Growth." *Canadian Journal of Economics and Political Science,* 29 (2): 141–58.

Webber, Jeremy. 2015. *The Constitution of Canada: A Contextual Analysis.* Oxford: Hart Publishing.

Weibust, Inger. 2010. "The Great Green North? Canada's Bad Environmental Record and How the Feds Can Fix It." In *The Case for Centralized Federalism,* edited by Gordon DiGiacomo and Maryantonnet Flumian. Ottawa: University of Ottawa Press.

Whitcomb, Ed. 2017. *Rivals for Power: The Contentious History of the Canadian Federation.* Toronto: James Lorimer.

Wilson, James Q. 1980. *The Politics of Regulation.* New York: Basic Books.

Winfield, Mark. 2012. *Blue-Green Province: The Environment and the Political Economy of Ontario.* Vancouver: UBC Press.

Winfield, Mark and Douglas Macdonald. 2008. "The Harmonization Accord and Climate Change Policy: Two Case Studies in Federal-Provincial Environmental Policy." In *Canadian Federalism* (second edition), edited by Grace Skogstad and Herman Bakvis. Don Mills: Oxford University Press.

– 2012. "Federalism and Canadian Climate Change Policy." In *Canadian Federalism* (third edition), edited by Grace Skogstad and Herman Bakvis. Don Mills: Oxford University Press.

Wingrove, Josh. 2012. "Oliver 'supportive' of Redford's proposed national energy strategy." *The Globe and Mail*, May 25, 2012.

winnipegconsensus.org. 2011. Website providing information on the Winnipeg and Banff meetings, site hosted by International Institute for Sustainable Development.

The Winnipeg Consensus. n.d. "Sparking a National Dialogue on Canada's Clean Energy Future." Paper in author's possession.

Working Group on Carbon Pricing Mechanisms. n.d. *Final Report.* www.canada.ca /content/dam/eccc/migration/cc/content/6/4/7/64778dd5-e2d9-4930-be59 -d6db7db5cbc0/wg_report_carbon-20pricing_e_v4.pdf.

Index

West-East divide, 90–100
   Alberta and Saskatchewan likely to
      resist future national climate
      policymaking, 262
   Alberta emission increases undercut
      reductions elsewhere, 95–8, 259
   Alberta's influence on all five energy
      and climate national programs,
      236, 238
   asymmetrical, 238, 240, 150
   differing fossil fuel energy interests,
      91–3, 233, 274
   higher per-capita emission
      reduction costs in Alberta and
      Saskatchewan, 8, 13, 91, 94, 106,
      107, 173, 234, 240, 257
      Alberta, 265, 272
   Brad Wall argument, 94, 229
   in 2002 federal discussion paper,
      166–7
   in any future national climate
      policymaking, 263
   largely due to Government of Canada
      actions, 238
      widened by National Energy
         Program, 115, 127, 131
      widened by Ottawa's refusal to be
         bound by JMM target, 1997, 147
   lessons from all cases, 235–8
   lessons from Canadian Energy
      Strategy, 197–8
   lessons from first national climate
      change process, 149–50
   lessons from national energy politics,
      1973 to 1981, 127

lessons from Pan-Canadian
   Framework, 228
lessons from second national
   climate change process,
   172–3
need for new national dialogue,
   257–61
not necessarily symmetrical, 149,
   172, 228, 235, 237
zero-sum game, 94, 104. *See also*
   allocation of total GHG
   emission reduction
   in any future national climate
      policymaking, 239, 240
   in national energy politics, 1973
      to 1981, 92, 114–15, 130, 153,
      237, 272
   leads to equal motivation,
      symmetry, 128
   not in first national climate
      process, 149–50
western alienation, 30, 98–100, 272
   definition, 99
   does not apply equally to all four
      western provinces,
      12, 99
   nonmaterial as well as material
      interest, 99
West, Steve (Alberta energy minister),
   146
wind energy, 11, 16, 18, 19, 22
Wynne, Kathleen (Ontario premier), 58,
   82, 223
   supporting role, PCF, 231
   Vancouver FMM, 209

www.ingramcontent.com/pod-product-compliance
Lightning Source LLC
Chambersburg PA
CBHW030236030426
42336CB00009B/129